Translating &
Understanding
the
Old Testament

Translating & Understanding the Old Testament

ESSAYS IN HONOR OF
HERBERT GORDON MAY

EDITED BY

Harry Thomas Frank, *Oberlin College*

AND

William L. Reed, *Texas Christian University*

𝄞 ABINGDON PRESS

NASHVILLE   NEW YORK

TRANSLATING AND UNDERSTANDING THE OLD TESTAMENT

ISBN 0-687-52414-X
Library of Congress Catalog Card Number: 75-115354

SET UP, PRINTED, AND BOUND BY THE
PARTHENON PRESS, AT NASHVILLE,
TENNESSEE, UNITED STATES OF AMERICA

DEDICATED TO
HERBERT GORDON MAY
*on the occasion of his retirement
from Oberlin after thirty-five
years of distinguished service,*
and to
HELEN ISABELLE MAY
*his faithful companion
of forty-two years*

Contents

Translating and Understanding the Old Testament

AN OPEN LETTER TO
HERBERT GORDON MAY

This book is a tribute to you as a scholar and as a person. Two years ago the Haskell Lectureship Committee of Oberlin College, recognizing your thirty-five years of service to the Oberlin Graduate School of Theology and to the College, decided to expand the 1969-1970 Haskell Lectures and offer them to you as a token of appreciation and esteem. At the same time a question was raised concerning the debt owed to you by a generation of scholars and students, in this country and abroad. Inquiry led to discovery of two things. First, colleagues, in America and Europe, were discussing appropriate ways of honoring you. Neither group had been in contact with the other; each graciously cooperated here. Second, there was, not surprisingly, a considerable outpouring of personal regard for you. Both of these could have been anticipated by anyone who knows of the quality and breadth of your contribution to the study of the Old Testament, its text and environment, and to anyone who has known you and worked with you.

Rock-hewn New Englander, gracious in manner, rigorously honest in your pursuit and evaluation of scholarly evidence, you have made major contributions in at least four areas: theology, archaeology, cartography, and translation of the Scriptures. Before you assumed your teaching post you were the author of four essays which continue today to be cited in scholarly writings. This was but an indication of what became continuous activity, and which even now, on the verge of your retirement, contains great promise.

At the same time you have never been merely a *Stubengelehrter*. Hundreds of students testify to your skill as a teacher, and remember with pleasure the unhurried scholarly and personal counsel offered in the privacy of your study. Moreover, your interest in the church has been evidenced by personal dedication, literary activity in practical journals, and innumerable appearances before various groups.

Within these covers are the labors of love of a number of distinguished contributors: Protestant, Catholic, and Jew; of several nations and various opinions. We are united in this undertaking by our regard for you as a scholar, and our respect for you as a man.

You, above all, will find it appropriate that in thinking of you we have not forgotten Helen, whose name we join with yours in our personal feelings and formal dedication.

With appreciation and affection,

Harry Thomas Frank

William L. Reed

HERBERT GORDON MAY

CURRICULUM VITAE

Born: December 26, 1904, at Fair Haven, Vermont, to Charles Leon
May and Mabel Maria (Cottrill)

Wesleyan University, A.B., 1927; University of Chicago, M.A., 1929;
Chicago Theological Seminary, B.D., 1930; University of Chicago,
Ph.D., 1932; D.D., Wesleyan University, 1952

Married Helen Isabelle Porter, February 11, 1928; children—Gola
Joyce Kina (born in Jerusalem, July 29, 1933), and Helen Emily
("Gale") (born in Oberlin, October 26, 1941)

Minister, First Congregational Church, Melvin, Illinois, 1928-1929

Blatchford Fellow, University of Chicago, 1930-1931

Fellow of the Oriental Institute of the University of Chicago, 1931-
1934

Epigrapher of the Megiddo Archaeological Expedition, 1931-1934

Assistant Professor of Old Testament Languages and Literature,
Oberlin Graduate School of Theology, 1934-1938

Lecturer, Summer School for Clergy, Macdonald College, Quebec,
1938

Associate Professor of Old Testament Languages and Literature,
Oberlin Graduate School of Theology, 1938-1946

Carew Lecturer, Hartford Theological Seminary, 1939

Member, Standard Bible Committee, 1945-

Charles Grandison Finney Professor of Old Testament Languages and
Literature, Oberlin Graduate School of Theology, 1946-

Lecturer, Garrett Bible Institute, summer, 1947

Crozer Lecturer, Crozer Theological Seminary, 1950

Lecturer, Union Theological Seminary (New York), summer, 1952,
1956, 1959

Honorary Lecturer, American Schools of Oriental Research (Jerusalem), 1959-1960

Chairman, Standard Bible Committee, 1966-

Joint Professorship, Oberlin College and Vanderbilt University, 1967-

Member: Society of Biblical Literature (President, 1962) ; American Schools of Oriental Research (Trustee) ; American Archaeological Society; American Oriental Society (President Mid-West, 1947) ; American Academy of Religion; National Association of Professors of Hebrew; World Union of Jewish Studies; *etc.*

Editorial Board: Vetus Testamentum; Journal of Biblical Literature (Old Testament Book Review Editor, 1948-1952) ; Journal of Religious Education (1948-1956)

Bibliography of Publications of Herbert Gordon May

A. BOOKS

Material Remains of the Megiddo Cult. University of Chicago Press, 1935.

Culture and Conscience (with W. C. Graham). University of Chicago Press, 1936.

A Remapping of the Bible World: Nelson's New Bible Maps (with C. C. McCown). 40 maps. Camden, N. J.: Thomas Nelson & Sons, 1949.

Our English Bible in the Making. Philadelphia: Westminster Press, 1952.

Ezekiel: Introduction and Exegesis, Interpreter's Bible, Vol. VI. Nashville: Abingdon Press, © 1956, 41-338.

Interpreter's Dictionary of the Bible, Vols. I-IV (Associate Editor). Nashville: Abingdon Press, 1962.

Oxford Bible Atlas (Editor, with assistance of W. R. Hamilton and G. N. S. Hunt). London and New York: Oxford University Press, 1962.

Oxford Annotated Bible, Revised Standard Version (Coeditor, with Bruce Metzger). New York: Oxford University Press, 1962.

Our English Bible in the Making, Revised Edition. Philadelphia: Westminster Press, 1965.

Oxford Annotated Bible with the Apocrypha (Coeditor, with Bruce Metzger). New York: Oxford University Press, 1965.

B. BOOK CONTRIBUTIONS

Twentieth Century Encyclopedia of Religious Knowledge, L. A. Loetscher, ed.:
"Fertility Cults," I, 426.
"Gods and Goddesses Mentioned in the Old Testament," I, 464-65.
"High Places," I, 510.
"Philistines," II, 877.

"Some Historical Perspectives," *A Stubborn Faith,* E. C. Hobbs, ed., Dallas: Southern Methodist University Press, 1956, 100-116.

"Synagogues in Palestine," *The Biblical Archaeologist Reader,* G. E. Wright and D. N. Freedman, eds., Anchor Books, 1961, 229-50.

"Individual Responsibility and Retribution," *HUCA* XXXII (1961), 107-20.

"The King in the Garden of Eden: A Study of Ezekiel 28:12-19," *Israel's Prophetic Heritage.* New York: Harper & Row, 1962.
Interpreter's Dictionary of the Bible (1962), 122 major and cross-reference articles.
Encyclopaedia Britannica (1962)
    "Ezekiel, Book of"
    "Hosea, Book of"
    "Jashar, Book of"
Peake's Commentary on the Bible (1962). London, Toronto, and New York: Thomas Nelson and Sons—
    "History of Israel to the Exile," pp. 115-25.
    "Joshua," pp. 289-303.
Sundry articles in *The Interpreter's Dictionary of the Bible,* 1962.
"The Bible and the Faith of the Christian," reprinted in H. E. Beck, *Our Biblical Heritage.* Philadelphia, United Church Press, 1964, pp. 102-5.
Oxford Annotated Apocrypha. New York: Oxford University Press, 1965.
    "Introduction and Annotations of the Book of Baruch."
    "Introduction and Annotations of the Letter of Jeremiah."
"Response to Kapelrud's 'The Role of the Cult in Old Israel,' " *The Bible in Modern Scholarship,* edited by J. P. Hyatt. Nashville: Abingdon Press, 1965.
The Interpreter's One Volume Commentary on the Bible. Nashville: Abingdon Press (in press):
    "The Fertile Crescent and Its Environment."
    "The Peoples of the Old Testament World."
    "Greece and Rome in the Biblical World."
    "The Book of Ruth."

C. ARTICLES IN SCHOLARLY JOURNALS

"The Evolution of the Joseph Story," *AJSL* XLVII (1931), 83-93.
"The Fertility Cult in Hosea," *AJSL* XLVIII (1932), 73-93.
"An Inscribed Jar from Megiddo," *AJSL* L (1933), 10-14.
"A Supplementary Note on the Ivory Inlays from Samaria," *PEFQS* (1933), 88-89.
"The Seal of Elamar," *AJSL* LII (1936), 197-99.
"The Relation of the Passover to the Festival of Unleavened Cakes," *JBL* LV (1936), 65-82.
"Interpretation of the Names of Hosea's Children," *JBL* LV (1936), 285-91.
"The Ark—A Miniature Temple," *AJSL* LII (1936), 215-34.
"Some Aspects of the Solar Worship at Jerusalem," *ZAW* XIV (1937), 269-81.
"The Departure of the Glory of Yahweh," *JBL* LVI (1937), 309-30.
"A Key to the Interpretation of Zechariah's Visions," *JBL* LVII (1938), 173-84.
"Ephod and Ariel," *AJSL* LVI (1939), 44-69.
"Three Hebrew Seals and the Status of Exiled Jehoiakin," *AJSL* LVI (1939), 146-48.
"Ruth's Visit to the High Place at Bethlehem," *JRAS* (1939), 75 ff.

"The Sacred Tree on Palestinian Painted Pottery," *JAOS* LIX (1939), 251-59.

"The Old Testament as Content for Religious Education," *RE* XXIV (1939), 37-43.

"The Creation of Light in Genesis 1:3-5," *JBL* LVIII (1939), 203-11.

"Religious Education Aims in Teaching Old Testament in Church Schools," *RE* XXXV (1940), 117 ff.

"*al* in the Superscriptions of the Psalms," *AJSL* LVIII (1941), 70-83.

"Pattern and Myth in the Old Testament," *JR* XXI (1941), 285-99.

"The Patriarchal Idea of God," *JBL* LX (1941), 113-28.

"The God of My Father," *JBR* IX (1941), 155-58, 199-200.

"Jeremiah's Biographer," *JBR* X (1942), 195-201.

"Towards an Objective Approach to the Book of Jeremiah," *JBL* LXI (1942), 139-55.

"The Two Pillars Before the Temple of Solomon," *BASOR* No. 88 (1942), 19-27.

"Biblical Archaeology and Visual Education," *RE* XXXVIII (1943), 115-99.

"The Ten Lost Tribes," *BA* VI (1943), 55-60.

"Synagogues in Palestine," *BA* VII (1944), 1-20.

"A Sociological Approach to Hebrew Religion," *JBR* XII (1944), 98-106.

"Lachish Letter IV: 7-10," *BASOR* No. 97 (1945), 22-25.

"Biblical Archaeology and Religious Education," with L. Stidley, *RE* XL (1945), 235-45.

"Moses and the Sinai Inscriptions," *BA* VIII (1945), 93 ff.

"The Chronology of Jeremiah's Oracles," *JNES* IV (1945), 217 ff.

"Hebrew Origins and Religious Education," *RE* XLI (1946), 76 ff.

"Theological Universalism in the Old Testament," *JBR* XVI (1948), 100-101.

"Report from Board of Trustees of American Schools of Oriental Research to the Society of Biblical Literature," *JBL* LXXI (1952), xxvii-xxx.

"Some Religious Education Values of the Revised Standard Version," *RE* XLVII (1952), 272-77.

"Prometheus and Job," *Anglican Theological Review,* XXXIV (1952), 240-46.

"The Geography of the Old Testament and the Revised Standard Version," *An Introduction to the Revised Standard Version of the Old Testament,* 1952, pp. 41-49.

"The Revised Standard Version in the Classroom," *JBR* XXI (1953), 174-79.

"The Righteous Servant in Second Isaiah's Songs," *ZAW* LXVI (1954), 236-44.

"Some Cosmic Connotations of *Mayim Rabbim,* 'Many Waters,'" *JBL* LXXIV (1955), 9-21.

"Report of the Society's Representative on the Board of Trustees of the American Schools of Oriental Research," *JAOS* LXXV (1955), 276-77.

"Report of the Society's Representative on the Board of Trustees of the American Schools of Oriental Research," *JAOS* LXXVI (1956), 254-55.

"Report of the Society's Representative on the Board of Trustees of the American Schools of Oriental Research," *JAOS* LXXVII (1957), 300-301.

"A Flying Trip to the Near East," *Bulletin, Graduate School of Theology* IV, No. 1 (1958), 4-6.

"Report of the Society's Representative on the Board of Trustees of the

American Schools of Oriental Research," *JAOS* LXXVIII (1958), 229-30.
"Report of the Society's Representative on the Board of Trustees of the American Schools of Oriental Research," *JAOS* LXXIX (1959), 221-22.
"Report of the Society's Representative on the Board of Trustees of the American Schools of Oriental Research," *JAOS* LXXX (1960), 293-94.
"Report of the Society's Representative on the Board of Trustees of the American Schools of Oriental Research," *JAOS* LXXXI (1961), 349-51.
"Report of the Society's Representative on the Board of Trustees of the American Schools of Oriental Research," *JAOS* LXXXII (1962), 478-79.
"Out of the Life of a People," *IJRE* XXXVI, No. 6 (1963), 6-8, 58.
"Cosmological Reference in the Qumran Doctrine of the Two Spirits and in Old Testament Imagery," *JBL* LXXXII (1963), 1-14.
"Report of American Oriental Society Representative on the Board of Trustees of the American Schools of Oriental Research," *JAOS* LXXXIV (1964), 321-22.
"The Revised Standard Version After Twenty Years," *McCormick Quarterly*, May, 1966.
" 'This People' and 'This Nation' in Haggai," VI, XVIII (1968), 190-97.

D. BOOK REVIEWS IN SCHOLARLY JOURNALS

Wooley, C. L., *Abraham,* in *RL* 1937, pp. 463-64.
Harris, C. W., *The Hebrew Heritage,* in *RL* 1937, pp. 148-49.
Causse, E., *Du Groupe Ethnique à la Communauté Réligieuse,* etc., in *JR* XIX (1939), 248-50.
Greenstone, J. H., *Numbers with Commentary,* in *JR* XX (January, 1940), 100-101.
Hebrew Union College Annual, XIV, 1939, in *JR* XX (April, 1940), 185-87.
Haller, Max, and Galling, Kurt, *Die Fünf Megilloth, Handbuch zum Alten Testament,* in *JR* XXI (1941), 61-64.
Cohon, B. D., *The Prophets, Their Personalities and Teachings,* in *JSS** 1941, pp. 214-15.
Siegman, E. F., *The False Prophets of the Old Testament,* in *JSS** 1941, pp. 215-16.
Hebrew Union College Annual, XV, 1941, in *JR* XXII (1942), 115-18.
Albright, W. F., *Archaeology and the Religion of Israel,* in *JSS** 1942, pp. 400-401.
Burrows, M., *What Mean These Stones?* in *JBL* LXI (1942), 283-89.
Hebrew Union College Annual, XVI, 1941, in *JR* XXIII (1943), 66-68.
Wright, G. E., *The Challenge of Israel's Faith,* in *JBL* LXIII (1944), 413-18.
McCown, C. C., *Ladder of Progress in Palestine,* in *JR* XXIV (1944), 300-301.
Wach, J., *Sociology of Religion,* in *JBR* XII (1944), 249-50.
Hebrew Union College Annual, XVII, 1942-43, in *JR* XXIV (1944), 139-40.
Albright, W. F., *The Excavation of Tell Beit Mirsim, III. AASOR, XXI-XXII,* in *JBL* LXIII (1944), 191.
Wolfe, R., *Meet Amos and Hosea,* in *JBL* LXIV (1945), 274-76.
Irwin, W. A., *The Problem of Ezekiel,* in *JNES* IV (1945), 61-64.
Wright, G. E., and Filson, F. V., *Historical Atlas to the Bible,* in *OTR* II, No. 3 (1945), 27-28.

Bibliography of Publications

Morgenstern, J., *Ark, Ephod, and Tent of Meeting,* in *JNES* V (1946), 279-80.

Finegan, J., *Light from the Ancient Past,* in *RL* XVI (1946-1947), 153-59.

Burrows, M., *Outline of Biblical Theology,* in *OTR* IV, 1947.

Humbert, P., *Études sur le récit du paradis et de la chute dans la Genèse,* in *JBL* LXVI (1947), 228-34.

Glueck, N., *The River Jordan,* in *AJA* LI (1947), 106-7.

Rylaarsdam, J. C., *Revelation in Jewish Wisdom Literature,* in *JR* XXVII (1947), 60.

Humbert, P., *Problèmes du Livre d'Habacuc,* in *JNES* VII (1948), 58-61.

McCown, C. C., et al., *Excavations at Tell en-Nasbeh,* in *JR* XXVIII (1948), 134-35.

Matthews, I. G., *Religious Pilgrimage of Israel,* in *JBR* XVI (1948), 126-28.

Danniel, B., *Jesus, Jews, and Gentiles,* in *RE* XLIII (1948), 189.

Gerleman, G., *Contributions to the Old Testament Terminology of the Chase,* in *JBL* LXVII (1948), 188.

Hebrew Union College Annual, XX, 1947, in *JBL* LXVII (1948), 184-86.

Gordon, C., *Lands of the Cross and Crescent,* in *RE* XLIII (1948), 189.

Westminster Press, *Bible Study Projects with the Use of Maps,* in *RE* XLIII (1948), 184-85.

Alleman, H. C., and Flack, E. E., *Old Testament Commentary,* in *RE* XLIII (1948), 250.

Montgomery, J. A., *The Bible, the Book of God and of Man,* in *RE* XLIV (1949), 124.

Leslie, E. A., *The Psalms,* in *RE* XLIV (1949), 189.

Baab, O., *The Theology of the Old Testament,* in *CQ* XXVI (1949), 342-44.

Reed, W., *The Asherah in the Old Testament,* in *JBL* LXVIII (1949), 376-79.

Hyatt, J. P., *Prophetic Religion,* in *RE* XLIV (1949), 256.

Williams, G., *The Student's Commentary on the Holy Scriptures,* in *RE* XLIV (1949), 376.

Watts, H. H., *The Modern Reader's Guide to the Bible,* in *RE* XLIV (1949), 371.

Patterson, J., *The Goodly Fellowship of the Prophets,* in *RE* XLIV (1949), 313-14.

Flight, J., *The Drama of Ancient Israel,* in *JBL* LXIX (1950), 199.

Irwin, W. A., and Wikgren, A., *The Ancestry of Our English Bible* (I. M. Price), in *RE* XLV (1950), 253-54.

Ginzberg, L., *Jubilee Vols. I and II,* in *JNES* IX (1950), 57-58.

Heidel, A., *Gilgamesh Epic and Old Testament Parallels,* in *RE* XLV (1950), 122.

Buber, M., *The Prophetic Faith,* in *JBR* XVIII (1950), 131-32.

Morgenstern, J., *As a Mighty Stream,* in *JBL* LXIX (1950), 199.

Matthews, C. D., *Palestine-Mohammedan Holy Land,* in *JBL* LXIX (1950), 200.

Knox, R., *The Old Testament, Vol. I: Genesis to Esther,* in *RE* XLV (1950), 63.

Lewy, I., *The Birth of the Bible,* in *JBR* XVIII (1950), 250-52.

Hammond and Co., *Atlas of Bible Lands,* in *RE* XLV (1950), 319.

East-West Library, *The Books of the Maccabees,* in *RE* XLV (1950), 253.

Rowley, H. H., *The Growth of the Bible,* in *JBL* XLIX (1950), 407.

Mould, E., *Bible History Digest,* in *RE* XLV (1950), 379.

Hebrew Union College Annual, XXI, 1948, in *JNES* IX (1950), 263-64.

Pritchard, J. B., ed., *Ancient Near Eastern Texts,* in *RE* XLVI (1951), 191-92.

Albright, W. F., *The Biblical Period,* in *JBL* LXX (1951), 175.

Howie, C. G., *The Date and Composition of Ezekiel,* in *JBL* LXX (1951), 168-70.

Rowley, H. H., *From Joseph to Joshua,* in *JBL* LXX (1951), 170-71.

Tobler, A. J., *Excavations at Tepe Gawra,* in *JBL* LXX (1951), 175.

Gordis, R., *The Wisdom of Koheleth,* in *RE* LXVI, (1951), 190-91.

Reifenberg, A., *Ancient Hebrew Seals,* in *RE* XLVI (1951), 192.

Bewer, J. A., *Book of Isaiah, Vol. I, Chs. 1-39; Book of Isaiah, Vol. II, Chs. 40-66,* in *JBL* LXX (1951), 174.

Bewer, J. A., *The Book of Isaiah, Vol. I, Chs. 1-39,* in *RE* XLVI (1951), 188.

Wright, G. E., *The Old Testament Against Its Environment,* in *JBL* LXX (1951), 321-23.

Cunliffe-Jones, H., *Deuteronomy: Introduction and Commentary,* in *JBL* LXX (1951), 344.

Fischel, W., ed., *Semitic and Oriental Studies,* in *JBL* LXX (1951), 344.

Rowley, H. H., ed., *Book List 1951: The Society for Old Testament Study,* in *JBL* LXX (1951), 344.

Brannon, C. H., *An Introduction to the Bible,* in *JBL* LXX (1951), 344.

Rypins, S., *The Book of Thirty Centuries,* in *RE* XLVII (1952), 63-64.

Rowley, H. H., ed., *The Old Testament and Modern Study,* in *JBL* LXXI (1952), 118.

Bewer, J. A., *The Book of Jeremiah, Vol. II,* and Grant, F. C., *The Gospel of Mark,* in *RE* XLVII (1952), 367.

Terrien, S., *The Psalms and Their Meaning for Today,* in *RE* XLVII (1952), 302-3.

Pope, H., *English Versions of the Bible,* in *RE* XLVII (1952), 241.

Robertson, E., *The Old Testament Problem: A Reinvestigation,* in *JNES* XII (1952), 65-67.

Dupont-Sommer, A., *The Dead Sea Scrolls,* in *RE* XLVIII (1953), 53-54.

Butterworth, C. C., *The English Primers, 1529-1545,* in *RE* XLVIII (1953), 202.

Parker, R. A., *The Calendars of Ancient Egypt,* in *JBL* LXXII (1953), 142.

Neufeld, E., *The Hittite Laws, Translated into English and Hebrew with Commentary,* in *JBL* LXXII (1953), 142.

Levene, A., *The Early Syrian Fathers on Genesis,* in *JBL* LXXII (1953), 142-43.

Hedegard, D., *Seder R Amran Gaon,* Part I, in *JBL* LXXII (1953), 143.

Gleave, H. C., *The Ethiopic Version of the Song of Songs,* in *JBL* LXXII (1953), 143.

Hart, H. St. J., *A Foreword to the Old Testament,* in *JBL* LXXII (1953), 143.

Bialik Institute, *Dictionary of Ceramic Terms,* in *JBL* LXXII (1953), 143.

Rypins, S., *The Book of Thirty Centuries,* in *JBL* LXXII (1953), 209.

Irwin, W. A., *The Old Testament—Keystone of Human Culture,* in *RE* XLVIII (1953), 441.

Montgomery, J. A., *A Critical and Exegetical Commentary on the Book of Kings,* in *RE* XLVIII (1953), 442-43.

Irwin, W. A., *The Old Testament—Keystone of Human Culture,* in *JBL* LXXII (1953), 272-73.

Peters, B., *The Private Lives of the Prophets and the Times in Which They Lived,* in *RE* XLIX (1954), 228-29.

Barrois, A. G., *Manuel d'Archéologie Biblique,* in *JAOS* LXXIV (1954), 94-96.

Wentzel, E. D., *Song of the Earth,* in *RE* XLIX (1954), 367.

Frost, S. B., *Old Testament Apocalyptic,* in *JBL* LXXIII (1954), 242-44.

Orlinsky, H. M., *Ancient Israel,* in *JAOS* LXXIV (1954), 268-69.

New World Translation of the Hebrew Scriptures, in *RE* L (1955), 139-40.

Orlinsky, H. M. *Ancient Israel,* in *RE* L (1955), 140.

Karraker, W. A., *The Bible in Questions and Answers,* in *RE* L (1955), 142.

Snaith, N. H., *et al., The Interpreter's Bible, Vol. III,* in *RE* L (1955), 208.

Honor, L. L., *Book of Kings I,* in *RE* L (1955), 266.

Goldman, Solomon, ed., *Iggeret Teman (Letters to the Jews of Yemen),* in *RE* L (1955), 271.

Bewer, J. A., *The Book of Daniel,* in *RE* L (1955), 272.

Gordis, R., *The Song of Songs; a Study, Modern Translation and Commentary,* in *JNES* XIV (1955), 207-8.

The Holy Scriptures According to the Masoretic Text, by Jewish Publication Society of America, in *RE* LI (1956), 78.

Torrey, C. C., *The Chronicler's History of Israel: Chronicles-Ezra-Nehemiah, Restored to Its Original Form,* in *JNES* XV (1956), 51.

Pritchard, J. B., *The Ancient Near East in Pictures Relating to the Old Testament,* in *JBL* LXXV (1956), 77-78.

Wilson, E., *The Scrolls from the Dead Sea,* in *RE* LI (1956), 228-29.

Williams, W. G., *The Prophets-Pioneers to Christianity,* in *RE* LI (1956), 319-20.

Tufnell, Olga, *Lachish III (Tell ed-Duweir), The Iron Age,* in *JBL* LXXV (1956), 342-44.

Gaster, T. H., *The Dead Sea Scriptures in English Translation,* in *RE* LII (1957), 74.

Parrot, A., *Nineveh and the Old Testament,* in *RE* LII (1957), 78.

Robinson, H. W., *The Cross in the Old Testament,* in *RE* LII (1957), 160.

Wright, G. E., *Biblical Archaeology,* in *RE* LII (1957), 473.

Bamberger, B. J., *The Story of Judaism,* in *RE* LIII (1958), 77-78.

Snaith, N. H., *The Jews from Cyrus to Herod,* in *RE* LIII (1958), 235.

Lamsa, G. M., *The Holy Bible from Eastern Manuscripts,* in *JBR* XXVI (1958), 326-27.

Pfeiffer, R. H., *The Hebrew Iliad,* in *RL* XXVIII (1958), 152-53.

Cross, F. C., Jr., *The Ancient Library of Qumran and Modern Biblical Studies,* in *JBL* LXXVIII (1959), 78-80.

Anderson, G. W., *Critical Introduction to the Old Testament,* in *JBR* XXVII (1959), 340-44.

Zimmerli, W., and Jeremias, J., *The Servant of God,* in *JNES* XVIII (1959), 229-30.

Thomas, D. W., *Documents from Old Testament Times,* in *JSS* V (1960), 72-73.

Tufnell, Olga, *Lachish IV (Tell ed-Duweir), The Bronze Age,* in *JBL* LXXIX (1960), 66-67.

De Vaux, R., *Les Institutions de l'Ancien Testament, Vol. I,* in *JNES* XX (1961), 208-9.

Join-Lambert, M., *Jerusalem,* in *JNES* XX (1961), 212-13.

Wright, G. E., ed., *The Bible and the Ancient Near East,* in *JR* XXXI (1961), 155-56.

Pfeiffer, R. H., *Religion in the Old Testament,* in *JBR* XXX (1962), 57-60.

Noth, Martin, *Exodus, A Commentary,* in *RL* XXXII (1962-63), 142-43.

Douglas, J. D., ed., *The New Bible Dictionary,* in *JBR* XXXI (1963), 138-40.

Heschel, Abraham, *The Prophets,* in *Union Seminary Quarterly Review* XVIII (1963), 405-6.

De Vaux, R., *Les Institutions de l'Ancien Testament, II,* in *JNES* XXII (1963), 202-4.

Leslie, E. A., *Isaiah: Chronologically Arranged, Translated, and Interpreted,* in *JR* XXXIII (1963-64), 147-48.

Greenslade, S. L., ed., *The Cambridge History of the Bible: The West from the Reformation to the Present Day,* in *JBR* XXXII (1964), 365-67.

Davies, W. D., *The Setting of the Sermon on the Mount,* in *JR* XXXIV (1964-65), 316-17.

Harrelson, W., *Interpreting the Old Testament,* in *RL* XXXIV (1965), 316-17.

Albright, W. F., *History, Archaeology, and Christian Humanism,* in *JBR* XXXIII (1965), 262-64.

Burrows, M., *Diligently Compared—the Revised Standard Version and the King James Version of the Old Testament,* in *JBL* LXXXIV (1965), 445-46.

Knight, G. A. F., *Deutero-Isaiah—A Theological Commentary on Isaiah 40-55,* and J. D. Smart, *History and Theology in Second Isaiah—A Commentary on Isaiah 35, 40-66,* in *RL* XXXV (1966), 303-4.

Parrot, André, *Abraham and His Times,* in *RL* XXXVIII (1969), 294-95.

Reicke, Bo, *The New Testament Era,* in *RL* XXXVIII (1969), 299-300.

E. ARTICLES IN POPULAR PUBLICATIONS

"Spoils of the Spade at Armageddon," *ILN* (May 26, 1934), pp. 836 ff.

"The Meaning of Genesis," *Adult Bible Class Magazine,* April, 1937.

"The Call of Israel," *Adult Bible Class Quarterly,* VI (1943), 13 ff.

"Solomon in All His Glory," *Elyria Masonic News,* I, No. 2, p. 1.

"Biblical Archaeology and Religious Education," with L. Stidley, *Religious Digest* (October, 1945), pp. 25 ff.

"This Nation Is Thy People," *Pilgrim Adult Bible Class Quarterly,* IX (1946), 3 ff.

"A Chat About the Old Testament," *The Christian Sun,* No. 98 (1946), pp. 5, 23.

"God Speaks Through the Prophets," *The Highroad,* V (1946), 22-32. A series of five articles for Church School students.

"God Speaks Through the Prophets," *The Church School,* V (1946), 21-28. A series of five articles for Church School teachers.

"The Prophet Micah," *Christian Action,* III (1948), 2 ff.

"Jeremiah," *Current Christian Thought,* VIII (1948), 11-13.

"Jeremias," *El Sendero de la Verdad,* III (1949), 2-5.

"God Speaks Through the Prophets," *Workers With Youth,* V (1952), 29-40.

"The Revised Standard Version," *PUQ* III (1952), 5-9.

"Newest Version of Oldest Writing," *Adult Student,* XI (1952), 5-9.

"The Bible and the Faith of the Christian," *CR* XIII, No. 9 (1952), 3-5.

"The Bible in English," *The Christian Home,* II (1952), 4-6, 48-49.

"The Revised Standard Version," *The Church in the Home,* III (1952), 4-8.

"Some Twentieth Century Translations of the Bible," *Publishers Weekly,* CLXII (1952), 648-91.

"Old Testament Devotional Materials (The Psalms)," *Adult Teacher,* V (October, 1952), pp. 32-45; (November, 1952), pp. 29-45; (December, 1952), pp. 30-43.

"John's Gospel and Its Bearing on Today," *Adult Teacher,* VI (1953), 9-12.

"The Significance of the Elijah-Elisha Stories," *PUQ* IV (1954), 6-9.

"The Christian View of God," *Kindergarten Teacher's Guide,* V (1955), 8-11.

"From Jeremiah to Nehemiah—Defeat and Reconstruction," *PUQ* V (1955), 3-5.

"The Kingdom of Judah and Its Kings," *PUQ* V (1955), 5-8.

"The Revelation of God in the Old Testament," *CR* XVII, No. 1 (1956), 3-4.

"A Good Time to Be Alive," *CR* XVII, No. 6 (1956), 11-12.

"Life and Its Problems in Early Israel," *PUQ* VIII (1958), 5-9.

"Pathways of Israel to the Knowledge of God," *PUQ* IX, No. 4 (1959), 3-5.

"George David Hubbard, 1871-1958," *Current Religious Thought,* 3rd Series, I, 3-5.

"The Times of the Prophets," *PUQ* X, No. 4 (1960), 3-5.

"The Book of Books," *CSW* XII, No. 2 (1961), 7-8.

"The Old and the New Covenant," *CSW* XII, No. 3, (1961), 7-8.

"The Bible in English," *CSW* XII, No. 4 (1961), 10-12.

"The Bible, A Prophetic Book," *CSW* XII, No. 5 (1962), 7-9.

"The Bible and Archaeology," *CSW* XII, No. 6 (1962), 7-9.

"The Bible and Geography," *CSW* XII, No. 7 (1962), 7-10.

"Nahum-Habakkuk-Zephaniah," *Reader's Guide, Old Testament,* No. 15 (1962), pp. 1-6.

"The Bible in the United Church Curriculum," *CSW* XIII, No. 11, pp. 13-15, 35.

"Lessons in Living," *Christian Adventure,* III, No. 4 (1964), 18-32.

"Laments and Penitence in the Psalms," "Thanksgiving in the Worship of Israel," "The Law and Wisdom Themes in Israel's Worship," "Trust in the Lord—a Theme in Israel's Worship," *Adult Teacher,* Vol. XIX, No. 12 (1966).

"The Psalms," *Reader's Guide, Old Testament,* No. 21 (1967), pp. 1-5.

F. BOOK REVIEWS IN POPULAR PUBLICATIONS

Belloc, H., *The Battleground,* in *C* I (1936), 897-900.

Zeitlin, J., *Disciples of the Wise,* in *USQBL* II, No. 1 (1945), 18.

Torrey, C. C., *The Apocryphal Literature,* in *USQBL* II, No. 1 (1946), 20.

Archer, J. C., *The Sikhs in Relation to Hindus, Moslems, Christians, and Ahmadiyyas,* in *USQBL* II, No. 2 (1946), 90-91.

Longacre, L. B., *The Old Testament: Its Form and Purpose,* in *C* XI, 1946.

Arpee, L., *A History of Armenian Christianity,* in *USQBL* II, No. 3 (1946), 184-85.

Glueck, N., *The River Jordan,* in *USQBL* II, No. 3 (1946), 215-16.

Case, S. J., *Origins of Christian Supernaturalism,* in *USQBL* III, No. 1 (1947), 28-29.

Fite, W., *Jesus the Man,* in *USQBL* III, No. 1 (1947), 30.

Clinchy, R., *Faith and Freedom,* in *USQBL* III (1947), 248.

Cuninggim, M., *The College Seeks Religion,* in *USQBL* IV (1948), 27-28.

Willoughby, H. R., ed., *The Study of the Bible Today and Tomorrow,* in *USQBL* IV (1948), 148.

Baughman, F., *Jeremiah for Today,* in *Advance,* CXLI (April, 1948), 25.

Wischnitzer, R., *The Messianic Theme in the Paintings of the Dura Synagogue,* in *USQBL* IV (1948), 257-58.

Harmon, N. B., *The Organization of the Methodist Church,* in *USQBL* IV (1948), 282.

Rach, M., *Report to Protestants,* in *USQBL* V (1949), 36-37.

Weigle, L. A., *The English New Testament from Tyndale to the RSV,* in *USQBL* V (1949), 174-75.

Latourette, K. S., *The Emergence of a World Christian Community,* in *USQBL* V (1949), 172.

Clark, E. T., *The Small Sects in America,* in *USQBL* V (1949), 459-60.

Pfeiffer, R. H., *History of New Testament Times,* in *USQBL* VI (1950), 33-34.

Matthews, C. D., *Palestine-Mohammedan Holy Land,* in *USQBL* VI (1950), 31-32.

Thompson, C. R., *Inquisitio de Fide,* in *USQBR* VI (1950), 420-21.

Pauck, W., *Heritage of the Reformation,* in *USQBR* VI (1950), 295.

Bailey, A. E., *The Gospel in Hymns,* in *USQBR* VI (1950), 163-64.

Everett, J. R., *Religion in Human Experience,* in *USQBR* VI (1950), 421.

Lewisohn, L., *The American Jew,* in *USQBR* VII (1951), 36.

Kennard, J. S., *Render to God,* in *USQBR* VII (1951), 35-36.

Casson, L., and Hettich, E., *Excavations at Nessana,* in *USQBR* VII (1951), 9-10.

Glueck, N., *Explorations in Eastern Palestine, IV,* in *USQBR* VII (1951), 230.

Prichard, J., *Ancient Near Eastern Texts,* in *USQBR* VII (1951), 149.

McNeill, J., *History of the Cure of Souls,* in *USQBR* VII (1951), 251.

Thiele, E. R., *The Mysterious Numbers of the Hebrew Kings,* in *USQBR* VII (1951), 363.

Buttrick, G., ed., *The Interpreter's Bible, Vol. VII,* in *USQBR* VIII (1952), 40-41.

Bibliography of Publications

Kraeling, C. H., *John the Baptist,* in *USQBR* VIII (1952), 41.

Baron, S. W., *A Social and Religious History of the Jews, Vols. I and II,* in *USQBR* VIII (1952), 139-40.

Jeffery, A., *The Quran as Scripture,* in *USQBR* VIII (1952), 380.

The Interpreter's Bible, Vols. I and VIII, in *USQBR* IX (1953), 49-50.

Latourette, K. S., *A History of Christianity,* in *USQBR* IX (1953), 436.

Craig, C. T., Short, J., *et al., Corinthians, Galatians, and Ephesians, The Interpreter's Bible, Vol. X,* in *USQBR* IX (1953), 307.

Gaster, T. H., *Festivals of the Jewish Year,* in *The Pastor,* XVII (1954), 39-40.

Micklem, N., Marsh, J., *et al., Leviticus–Samuel, The Interpreter's Bible, Vol. II,* in *USQBR* X (1954), 64-65.

Chester, A. G., *Hugh Latimer,* in *USQBR* X (1954), 151.

Johnson, E., *Under Quaker Appointment,* in *USQBR* X (1954), 151.

Foley, A. S., *Bishop Healy—Beloved Outcaste,* in *USQBR* X (1954), 294-95.

Gurian, W. and Fitzsimons, M. A., *The Catholic Church in World Affairs,* in *USQBR* X (1954), 353-54.

Macgregor, G. H. C., *et al., The Interpreter's Bible, Vol. III,* in *USQBR* X (1954), 355.

Herklots, H. G. G., *How Our Bible Came to Us,* in *WB* XIII (1954), 7-8.

Craig, C. T., *et al., The Interpreter's Bible, Vol. X,* in *USQBR* X (1954), 517.

Katsh, A. I., *Judaism in Islam,* in *USQBR* X (1954), 517-18.

Kleist, J. A., *The New Testament Rendered from the Original Greek, Part I, The Four Gospels,* in *USQBR* X (1954), 519-20.

Rouse, R., *et al., A History of the Ecumenical Movement,* in *USQBR* X (1954), 521.

West, W. G., *Barton Warren Stone,* in *USQBR* XI (1955), 19.

Ahern, P. H., *The Life of John J. Keane,* in *USQBR* XI (1955), 167.

Pritchard, J. B., *The Ancient Near East in Pictures Relating to the Old Testament,* in *USQBR* XI (1955), 199-200.

Grant, R. M., *The Sword and the Cross,* in *USQBR* XI (1955), 221.

McCullough, W. S., *et al., The Interpreter's Bible, Vol. IV, Psalms and Proverbs,* in *USQBR* XI (1955), 222.

The Jewish People, Past and Present, IV, in *USQBR* XI (1955), 331.

Barrow, J. G., *A Bibliography of Bibliographies in Religion,* in *USQBR* XI (1955), 426-27.

Scott, E. F., *et al., The Interpreter's Bible, Vol. XI, Philippians to Hebrews,* in *USQBR* XI (1955), 480.

Goldwin, J., *'The Fathers' According to Rabbi Nathan,* in *USQBR* XI (1955), 479.

Neil, W., *The Rediscovery of the Bible,* in *WB* XIV (1955), 6-7.

Knox, John, *The Early Church and the Coming Great Church,* in *USQBR* XI (1955), 359-60.

Shaw, J. M., *Pulpit Under the Sky; A Life of Hans Nielsen Hauge,* in *USQBR* XII (1956), 9-10.

Reidy, M. F., *Bishop Lancelot Andrewes, Jacobean Court Preacher,* in *USQBR* XII (1956), 52-53.

Clark, R. D., *The Life of Matthew Simpson,* in *USQBR* XII (1956), 134-35.

Forbush, B., *Elias Hicks, Quaker Liberal,* in *USQBR* XII (1956), 136-37.

Heschel, A. J., *God in Search of Man,* in *USQBR* XII (1956), 182-83.

Buttrick, G., ed., *The Interpreter's Bible, Vol. V,* in *USQBR* XII (1956), 183.

Noerdlinger, H. S., *Moses and Egypt,* in *New Christian Advocate,* I, No. 3, pp. 76, 78.

Wheaton, E. W., *Everyday Life in Old Testament Times,* in *WB* XV (1956), 5-6.

Bewer, J. A., *The Prophets,* in *Advance,* 149, No. 2, p. 18.

Anderson, B. W., *Understanding the Old Testament,* in *WB* XVI, No. 4 (1957), 5-6.

Price, Sellers, and Carlson, *Monuments of the Old Testament,* in *WB* XVIII, No.1 (1958), 11-12.

Henshaw, T., *The Latter Prophets,* in *I,* XIII (1959), 359-60.

Guthrie, H. H., Jr., *God and History in the Old Testament,* in *WB* XIX, No. 4 (1960), 2-3.

Muilenburg, J., *The Way of Israel,* in *WB* XXI (1962), 2-3.

Achtemeier, Paul and Elizabeth, *The Old Testament Roots of Our Faith,* in *CSW* XIII, No. 3 (1962), 20, 24.

Newman, M. L., *The People of the Covenant: A Study of Israel from Moses to the Monarchy,* in *WB* XXII, No. 2, pp. 3-4.

Speiser, E. A., *Genesis (Anchor Bible),* in *The Christian Century,* LXXXI (1964), 1434-36.

Staack, H., *Living Personalities of the Old Testament,* in *United Church Herald,* VII, No. 2 (1964), 31-32.

List of Abbreviations

AASOR—Annual of the American Schools of Oriental Research
AJA—American Journal of Archaeology
AJSL—American Journal of Semitic Languages and Literatures
ANET—J. B. Pritchard, *Ancient Near Eastern Texts Relating to the Old Testament* (2nd ed.)
Arch.—Archaeology
ASV—American Standard Version
ATD—Das Alte Testament Deutsch
AthANT—Abhandlungen zur Theologie des Alten und Neuen Testaments
ATR—Anglican Theological Review
AV—Authorized Version
BA—The Biblical Archaeologist
BASOR—Bulletin of the American Schools of Oriental Research
BGBE—Beiträge zur Geschichte der biblischen Exegese
Bi. et Or.—Biblica et Orientalia
Bi. Or.—Bibliotheca Orientalis
BIES—Bulletin of the Israel Exploration Society
BK—Bibel und Kirche
BWANT—Beiträge zur Wissenschaft vom Alten und Neuen Testament
BZ—Biblische Zeitschrift
BZAW—Beihefte zur Zeitschrift für die alttestamentliche Wissenschaft
C—Christendom
CAH—Cambridge Ancient History
CBQ—Catholic Biblical Quarterly
CQ—Crozer Quarterly
CR—Children's Religion
CSW—Church School Worker
EB—Encyclopaedia Biblica
EI—Encyclopaedia of Islam

E.T.—English Translation
EV(V)—English Version(s)
Ev. Theo.—Evangelische Theologie
FRLANT—Forschungen zur Religion und Literatur des Alten und Neuen Testaments
GJ—Geographical Journal
HAT—Handbuch zum Alten Testament
HUCA—Hebrew Union College Annual
I—Interpretation
IB—The Interpreter's Bible
IDB—The Interpreter's Dictionary of the Bible
IEJ—Israel Exploration Journal
IJRE—International Journal of Religious Education
ILN—Illustrated London News
JAOS—Journal of the American Oriental Society
JBL—Journal of Biblical Literature
JBR—Journal of Bible and Religion
JCS—Journal of Cuneiform Studies
JEA—Journal of Egyptian Archaeology
JNES—Journal of Near Eastern Studies
JPOS—Journal of the Palestine Oriental Society
JPSV—Jewish Publication Society Version
JQR—Jewish Quarterly Review
JR—Journal of Religion
JTS—Journal of Theological Studies
JSS*—Jewish Social Studies
JSS—Journal of Semitic Studies
KB—Köhler-Baumgartner
NKZ—Neue kirchliche Zeitschrift
OTR—Oberlin Theological Review
PEFQS—Palestine Exploration Fund Quarterly Statement
PEQ—Palestine Exploration Quarterly
PJB—Palästina Jahrbuch
PSBA—Proceedings of the Society of Biblical Archaeology
PUQ—Pilgrim Uniform Quarterly
Q—Qere
RB—Revue biblique
RE—Religious Education
RES—Répertoire d'épigraphie sémitique
RHPR—Revue d'histoire et de philosophie religieuses
RL—Religion in Life
RSV—Revised Standard Version
ST—Studia Theologica
SVT—Supplements to Vetus Testamentum

TLZ—Theologische Literaturzeitung
TVT—Tijdschrift voor Theologie
TZ—Theologische Zeitschrift
USQBL—United States Quarterly Book List
USQBR—United States Quarterly Book Review
VT—Vetus Testamentum
WB—Westminster Bookman
WZKM—Wiener Zeitschrift für die Kunde des Morgenlandes
ZA—Zeitschrift für Assyriologie und verwandte Gebiete
ZAW—Zeitschrift für die alttestamentliche Wissenschaft
ZDPV—Zeitschrift des deutschen Palästina-Vereins

The Standard Bible Committee
LUTHER A. WEIGLE

The American Standard Version of the Bible, a variant of the Revised Version of 1881-1885, was published by Thomas Nelson & Sons in 1901 and copyrighted to protect the text from unauthorized changes. In 1928 the copyright was transferred to the International Council of Religious Education, a body in which the educational boards of forty of the major Protestant denominations of the United States and Canada were associated. That body appointed an American Standard Bible Committee of scholars to have charge of the text, and authorized it to undertake further revision if deemed necessary. The charter of the Committee contains the provision that "all changes in the text shall be agreed upon by a two-thirds vote of the total membership of the Committee"—a more conservative rule than had governed revision hitherto, which required only a two-thirds vote of members present.

The work of the American Standard Bible Committee was begun in 1930; it was suspended in 1932 because of lack of funds to provide for the expense of travel and secretarial service for the comprehensive revision which it decided to undertake. In 1937 the necessary budget was provided, and the revision proceeded, with the authorization of the following vote of the International Council of Religious Education: "There is need for a version which embodies the best results of modern scholarship as to the meaning of the Scriptures, and expresses this meaning in English diction which is designed for use in public and private worship and preserves those qualities which have given to the King James Version a supreme place in English literature. We, therefore, define the task of the American Standard Bible Committee to be that of revision of the present American Standard Bible in the light of the results of modern scholarship, this revision to be designed for use in public and private worship, and to be in the direction of the simple, classic English style of the King James Version."

The Committee worked in two Sections, one dealing with the Old Testament and one with the New Testament. In the experimental period, 1930-1932, five meetings, each of two- or three-days duration, were held in New York. At the first of these Luther A. Weigle was elected chairman of the Committee, and the officers of the Sections were chosen: for the Old Testament, John R. Sampey as chairman and F. C. Eiselen as secretary; for the New Testament, James H. Ropes as chairman and Henry J. Cadbury as secretary. When the decision was reached in 1932 to recommend that revision of the American Standard Version be undertaken, Ropes dissented and resigned, and when the work began in 1937 Sampey asked that he be replaced by Kyle Yates, his associate on the faculty of the Southern Baptist Theological Seminary at Louisville. So the practice of having separate chairmen for the Sections lapsed, the meetings of the Sections were scheduled at separate times and places, and Luther A. Weigle, as chairman, and James Moffatt, as executive secretary, were officers and voting members of both Sections.

The first death in the membership of the Committee was that of Alexander R. Gordon, Montreal, in March 1931, who was succeeded by William R. Taylor, Toronto. Other deaths were those of J. M. P. Smith, 1932; A. T. Robertson, 1934; and F. C. Eiselen in May 1937. Four other members—William P. Armstrong, James A. Montgomery, Andrew Sledd, and Charles C. Torrey—resigned because they were not willing to undertake a task which would continue for at least seven or eight years. When the Committee met at Union Theological Seminary, New York, December 3-4, 1937, the only original members present were Julius A. Bewer, Henry J. Cadbury, Edgar J. Goodspeed, James Moffatt, John R. Sampey, and Luther A. Weigle. To these were added Walter Russell Bowie, George Dahl, Frederick C. Grant, William A. Irwin, Willard L. Sperry, William R. Taylor, and Leroy Waterman. In early 1938 Millar Burrows, Clarence T. Craig, and Abdel Ross Wentz were elected to the membership of the Committee. It should be stated that Bowie, Sperry, Wentz, and Weigle were members chosen under the provision contained in the action of the Council which established the Committee: "that not less than three and not more than five of the fifteen members of the Committee be chosen with a view to their competence in English literature, or their experience in the conduct of public worship or in religious education." The other members, six in each Section, were chosen for their competence in biblical scholarship. Sperry was assigned to the Old Testament Section, Bowie and Wentz to the New Testament Section.

With the Committee was associated an Advisory Board of representatives chosen by each of the forty denominations affiliated with the International Council of Religious Education. The members of this Board were consulted with respect to the principles underlying the revision; they were afforded opportunity to review and make suggestions concerning the drafts of the work in progress.

The New Testament Section convened thirty-one times in the six years 1937-1943, in meetings covering one hundred and forty-five days, with sessions scheduled from 9 A.M. to noon, 2:30 to 5:30 P.M., and 7:30 to 9:30 P.M. The meetings were usually at Union Theological Seminary in New York, at the Yale Divinity School in New Haven, or in the summers at the Northfield Hotel, East Northfield, Massachusetts. For a week in June 1938, and again for two weeks in the summer of 1939, we met as the guests of Professor and Mrs. Edgar J. Goodspeed at their summer home on Paradise Island, Plum Lake, Sayner, Wisconsin.

The initial draft of the revision of each of the books of the New Testament was prepared by one or two members of the Section, to whom it was assigned. This draft was then typed, and a copy sent to each member of the Section, for study prior to the meeting at which it would be considered. It was then discussed, verse by verse, in sessions of the Section. A new draft, prepared by Dr. Moffatt, in the light of the decisions then reached, was mimeographed and distributed for further study. At subsequent sessions of the Section, these mimeographed drafts were again discussed, verse by verse, and suggestions submitted by members of the Advisory Board and others were considered. A revised set of the mimeographed drafts was then submitted to the members of the Old Testament Section, who were given opportunity to record their dissent from any proposed change. At a meeting held in Northfield, August 15-29, 1943, the typescript of the entire New Testament was once more reviewed and the votes and comments of the members of the Old Testament Section were considered. The revised typescript was then placed in the hands of a smaller editorial committee, charged to prepare it for the press and supervise its publication, which took place on February 11, 1946. Meanwhile, we had suffered our greatest loss in the death of Professor James Moffatt on June 27, 1944. A scholar of rare judgment and learning, he brought to the work of both Sections the rich resources of his training and experience as a translator and the genius and devotion of a really great soul.

It is a matter of regret that there is no chapter by Moffatt in the 72-page paperbound *Introduction to the Revised Standard Version of the New Testament* which was also published in February 1946, containing essays by each of the other members of the New Testament Section.

The work of the Old Testament Section had proceeded along similar lines, though more slowly. At the meeting held in New York, June 14-30, 1943, Millar Burrows was added to this group, attending every session and assuming a full share thereafter of the work upon the revision of the Old Testament. In 1945 this Section was substantially reinforced by the election of five new members of the Committee: William F. Albright, J. Philip Hyatt, Herbert G. May, James Muilenburg, and Harry M. Orlinsky. In 1947 one more member was added in the person of Fleming James, who made his home in New Haven and became executive secretary of the Old Testament Section.

In 1937-1944 sixteen meetings of the Old Testament Section had been held; in 1945-1951, with the added membership, there were twenty-six meetings. In the earlier period, three meetings were at the University of Michigan, Ann Arbor; the other meetings of that period and all meetings of the later period were at Union Theological Seminary, the Yale Divinity School, or the Northfield Hotel. In all, the Old Testament Section held forty-two meetings, covering three hundred and fifty-two days; twelve of these meetings were of two weeks or more. The Revised Standard Version of the Bible, containing the Old and New Testaments, was published on Sept. 30, 1952.

On the same date was published a 92-page paperbound *Introduction to the Revised Standard Version of the Old Testament,* containing essays by eleven members of the Old Testament Section and edited by its chairman. Again, it is a matter of regret that there are no chapters by William R. Taylor, who had been chiefly responsible for the translation of the Psalms but died on February 24, 1951, or by Julius A. Bewer, who had been an active member of the Committee from its beginning until the completion of its work but was now suffering from what was destined to be his last illness.

In response to the request of the General Convention of the Protestant Episcopal Church, October 1952, the Division of Christian Education of the National Council of the Churches of Christ in the U.S.A., into which the International Council of Religious Education had merged, organized a committee of scholars to undertake revision of the English translation of the Apocrypha; its publication was authorized by the General Board, NCCCUSA, December 12, 1952. The scholars accepting this assignment were Millar Burrows, Henry J. Cadbury, Clarence T. Craig, Floyd V. Filson, Frederick C. Grant, Bruce M. Metzger, Robert H. Pfeiffer, Allen P. Wikgren, and Luther A. Weigle who was appointed chairman. Five of these scholars were already members of the Standard Bible Committee, and the other four were promptly recognized as members, assigned to their appropriate Section.

A great loss was sustained in the death, August 20, 1953, of Dean Craig. In 1954, J. Carter Swaim became Executive Director of the Department of the English Bible, in the Division of Christian Education, and was added to the membership of this Committee.

The work involved the preparation and circulation of mimeographed drafts of translation, the discussion and resolution of all disputed points in face-to-face conference, the circulation of new drafts embodying the decisions reached in conference, and a final review of each book in the light of written agenda proposed by the members of the Committee and of the Advisory Board made up of representatives appointed by denominations which accepted the invitation to review the drafts. This procedure was similar to that followed by the Committee which prepared the Revised Standard Version of the Bible, containing the Old and New Testaments; in general, similar principles of translation were followed.

Meetings of the Apocrypha Committee were held at the Yale Divinity School, January 30-31, June 22 to July 3, and December 18-23, in 1953, and December 7-9, 1956. Most of the conferences, however, were held at the Hotel Northfield, East Northfield, Massachusetts, where the Committee was in session over the following periods: August 17-29, 1953; June 14-26 and August 16-28, 1954; June 13-25 and August 15-27, 1955; June 11-23, 1956.

The Revised Standard Version of the Apocrypha was published in 1957. The Preface states that "No attempt has been made to provide introductions to the various books of the Apocrypha, as here translated. The scholar will not need them, and for the general reader there are admirable recent books on the Apocrypha by Charles C. Torrey, Edgar J. Goodspeed, Robert H. Pfeiffer, and Bruce M. Metzger. We gladly acknowledge our debt, not only to the scholars who throughout the centuries have made competent studies of these books, but also to the former English translations, especially the King James Version of 1611, the English Revised Version of 1895, and Goodspeed's translation of 1938."

The purpose of the Standard Bible Committee and the assignment of responsibility are stated as follows in the memorandum dated November 23, 1953, signed by Gerald E. Knoff and Luther A. Weigle:

The purpose of the Committee is:

1. To have charge of the text of the American Standard Version of the Bible, and the Revised Standard Version of the Bible.

2. To recommend to the Division when, in its judgment, revision of the texts of these Versions should be made, or any other projects in the translation of the Bible or related books from the ancient languages should be undertaken.

3. To make such revisions or new translations as may be authorized by the Council upon recommendation of the Division.

It is understood:

(1) That the copyright of the American Standard Version, the Revised Standard Version, and all revisions or new translations made by the Committee are the property of the Division.

(2) That responsibility to determine the wording of the text of these versions, revisions, or new translations rests solely upon the Committee.

(3) That responsibility for the budget of the Committee, for authorization of work to be undertaken by the Committee, for publication, and general policy, rests solely upon the Division.

Throughout the work of translation, 1937-1956, the Standard Bible Committee met by Sections, at dates so arranged that the chairman of the Committee could serve as chairman of each of the Sections.

Since the completion of the translations, the work of the Standard Bible Committee has been done largely by correspondence, publication, and conference with interested parties such as, to cite notable examples, the Advisory Committee on English Bible Versions appointed by The Lutheran Church–Missouri Synod, and the committee of scholars representing the Catholic Biblical Association of Great Britain.

A general meeting of the Standard Bible Committee was held at Union Theological Seminary, New York, December 30, 1954, to consider the proposal of the Catholic Biblical Association of Great Britain. The proposal was approved, and the Committee on the Apocrypha was authorized to consider and to grant permission for the changes in the text of the Revised Standard Version of the New Testament requested by the editorial committee of the Catholic

Biblical Association of Great Britain. This was done by the Committee on the Apocrypha at its meeting in Northfield, June 25, 1955.

A general meeting of the Standard Bible Committee was held at the Yale Divinity School, June 9-16, 1959. This had been preceded by a mail vote upon an extensive agenda made up of criticisms and suggestions submitted by various readers from 1952 to 1959 which were of sufficient plausibility to warrant consideration by the Committee. As a result of this mail vote and the decisions reached in the eight-day meeting, a few corrections and changes in the text of the Revised Standard Version were authorized, a list of which was sent to each of the licensed publishers on October 1, 1959. Thomas Nelson & Sons made these corrections and changes in 1960, and the other publishers incorporated them in all editions, beginning September 30, 1962. These changes are described in a new paragraph inserted toward the close of the Preface, which reads as follows:

"These principles were reaffirmed by the Committee in 1959, in connection with a study of criticisms and suggestions from various readers. As a result, a few changes have been authorized for the present and subsequent editions. Most of these are corrections of punctuation, capitalization, or footnotes. Some changes of words or phrases are made in the interest of consistency, clarity, or accuracy of translation. Examples of such changes are 'from,' Job 19.26; 'bread,' Matthew 7.9, 1 Corinthians 10.17; 'is he,' Matthew 21.9 and parallels; 'the Son,' Matthew 27.54, Mark 15.39; 'ask nothing of me,' John 16.23; 'for this life only,' 1 Corinthians 15.19; 'the husband of one wife,' 1 Timothy 3.2, 12; 5.9; Titus 1.6."

In 1960 ten new members were elected to the Standard Bible Committee: (1) as Old Testament scholars, Raymond A. Bowman, Frank M. Cross, Robert C. Dentan, Marvin H. Pope, Alfred von Rohr Sauer; (2) as New Testament scholars, Francis W. Beare, Sherman E. Johnson, John Knox; (3) chosen for competence in English literature, the conduct of public worship, or Christian education, Theodore O. Wedel, Amos N. Wilder.

A general meeting of the Standard Bible Committee was held at the Yale Divinity School, June 16-19, 1965, with sixteen members present. The agenda was based upon correspondence during the preceding six years, upon the careful study of the Revised Standard Version of the Old Testament by Millar Burrows, and upon items submitted by Herbert G. May.

It was understood that the Committee has no authority to make changes at the present time, since we are pledged to the publishers to leave the text unchanged for ten years. Yet substantial progress was made in rejecting many items upon the agenda, in definitely assigning other items to one of the Sections or to individual members for study and report, and in recording present approval of other items while recognizing that no such approval can be regarded as final.

There was general agreement that the Committee should plan to meet in 1968 and at two-year intervals thereafter, and general agreement that the Revised Standard Version is so important, as the representative in our time of the Tyndale–King James tradition and as a bridge linking Catholic and Protestant, that it must not be dealt with hastily. If and when the time comes that further revision should be desirable, in the judgment of the Standard Bible Committee, it will follow the procedure outlined in the paragraphs of the memorandum which has been quoted.

On May 3, 1966, the Catholic Edition of the Revised Standard Version of the Bible was published in Edinburgh and London, followed on July 1, 1966, by its publication in America and Australia. The preparation and publication of this edition are a Catholic project, undertaken at Catholic initiative, edited by Catholic scholars, and bearing the approval of the Catholic Church. It is a Catholic project with which the Standard Bible Committee and the Division of Christian Education are gladly cooperating.

A full account of the project, from its inception in 1953 until the present, has been published by Father Reginald Fuller, D.D., of the Catholic Biblical Association of Great Britain, editor of the Catholic Edition of the Revised Standard Version of the Bible, in his Introduction to the published volumes and in articles which he wrote for publication in *The Tablet,* London, and in the *Catholic Ecumenical Review* which now bears the name *One in Christ.* The article in the second of these publications is entitled, "The Revised Standard Version Catholic Edition and Its Ecumenical Significance."

On May 26, 1966, the *New York Times* carried a front-page article with the news that Richard Cardinal Cushing, Archbishop of Boston, had given his official *imprimatur* to the Oxford Annotated Bible with the Apocrypha. This is an important addition to the approvals already given for the use of the Catholic Edition of the Revised Standard Version of the Bible.

The Oxford Annotated Bible was first published in 1962 by the Oxford University Press. The Revised Standard Version is used as its text, and it is equipped with general and special introductory articles, extensive annotations at the bottom of each page, and a new set of maps. The editors are Dr. Herbert G. May, Professor of Old Testament, Oberlin Graduate School of Theology, and Dr. Bruce M. Metzger, Professor of New Testament, Princeton Theological Seminary. This volume immediately won praise and wide use, especially by ministers and by students in colleges, universities, and theological seminaries. One Catholic college, the Jesuit College of the Holy Cross in Worcester, Massachusetts, promptly adopted it as the required text for all its biblical courses. In 1965 the Oxford University Press produced the Oxford Annotated Apocrypha, and later in that year the two volumes were published together as the Oxford Annotated Bible with the Apocrypha.

Because of a growing acceptance of this volume in Catholic circles, the Oxford University Press decided to approach Cardinal Cushing for his formal approval of this edition of this Bible. He expressed his willingness to consider the request if a joint committee of Catholic and Protestant scholars reviewed the matter and made recommendations. This committee consisted of Father Philip J. King, Professor of Sacred Scriptures, St. John's Seminary, Boston, and Father W. Van Etten Casey, S.J., Professor of Theology, Holy Cross College, Worcester, Massachusetts, who, together with Father Eugene H. Maly, Mount St. Mary's Seminary of the West, Norwood, Ohio, consulted with the editors, Dr. May and Dr. Metzger.

This informal committee reached full agreement on all details. They decided that no changes were desirable or necessary in the text or footnotes of the Revised Standard Version or in the general or special introductory articles except for that upon Ecclesiastes. A few minor changes were made in the annotations. These consisted chiefly of adding a brief explanation to particular phrases or verses to indicate where the Catholic interpretation differs from the Protestant interpretation.

Two weeks after the committee submitted its recommendations, Cardinal Cushing granted his endorsement in the form of an *imprimatur* to the Oxford Annotated Bible with the Apocrypha. He also expressed his "pleasure to be associated with this ecumenical venture which should have far-reaching fruitful results."

In my judgment, the far-reaching fruitful results which Cardinal Cushing envisages are assured in due time. The two avenues toward common use of the Revised Standard Version of the Bible by Catholics and Protestants are complementary and mutually reinforcing, rather than competitive. Catholic Edition is a part of the copyrighted title of the edition of the Revised Standard Version prepared by the Catholic Biblical Association of Great Britain with our consent. No other edition can use that title, which was proposed at the conference in London, 1954, when Dom Bernard Orchard, O.S.B., the Reverend Reginald C. Fuller, D.D., L.S.S., and their associates met with Dr. Peter Morrison, Dr. Gerald E. Knoff, and myself. The decision to adopt it and go ahead with the project was easily reached by the Standard Bible Committee and the Division of Christian Education, but ten years of hard work to perfect the plan, to surmount opposition, and to secure ecclesiastical approval lay before Fathers Orchard and Fuller. The present approval of the Oxford Annotated Bible with the Apocrypha rests largely upon their success. We must not forget that Cardinal Cushing wrote the Foreword for the American printing of the Catholic Edition of the Revised Standard Version of the Bible, as well as granted the *imprimatur* for the Oxford Annotated Bible with Apocrypha: Revised Standard Version.

These two volumes are complementary for two reasons. One is that they are of a different scope; the Catholic Edition is simply a Bible, with only the brief explanatory notes which canon law requires, while the Oxford Annotated affords ample help to the student of the Bible. The other reason is that the difference between the two volumes clearly pinpoints the major differences that remain between Catholic and Protestant views of the Scriptures. These are concerned with the canon of the Old Testament, and with the degree to which Catholic usage and doctrine should be reflected in the New Testament. I have no doubt that, in due time, Catholics and Protestants will come to closer agreement with respect to these matters, but there is no good to be gained by undue hurry. And in the meantime, it is good that both Catholics and Protestants should be kept aware of these differences and of how small they are in comparison with the great truths which we hold in common.

At the annual meeting of the Program Board of the Division of Christian Education, February 1966, Paul S. Minear was elected to membership in the Standard Bible Committee, assigned to the New Testament Section, and Herbert G. May was elected as chairman of the Committee. Professor May accepted this post with the understanding that he would not devote full time to it until his retirement in 1970 from the faculty of Oberlin College, and that until then Luther A. Weigle would continue in active service as vice-chairman of the Committee in charge of its office at the Yale Divinity School.

The Standard Bible Committee

A six-day meeting of the Standard Bible Committee was held at the Yale Divinity School, June 17-22, 1968, attended by seventeen members, under the chairmanship of Professor Herbert G. May.

This meeting was of especial significance because it is the first meeting of the Standard Bible Committee to engage the presence and participation of Roman Catholic biblical scholars. Hitherto, our cooperation with Catholic scholars has been by conferences and correspondence. But at the meeting in June, 1968, three Catholic scholars were present, not as observers or conferees, but as participants with full freedom of initiative and discussion and with right to vote. They were invited with the approval of the RSV Policies Committee and the Program Board of the Division of Christian Education. They and three others who could not be present at this meeting were nominated by an *ad hoc* committee composed of Professor May, Dean Weigle, Dr. Knoff, Professor Metzger, and Professor Minear.

Dean Weigle introduced and welcomed to the Committee the Catholic participants from Great Britain (Dom Bernard Orchard and Dr. Reginald Fuller) and Canada (Professor David M. Stanley), and expressed the regrets of the Catholic scholars from the United States who were unable to be present at this meeting. There was a general discussion of Catholic participation in the Revised Standard Version of the Bible. Fathers Orchard and Fuller described their experiences in connection with the Catholic Edition of the Revised Standard Version; Professor Paul Minear gave a description of the service of Investiture of Dr. Weigle into the Knighthood of St. Gregory the Great; and Professor Bruce Metzger reported on the granting of an *imprimatur* to the Oxford Annotated Bible with the Apocrypha.

The problem of a "You-Your" edition of the Psalms and of the entire RSV Bible was discussed. It was the sentiment of the Committee that now was not the time to make a decision, for the liturgical practices closer to the time of the publication of an updated Revised Standard Version should be taken into consideration. Perhaps by 1976 the situation will be clearer. It was recognized that the "You-Your" forms were becoming increasingly popular, and that a different situation may face us in 1976 than that which caused the original decision to be made in the 1930's. It was voted to concur in the present decision of the RSV Policies Committee to grant permission for such changes only in response to application from a specific publisher, for specific passages intended for liturgical use, and only if opportunity is given for review of the text by a subcommittee, comprising Drs. May, Weigle, Wedel, and Wilder.

Substantial progress was made in dealing with the extensive agenda, both in plenary sessions of the Committee and in separate sessions of the Old Testament Section and the New Testament Section. In addition to suggestions arising from Professor Millar Burrows' thorough study of the RSV Old Testament, we had before us a body of suggestions arising in connection with Professor Burton H. Throckmorton's editing of the recently published Third Edition of his Gospel Parallels. There were also suggestions arising from the growing use of the Revised Standard Version by Catholics; suggestions made by a study committee of The Lutheran Church–Missouri Synod; suggestions made by a similar study committee of the Christian Reformed Church; besides questions and suggestions contained in letters of individual correspondents from June 1965 to June 1968. The Committee made plans to meet again in 1970, 1972, 1974, and 1976.

The six Roman Catholic biblical scholars who were elected by the Program Board to the membership of the Standard Bible Committee are:

Dom Bernard Orchard, O.S.B., St. Benedict's School, Ealing, London, England

The Reverend Reginald Fuller, D.D., St. Mary's College, Twickenham, Middlesex, England

The Reverend Professor David M. Stanley, S.J., Regis College, Willowdale, Ontario, Canada

The Reverend Professor Joseph A. Fitzmyer, S.J., Woodstock College, Woodstock, Maryland

The Reverend Professor John L. McKenzie, S.J., University of Notre Dame, Notre Dame, Indiana

The Reverend Professor Eugene H. Maly, S.S.D., Mount St. Mary's Seminary, Norwood, Ohio

I do not undertake to list or describe the outstanding contributions which Professor Herbert G. May has made to the editing and the growing use of the Revised Standard Version of the Bible since he became a member of the Standard Bible Committee twenty-five years ago. Some of these are known to the public—his book on *Our English Bible in the Making,* his share in *The Interpreter's Bible* and *The Interpreter's Dictionary of the Bible,* his editing of *The Oxford Bible Atlas* and, with Bruce Metzger, *The Oxford Annotated Bible with the Apocrypha.* Others are to be found only in the records of the Standard Bible Committee—notably the fact that he came to New Haven and worked with me throughout the months of July and August 1951, in our final editing of the typescript of the Revised Standard Version of the Old Testament to be placed in the hands of the publishers. When my advancing years made it advisable that a new chairman be chosen for the Standard Bible Committee, Professor May was a natural choice. The decision of the nominating committee was unanimous, and he was elected chairman in 1966. I rejoice in his acceptance of the responsibility that I carried for so long, and I have high hope for the future service of the Revised Standard Version of the Bible, under his leadership of the Standard Bible Committee, in the new ecumenical climate of the years that lie ahead.

The Terminology of Adversity
in Jeremiah

JAMES MUILENBURG

Among the scholars who have directed their attention to a study of
the book of Jeremiah and have helped us to come to an understanding not only of the character of the book as a whole, but also
of the nature of the composition of its several strata or streams of
tradition, the name of Herbert May holds a place of distinction.[1]
It is no little satisfaction to do honor to one whom the writer is
proud to count among his most treasured friends, a colleague on the
Revised Standard Version committee, and a teacher whose influence
has extended far beyond the confines of the classroom and, indeed,
of his own land.

Whenever one undertakes to read through the book of Jeremiah
and to gain a synoptic view of its contents, he cannot but be impressed
by the vast scope of the materials associated with his name,[2] by the
diversity of the literary genres and the stylistic versatility of their
formulations, by the many personal crises which evoked the prophet's
poignant response, by the momentous historical events of a distraught
and turbulent international age, and by the large number of symbols
and images whereby Jeremiah seeks to body forth his prophetic
message.

It is the purpose of this modest offering to Professor May to call
attention first of all to the presence of semantic or lexical motifs
which persist throughout the prophet's *ipsissima verba* and to the

[1] H. G. May, "Towards an Objective Approach to the Book of Jeremiah: The
Biographer," *JBL* LXI (1942), 139-56; "Jeremiah's Biographer," *JBR* X (1942),
195-201; "The Chronology of Jeremiah's Oracles," *JNES* IV (1945), 217-27; "Individual Responsibility and Retribution," *HUCA* XXXII (1961), 107-20.

[2] Of the 1434 pp. in Kittel's *Biblia Hebraica,* 108 pp. are given to the book of
Jeremiah.

imagery which accompanies them, but, more particularly, to focus upon one field of speech and symbol which appears to the writer to have received less attention than it deserves. Among these motifs one recognizes, for example, the constant tensions between the language of *mendacity* and the language of *veracity*, between what is spurious and what is authentic, between truth and falsehood.[3] Nowhere is this language employed more profusely than with Jeremiah,[4] and what makes it so impressive is that it enters into every literary genre, whether one thinks of the lawsuits with their indictments, or of the laments and confessions, or of the castigations of the false prophets, or of the exhortations and sermons. More significantly, it penetrates Jeremiah's own self-awareness, his interior conflicts, the authenticity of his credentials as Yahweh's appointed and commissioned covenant mediator, which he is called upon to defend against his detractors, and supremely his dialogical encounters with Yahweh (cf. 15:18; 20:7). Closely related to the semantic field of mendacity and veracity is the speech of fidelity and infidelity, of commitment and trust, on the one hand, and of faithlessness and disloyalty on the other, where the familial symbol of father-son and the nuptial symbol of husband-bride are frequently invoked, and in varying contexts. Also closely related are the tensions between apostasy and repentance, the two ways of turning. The verb *šûb* is one of the most frequently employed, and with great versatility and in a great variety of syntactical constructions, connotative nuances, and stylistic forms.[5]

Accompanying these and other persisting semantic motifs and frequently illuminating them are numerous figures of speech. The book of Jeremiah fairly teems with images and symbols of many different kinds. Simile and metaphor, apostrophe and personification, metonymy and synecdoche, parable and vision, and not a few symbolic ac-

---

[3] Martin A. Klopfenstein, *Die Lüge nach dem Alten Testament* (Zürich and Frankfort, 1964).

[4] While Jeremiah employs a considerable number of words to express different kinds of mendacity, such as מרמה (5:27; 9:5, 7), תרמית (8:5; 14:14 [Q]; 23:26), and שוא (2:30; 4:30; 6:29), we confine ourselves to the one word which appears more frequently than any other, the word שקר. It will be observed that it pervades all his prophecies, and, what is more, it is preserved in the prose narratives of Baruch, which, as we shall see, is in many ways surprising since this is by no means always the case: 3:10, 23; 5:2, 31; 6:13–8:10; 9:2, 4 (E.T. 3, 5); 13:25; 14:14; 16:19; 20:6; 23:14, 25, 26, 32; 27:10, 14, 15, 16; 28:15; 29:9, 21, 23, 31. The little poem of 9:1-7 (E.T. 9:2-8) is a superb example of the motif. Here the terminology of truth and falsehood is exceptionally rich and the imagery especially striking.

[5] William L. Holladay, *The Root Šûbh in the Old Testament* (Leiden, 1958), pp. 128-39.

tions[6] punctuate and interpret the prophecy from beginning to end. In this respect Jeremiah is not unlike his spiritual predecessor, the prophet Hosea, with whom he shows himself akin in other ways.[7] Notable among these spheres of imagery is the motif of *water* or *rain*.[8] This is not at all surprising because throughout his prophetic career Jeremiah wages unwearying battle against the cults of fertility. Already in one of his earliest poems we encounter a striking instance of the motif, precisely where the pericope reaches its impressive climax:

> For two evils my people have committed:
>> they have abandoned me,
>> the fountain of living water,
> to hew for themselves cisterns,
>> broken cisterns,
>> that can hold no water.   2:13; cf. 3:3; 5:22, 24; 6:7; 18:23 (E.T. 9:1); 13:1 ff.; 14:3 ff.; 15:18; 17:8; 18:14; 31:35.

Of quite a different order, but in many ways equally revealing, are the repeated references to birds.[9] Sometimes these are general and rather stereotyped (7:33; 9:10; 12:4; 15:3; 16:4; 19:7; 34:20) and may have their prototypes in the curses and maledictions of other texts from the ancient Near East. At other times, however, they are very moving and impressive formulations. When Jeremiah thinks of the passing away of the world, he characteristically mentions the birds. The most telling of these passages appears in the heart of a poem describing the return of the created universe to primeval chaos:

> I looked on the earth, and lo, it was chaos and waste,
>> and to the heavens, and they had no light.
> I looked on the mountains, and lo, they were quaking,
>> and all the hills moved to and fro.
> I looked, and lo, there was no man,
>> and all the birds of the sky had fled. 4:23-25; cf. 9:9 (E.T. 10).

---

[6] H. W. Robinson, "Prophetic Symbolism" in *Old Testament Essays* (Papers read before the Society for Old Testament Study), (1927), pp. 1-17; G. Fohrer, *Die symbolischen Handlungen der Propheten, AThANT* XXV (Zürich, 1953).

[7] Karl Gross, "Die literarische Verwandtschaft Jeremias mit Hosea," Dissertation Berlin, 1930; *idem,* "Hoseas Einfluss auf Jeremias Anschauungen," *NKZ* XLII (1931), 327-43.

[8] H. Kaupel, *Das Wasser in der Bildersprache der Propheten, BK,* 1949; Philippe Reymond, *L'Eau, sa Vie, et sa Signification dans l'Ancient Testament,* Supplements to Vetus Testamentum VI (1958); Otto Kaiser, *Die mythische Bedeutung des Meeres in Ägypten, Ugarit, und Israel, BZAW* LXXVIII (1962); L. Alonso Schökel, *Estudios de Poetica Hebrea* (1963), pp. 269-307.

[9] G. R. Driver, "Birds in the Old Testament," *PEQ* LXXXVII (1955), 129-40.

In a text of quite another kind Jeremiah contrasts poignantly the homing instinct of the birds with the conduct of the people:

> Even the stork in the heavens
> knows her times;
> and the turtledove, swallow, and swift
> keep the time of their coming;
> but my people know not
> the ordinance of Yahweh. 8:7; cf. 5:27.

Much more extensive is the frequent reference to animals. While the beasts of the field are sometimes mentioned in the same stereotyped fashion as the birds, it is much more characteristic of the prophet to give us their names and to speak of them with discernment, i.e. with features which characterize each.[10]

We turn now to the area of our central interest, the semantic field of adversity and affliction in Jeremiah. Especially within recent years attention has been focused upon Baruch's passion narrative,[11] but, as we shall have occasion to observe, the vocabulary of suffering and pain and grief is actually more abundant in Jeremiah's own words. The richness of the prophet's terminology is all the more noteworthy because so often the relevant terms are concentrated within the narrow compass of a single strophe or literary genre (note, e.g., 8:18-23 [E.T. 8:18–9:1]). The survey which follows does not profess to be in any way complete. We omit, for example, the extensive lexical field of wrath and anger, which is as revealing for a grasp of the prophet's theology as for an insight into the interior conflicts and tensions which the oracles portray.[12]

1. Sickness and wounds.

The two words are not infrequently associated in the Old Testament, and for good reason since to the ancient Hebrew the wounded

---

[10] Note, e.g., the *lion* (2:15, 30; 4:7; 5:6; 12:8; cf. 25:38), the *leopard* (5:6; 13:23), *horse* or *stallion* (4:13; 5:8; 8:6, 16; 12:5); the restive young *camel* (2:23), *ass* (14:6; 22:19), the *calf* (14:5; 31:18), *jackal* (9:11; 10:22; 14:6); *snakes* (8:17). For ancient Near Eastern parallels to ravening animals as instruments of punishment, see D. R. Hillers, *Treaty-Curses and the Old Testament Prophets. Biblica et Orientalia.* No. 16 (1964), pp. 54-6. See also F. S. Bodenheimer, *Animal and Man in Bible Lands.* Collection des Travaux de l'Académie Internationale d'Histoire des Sciences, 1960.

[11] Heinz Kremers, "Leidensgemeinschaft mit Gott im Alten Testament," *EvTh* XIII (1953), 122-40.

[12] Abraham Heschel, *The Prophets* (New York, 1955), pp. 106-7, 115-17.

person is understood to be sick (cf. 6:7; 10:19).[13] Chief among the words used for *wound* is the noun שבר, which appears frequently and always in strategic collocations. The verb form is one of the most commonly employed in the Old Testament, most often with the meaning of *break* or *shatter*. Jeremiah employs it in this sense too (2:13; 19:10-11; cf. 28:12-13). The noun may be rendered *fracture, breach, shattering, crash, blow,* and so, in a more extended sense, *disaster* or *destruction.* It is used graphically in military contexts, as in the poems on the northern foe:

> For I bring evil from the north,
> and great destruction (ושבר גדול). 4:6b.

> Disaster follows hard upon disaster (שבר על־שבר),
> the whole land is laid waste. 4:20; cf. 6:1.

But it is most characteristically and frequently used with the meaning of *wound* [14]:

> They have healed the wound (שבר) of my people but lightly,
> saying, "Peace, peace,"
> when there is no peace. 6:14—8:11.

> Because of the wound (שבר) of the daughter, my people,
> am I wounded (השברתי),
> I mourn, and dismay has seized me. 8:21; cf. 14:17.

Only the original Hebrew is able to reveal the passion and poignancy of some of the formulations. We content ourselves with two examples:

> אוי לי על־שברי נחלה מכתי
> ואני אמרתי אך זה חלי ואשאנו 10:19.

Here in this remarkably condensed and pregnant outcry we encounter several characteristics of Jeremiah's style: the pervasive assonance reflecting the prophet's grief, the citation of his own words, "Woe is me! This is my affliction" (RSV. lit. "my sickness"), and the concentration of key words of suffering and pain. It will be noted that

---

[13] Josef Scharbert, *Der Schmerz im Alten Testament,* Bonner Biblische Beiträge, herausgegeben von F. Nötscher und Th. Schäfer (Bonn, 1955), pp. 98, 108. Cf. Ludwig Köhler, *Hebrew Man* (London, 1956), p. 18: "We must, however, point out here that the Old Testament contains no expression of opinion at all as to what is healthy and what is sick. . . . Furthermore the language of illness is very little developed."

[14] Johannes Pedersen, *Israel: Its Life and Culture, I-II* (London, 1926), p. 313: "Evil is in its strongest form a breach, *shebher,* an infringement upon the whole, which is peace. Breaches are most frequently mentioned in the prophets, in particular Jeremiah. His whole soul is scarred with breaches (10:19) because his people are broken." Cf. 8:21; 14:17; 30:12.

the word שבר is parallel with מכה, which appears frequently in Jeremiah in similar contexts (6:7; 14:17; 15:18; 19:8; 30:12, 14, 17). A second example, likewise autobiographical and burdened with the weight of sorrow, is given in the laconic lament concerning the prophets:

> My heart is broken (נשבר) within me.[15]
> all my bones are shaking;
> I am like a drunken man,
> like a man overcome by wine,
> because of Yahweh
> and because of his holy words.   23:9.

Again the assonance of grief is heard, but now accompanied, as so often in Jeremiah, by a vivid figure.

As we have observed, the motif is characteristically employed in rhetorically significant contexts, as in the concluding imprecation of the confessional lament of 17:14-18:

> Bring upon them the day of evil;
> destroy them with a double destruction (שברון שברם).   17:18*b*.

Our final passage is so rich in the terminology of affliction that it might be taken as an expression *in nuce* of the general theme to which we are addressing ourselves:

> For thus Yahweh is saying[16]:
> "Your hurt is incurable (אנוש לשברך),
> your wound is grievous (נחלה מכתך).
> There is no[17] medicine for your wound (מזור),
> no healing for you.
> All your lovers have forgotten you;
> they care nothing for you;
> for I have dealt you the blow (מכת) of an enemy,
> the punishment of a merciless foe,
> because your guilt is great,
> your sins flagrant.
> Why do you cry out over your hurt (שברך),
> your pain (מכאבך) is incurable."   30:12-15*a*.

[15] For the psychical functions of physical organs, see J. Pedersen, *op. cit.*, pp. 150 ff. and *passim;* H. W. Robinson, "Hebrew Psychology," in A. S. Peake (ed.), *The People and the Book* (Oxford, 1925), pp. 262-64; A. R. Johnson, *The Vitality of the Individual in the Thought of Ancient Israel*, 2nd ed. (Cardiff, 1964), pp. 75-87; J. Scharbert, *op. cit.*, pp. 93-97.

[16] Johannes Hempel, *Heilung als Symbol und Wirklichkeit im biblischen Schrifttum* (Göttingen, 1965), p. 311: "Die Heilkunde des AT gehört in den

The lexical data for wounding and healing here are ample and diverse. One half of the words concern these motifs. The key words appear in crucial contexts. The two most important, with which we have already become familiar, שבר and מכה, appear in the opening bicola and are then repeated climactically and chiastically, the second in the motivating clause of 14*a*, the first in the outcry of lament in 15*a*. But to these two words for "wound" Jeremiah now adds a third, מזור. It should properly be rendered "ulcer" or "boil" (so KB *ad loc.*) [18]. The final colon introduces still another term of affliction, employed in this form only once elsewhere in Jeremiah, but there illuminatingly in the description of Baruch's adversities (45:3): incurable *your pain* (מכאבך; cf. 15:18) .[19]

2. *Travail and anguish.*

A lexical field, more limited in extent than the foregoing, but equally revealing, is the terminology associated with anguish and anxiety. It is here that we encounter one of the most striking features of Jeremiah's speech and thought, his constant preoccupation with the mystery and perplexity of his birth. Already in the opening words of his call we listen to the solemn words of appointment and the prophet's anguished expostulation:

> Before I fashioned you in the body I knew you,
>> before you came forth from the womb I set you apart,
>> a prophet to the nations I have appointed you.
> Ah, Lord Yahweh!
>> Behold, I cannot speak,
>> for I am only a boy.   1:5-6.

The words were remembered and on many an occasion conditioned the cast of Jeremiah's mind and the texture of his reflections. His

Zusammenhang mit der altorientalischen Volksmedizin, aber gerade auf deren Hintergrund zeigt sich ihre religionsgeschichtliche Sonderstellung. Sie konzentriert Krankmachen und Heilen auf ihren Gott, seinen Willen und seine (prophetischen) Werkzeuge, die sich im Töten und Heilen als solche legitimieren und seine souveräne Macht repräsentieren." See also G. von Rad, *Old Testament Theology*, I (New York, 1962), 274. For parallels in the treaty curses, see D. R. Hillers, *op. cit.*, p. 65.

[17] Deleting "to uphold your cause," which intrudes upon the metaphor and may be a marginal gloss.

[18] See Mitchell J. Dahood, "Philological Notes on Jer. 18:14-15," *ZAW* LXXIV (1962), 208. Cf. Hos. 5:13.

[19] Scharbert, *op. cit.*, pp. 45-47. Cf. 51:8; Isa. 53:3-4; Pss. 32:10; 38:18 (E.T. 17); Job 33:19. For Near Eastern parallels in the treaty curses, see D. R. Hillers, *op. cit.*, p. 65.

anguish is concentrated in his being born, born to be the kind of man he was. It comes to its most poignant expression in the confessional laments, which are for all the world personal commentaries on his birth. Thus, in one of the most impassioned of these personal disclosures he cries out:

> Woe is me, my mother, that you gave me birth,
>> a man of strife and a man of contention with the whole land. 15:10.

Surely this is one of the most inward of Jeremiah's woes, and its force is enhanced, as in similar contexts, by the assonance of sorrow. In another confession he utters his desperation even more outspokenly and daringly:

> Cursed be the day
>> on which I was born!
> The day my mother gave me birth,
>> let it not be blessed!
> Cursed be the man
>> who brought the news to my father,
> "A son is born to you,"
>> making him very glad. . . .
> Why did I come forth from the womb
>> to see toil and sorrow,
>> and spend my days in shame? 20:14-15, 18.

The same motif comes to expression in contexts of quite a different kind, notably in the poems about the northern foe. In the final lines of a succession of poems where the prophet's lyrical gifts reach their culmination we are given a picture that is almost ghastly in its effects, where the assonance again reenforces the wording:

> For I heard a cry as of a woman in travail (חולה),
>> anguish (צרה) as of one bringing forth her firstborn child.
> The cry of the daughter Zion gasping for breath,
>> stretching out her hands,
>> "Woe is me! I am fainting before murderers." 4:31.

But nowhere are the anguish and torment and distraughtness of the prophet portrayed more passionately than in the lament of 4:19 ff.[20]

> O my bowels, my bowels! I writhe! (read אוחילה),
>> O walls of my heart!
> My heart is beating wildly,

---

[20] See D. R. Hillers, "A Convention in Hebrew Literature: The Reaction to Bad News," *ZAW* LXXVII (1965), 86-90.

> I cannot keep silent,
> for you have heard, O my soul, the sound of the trumpet,
> the alarm of war.   4:19.

The language penetrates other formulations too:

> What will you say when they set as head over you
> those whom you yourselves have taught
> to be friends to you?
> Will not pangs (חבלים) take hold of you,
> like those of a woman in travail (אשת לדה) ?
>   13:21 [21]; cf. 6:24; 22:23.

The word *distress* or *trouble* (צרה) often appears in related contexts (4:31; 6:24; 15:11). It may be well to remind ourselves that this terminology is all but absent in the Baruch prose narratives.

3. *Horror, terror, and desolation.*

The motifs are already anticipated in the prophet's call:

> Do not be dismayed (אל-תחת) by them,
> lest I dismay you (אחתך) before them.   1:17*b*.

On more than one occasion the lines are echoed, and in similarly personal contexts:

> Let those be put to shame who persecute me,
> but let not me be put to shame.
> Let them be dismayed (יחתו),
> but let not me be dismayed (אחתה).
>   17:18*ab;* cf. 14:4, 8; 16:19; 30:10.

In the great lament we have already cited the thought is very much the same, although a different word is used:

> On account of the wound of the daughter, my people, am I wounded,
> I mourn, and dismay (שמה) has seized me.   8:21.

Jeremiah was destined to be a messenger of judgment, so much so that his enemies taunt him with the name "Terror on every side" (מגור מסביב), a sentence he himself employed in his poems on the foe from the north (6:25) and in the title he gave to Pashhur when he was imprisoned in the upper Benjamin Gate of the Temple (20:1-4). It is revealing that he should refer to the nickname in his confessional disclosures:

---

[21] So RSV. The rendering is conjectural.

> For I hear many whispering,
>   "Terror on every side!"
> "Denounce him! Let us denounce him!"
>   say all my familiar friends,
>   watching for my fall.   20:10.

Our motifs are amply illustrated in numerous passages. Singularly, they appear in the climax of the indictment in the opening poem:

> Be appalled (שׁמּוּ) , O heavens, at this,
>   bristle with horror (שׂערוּ) , be utterly desolate (חרבו מאד) . 2:12.

Such terminology appears elsewhere:

> An appalling and horrible thing (שׁמה ושׁערורה)
>   has happened in the land:
> the prophets prophesy falsely,
>   and the priests rule at their direction.   5:30-31a; cf. 23:14.

One of the words most frequently employed by Jeremiah, nearly always in referring to the destruction of the land, is שׁמם and its congeners, above all the noun שׁממה.

> Hark! a rumor! it comes!
>   a great commotion out of the north country
> to make the cities of Judah a desolation (שׁממה) ,
>   a lair of jackals.   10:22.

An even more eloquent instance of the motif appears in the heart of one of the most piercing of the divine self-disclosures:

> Many shepherds have destroyed my vineyard,
>   they have trampled down my portion,
> they have made my pleasant portion
>   a desolate wilderness (למדבר שׁממה) .
> They have made it (Syr., Targ., Vulg.) a desolation (שׁממה) ,
>   desolate (שׁממה) , it mourns to me.
> The whole land is made desolate (נשׁמה) ,
>   but no man lays it to heart.   12:10-11; cf. also 4:27; 6:8.

The noun שׁמה, always employed in contexts of judgment, is used similarly:

> The lions have roared against him,
>   they have roared loudly.
> They have made his land a waste (שׁמה) ,
>   his cities are in ruins, without inhabitant.   2:15; cf. 4:7.

But the word can also denote a dreadful and terrifying event. One example must suffice:

> ... making their land a terror (שמה),
>> a hissing for ever.
> Every one who passes by it is horrified (ישם)
>> and shakes his head.   18:16; cf. 19:8.

Jeremiah also knows the language of fear and trembling, of dread and anxiety. In a passage whose precise meaning is much controverted he portrays these sensations vividly, not only by the key words of affliction and pain, but also by the imagery with which he accompanies them:

> We hear a cry of panic (חרדה),
>> of terror (פחד) and no peace.
> Ask now and see,
>> can a man bear a child?
> Why then do I see every man
>> his hands on his loins, like a woman in labor?
> Why has every face turned pale?   30:5-6.

4. *Abandonment, rejection, and alienation.*

Among the most characteristic literary genres in the book of Jeremiah are the lawsuits with their indictments and verdicts. In these the charge launched against Judah is that she has *abandoned* or *forsaken* Yahweh. The verbal key word עזב is more frequently used than any other, for it is the antonym par excellence of the election. It is also a covenant word since it signifies the cancellation of the covenant bond. In a climactic context associated with the prophet's call, the word appears in a bicolon which summarizes all the indictments which are to follow:

> So I will pronounce my judgments against them
>> on account of all their evil in abandoning me (עזבוני).   1:16.

The lawsuits which follow (2:1–4:4) perpetuate the charge. In the climax of the first (2:1-13) it is formulated even more dramatically and succinctly: *me have they abandoned* (2:13ab). In precisely the same rhetorical collocation, the two strophes of the following poem stress the indictment with great effectiveness:

> Is it not this you have brought upon yourself,
>> your abandoning (עזבך) Yahweh your God?   2:17.
> Realize how evil and bitter is
>> your abandoning (עזבך) Yahweh your god.   2:19b.

The poems included in the lyrical sequence on the foe from the north preserve the crucial function of the motif in similar fashion:

> How can I forgive you?
> Your children have abandoned me (עֲזָבוּנִי)
> and have sworn by no-gods.   5:7a

Again and again the people ask Jeremiah why it is that Yahweh has sent his terrible judgment upon them, why the land has been devastated and the city destroyed, and his reply is always the same: *they have abandoned their God.* It is true that some of these formulations bear the imprint of deuteronomic recasting, but the thought is certainly central to Jeremiah himself. The following text is illustrative:

> And when you tell this people all these words, and they say to you, "Why has Yahweh pronounced all this great evil against us? What is our iniquity? What is the sin we have committed against Yahweh our God?" then you shall say to them: "Because your fathers have abandoned (עָזְבוּ) me and not kept my law.
>
> 16:10-11; cf. 9:11-13 (E.T. 9:12-14) ; 19:3-4; 22:8-9.

When we turn to the second verb which Jeremiah uses to describe Judah's defection from Yahweh, we observe that the relevant texts have the same cumulative and decisive character. The verb מאס performs the same function as the word עזב and is present in similar contexts. It is usually rendered "refuse" or "reject."

> Hear, O earth!
> Behold, I am bringing disaster upon this people,
>   the fruit of their devices,
> because they have not given heed to my words;
>   and as for my law, they have rejected it (וִמְאָסוּ) .   6:19.

In the final pericope of the poems on the northern foe (6:27-30) and in the climactic conclusion, Jeremiah plays upon the word in dramatic fashion. He had been appointed an assayer and tester among his people. The imagery of refining is vividly described. The prophet's efforts are all to no avail, so the judgment is pronounced:

> Refuse silver (כֶּסֶף נִמְאָס) they shall be called,
> because Yahweh has refused (מָאַס) them.
>
> 6:30; cf. the judgment upon the wise in 8:8-9.

The verb נתש, to "pluck up" or "uproot," belongs to the terminology of rejection. It is already sounded in the series of parallel verbs in the prophet's call (1:10) and is echoed in related series over and over again as a leitmotif (18:7; 24:6; 31:28; 42:10; 45:4). In a prose passage which does not belong to Jeremiah but is consonant with his thought elsewhere, Yahweh addresses his people in the first person:

Behold, *I will pluck them up* (נתשם) from their land, and *I will pluck up* the house of Judah from among them. And after *I have plucked them up*, I will again have compassion on them, and I will bring them again each to his heritage and each to his land. . . . But if any nation will not listen, then *I will utterly pluck it up* and destroy it, says Yahweh.

12:14*b*-17.

We observe here one of the most common literary features of Old Testament rhetoric, the propensity to employ the same or similar semantic terms in clusters. We may cite one example where it is not difficult to hear the authentic accents of the prophet:

Hast thou utterly rejected (המאס) Judah?
Does thy soul loathe (געלה) Zion?
Why hast thou smitten us
so that there is no healing for us?
Do not spurn us (תנאץ), for thy name's sake;
do not dishonor (תנבל) thy glorious throne;
remember and do not break thy covenant with us.   14:19, 21.

Judah's rejection of Yahweh has left him no alternative but to reject her. Interestingly, his pronouncements of judgment are formulated stylistically much as in the deuteronomically colored passages cited above (e.g. 23:33, 39). In an interior divine self-disclosure, throbbing with *pathos* and with the conflict between covenant love and covenant judgment, Yahweh speaks:

I have abandoned (עזבתי) my house,
I have forsaken (נטשתי) my heritage;
I have given the beloved of my soul
into the hands of her enemies.   12:7; cf. 7:29.

Much in the same spirit Yahweh admonishes Jerusalem in a climactic context:

Be warned, O Jerusalem,
lest I be alienated (תקע) from you;
lest I make you a desolation,
an uninhabited land.   6:8.

Only here among the prophets does the verb יקע occur. RSV renders "be alienated," which doubtless gives the nuance required, but Köhler-Baumgartner define it "turn one's back in disgust" (so Bright, *ad loc.*).

The Terminology of Adversity in Jeremiah

5. Grief and mourning.

In the foregoing survey of some of the major areas of affliction and adversity, we have not infrequently come upon passages where Jeremiah gives voice to his sorrow and pain. It is often said that Jeremiah is the most subjective of the prophets, and it is true that he speaks more of himself and more intimately and inwardly than the other messengers of Yahweh. Our closest parallels to his way of speaking, to the literary genres in which he records his grief, and to many of the most characteristic key words are to be found in the book of Psalms, upon which, it is sometimes averred, he exerted his influence. The task before us now is to scrutinize the lexical deposit of suffering, to record how and where the words appear, and to call attention once more to the interior continuities of the prophet's utterances.

We shall speak first of all of a series of elemental words, exclamations, and shouts and assonant sounds, which Jeremiah uses in situations that evoke his astonishment and revulsion. To the first of these we have already referred, the expostulation of protest on the occasion of his call to be a prophet:

> Ah (אהה), Lord Yahweh!
> Behold (הנה), I cannot speak,
> for (כי) I am only a boy.   1:6.

Each of the introductory particles appears elsewhere in similar contexts. The first belongs to the class of words described many years ago by Rudolf Otto as *numinose Urlaute*, numinous elemental sounds. When Yahweh reveals the appalling disaster that is to befall the leaders of Judah at the coming of the foe from the north, Jeremiah cries out in the same way: "Ah (אהה), Lord Yahweh, you have surely deceived this people" (4:10). When he is denied the office of intercessor and the prophets deceive the people by their optimistic assurances, he registers his protest in identical manner (14:13). It is interesting to observe that Baruch preserves the expression (32:17).

The second particle is the outcry of אוי, "Woe!" We listen to it in the poems on the foe from the north. In our first example, it is accompanied by other ejaculatory words:

> Behold (הנה), he comes up like clouds,
> his chariots like whirlwind;
> His horses are swifter than eagles—
> Woe to us (אוי לנו) for (כי) we are ruined!
> Wash your heart from evil, O Jerusalem,
> that you may be saved.

> How long (עד־מתי) shall evil thoughts
> lodge within you?   4:13-14; cf. 13:27.

The second example is drawn from the same historical situation, but here it appears in a series of shouts before the relentless advance of the foe:

> Woe to us (אוי לנו), for the day declines,
> for the shadows of evening lengthen.   6:4*b*.

We hear the words again in the dying shriek of the prostitute:

> Woe is me (אוי־נא לי)! I am fainting before my murderers!   4:31*c*.

Finally, Jeremiah opens one of his most stirring confessions with the cry,

> "Woe is me (אוי־לי), my mother."   15:10*a*; cf. also 4:13 and 45:3.

The word הוי, "alas," is used with the same frequency. The one instance we shall cite is notable not only for its impressive repetition, but also for the extraordinary economy of the cola:

> They shall not lament for him,
> "Alas, my brother," or "Alas, sister!"
> They shall not lament for him,
> "Alas, lord," or "Alas, his majesty!"   22:18*bc*; cf. 23:1; 30:7; 34:5.

The cry, עד מתי, "How long," which appears in the laments of the Psalter and in other texts from the ancient Near East, is present in Jeremiah too. In the final words of a shattering lament Jeremiah cries out:

> How long must I see the standard,
> and hear the sound of the trumpet?   4:21; cf. 4:14 cited above.

In more plaintive mood he bewails the drought:

> How long will the land mourn,
> and the grass of the field wither?   12:4*a*.

Poignantly he speaks to his people:

> How long will you waver,
> O faithless daughter?   31:22*a*; cf. 13:27; 23:26.

The word קול is sometimes used as an interjection, "hark," and introduces the messages of destruction and woe, as in 3:21; 8:19; 10:22; 25:36. At other times it is used in the familiar sense of "voice," but mostly in contexts of indictment and affliction (4:15-16; 9:21 [E.T.

19]). The word הנה, "behold," similarly often introduces messages of judgment and doom (1:15; 2:35; 4:13; 5:15; 6:10*b;* 8:15; 9:14 [E.T. 15]; 10:18, etc.).

The prophecies of Jeremiah present us with a veritable thesaurus of terms designating sorrow, mourning, and wailing. They not only contain laments and dirges, but also employ the *termini technici* for the literary genre. The prophet calls upon the people to cut off their hair and to raise a קינה on the bare heights (7:29*a*), or to take up a בכי and נהי for the mountains, a קינה for the pastures of the wilderness (9:9 [E.T. 9:10]). Yahweh instructs him to call for the professional mourning women מקוננות to come that they may lift up a נהי over the people, and Jeremiah addresses the women with solemn summons:

> Hear, O women, the word of Yahweh,
> let your ear receive the word of his mouth;
> teach your daughters a lament (נהי)
> and each to her neighbor a dirge (קינה). 9:19 (E.T. 9:20).

Among the terms denoting grief or sorrow, the noun יגון, which appears relatively seldom, is found in crucial contexts and expresses in a word the motif which is elsewhere amplified and elaborated. The opening colon of the great lament of 8:18-23 (E.T. 8:18–9:1) is corrupt and requires emendation (see BH *ad loc.*), but does not involve the alteration of our word:

> My grief (יגון עלי) is beyond healing,
> my heart is sick (דוי) within me. 8:18.

In a final outburst of anguish and grief in a confessional lament Jeremiah cries out:

> Why, O why did I come forth from the womb
> to see toil (עמל) and sorrow (יגון)! 20:18.

In the closing pericope of what was doubtless at one time the conclusion to the original form of the book, Yahweh significantly quotes Baruch's tale of travail and agony:

> Woe is me! for Yahweh has added sorrow (יגון) to my pain (מכאבי);
> I am weary with my groaning (אנחתי), and I find no rest. 45:3.

We observe once more that the language of suffering is concentrated, that the cry of "Woe!" is motivated by a chronicle of affliction, and, above all, that God himself endures a grief incalculably greater than Baruch's.

An examination of the nomenclature of mourning reveals the diversity of the linguistic data. Translations seldom do sufficient justice to the nuances and connotations of the words or to their precise function in a particular context. Thus the same word is often employed where the Hebrew has several different words with a variety of meanings or shades of meaning. One should always be on the lookout for *le mot juste,* especially in parallel lines, but also where the same word is employed within a single literary unit or literary genre. We now cite several instances of the motif of mourning. The first is drawn from a graphic description of the foe from the north and constitutes its climax:

> For this gird you with sackcloth,
> lament (ספדו) and wail (הילילו).   4:8; cf. 8:21.

The final verb gains its force by the assonance of the onomatopoeia, but also by the fact that it underlines and accentuates the preceding parallel verb. Our second example is also taken from the poetic sequence of the northern foe and brings the poem to its finale:

> O Daughter, my people, gird on sackcloth,
>   and roll (התפלשי) in ashes;
> make mourning (אבל עשי) as for an only son,
>   most bitter lamentation (מספד תמרורים),
> for suddenly the destroyer
>   will come upon us.   6:26; cf. 12:11; 14:2.

Each of the first four cola contains a predication of mourning and is brought to a dramatic focus by the concluding motivation. Our third exemplar (16:1-9) is of a quite different order. The pericope is a prose narrative. The formulation is to be ascribed to the deuteronomic or scribal editor, but there is no reason to question its authenticity. Jeremiah is forbidden to enter the house of mourning (בית מרזח). He is not to lament (לספוד) or bemoan (תנד) his fellow countrymen. The dead are not to be buried or lamented (יספדו). No one shall lament for the people or lacerate himself (יתגדד) or make himself bald (יקרח) for them. The verb *mourn* (אבל) is sometimes paralleled with the verb לדר, to put on black, as in 4:28 (cf. also 8:21; 14:2). At other times it is linked with the verb נוד, to move to and fro in the manner of those who mourn:

> Who will have pity (יחמל) on you, O Jerusalem,
>   or who will bemoan (ינוד) you?   15:5a; cf. 16:5.

Even more impressively:

Weep not (אל־תבכו) for the dead,
   and do not bemoan him (אל־תנדו) ;
but weep bitterly (בכו בכו) for him who goes away,
   for he shall return no more
      to see his native land.   22:10; cf. 31:18.

The sound of weeping is heard elsewhere, especially in the confessional lament of the long liturgy of 3:1–4:8:

A voice is heard on the bare heights,
   the weeping (בכי) and pleading (תחנוני) of Israel's sons,
because they have perverted their way,
   they have forgotten Yahweh their God.   3:21.

And again in the lament to which we have had occasion to refer before:

O that my head were waters,
   and my eyes a fountain of tears,
that I might weep (אבכה) day and night
   for the slain of my daughter, my people. 8:23 (E.T. 9:1) .

And finally in the pathetic lines from the Little Book of Comfort:

A voice is heard in Ramah,
   lamentation (נהי) and bitter weeping (בכי תמרורים) ,
Rachel is weeping (מבכה) for her chidlren:
   she refuses to be comforted because they are not.
               31:15; cf. 9:9 (E.T. 9:10; 31:9) .

If we are to release our study from exclusively semantic confinement, then it becomes imperative that we take account of the style, rhetoric, and literary types of the materials that have come under our inspection. Now the most obvious reflection to make is that they are clothed in the rhythms, parallelisms, and structures of ancient Hebrew poetry. The terminology of adversity is woven into the patterns of the rhetorical forms. Its key words often determine the articulation and movement of the literary unit. The other prophets, to be sure, also employ poetry for their proclamations, but in Jeremiah the lyrical impulse is more native, more inward, more existential. In not a few contexts, as in the poems on the foe from the north and sometimes in the laments, he is more poet than prophet.[22] The prophet's

---

[22] G. von Rad, *Old Testament Theology*, II (Edinburgh, 1965) , 201: "This again shows us that Jeremiah is much more keenly inflamed, and in an entirely novel way, by a poetic impulse which exists quite independently from prophecy. It also raises the question of how we are to evaluate this remarkably large increase of the element of pure poetry."

feelings and reflections are transmuted into free lyrical verse, in striking contrast to the so-called deuteronomic sections and the biographical narratives of Baruch.[23] Nowhere is this more clear than in the speech of adversity and affliction. There is nothing contrived or studied about it. It records itself variously: in exclamations and interjections, in emphatic particles, in passionate shouts and urgent expostulations and warnings, and, above all, in extraordinarily striking assonances. Yet all these are couched in the forms and patterns characteristic of Hebrew poetry.

We have called attention from time to time to the affinities of Jeremiah's speech and literary types with the language, forms, and images encountered in the literatures of the other peoples of the ancient Near East. These relationships cannot of course be denied. It is very clear that Jeremiah has been influenced by such predications. But it is important to point out that while he does indeed make use of conventional forms and conventional semantic property, he is by no means dominated by them. He is not simply a borrower; it is even doubtful whether he was aware of appropriating "foreign" modes of speech. Rather, he subordinates them to his own unique manner of speaking, to his own experiences, and to his own literary propensities. We are to think here, then, as in the case of his employment of the conventional literary types among his own people, not so much of conscious literary borrowing, but rather of spiritual and cultural affinity. It has been pointed out by G. von Rad that in the so-called confessions of the prophet the formulation and style vary considerably. While they are indeed related to the *Gattung* of the individual lament, "Jeremiah interpenetrated the conventional usage of the old cultic form with his own concern as a prophet, and transformed it." [24] But more than that, the dialogical and conversational manner of the prophet emerge more strikingly than anywhere else in the Old Testament. His capacity for empathy, both social and cosmic, his profound sympathy with his own people, despite their waywardness and infidelity, his ability to identify himself interiorly with their afflictions

---

[23] Ernst Cassirer, *Language and Myth* (New York, 1946), pp. 34-35: "The modern science of language, in its efforts to elucidate the 'origin' of language, has indeed gone back to Hamann's dictum, that poetry is 'the mother tongue of humanity'; its scholars have emphasized that speech is rooted not in the prosaic, but in the poetic aspect of life, so that its ultimate basis must be sought not in the preoccupation with the objective view of things and their classification according to certain attributes, but in the primitive power of subjective feeling."

[24] G. von Rad, *op. cit.*, p. 201.

are after all more significant than all the many parallels, impressive as they often are, that may be adduced to his utterances.[25]

Closely related to the terminology of sickness, pain, and indeed every manner of affliction is the pervasive motif of healing and of Yahweh as Israel's Physician.[26] Here again the prophet is strongly under the influence of his spiritual predecessor Hosea (5:13; 6:1; 7:1; 11:3; 14:4). The motif is an ancient one and has its roots in the traditions associated with Moses. In the diminutive pericope immediately following the Song of Miriam which is formulated in deuteronomic style, the finale is given as a divine first-person self-asseveration, "For I am Yahweh, your Healer" (Exod. 15:26). As we should expect, the pleas for healing are heard in the prayers and laments, and thanksgivings are raised for restoration to health and well-being. Given the psycho-physical character of Israel's mentality, it is not surprising that the terminology is frequently employed for forgiveness. As in Hosea, apostasy is understood as sickness. In the very heart of the great liturgy of 3:1–4:4, Yahweh pleads with his recreant sons:

> Return, O faithless sons,
> I will heal your faithlessness.   3:22.

The false prophets heal the wound of the people only lightly, promising health and restoration when there is none (6:14–8:11). Poignantly the people cry out that Yahweh has smitten them so that there is no healing for them (14:19). In one of his confessions Jeremiah cries out that his wound is incurable, refusing to be healed (15:18), and in another he pleads passionately for healing:

> Heal me, O Yahweh, and I shall be healed,
> save me, and I shall be saved;
> for Thou art my praise.   17:14.

Similarly in a moving lament he gives vent to his grief:

> Is there no balm in Gilead?
> Is there no physician there?
> Why then has the health of the daughter, my people,
> not been restored?   8:22; cf. 30:13, 17.

[25] The list of parallels could be greatly extended beyond those we have cited. See *inter alia* Geo. Widengren, *The Accadian and Hebrew Psalms of Lamentation as Religious Documents; a Comparative Study* (Stockholm, 1937), p. x; Adam Falkenstein and Wolfram von Soden, *Sumerische und Akkadische Hymnen und Gebete* (Zürich, 1953).

[26] J. J. Stamm, *Erlösen und Vergeben im Alten Testament* (Bern, 1940), pp. 78-84; Johannes Hempel, "Ich bin der Herr, dein Arzt," *TlZ* (1957), cols. 809-26; *Heilung als Symbol und Wirklichkeit im biblischen Schrifttum.*

Theologically, all the outcries and fervent pleas and poignant plaints have their *raison d'être,* their setting or context, and their presuppositions in the faith that there is One who hears the words of his servants. He is their healer who knows their afflictions and adversities, and knows them more deeply than they do.

The profuse terminology of adversity and affliction in Jeremiah is to be explained, at least in part, by the interior conflicts within the prophet himself. From the very beginning he was fashioned and set apart (1:5 הִקְדַּשְׁתִּיךָ) to be the prophet of Yahweh to an apostate age, to be separated from normal human relationships, and to stand over against the leaders of Judah. Yet the radical paradox which underlies his prophetic activity and ministry is that he feels himself deeply drawn to those upon whom he is called to pronounce judgment. His mission as Yahweh's prophet conflicts with his mission as intercessor for the people, an office which was obviously congenial to him, but one which he is denied again and again. There were many prophets in Jeremiah's time, but he finds himself pitted over against them. He denies that they have been called and sent by Yahweh. His ministry is closely connected with the Temple and its precincts, but he is excluded from them and on one occasion is placed in the stocks. During the Babylonian siege he urges the king to capitulate and is even suspected of going over to the enemy. His familiar friends reject him and cry out in denunciation and derision against him. He laments that it is his cruel fate to sit alone, filled with the divine indignation and unsupported by any solace from man or God (15:17). His foes are those of his own household (12:6). He is unsustained and uncomforted by wife and children. But, above all, he is torn and shattered by the sense of the apparent absence and neutrality of God. All the forces that make for solidarity and community for which he so deeply longed are withdrawn from him. It is his destiny to walk alone. His afflictions are the afflictions of an isolated soul, and they are doubtless accountable for the language he employs to body forth his message.

Finally, the terminology of adversity has its explanation in the character of Jeremiah's mission and calling. Like the prophets before and after him he is under the compulsion of the divine imperative to speak all that is commanded him. And like them he is to suffer the pain of rejection and obloquy and persecution. Isaiah of Jerusalem too was warned that all his prophetic preaching would be of no avail, that throughout his long career he would encounter naught but stubborn resistance and deafness, but that he must nevertheless persist in proclaiming the divine word of judgment against his own people.

Ezekiel is also sent to a stubborn and rebellious people, and in his call receives from God's hand a scroll inscribed on both sides "with mourning, lamentations, and woe," which he devours at Yahweh's command, thus taking to himself the words that he is to utter. But the autobiographical accounts are relatively limited. With Jeremiah it is otherwise. He is sent to speak all that he is commanded to speak, but is admonished not to fear, for Yahweh will be with him to deliver him from his foes. Yahweh will make him "a fortified city, an iron pillar, and bronze walls against the whole land" (1:18; cf. 15:19-20). He is to live his prophetic life under the abiding assurance that he is speaking for God, and that the divine will and purpose will prevail. God's strength will be sufficient to meet Jeremiah's weakness. None of the prophets was so little "a man of iron" as Jeremiah. It is revealing that he so often employs the verb יכל, "to be able." Over against Jeremiah's inability and frailty stand the ultimate power and sovereignty of God. Over against his "failures" stand the vindication and "success" of the divine Victor. Yet, despite the frequent assurances of divine help and support, these are shrouded and concealed from him. Upon occasion he could rejoice in Yahweh's nearness (15:16) and that the only legitimate source of human pride and glorying was to know and understand Yahweh "who practices covenant love, justice, and righteousness in the earth" (9:23-24). The apostle Paul knows these words (II Cor. 10:17), but despite all his "boastings," all the adversities and afflictions he had suffered, he is left with nothing but his weakness. Of these he dares to boast, and in his darkest hour he is solaced by the words which came to him, "My grace is sufficient for you, for my power is made perfect in weakness" (II Cor. 12:9)

The Participle of the Immediate Future and Other Matters Pertaining to Correct Translation of the Old Testament

WILLIAM F. STINESPRING

This paper is presented to Herbert G. May in consideration of his efforts toward better translations of the Bible.

My first contention is that the use of the so-called participle (usually active) in biblical Hebrew and Aramaic as a pure verb (hence no longer a participle in function) to express the immediate future is recognized by the grammarians but often neglected by the translators. In two previous papers I made similar claims with respect to two other idioms in the Old Testament.[1]

First let us have a look at the conclusions of grammarians. Ronald J. Williams[2] gives as usage number one under the heading *Participle* "to express continuous action, either in the present or in the past." Usage number two is stated as "to indicate imminent action," with Gen. 6:17; 20:3, and I Kings 20:13 suggested as examples. Williams then lists eight other uses of the participle, thus showing that he gives high priority to "imminent action" by placing it second in a list of ten.

Gesenius-Kautzsch-Cowley[3] put third under the caption "the participle as predicate" the usage "to announce future actions or events"; then they add these words: "but especially often . . . if it is intended

---

[1] "The Active Infinitive with Passive Meaning in Biblical Aramaic," *JBL* LXXXI (1962), 391-94; "No Daughter of Zion: A Study of the Appositional Genitive in Hebrew Grammar," *Encounter* XXVI (1965), 133-41.

[2] *Hebrew Syntax: An Outline* (Toronto, 1967), p. 42.

[3] E. Kautzsch, *Gesenius' Hebrew Grammar,* 28th ed., rev. and trans. by A. E. Cowley (Oxford, 1910), § 116 *p*, pp. 359-60.

to announce the event as imminent, or at least near at hand (and sure to happen), when it is called *futurum instans*." I might add that sometimes there is also a connotation or implication of threat. About twenty-five examples are listed, and there is a cross reference to Sect. 112 *t*, where it is pointed out that this usage of the participle is sometimes followed by the *waw-consecutive* perfect, thus attesting to its futurity. About ten examples are given, some of which also appear in the list of twenty-five previously mentioned.

Paul Joüon puts the matter thus[4]:

> L'emploi du participe pour exprimer le futur prochain et, d'une façon général, le futur, est une extension de l'emploi du participe comme présent. L'action future, surtout l'action prochaine, est représentée comme s'accomplissant déjà.

I more or less agree with this statement. Joüon offers seven examples, as follows: Gen. 7:4; 19:13, and 20:3; Deut. 1:20; II Sam. 20:21*b* (passive), I Kings 20:13, and II Kings 4:16.

G. Bergsträsser[5] has a similar statement, supported by about thirty-five examples. He suggests that the English locution "going to" as in "I am going to eat" would be a better translation than the simple future. I believe that the best translation in most cases would be the idiom "about to" as in "I am about to eat," "the land which you are about to possess," and the like.

It seems unnecessary to multiply references to grammatical works, since they mostly agree. It remains to see what the translators have done, by examining their renderings of some of the examples given by our grammarians. The first example is from Gen. 6:17, suggested by at least three of the grammarians consulted. KJV translates as follows: "And behold, I, even I do bring (מביא) a flood of waters upon the earth. . . ." The essential words are "I do bring" as a translation of מביא following the personal pronoun. ASV and the old JPSV[6] have the same words, Douay and RSV say "I will bring," Moffatt has "I am sending"; only AT [7] and the new JPSV [8] say "I am about to bring," which seems to me exactly right.

[4] *Grammaire de l'Hébreu Biblique*, 2nd ed. (Rome, 1947), § 121 *e*, p. 339.
[5] *Hebräische Grammatik*, II. Teil: Verbum (Leipzig, 1929; reprinted Hildesheim, 1962), § 13 *h*, p. 72.
[6] *The Holy Scriptures According to the Masoretic Text* (Philadelphia, 1917).
[7] J. M. P. Smith and E. J. Goodspeed, *The Complete Bible: An American Translation* (Chicago, 1939).
[8] *A New Translation of the Holy Scriptures:* First Section, The Torah (Philadelphia, 1962). Other sections of this version are yet to appear. The editor-in-chief is Dr. Harry M. Orlinsky.

Let us take one more example from Genesis, viz. 20:3, listed by all four of the grammarians mentioned above.

KJV: But God came to Abimelech in a dream by night, and said to him, Behold, thou *art but* a dead man, for the woman which thou hast taken; for she *is* a man's wife.[9]

The relevant words are "Behold, thou *art but* a dead man," הנך מת in Hebrew. Other readings are: ASV, the same; old JPSV, "Behold, thou shalt die"; Douay, "Lo, thou shalt die"; RSV, "Behold, you are a dead man"; Moffatt, simply, "You are a dead man"; AT, "You are going to die"; new JPSV and JB,[10] "You are to die"; Knox,[11] "Thy life is forfeit." None of these have my preferred idiom, which would be "about to die," though AT comes close in meaning with its "going to die." But I prefer "You are about to die" because it seems to call for quick action; Monsignor Knox's eloquent phrase, "Thy life is forfeit," also commends itself although it may be too highbrow for most readers.

The beginning of Deuteronomy is a good place to find examples of this idiom. Things are about to happen: Moses is about to give (or repeat) the Law, he is about to die, the people are about to cross over to their inheritance. The grammarians have mostly overlooked these passages, though Joüon does mention 1:20. In this verse, only AT has my preferred wording, thus: "You have reached the highlands of the Amorites, which the LORD our God is about to give us." To be sure, "is giving," "intends to give," or simply "to give" are not wrong, though I prefer the "about to" idiom in most cases, but of course not in all—"all" being a bad word in my vocabulary.

What I mean is to be seen very clearly in Jon. 1:3. KJV says, "Jonah . . . went down to Joppa; and he found a ship going (באה) to Tarshish." And so some other versions. But AT, Knox, and JB have "bound for" instead of "going to." This is good, since the Random House Dictionary defines the idiom "bound for" as meaning "going or intending to go." Yet to translate "about to go to Tarshish" is much more exact. For to say "going" may imply that the ship was already in motion, in which case Jonah would have missed the boat, as most of the translators seem to have done. And "intending to go" does not necessarily imply intending to go *very soon*, to say nothing of the unnecessary personification in this case.

In spite of my admiration for Moffatt's translation, and my praise

---

[9] In KJV italicized words are words supplied by the translators.
[10] *The Jerusalem Bible* (Garden City, N. Y., 1966).
[11] R. A. Knox, *The Holy Bible: A Translation from the Latin Vulgate in the Light of the Hebrew and Greek Originals* (New York, 1956).

of him in a previous paper,[12] I must say that this time Moffatt is worst of all with his "ship there sailing for Tartessus." One can just see that ship about a mile out at sea under full sail heading away from Joppa, with Jonah standing disconsolately on the shore. Only a helicopter could have caught that ship. But maybe Moffatt did not mean to rule out that means of transportation (even in 1925); for he translates the preceding sentence thus: "But Jonah went away to fly [sic!] to Tartessus, from the presence of the Eternal."

We conclude our examples with two from Aramaic. First, Dan. 2:13a, which reads in the KJV, "And the decree went forth that the wise men should be slain." This makes excellent sense, but the second clause, וחכימיא מתקטלין, is probably co-ordinate rather than subordinate, as shown in ASV, old JPSV, and AT, which translate "and the wise men were to be slain" (Moffatt has "killed" instead of "slain"). They should have said "and the wise men were *about* to be slain" (or "killed") to keep the imminent, threatening connotation. The least satisfying version in this case is Douay, which says flatly "the wise men were slain." This is inaccurate in the light of vss. 24 and 48, which show that the wise men survived and suffered no penalty except to have Daniel made their chief. JB agrees in sense with KJV, and Knox is very free while getting the meaning quite well.

The last example is from Matt. 6:8 in the Peshitta version of the Syriac,[13] which of course has affinities with biblical Aramaic. The Greek may be translated literally thus: "Be not therefore like them [the heathen]; for your Father knows what things you have need of before you ask him." Instead of "what things you have need of" (ὧν χρείαν ἔχετε in Greek), the Syriac has in the second clause the participial expression *māná methbeʿē lᵉkhōn,* so that the whole clause may be translated, "for your Father knows what is about to be sought by you before you ask him." Thus the *ethpeʿēl* participle of the immediate future renders the thought of the passage in a very clear manner with a good Semitic idiom. (The contextual question is about excessive use of words rather than about needs.)

This is the third of a series of studies on biblical grammar.[14] The first had to do with the use of the active infinitive with passive meaning in biblical Aramaic. It showed that neither the grammarians nor the translators understood this usage very well, and that too often the

---

[12] See n. 1, sec. item. pp. 138-39. Moffatt's translation of the Old Testament appeared first in two vols., Vol. I, 1924; Vol. II, 1925.

[13] The edition used was *The New Testament in Syriac,* ed. Kilgour (London, 1919, reprinted 1950).

[14] See n. 1, above.

translation was active when it should have been passive.[15] The second study dealt with a Hebrew locution, בת ציון, usually translated "the daughter of Zion," and similar expressions in the Hebrew Bible.[16] I tried to show by grammatical analysis that Zion did not have a daughter, but was itself or herself the daughter, because Zion in the genitive case is here an appositional genitive, not a possessive genitive. It appeared that the grammarians have more or less understood this fact, while the translators have mostly been neglectful of it, with the exception of Moffatt and the new JPSV. The proper translation would be "daughter Zion" or "maiden Zion," a term of endearment.[17] In this third study the same type of thing appears: The grammarians are well aware of the participle of the immediate future, while the translators are just barely beginning to recognize it.

This plea for more care in Bible translations can be well illustrated by a few words about the "Red Sea" blunder. This name, "the Red Sea," occurs about twenty-two times in the conventional translations of the Old Testament as a rendering of the Hebrew term *yam sûph,* following the practice of the Greek versions, which have ἡ ἐρυθρὰ θάλλασσα in these places.

Yam sûph, however, never means "the Red Sea" as that term is understood today (this can be seen by consulting any map of the area). There seem to be three possible meanings: (1) any one of a series of marshes and small lakes along the route of the present Suez Canal; (2) the Gulf of Aqabah; (3) the Gulf of Suez. The latter two are, of course, arms of the Red Sea, but are never included in modern usage in the geographical term "Red Sea."

So what should be done? That amazing man, James Moffatt, adopted a very simple solution in his 1924-25 translation of the Old Testament: he changed "Red Sea" to "Reed Sea." This change had the virtue of getting rid of the incorrect and misleading "Red Sea," and was at the same time a rather literal translation of the Hebrew words *yam sûph* ("sea of reeds," *sûph* being an Egyptian word referring to the

---

[15] E.g., in Dan. 5:7, where RSV has, "The king cried aloud *to bring in* the enchanters, the Chaldeans, and the astrologers," AT has the correct passive translation of the infinitive, thus: "The king called aloud for the enchanters, the Chaldeans, and the astrologers *to be brought in.*"

[16] Some typical passages are Isa. 1:8; 37:22; Jer. 4:31; 6:2, 23; Lam. 2:1, 4, 8, 10, 13, 18.

[17] Other variations of the idiom are "maiden Jerusalem," "maiden Judah," "the maiden, my people," "the virgin girl Zion," "virgin Israel"; all these are terms of endearment. The Hebrew word *bath,* literally "daughter" or "girl," may also be used in pity or even hatred for an enemy that is doomed to destruction, as for example, "O 'virgin' vixen Babylon" (the word "virgin" being sarcastic) and "O hussy Chaldea" in Isa. 47:1; also "O 'virgin' vixen Egypt" in Jer. 46:11.

papyrus plant). *Yam,* however, may refer to any kind of a body of water, such as a marsh, a lake, a gulf, a sea, or even a river.[18]

Moffatt attempted no distinction between the three (or more?) meanings of the Hebrew term. Perhaps this cautious approach was wise, since the distinction is fraught with difficulties both geographical and theological. The first meaning mentioned above (area of the Suez Canal) seems appropriate in about thirteen passages. In about seven passages the Gulf of Aqabah seems to be clearly indicated. Two passages may have reference to the Gulf of Suez, though the matter is doubtful. But in no case is there any possible reference to the Red Sea, that great body of water more than twelve hundred miles long, in places about 125 miles wide, nearly a mile and a half deep, and much too far to the south to have any connection with *yam sûph* or the fleeing Israelites. I like to take my miracles straight, but this one overwhelms the imagination. Even the Gulf of Suez, about two hundred miles long and from twenty to forty miles wide, is a fairly formidable body of water. Small wonder, then, that the first meaning mentioned above is most appropriate in the tradition of the miraculous crossing. The use of *yam sûph* as a name for the Gulf of Aqabah may be from an entirely different tradition.

All this is made clear in many commentaries.[19] My complaint is with the translators, not the commentators. A search through six or eight "modern" translations published in this century, including AT and RSV, both of which are pretentiously up-to-date, shows that only three of these versions have taken account of the facts just presented. Moffatt's courageous correction of 1924 has already been noted. In the new JPSV Pentateuch translation of 1962,[20] *yam sûph* is rendered as "the sea of Reeds," with the following footnote added at its first occurrence in Exod. 10:19: "Traditionally, but incorrectly, 'Red Sea.' " Here we have factuality of the highest order, stated in the plainest and simplest terms.[21] By contrast, the Old Testament section of AT appeared in 1927 with "the Red Sea" in all the relevant passages, and subsequent revisions brought no change. Likewise RSV, the Old Testament section of which appeared in 1952. Finally, there is JB (1966),

---

[18] In RSV, Isa. 19:5, this word is translated "Nile," a commendable departure from the habit of always rendering *yam* as "sea."

[19] One of the latest is M. Noth, *Exodus* (Philadelphia, 1962), pp. 11, 107-8.

[20] See n. 8 above.

[21] Also to be commended is the plain statement of the translator, J. S. Bowden, of Noth, *op. cit.,* on p. 11: "This term ['the sea'] will be used throughout in place of the traditional 'Red Sea,' which is not an accurate translation of the Hebrew text and has a confusing effect on any discussion of the route of the Exodus."

which uses "the Sea of Reeds" without comment, thanks, no doubt, to the French version from which JB is derived.[22]

As an American Protestant, I should like to pay my respects to the memory of that doughty Scot, James Moffatt, and to commend the Jewish editors of JPSV and the Roman Catholic editors of JB for their efforts toward a better English translation of the Bible. But no translation is perfect, and in some respects the American Protestant versions, such as AT and RSV, are better, as I have indicated above and elsewhere. Continual new translations will be needed, and all parties should consult one another and work together for an increasingly correct English Bible.

[22] *La Sainte Bible traduite en français sous la direction de l'École Biblique de Jerusalem* (Paris, 1956). This version uses "la mer des Roseaux" throughout. It may be noted here that Martin Luther, with an eye to the Hebrew rather than the Greek, rendered *yam sûph* as "Schilfmeer," an exact equivalent of Moffatt's "Reed Sea." "La Mer de Jonc" in E. Dhorme's French translation (1956) also comes very close to the mark.

Some Remarks Concerning and Suggested by Jeremiah 43:1-7

P. A. H. DE BOER

The seven verses which are the subject of this contribution belong to a fairly long piece of prose which deals with the conquest of Jerusalem and what happened directly afterward. Neither the translation nor the explanation of these verses is made more difficult by uncertainties concerning the historical background of the text. The Hebrew text of this part of the Old Testament shows very little irregularity and indicates a period in which a very great deal of the Old Testament obtained the form in which material from earlier periods had been reedited. Since no truly ancient witness to the text is preserved, a precise dating remains a guess. The oldest witnesses of the first translations are uniform to a great degree.

Yet an attempt to translate this passage faces all sorts of difficulties. Because a comparison of the old and modern translations does not bring all the difficulties to light, I have given my own translation; one in which an explanation is added in those places where it is different from the usual and generally similar translations. Finally, a few opinions about the editing of this passage follow, wherein differentiation is made between literature which describes events and literature which has at its kernel oracles concerning these events.

I

AN ATTEMPT AT TRANSLATION

Jer. 43:1-7 (1) When Jeremiah had completely transmitted the message from their God YHWH, with which their God YHWH had sent him to them, to them all—the whole message— (2) Hoshaiah's son Azariah and Kareah's son Johanan, and everyone, excitedly talking, said to Jeremiah: "Thou art an impostor. Our God YHWH has not sent you to say: Thou shalt not enter Egypt to remain there. (3) It is Neriah's son Baruch who has set you against us to deliver us to the Babylonians, who will take us to Babel in exile, which ends in death."

(4) And Kareah's son Johanan and all the commanders of the forces and all those—they did not obey YHWH's command to remain in the region of Judah.

(5) And Kareah's son Johanan and all the commanders of the forces took all the remnant of Judah, those returned from all the nations whither they had been driven to remain in the region of Judah, (6) men, women, and children, the court, and all those who by the aid of the head of the bodyguard, Nebuzaradan, had found shelter with Ahikam's son, Saphan's son Gedaliah—and the prophet Jeremiah and Neriah's son Baruch. (7) They now went into the region of Egypt—for they did not obey YHWH's command—and came to (*or* in) Tahpanhes.

II

SOME EXPLANATIONS

In this translation the word עַם ("people") occurring in vss. 1 and 4 is not used. The expression כל־העם is rendered by "them all," for the author of this part was not of the whole population of the area of Judah. The assembly, for whom YHWH's command is intended, are those who are planning to leave for Egypt and, owing to the development of affairs after the murder of Gedaliah, have gathered together in a place somewhere near Bethlehem. In vss. 4-5 this is made more explicit. The group consists of commanders and their gangs, among whom Johanan is the leading figure, and those who had remained at Mizpah under Gedaliah, insofar as they had survived at the time of Gedaliah's murder. A third group of those to whom the prophet directs YHWH's message are those who had been able to return from exile to join up with Gedaliah.

Not everyone became an exile with the arrival of the Babylonians. In Jer. 40:7-8 we have a summary of those who were left in the land. The use of the expression כל־שארית יהודה in vs. 5 of our passage must not allow us to forget that there were population groups who, with the coming of the Babylonians, certainly got a new government but not a new dwelling or a new style of living. Moreover, a not unimportant number of the population of the destroyed city of Jerusalem will have sought and found their refuge in areas nearby.

The verb גור, "stay as a stranger who is domiciled somewhere," generally with the idea of being admitted or received as a refugee, is used in vs. 2 for the proposed stay in Egypt, whither people sought to escape and where they hoped to get permission to stay. It is noticeable that the same verb (גור) is also used for the sojourn, in the Judean region, of those who returned from foreign parts and are mentioned as "the whole remnant of Judah" in vs. 5. The Greek, Syriac, and Aramaic translations of this fifth verse have clearly expressed this meaning. They use, respectively, the following verbs to render גור: κατοικεῖν, "to establish oneself, to settle down," also: "to found a colony"; 'mr, "to stay with as a stranger"; the *Ittaf.* of יתב, "to settle as a foreigner, to get permission to reside." We ought to discriminate between the region of Judah and its more or less permanent population, and what the author of this passage calls "the people" or "the remnant of Judah." The term "the region of Judah" is used in the foregoing translation in order to differentiate between Judah as the name of an area and as the name for those to whom the author confined himself. Not only in our passage but also elsewhere in the Old Testament these definitions for people and country ought to be more closely specified.[1]

Several sentences of the passage with which we are concerned leave the impression, after reading them, that they are a patchwork. In vs. 1, את כל־הדברים האלה is clearly an addition. It is also striking that a liberal use has been made of the word כל; in the seven verses of this passage it occurs eight times.

In the second verse, there are also additions. In this essay it is not my intention to go into supposed changes in the text. In the translation an attempt has been made to render all the words in the text into English. However, this does not mean that I presuppose that the original reading of the verse has been preserved. At any rate, a more or less possible sentence is achieved if the adjective with "men," הזדים, is recognized as having an adverbial meaning: the men talk in an excited way. This translation of זד, "excited," certainly expresses the fact that the normal limits of conversation are being exceeded—thus acknowledging the meaning of the root זוד/זיד, "to cook, cook over"—but not that this is condemned on religious or moral grounds. The usual translation "recklessly, audaciously, impudently," does just this. Even though זד did contain an element of blame (which cannot with certainty be deduced from the few places where it occurs), it

---

[1] L. Rost, "Die Bezeichnungen für Land und Volk im Alten Testament," in *Festschrift Procksch* (Leipzig, 1934), pp. 125-48, is instructive in this regard.

fits less well in the context of the passage in question. Johanan and his men may doubt Jeremiah's authority, but neither here nor in previous passages are they pictured as reckless fellows who audaciously rebel against YHWH. They seem more panic-stricken than presumptuous.

שֶׁקֶר, "lie," vs. 2*b,* has been rendered by "deceit," and I have tried to express the directness of the reaction to Jeremiah's words by letting the words and the speaker be expressed together: "Thou art an impostor." I refer to an obesrvation made by Klopfenstein who calls (*sheker*) "zwar eine Wortlüge . . . , aber nicht nur im negativen Sinn 'Unwahrheit,' sondern im positiv-aktiven Sinn 'Betrug.' " [2]

The verb בוא, "come, enter, reach," is used once in vs. 2 and twice in vs. 7. The old translations have rendered the Hebrew verb's meaning exactly. The Septuagint uses in all three places εἰσιέναι. The Peshiṭta uses '*al;* "to enter," in vs. 2 and '*ata*', "to come, to get to," in vs. 7. So also the Targum. The Vulgate uses *ingredere* in vs. 2 and vs. 7*a,* and *venire* in vs. 7*b.* In some recent translations the meaning "go to, to proceed to," at least in the vss. 2 and 7*a,* is attached to the verb בוא. This is done, among others, by A. Gélin in *Bible de Jérusalem,* in the RSV, in the version of the Dutch Bible Society, by J. A. Grispino in the *Confraternity Version.* In Brown-Driver-Briggs' *Lexicon,* the meaning "go, go to" is given. The evidence for this meaning of the verb is not convincing, however. Ps. 26:4, where the verb occurs with the preposition עם, and Prov. 22:24, where it appears with את, give the meaning "to come together with" a good sense, which moreover is in agreement with the parallel expressions ישב עם and התרעה את. The verb occurs several times after the imperative of the verb הלך, "to go." Thus it does in Isa. 22:15 where the RSV translates: "Come, go." But even in these cases, בוא keeps its own meaning. The translation of Isa. 22:15 should be *vade ingredere* (Vulgate) . There exists one expression, preserved in Jon. 1:3, which seems to support the meaning "to go" for the verb בוא. It concerns the shipping term אניה באה תרשיש. In early translations the term was rendered by verbs meaning "to go": βαδίζον εἰς in the Greek of the Septuagint, דאזלא בימא in the Targum, *euntem in Tharsis* in the Vulgate. But it seems to me that in this expression also בוא does not mean "to go" but "come," "arrive." Jonah found a ship in the harbor of Joppa "bound for Tarshish." "Destined for," "bound for" are still the normal shipping terms. The expression does not refer to the journey, "the going," but

---

[2] M. A. Klopfenstein, *Die Lüge nach dem Alten Testament, ihr Begriff, ihre Bedeutung, und ihre Beurteilung.* Thesis Bern (Zürich, 1964) , p. 102.

to the arrival, the goal of the voyage. In II Chron. 9:21 two verbs in connection with ships occur, הלך and בוא, distinguishing the journey of the ship (הלך) and its arrival (בוא). The parallel text in I Kings 10:22 only uses the verb בוא. In Jer. 43 the author is not interested in the journey to, but the stay in Egypt.

The literal translation of vs. 3 (end) is: "to kill us and to carry us into exile to Babel." The old translations all have the same sequence and join the two expressions by "and," *et*. We can find this literal rendering in several recent translations: the version of the Dutch Bible Society; E. Dhorme (Pléiade); B. N. Wambacq, Commentary (1957). However, there are also others who take the two phrases, about an expected death and about exile, as alternatives, changing the copulative *et* to *aut*. This is done, among others, by the Leiden Translation (1901); Volz, Commentary; Rudolph, Commentary; Gélin; RSV; Grispino. There is no language problem here, as *waw* can be rendered by *aut* in many places. One can also ascertain that when it is taken as an alternative the sense becomes more vivid. Yet the anticlimax remains.

The two infinitives with *lamed,* להמית and להגלות, are dependent on the previous phrase, i.e. the delivery into the power of the Babylonians. The opinion of these Judean men is that the consequence of this delivering into Babel's power will mean their death, their exile. In my translation, "exile which ends in death," I treat the two infinitives as belonging closely together, expressing one thought. That two verbal forms, whether or not joined by *waw*, can render one thought, and that in this way the first possesses an adverbial meaning, is a well-known feature of Hebrew style. In the detailed work on syntax by Eduard König and in Paul Joüon's useful *Grammaire,* to mention but a couple of studies, one can find examples of the adverbial meaning of verbs used in connection with other verbs.[3] This aspect is not limited to the *hiphil* forms of the verb, though these are the most clearly distinguishable, which also found their way into translations. T. J. Meek, dealing with the coordinate adverbial clause in Hebrew, refers to the common construction in Arabic, the so-called *hāl*-clause, expressing the state, condition, and also the manner in which the action of the main clause takes place.[4] In a study of II Sam. 12:25 I have summed up a fairly large number of cases of וישלח followed by

[3] Eduard König, *Historisch-Comparative Syntax der hebräischen Sprache* (Leipzig, 1897), pars. 332x, 361, 369. Paul Joüon, *Grammaire de l'hébreu biblique*, 2nd ed. (Rome, 1947), pars. 102g, 54d, "hifil adverbial."

[4] In *JAOS* XLIX (1929), 156-59.

a verbal form which carries the main thought of the sentence, like the Greek ἀποστέλλειν.[5] To mention yet a few more examples of this figure of speech, besides those mentioned in the literature referred to, I would point to the combination frequently in use: ויען ויאמר, usually rendered literally: "and he answered and said." Sometimes one finds: "and he answered," a single translation of the double expression. So one reads "and he answered" in RSV, Gen. 18:27; and the same, rendering the term ויען לאמור in Gen. 42:22. But in both cases the translators have wrongly chosen to translate the first verb of the combination. From the context, too, it seems to be clear that in Gen. 18 Abraham does not answer but "addresses the word to." And in Gen. 42:22 Reuben does not answer his brothers but addresses the word to them. Recognition of the adverbial meaning of one of the verbs, in this case of the verbal form ויען, would improve the translation of many sentences in both Old and New Testament. In Ps. 27:7*b* the psalmist begs: וחנני וענני. The translations render this literally: *miserere mei et exaudi me.* Here also an adverbial meaning for the first of the two verbs would express the unity of thought better. One could translate: "answer me mercifully."

Where in Jer. 43:3 we note the unity of thought expressed in two verbal forms, the two infinitives המית and הגלות, the first infinitive has an adverbial value connected to the carrying off into exile. Exile is feared as a fatal business, leading to ruin. "Exile which ends in death" is an attempt to do this figure of speech justice.

In the Syriac version of vs. 5, "all commanders of the forces" are counted in with those whom Johanan took. Probably the singular form of the verb has caused this rendering. Although "and all commanders of the forces" may be an addition, it more likely should be considered as belonging to the subject of the sentence. I have translated the verb as a plural, just as in vs. 4: "they did not obey." Those who are taken by Johanan are those who are led by him and his colleague commanders. In vs. 6 they are listed. The verb לקח indicates that those who are taken with them are carried away; not, however, that the carrying away takes place against their will. The picture of Jeremiah and Baruch being dragged away against their will cannot be derived from the wording of vss. 5 ff. It does not recognize the additional character of the last line of vs. 7 and tries to clear Jeremiah and Baruch of all blame.

Instead of "the daughters of the king," the princesses, which is the translation of the Hebrew text and also that of the Greek, Aramaic,

[5] In *Festschrift Vriezen* (Wageningen, 1966), pp. 27-28.

and Latin, I have translated: "the court," a rendering of בית המלך. This is the reading of the Peshiṭta. Although I cannot give an absolutely convincing argument for choosing the Syriac reading, there are some indications that we should bear in mind the possibility that the handing down of the Hebrew text and the translations which depend on it do not preserve the original reading.

The phrase בנות המלך appears, apart from Jer. 43:6, also Jer. 41:10 and II Sam. 13:18; בנות מלכים occurs in Ps. 45:10. The two last-mentioned references deal with the splendor of the robes and the beauty of the princesses. Jer. 41:10 uses the expression similarly in a summary. The Syriac translation of Jer. 41:10 does not have this phrase.

The context of Jer. 43 preserves another summary which has even more similarity with our vs. 6, Jer. 41:16. The second part of this verse runs: "soldiers, women, children, and eunuchs" (סרסים). The Syriac translation renders this word with *mhymn'*, "the trusted ones." The eunuchs belonged to the court as servants and guarded the house of the king. Instead of the princesses in the lists of Jer. 41:10 and 43:6, the text in Jer. 41:16 mentions the eunuchs. And this does make the list more understandable: the men, the women, the children, and the emasculated, the servants of the court. It is in no way strange that they are mentioned in such a summary. But the mentioning of the princesses does raise questions: Why are they mentioned and not the king's wives, not the princes? If the intention was to report that also among those who remained behind in the land there were members of the royal house, then it is possible that originally in place of בנת המלך: בית המלך was written. The change of one letter could be the reason for the form being preserved in the Hebrew tradition. In the old writings a *nun* is not very different from a *yodh*. The *plene* writing בנות is a later appearance. I offer my choice of the Syriac tradition, which finds some indirect support in the list in Jer. 41:16, for discussion.

III

REMARKS CONCERNING THE REDACTION

Paul Volz treated Jer. 42:1–43:7 as a unit, to which he gave the title: "Die Juden wandern trotz Jeremias Rat nach Ägypten." [6] He changes the sequence of the text by placing 43:1-3 before 42:19. Jeremiah's threat, that Egypt will not be a place of refuge but a place of death for "the remnant of Judah" (42:19-22), he considers a reaction of the

---

[6] *Der Prophet Jeremia,* Commentary, 2nd ed. (Leipzig, 1928), pp. 356-62.

prophet to the accusation: "Thou art an impostor." Many people have followed Volz's suggestion in their studies concerning Jeremiah. W. Rudolph has indicated this sequence of the reading in his treatment of the Hebrew text in the third edition of Kittel's *Biblia Hebraica* (1937), and in his well-known commentary the suggestion is accepted.[7]

This reorganization of the text seems attractive but at the same time raises new questions. Apart from the fact that the earliest history of the text preserves no witness that can be used to justify the change, it does seem strange that vs. 1 of chap. 43 so emphatically stresses that the oracle has come to an end and that Jeremiah has transmitted it in its entirety. In the passage 42:19-22, moreover, there is absolutely no reaction to the accusation of Jeremiah's falseness, nor to the accusation of Baruch's wicked intentions. Finally, changing the order makes an additional introductory sentence, such as "but Jeremiah said," or, "answered," necessary.

However, this attempt to strengthen the unity of a large passage makes it clear that Jer. 43:1-7 consists of two fragments. The lively, indeed, stirring style of the part which describes Jeremiah's share in what happened after the arrival of the Babylonians ceases after 43:3. Direct speech dominates this description. In 42:1-6 an oracle is asked for, promised, and accepted in advance; in 42:7-22 the oracle is given: If they stay in Judah, well-being is promised; should they settle in Egypt, they are doomed to total destruction. In 43:1-3, in just as emotional a manner, the veracity of the oracle is denied and Baruch accused.

The second part of Jer. 43:1-7, vss. 5-7, continues the report of the occurrences described in Jer. 40:7-16; 41:1-18. The information about Gedaliah's provincial governorship, his murder by Ishmael, Johanan's intervention and proposal to escape into Egypt, are continued in the same style in 43:5-7. Johanan and the other commanders carry away the group of Judeans who, because of the murder of Gedaliah, see no future for themselves in the land of Judah. Vs. 4 of chap. 43 attempts to connect up with the story that centers on the oracle. This verse omits Azariah, who does not appear in the report about what happened, but does come into the Jeremian passages, 42:1, and in 43:1-3 is the actual accuser of the prophet and Baruch. For Kareah's son Johanan is the leader after Gedaliah's death.

In vs. 6 the last line follows lamely. The words "and the prophet Jeremiah and Neriah's son Baruch" are obviously a redactional addi-

---

[7] *Jeremia*, Commentary, 2nd ed. (Tübingen, 1958) pp. 236-37.

tion. Just as in the report in II Kings 25 about the same events, Jeremiah does not appear in the fairly detailed report preserved in the book which bears his name. The subsidiary sentence in vs. 7, "for they obeyed not YHWH's command," comes from the same redactional hand. The last line, "and came to, *or* in Tahpanhes," may have served as connecting point for the prophetic story beginning in vs. 8.

Judging from style and content, the prophetic passages are independent units. Their connection with the description of events is secondary and stylistically weak. The intriguing question of whether the prophetic passages ought to be considered as a religious explanation of the events, or whether the events are to be taken as the fulfillment of prophecy—Zimmerli says, "das Geschehen ist verwirklichtes Wort, eingelöste Verkündigung"—is not solved by the exegesis of Jer. 43:1-7. The weak redactional links between the report of events and the oracles concerning these events indicate fairly independent circles, in which these two kinds of literature were handed down before they were joined together in the texts preserved for us.

The Literary Category of the Book of Jonah

MILLAR BURROWS

The odd little tale of Jonah is still understood and classified in a variety of ways. It is not the purpose of this paper to trace the history of its diverse interpretations. An interesting sketch of this history is given by Elias Bickermann.[1] My intention is to advocate a particular view. This may be conveniently approached, however, by a process of elimination.[2] The essential problem, of course, is not classification for its own sake, but an understanding of the book's literary form as an expression of the author's purpose and meaning.

The thesis (or assumption) that the book of Jonah is a record of historical facts might seem to require no refutation at this late date, but it is still championed by reputable scholars and therefore cannot simply be ignored. As recently as 1962 it has been valiantly defended by P. Alberto Vaccari, S.J. With evident distress he notes (pp. 236 ff.) that since the appearances of Feuillet's articles, which he mentions without deigning to name their author, there has been a tendency in Roman Catholic scholarship to relinquish the interpretation of Jonah as history and to take it as fiction of one kind or another. Among scholars who in their publications have moved from the former view to the latter he points especially to Fr. Nötscher and J. Schildenberger. The same tendency has been evident also in Protestant scholarship. For instance, in the 1898 edition of the Commentary on Obadiah and Jonah in the *Cambridge Bible for Schools and Colleges* T. T. Perowne

[1] At the end of this essay there is a list of works cited. References in the text are made by pages only or, when more than one publication of the same author is used, by titles (usually abbreviated) and pages.

[2] For searching the literature, taking notes, and having copies made of important articles and excerpts from books I am much indebted to the Rev. Theodore N. Swanson, Associate Professor of Old Testament at the Lutheran School of Theology in Chicago.

held that the book of Jonah could only be regarded as actual history (p. 51); but in the 1918 edition H. C. O. Lanchester declared, "In spite of all that has been written to the contrary there can be little doubt that the Book of Jonah is not to be taken as literal history" (p. 41).

In opposition to this tendency Vaccari (p. 238) quotes with approval a statement of G. Rinaldi that, if the book of Jonah is not history, there is no need to seek another category for it, because in that case it has no parallel. True, the book is in some ways unique; but it still represents a particular type of literature, just as the most extraordinary man belongs to a particular race and nation. Vaccari insists also, still following Rinaldi, that God is revealed in history, which is recorded in the Bible; and therefore concern for the historical basis of a narrative should have precedence over any other consideration (pp. 240-41). In both the Old and the New Testament, however, revelation is given also in parables, allegorical poems, and other forms of literature.

Recalling the declaration of the Pontifical Biblical Commission on June 23, 1905, that a biblical narrative which appears to be historical may not be considered fictitious unless there are solid arguments to prove that the author intended it as such, Vaccari claims that in the case of the book of Jonah there are no such solid arguments (p. 236). We can well agree that the real point at issue is what the author intended. The historical accuracy of his narrative is another question. No historian can give a completely accurate account of the past; but if his purpose is to write history, his work cannot be assigned to any other category. For the book of Jonah our main question is not what happened or could have happened, but how the writer intended his book to be understood.

Since it is seriously claimed, however, that the book is not only history but historically accurate, a few words must be said on that point. That some historical facts are included is clear. There is no reason to doubt that Jonah the son of Amittai was a real prophet, who predicted the territorial expansion of Israel under Jeroboam II as recorded in II Kings 14:25. Gath-hepher, from which he came, was a real town (Josh. 19:13); Joppa and Nineveh were real cities; and Tarshish, wherever it may have been, was a real place or area. If some of the events recounted in the book are not such as one might expect to find in a sober historical chronicle, that is true also of much that is included in the historical books of the Old Testament.

The first part of the story, though strange, is not incredible. The storm at sea and the measures taken to allay or outride it present no serious problem. Even the idea of pagan mariners calling upon Yahweh is in accord with the practice of polytheists everywhere under similar circumstances. The Babylonians could invoke a "god or goddess, known or unknown," and later the Greeks could dedicate an altar "To An Unknown God." Not until Jonah is picked up by the fish is our credulity taxed. From then on, however, the difficulties multiply.

The "great fish," of course, was not a whale. Its designation as such is merely an item in the history of translation and exegesis. An ancient Hebrew writer might have been so unscientific as to call a whale a fish; but this was not any creature known to ichthyology or to any branch of zoology.[3] It was a special fish, which Yahweh "appointed" for its particular purpose, like the plant and the worm later in the story. It not only had a mouth and a maw sufficiently capacious to accommodate a man; it evidently did not have, or was able to restrain, the normal flow of digestive juices and the muscular activity involved in digestion. Otherwise Jonah would hardly have survived the passage back to shore, even if some kind of ventilation had been provided.

More serious difficulties for a historical interpretation of the book are encountered when Jonah reaches Nineveh, which, we are told, was "an exceedingly great city of three days' journey" (3:3). Whether this refers to the circumference or, as commonly supposed, to the diameter of the city is not certain. In either event three days' journey, by a conservative estimate, would be something like fifty miles. The excavations at the site revealed an inner wall about seven and a half miles in length, enclosing less than three square miles. The greatest length of the walled city from north to south was about three miles; the width varied from about half a mile at the south to about a mile and a quarter at the north. An outer wall on the east increased the maximum width to about two miles.

Even these dimensions were probably more than those of the city in Jonah's time. Sennacherib, whose reign began nearly half a century after the death of Jeroboam II, claimed to have been the first to enclose Nineveh with a wall, and to have increased the circumference of the city from 9,300 to 21,815 cubits (Luckenbill, p. 170); that is, from less than three to more than six miles. On that basis a day's journey into the city (3:4) would have carried Jonah well past

---

[3] Cf. Eduard Haller, *Die Erzählung von dem Propheten Jona* (Theologische Existenz Heute, NF Nr. LXV [München, 1958]), p. 29 where the fish is "keine zoologische Spezies mehr."

the center of it, if not out into the country on the other side.[4] There was a large suburban area outside the wall; but even if what might today be called Greater Nineveh is assumed to be included, the description of it as a city of three days' journey, whatever that means, is clearly very generous.

The statement that there were more than 120,000 persons in Nineveh (4:11) seems modest enough.[5] The population in the time of Sennacherib has been estimated at about 300,000 (Olmstead, p. 326). Certainly Nineveh was a big city; the prophet from the little kingdom of Israel had never seen one like it.

But who was the "king of Nineveh" in whose reign such an extraordinary reformation was brought about by Jonah's preaching? Four emperors ruled over Assyria while Jeroboam II occupied the throne of Israel, and of course Jonah's prophetic activity did not necessarily begin or end with the reign of Jeroboam. That any one of the four, however, was called "the king of Nineveh" is doubtful. Conceivably a local administrator may have claimed that title; and of course a Hebrew writer might apply to a foreign ruler a designation not used by him or his subjects. That, however, is only conjecture.

The Assyrian records of the period refer to a solar eclipse, famine, pestilence, internal disorders, and even a serious military disaster. These calamities and the decline of the Assyrian power in the first half of the eighth century are taken by Vaccari (pp. 248-49) to show that the situation at Nineveh when Jonah went there was such as to favor foreign influence and a change of mind on the part of the citizens. No document yet discovered, however, tells of a sweeping mass conversion at Nineveh, obeying the God of the Hebrews in response to the preaching of a Hebrew prophet. Perhaps an event of this kind would not have been considered suitable for inclusion in the royal annals.[6]

It would be strange, however, that no trace whatever should be left in the subsequent history of the empire. The mighty goddess

---

[4] Alberto Vaccari, S.J., "Il Genere Letterario del Libro di Giona in Recenti Publicazioni," *Divinitas,* VI (1962), 252 suggests that the prophet went zigzag through the streets of the city for a day, proclaiming his message. This is not supported by the Hebrew.

[5] A. Lods, *The Prophets and the Rise of Judaism,* trans. by S. H. Hooke (New York, 1937), p. 335 speaks of "thousands of little children," but the "persons" (אדם) who do not know their right hand from their left cannot mean only the children.

[6] Haller, *op. cit.,* p. 9 remarks that such a revival would surely have been mentioned in the Old Testament books of Kings and Chronicles. Incidentally one wonders whether Jonah spoke Assyrian or the Ninevites understood Hebrew.

Ishtar and other native deities were still worshiped at Nineveh down to the fall of the city in 612 B.C., and Assyrian warfare was as ruthless as ever to the end. If the book of Jonah is an accurate historical record, the reformation must have been very superficial and temporary. That, however, would spoil the rest of the story. The reformation is represented as so sincere and complete that God abandoned his intention to destroy the city.

In support of the historical character of the book, Vaccari argues (pp. 242-48) that it fits the historical circumstances of Israel in Jonah's lifetime. He illustrates this by pointing out parallels between the story of Jonah and the lives of Elijah and Elisha, especially the latter's mission to Damascus, as well as the mission of Amos to the kingdom of Israel. Contacts in language and ideas with Amos also are adduced to show that in its doctrine of judgment and pardon the book of Jonah agrees with the early eighth-century prophets. One may recognize these parallels and contacts, however, and agree that they show the author's fidelity to the prophetic tradition, without inferring that his narrative is historical. Many who have quite different ideas of its literary character put no less emphasis on its echoes of the prophetic books and narratives.

Against any view that the story of Jonah is fictitious, Vaccari argues (pp. 238-39) that the minor forms of fiction do not give their protagonists names, and the major forms give them invented names, not those of such famous historical persons as Jonah. If the author had wished to create a typical representative of a prophet's shortcomings, he could have left him nameless or given him a common name like Simon or Joseph instead of using the name of the only minor prophet honorably mentioned in the books of Kings. No doubt he might have done so, but the use of a known yet not too well-known historical figure served to anchor the story in Israel's national tradition.

The choice of Jonah is explained by Wade (p. xcvii) as a result of the author's use of traditional material for the nucleus of his story. That there was any such material for him to use, however, is at best a very dubious conjecture. The most probable explanation of the facts is that the author chose Nineveh, far away and in ruins in his day, as a convenient example of a notoriously wicked Gentile city, and in the same way chose Jonah, about whom little was known, as the principal character of his story. E. M. Good even suggests that Jonah may have been chosen because he was "so obscure a figure that a new story about him would contradict nothing previously known" (pp. 41-42).

In short, the historical accuracy of the book cannot be successfully maintained. Nor can it be shown that the author intended to record history or wished to be understood as doing so. In the opinion of H. W. Wolff he deliberately omitted all historical data except the names of Jonah and his father precisely because it was not his intention to report history ("Gotteswort," p. 23).

T. H. Robinson well stated the conclusion to which all this points: One is not in a position to understand what the book of Jonah means until he has freed himself from the assumption that it is a historical document (p. 118). Moreover, as Haller points out (pp. 7-8), the demand for history as what really happened makes the mistake of regarding as real only what is historical in a journalistic sense, and of assuming that when one has accepted the story as historical in that sense he has heard its message.

Many other ways of classifying it have been proposed. Unfortunately, as Feuillet remarks ("Sens," pp. 340-41), these classifications themselves cannot be classified, because too often they are not expressed precisely and differ only slightly among themselves. To this we may add that many interpreters combine two or more terms to express their understanding of the nature of the book, and indeed there is no reason a priori to suppose that it is not a mixture of different kinds of composition. Certainly it must not be forced into any form defined in terms of classical or modern literature, or derived from the traditions of other peoples, ancient or modern, eastern or western, civilized or preliterary.

Jonah begins with a sentence resembling the introductory formulas used by the editors of several of the prophetic books, though not corresponding exactly to any of them. It is included in the prophetic canon and is presumably one of "the twelve prophets" mentioned by ben Sira (49:10). Obviously, however, it is not a book of prophecy. Its contents are by no means typical of the prophetic literature. Instead of a collection of a prophet's pronouncements on various occasions, with perhaps a brief biographical note now and then, we have here an extended narrative about a prophet with only a very concise summary of his message on one occasion. Aside from the declaration that Nineveh would be overthrown, the only words of Jonah reported are his remarks to the sailors and his peevish complaints to Yahweh.

Haller (pp. 11-12) considers the opening sentence a *Nachstilisierung* of a prophet's reception of Yahweh's word, differing from the usual formula in the fact that there is no mention of time or place. Actually the exact formula used in Jonah (לאמר . . . וי יהי דבר יהוה אל), as C. A. Keller points out (p. 330), is found in the stories about Elijah (I Kings 17:2, 8; 21:17; cf. 18:1). In other ways also the book of Jonah resembles these stories and those about Elisha and other prophets in I and II Kings. Keller (*loc. cit.*) finds here its closest literary analogies, and concludes that the book is in the first place the story of a prophet.

There is one notable difference, however, between the early stories and the book of Jonah. Elijah and Elisha and the rest (with the exception, perhaps, of the man of God in I Kings 13:1-32 and II Kings 23:17-18) are the heroes of the stories told about them. Jonah is anything but a hero. He appears rather as a pitiable and ludicrous caricature of a prophet.[7] Aage Bentzen, noting that Gunnar Hylmö classifies Jonah with the devotional legends of the prophets,[8] points out that its form is peculiar, and it rebukes its main character instead of exalting him (vol. I, p. 239). Haller (pp. 8-9) assigns the book to the *Gattung* of prophetic legends, but adds that it differs from others in not being dated. The Elisha stories, however, often refer to "the king of Israel" and "the king of Syria" without names or dates.

Gerhard von Rad defines the literary category of Jonah as "a story told about a prophet," but one which differs from the earlier stories in being more didactic than they were. "Indeed," he says, "it seems to have been the last and strongest flowering of this old and almost extinct form" (p. 291). This at least has the merit of placing the book in a category indigenous to ancient Hebrew literature, and as far as it goes it is acceptable; it fails, however, to indicate the most distinctive literary feature of the story.[9]

Approached with an open mind and an attitude more appreciative than analytical, the book of Jonah reads like a fairy tale or a bit of simple folklore. Naïve and artless as it may appear, however, it is much more than that. Scholars who speak of legend or myth in connection with it refer to the author's material rather than the finished story. Feuillet observes that, far from resembling a popular

[7] Vaccari, *op. cit.*, p. 239 recognizes that Jonah "non fa bella figura" but takes this only as showing that unless the story is history it has no parallel in any literature. In *Los géneros literarios de la Sagraca Escritura* (Madrid, 1957), p. 103, note 16, he rejects the designation of Jonah as a caricature of a prophet.

[8] Gunnar Hylmö, *Gamla testamentets literaturhistoria* (Lund, 1908), p. 132.

[9] A more elaborate variation on the idea of a prophetic legend is offered by Haller, *op. cit.*, p. 50.

tale, the book manifestly comes from an educated Israelite, who conveyed his meaning by a masterly use of Scripture and a few items of folklore according to a well-considered plan ("Sens," p. 186; cf. "Livre," p. 18).

Many commentators note the widespread occurrence in folklore of man-eating monsters and similar marvels. T. K. Cheyne identified Jonah's fish with "the dragon of the subterranean ocean," to be understood here in a symbolic sense (col. 2568). Eissfeldt (p. 405) sees as the basis of the book two legends (in chaps. 1–3 and chap. 4 respectively), with which is interwoven the "mythological fairy-tale motif" of the fish. No mere compilation, however, would have the literary unity and originality of the book of Jonah. That the two "legends" ever existed independently, indeed, is questionable. The supposed compiler, in fact, is actually more than that, for Eissfeldt attributes to him "the broad universalism and tolerant humanity" of the final work.

Marti (p. 246) held that the author used many elements of tradition, reformulating them and subordinating them to his purpose, so that they did not affect the unity of the book. A skillful combination of various materials to produce a well-constructed and well-told story is recognized by Haller also (p. 7, note 8). In the use of the verb מנה he sees an indication of the way Yahwism could appropriate mythical material and demythologize it (p. 28, note 36). Loretz suggests that old traditions of the North Israelite–Phoenician area were reformulated by our author from a controlling theological point of view, producing something quite new (p. 28). Feuillet, on the other hand, finds any effort to discover pagan sources behind the book forced and unnecessary ("Livre," p. 15).

In any case, the story as we have it is a work of consummate artistry, told with a restraint and economy of language characteristic of the best biblical narratives. There is no splashing or smearing of colors; the picture is vividly drawn with a few swift strokes. At the end, having finished his tale, the author ties up the bundle and cuts the string with the neatness of a typical French short story. That some scholars can call this ending abrupt is amazing. It is perfect. Questions left unanswered are irrelevant to the purpose of the book.

As marks of the author's skill in narration, Wolff points to the artistic use of repetition and striking questions, particularly at the end of the story ("Jonabuch," col. 854).[10] Feuillet remarks that the

---

[10] In *Studien zum Jonabuch* (Biblische Studien, Heft 47 [Neukirchen-Vluyn, 1965]), pp. 29-58, H. W. Wolff has an extended section on "Die Jonaerzählung als sprachliches Kunstwerk."

absence of an explicitly stated moral is in conformity with the laws of the *genre parabolique.* He notes also, quoting H. Schmidt, the lack of any psychological observations explaining why the characters acted as they did, what they thought, or how they felt ("Sens," p. 340). To Schmidt's statement that the careful construction of the book is shown by the parallelism between its two halves, Feuillet adds that the first part is subordinated to the second, so that with Jonah's preaching at Nineveh a climax is reached (p. 342). This twofold structure, he says, brings out a striking antithesis: Jonah's prophecy is from God, yet it is not fulfilled (p. 344).

The book is manifestly a product of individual genius. It cannot be classified, therefore, according to the forms and types of folklore or oral tradition. The category to which it is assigned must be a literary category, though it may have developed from a simpler type found already in folklore.

Some interpreters are content with general designations, such as didactic fiction. Haller, who uses also a more specific classification of the story, says, "Sie ist eine *Lehrdichtung*" (p. 6). Weiser describes its *Gattung* as *Lehrdichtung* in the form of a *Tendenzerzählung* (p. 215). Undoubtedly it is didactic fiction, but that concept needs to be narrowed down to something more precise.

A native Israelite category considered appropriate by some critics is *midrash.* Karl Budde long ago made the ingenious suggestion (*ZAW* 1892, pp. 40 ff.) that the story of Jonah was an excerpt from the "Midrash of the Book of Kings" cited in II Chron. 24:27, and that it had originally followed what we now know as II Kings 14:21. The manner in which the book of Jonah begins, Budde thought, indicates that it is a continuation of something that originally preceded it.[11] The omission of the clause "who was from Gath-hepher" in Jon. 1:1 seemed to Budde to confirm this opinion.

Oswald Loretz accepts the classification of Jonah as *midrash* but remarks that Budde and others were wrong in regarding this form as a creation of rabbinic Judaism. It arose, he maintains, in the post-exilic period, when conditions required the presentation of Israel's traditions in a new form (p. 28). Obviously *midrash,* as the Chronicler used that term, antedated rabbinic Judaism. One may question, however, that the word had the same meaning for the Chronicler and the rabbis. More judicious is Feuillet's suggestion that in the way it uses Scripture the book of Jonah foreshadows the midrashic literature ("Livre," p. 18).

[11] Ezekiel also begins ויהי, as does Ruth.

Marti, though rejecting Budde's theory, described Jonah as a *midrash* "like Ruth, Tobit, and similar writings" (p. 245). G. A. F. Knight, after putting the book "in the same category of writings as the Prodigal Son," proceeds to describe it as "a Midrash upon the message of parts of Jeremiah and the second half of Isaiah" (pp. 51-52). Evidently the category of *midrash*, though perhaps applicable in some sense and to some degree, is not sufficiently precise, or perhaps not well enough understood by some of those who use it, to afford a satisfactory repository for the book of Jonah.

Much less appropriate, indeed quite misleading, is the old and still common idea that the story is an allegory. Jonah is Israel, say a great many interpreters. Most of them add that his involuntary sojourn in the belly of the fish represents the Babylonian Exile of the people of Judah, and his ejection on the shore their liberation and return to Palestine. The rest of the story is ordinarily supposed to refer to Israel's mission to the nations. Such an interpretation does not fit the story too well, and the more rigorously it is applied the less plausible it becomes. As Good says, "some pieces of the story will not fit any allegorical mold" (p. 40). Feuillet points out, for example, that Jonah's attitude in telling the sailors to throw him into the sea does not resemble that of the chosen people in exile; and the fish is not an instrument of punishment but of deliverance ("Sens," p. 334; "Livre," p. 15). In a sense Jonah may be said to represent Israel, or some party or tendency within Israel; but the book is not a figurative account of the nation's experience. Hans Schmidt (p. 470), while finding the closest analogy to the story of Jonah in the way Ezekiel uses ancient folktales in an allegorical fashion, qualifies this by adding that the traditional material used in Jonah is not allegorized but is connected with a historic person in such a way as to put a problem before the reader and leave him to solve it for himself.

It is possible, of course, to construct elaborate allegorical applications. The history of exegesis affords abundant proof that an ingenious interpreter can treat any narrative as an allegory and make it mean almost anything he wishes. The greatest weakness of this kind of exposition is that it is only to a small degree controlled by the text. Details which cannot be forced into the scheme are ignored; and minor, accidental resemblances are made to support the most fanciful applications.[12] The fish invariably receives undue prominence. The

---

[12] Cf. Haller, *op. cit.*, p. 13, note 16: "Die allegorisierende, spekulativ-typisierende Erweiterung der Jonaerzählung kann natürlich nicht ohne gewagte Überinterpretation da und spürbare Verkürzung dort geschehen."

repentance of the Ninevites is little emphasized, while the idea of Israel's repentance is injected without any support in the narrative.

Significance has been seen in the fact that the prophet's name means "dove" and his father's name is apparently derived from the root *'mt;* but "Dove son of Fidelity" is hardly an appropriate appellation for the prophet Jonah.[13] The patent fact of the matter is that these names were not invented by the author of our book: They are attested in II Kings 14:25 as the real names of a historic prophet and his father, and the choice of him as the chief character of the story carried with it the use of his full name to identify him.

The term allegory, like *midrash,* is often used very loosely. Good complains with reason that most of the proposed allegorical interpretations of Jonah are in fact "so general as scarcely to qualify as allegory in the strict sense at all" (p. 40). A genuine allegory, conceived and composed as such, follows a symbolic pattern on which interpreters can agree, even if they differ on details. The book of Jonah exhibits no such pattern. As Gottwald says, "no allegorical clue is provided and the reconstruction grows appallingly arbitrary" (p. 521). In short, the book does not naturally lend itself to a convincing allegorical interpretation. Indeed, as Feuillet says, making an allegory of it "takes from it all its freshness and life" ("Livre," (p. 15).

Some scholars propose what may be called quasi- or semiallegorical explanations. In Cheyne's interpretation *midrash* and mythology are combined with a symbolism verging on allegory. The great fish, identified with the primeval dragon, is taken as a symbol of "the all-absorbing empire of Babylonia which swallowed up Israel—not, however, to destroy it but to give it room for repentance" (col. 2568). The objections to this theory are well stated by Oesterley and Robinson, but their own interpretation is no more plausible: They regard the fish, in which Jonah was confined for three days, as a symbol of Nineveh, the city of three days' journey; his disgorgement is then a symbol of his departure from the repentant city (pp. 377-79).

Related to the idea of symbolism is H. W. Wolff's conception of the story of Jonah as *typisierende Dichtung,* the mariners and the Ninevites representing the heathen and Jonah the Israelites ("Jonabuch," col. 854). This, however, is only a part of Wolff's view. He finds the literary *Gattung* of the story in the "Weisheitliche Lehrerzählung,"

---

[13] E. M. Good, *Irony in the Old Testament* (Philadelphia and London, 1965), p. 42 suggests that by using the name Amittai our author was perhaps "making an ironic point." Why the name Jonah is not included in this suggestion is not apparent. Is the suggestion itself intended ironically?

which is marked by a mature art of narrative and a cosmopolitan culture (*ibid.*). These ideas are neatly combined in the description of the book given in the Sellin-Fohrer *Einleitung:* "Der Gattung nach ist das Buch . . . eine midraschartige Lehrschrift . . . , die von der Weisheitsliteratur beeinflusst ist" (pp. 485-86). The Wisdom element is not surprising, says Keller, commenting on Wolff's view, because all the categories of biblical literature are colored by that influence (p. 330).

Elsewhere Wolff calls the book of Jonah a *Novelle* and refers to the author as "unser Novellist" ("Gotteswort," p. 23). He elaborates this classification in his "Studien" (pp. 30 ff.). The distinguishing mark of the *Novelle* form, he says, is that the didactic motive is veiled by concentrating on the narrative and avoiding an explicit application or moral. Wolff's meticulous and finely drawn analysis produces some results which would have surprised the author of the book. On the whole, however, the classification as a *Novelle* is a satisfactory description of the general literary form; yet it still ignores the most distinctive characteristic of the book of Jonah, which Wolff himself is one of the few scholars to recognize.

More appropriate than any of the categories thus far noted, but still not quite precise, is the description of our story as a parable. With more or less qualification, and sometimes in combination with other categories, this has been adopted by many scholars.[14] Deden considers it well established (col. 876), and Good remarks that most commentators now accept it, though in calling the book a parable they often use the word "more or less loosely to mean a story with a didactic point" (p. 40). Feuillet uses it casually ("Sens," p. 352), but agrees with Joüon that the story does not actually resemble a parable ("Livre," p. 15).

An interesting refinement of the idea of the book as a parable is offered by Haller. He calls attention to the fact that the parable (*Parabel*) is only one of many kinds of comparisons (*Gleichnis*) in the New Testament: There are also allegories, metaphors, proverbs, *et al.*, "ja auch stilreine Beispielerzählungen" (p. 50). The *Beispielerzählung*, he explains, tells of something which really happens or may happen at any time. What distinguishes it from other kinds of *Gleichnis* is that its most varied details offer important points of

---

[14] E.g., J. A. Bewer, *A Critical and Exegetical Commentary on Jonah* (International Critical Commentary, XXV [New York, 1912]), 4; G. A. Smith, *The Book of the Twelve Prophets,* II (New York, 1901), 514; Aage Bentzen, *Introduction to the Old Testament,* 2nd ed., p. 147; J. D. Smart, "Introduction and Exegesis of the Book of Jonah," *Interpreter's Bible,* VI (New York and Nashville, 1956), 872.

comparison with the here and now (note 64). Accordingly the book of Jonah is described as "eine Beispielerzählung in der Form einer Prophetenlegende, weisheitlich-didaktisch intendiert" (p. 50).

The implications of this description appear in Haller's detailed exegesis, which, whatever else may be said of it, makes uncommonly enjoyable and edifying reading, abounding in statements one is tempted to quote. Sometimes the acute applications of small points in the story, taken as typical of universal human experience, seem almost as far-fetched as the wildest allegorical explanations, but they are basically different. Haller tries conscientiously to remain true to the story, and his exposition, based on human traits and experiences illustrated by the story, includes many keen and sound exegetical insights. By and large it is much more convincing than any allegorical interpretation. The assumption that applications can be found in details of the narrative, however, not only makes inevitable a good deal of fanciful eisegesis but also runs the risk of obscuring the central meaning of the whole story.

In all the categories we have reviewed there is some truth. Otherwise, no doubt, they would not have been proposed by competent scholars. None of them, however, quite hits the mark. The author of the book of Jonah was certainly not trying to conform to the rules of any recognized form. He might have said with Hans Sachs,

> "Wollt ihr nach Regeln messen,
> was nicht nach eurer Regeln Lauf,
> der eig'nen Spur vergessen,
> sucht davon erst die Regeln auf!" [15]

Nevertheless, I am convinced, there is a familiar type of literary composition into which, provided it is not too narrowly defined, the book of Jonah falls easily and naturally. I only wonder why it has not been generally applied to the book from the beginning of the literary study of the Old Testament.

Before naming it, let me recall an aspect of the story which has received much less attention than it deserves. This will require a brief review of the familiar story, beginning with Jonah's extraordinary reaction to his prophetic call. It was nothing unheard-of for a prophet to draw back from a task laid upon him because he felt his own inadequacy and incompetence. Moses had remonstrated with God when commanded to appear before Pharaoh on behalf of his people and to summon the Israelites to leave Egypt. Jeremiah, when called

[15] Richard Wagner, *Die Meistersinger*, Act I.

to prophesy, had protested that he was only a youth with no skill in speaking. Neither of them, however, scurried down to the nearest seaport, assuming that by sailing to the other end of the Mediterranean he could get away from God. Jonah did just that. "Nach Nordosten soll er, nach Südwesten geht er," says Haller (p. 15). He was in such a hurry to evade his unwelcome duty, or perhaps so exhausted by his precipitate flight to Joppa, that as soon as he was on board he went down into the hold and fell fast asleep. Haller draws attention to the word for sleep used here, which is from the same root as the noun used for Adam's deep sleep in Gen. 2:21 and Abraham's in 15:12, but "ist hier leicht ironisierend gewendet" (p. 19).

Good calls Jonah's effort to escape from God "an ironically perceived impossibility" (p. 43). "We are clearly intended," he says, "to perceive the incongruity between the prophet's confession of Yahweh as creator of the sea and his attempt to escape on the sea" (p. 45). The first readers and hearers of the story, we may be sure, were fully aware that the will of the Lord of all the earth could not be so easily thwarted. The very idea that any man would try to do it must have amused them. When the story was told to a group at the city gate, perhaps the post-exilic *sod* as Haller suggests (p. 10), or in the village guesthouse, surely a grin would spread over the faces of the audience at this point. They would exchange knowing looks and settle down to enjoy what was coming, thinking, "This is going to be good!"

The story continues: Yahweh raised a mighty tempest, the frightened sailors cast lots, and Jonah was thrown overboard; but Yahweh had ready the big fish which swallowed him, carried him back to land, and deposited him on the shore.[16] Thus forcibly convinced that there was no use trying to escape from his mission, Jonah picked himself up from the beach and set off on the journey of about a month to Nineveh.

With this beginning in mind, we can see that the exaggerated statement of the size of Nineveh is in keeping with the rest of the story, and we are prepared for the greater marvels still to come. Having arrived and entered the city, Jonah announced its impending overthrow. No doubt the anticipation of that well-deserved catastrophe would afford some compensation to a bitter and very tired prophet. But Jonah had reckoned without the king and people of Nineveh,

---

[16] We may pass over the inept effort of a well-meaning later writer to patch together an expression of Jonah's sentiments much less successful than the comparable additions to Daniel and Esther preserved in the Septuagint.

and without God. The people believed his dire prediction and at the command of the king himself proclaimed a fast. Not only the king and people but all their livestock were denied food and water and required to wear sackcloth. At this delightful touch surely those who first read or heard the story must have laughed aloud.

Jonah, however, was not at all gratified by the astounding success of his preaching. The repentance of the Ninevites and Yahweh's decision not to punish them after all made him, he felt, a false prophet. Nobody would ever believe him again. He was so angry that he wanted to die. Jeremiah complained mightily to the Lord, and Elijah asked that he might die; but their reasons were more worthy than Jonah's. His prayer that he might die, says Haller, is "fast lächelnd dargeboten," reminding us of the anger of a frustrated child (p. 44).

Hoping, perhaps, that when the king and people saw they were not going to be destroyed they would go back to their old ways, and the judgment he had foretold might still fall on them, Jonah went out to a place east of the city, made a booth, and sat down in its shade to see what would happen next. Apparently his leafy bower was not adequate for its purpose, or perhaps, as Haller supposes (p. 45), it soon withered. At any rate Yahweh had still further humiliation in store for Jonah. As he had appointed the fish, so now he appointed a plant to spring up and provide sufficient shade to make the disgruntled prophet comfortable and complacent. Whether it was a castor oil plant or not is of no consequence: It was a special plant, created *ad hoc* in one night (4:10).

Hardly had Jonah settled down to enjoy at ease what he hoped would still happen to the city, when two more acts of God came in quick succession. Yahweh appointed a worm which gnawed at the plant and made it wither; then he appointed a dry sirocco to make Jonah's plight still more wretched when the hot sun beat down upon him. Again Jonah begged Yahweh to take his life; but Yahweh replied with the eloquent question which ends the book.

With the whole story before us, we return to our main problem: What kind of literature is this? An important clue, indeed the decisive clue, is the fact that Jonah is everywhere made to appear ridiculous. With this goes the fact that most of the events related are wildly fantastic. Lack of attention to the central importance of the grotesque aspect of the story, I submit, is largely responsible for the variety and vagueness of current opinions about the book.

That there is humor in the story has not gone entirely unnoticed.

Bewer, for example, mentions its "kindly humor without sting or bitterness" (p. 423). Eissfeldt refers to the absurdity of Jonah's attitude when reproached by Yahweh (p. 405). The Jerusalem Bible (p. 1141) speaks of Jonah's "droll adventure," describes "the successive prodigies" as "like a succession of practical jokes," notes the "undisguised irony" with which the story is told, and says that it was "intended to amuse and instruct" (in that order, no doubt). Most commentators, however, either ignore the humorous element or mention it in a tone of apology, apparently assuming that anything in the Bible must have been meant to be read with earnest solemnity.

The same false assumption prevents many readers from appreciating the humor in the sayings of Jesus. Speaking of the "grim humor" of the book of Jonah, J. D. Smart observes that it is "very like the humor of Jesus with which he unmasked men's hypocrisies and follies" (pp. 872-73). The adjective "grim" seems to me inappropriate, but otherwise I heartily agree with this statement. The great crowds who heard Jesus gladly were composed mainly of common folk who could enjoy humor in a story, and especially the kind of humor which was characteristic of his way of speaking. This is the humor of deliberate hyperbole, which makes the object of attack ridiculous by incongruity and grotesque exaggeration. Surely few of Jesus' hearers listened with a straight face when he spoke of covering a lamp after lighting it, of carefully straining a gnat out of one's beverage and calmly swallowing a whole camel, or of a camel vainly trying to squeeze through the eye of a needle.

The book of Jonah is full of exactly this kind of humor. The whole narrative is composed in this vein. For its first readers this must have been as obvious as the same quality of Jesus' sayings was to his hearers. They would not assign the story to a standard literary category with a technical name,[17] but they would recognize it at once for what it was. We have a name for such compositions: The book of Jonah is a satire. In purpose and method it belongs to the same general type of literature as Don Quixote or Gulliver's Travels.

The words "satire" and "satirical" have been used by a few scholars in connection with the book of Jonah. Already in Thomas Paine's *Age of Reason*, as Bickermann reminds us (p. 33), the author's purpose is said to have been to satirize a prophet. Feuillet refers to the

---

[17] Wolff, *op. cit.*, pp. 76-78 suggests that they would have called it a *midrash*. He considers the *Novelle*, as he applies that term to the book of Jonah, a particular form within the wider category of *midrash* literature.

book as "cette satire" ("Sens," p. 347; "Livre," p. 20), and devotes Part II of his article on its meaning to "Le caractère satirique et parénétique, et l'actualité du livre de Jonas" ("Sens," pp. 346-52). Wolff remarks that Jonah is portrayed "ironisch und satirisch" as a type of contemporary Israelite ("Gotteswort," p. 23). This aspect of the story is especially stressed in the same author's "Studien" (pp. 78, 80). Both there and in "Gotteswort" (p. 23) he repeatedly uses the words *Satire, Satirik,* and *satirisch.*

Lods says explicitly, "The curious story of Jonah is a satire" (p. 15), and again, "The book of Jonah is an amusing satire" (p. 334). Equally clear and even more emphatic is the statement of Good: "The Book of Jonah is a satire. It portrays the prophet in order to ridicule him. . . . And the satire is through and through ironic. Its basis is a perception of incongruity" (p. 41). Again, "This is a satire, and the author deliberately overdraws his scene to highlight the irony of the peevish prophet's totally unexpected success. We are supposed to laugh at the ludicrous picture" (pp. 49-50).

The satirical tone of the story is not accidental or incidental; it is the very essence of the author's intention. The satirical attitude and manner of presentation produce a distinctive literary form deliberately employed by the author to accomplish his purpose. The spirit and conduct exemplified by Jonah *are* ridiculous, they *are* incongruous; and the author has chosen the most effective vehicle to demonstrate this.

The formal discipline of comparative *Literaturwissenschaft* may or may not recognize satire as a distinct category. No doubt it would be difficult to specify such formal characteristics as Wolff, for example, uses to classify Jonah as a *Novelle.* By the expression "literary category" I understand first of all the dominant spirit and intention of the work, and only secondarily the form which expresses that intention. A satire may be roughly defined as a caricature in words.

It is possible to apply the term too widely. Stinespring does this, it seems to me, when he points to "the prophets' bitter criticism of the corrupt society in which they lived" as the outstanding example of satire in the Bible, and characterizes the stories in Daniel 1–6 as satire. "The book of Jonah," he says, however, "presents a satire of a very different type" (pp. 727-28). I should prefer to restrict the term to that particular type.

The grotesque, fantastic elements in the book not only make an unspoiled reader smile; they also cut down to size a type of person, perhaps a particular group of persons, well known to the people for whom the book was written. Who were these persons? Of whom would the original readers have been reminded? Was the author portraying human nature in general, the people of Israel as he knew them, or any specific group within Israel in his time? A review of the qualities exemplified by Jonah should clarify the picture of the persons here pilloried, and perhaps help us to identify them. Jonah's character, of course, is not described. As usual in ancient Hebrew literature, it is shown by his acts and speech, and shown vividly. Deliberately exaggerated as the picture is, it is very real and human.

Among Jonah's faults we cannot number dishonesty or insincerity. He was no hypocrite. I see no reason to pronounce his declaration that he worshiped Yahweh "ein Credo, ein Katechismusbekenntnis" (Haller, pp. 21-22). Nor was he lacking in courage. Convinced by the storm and what followed it that his attempt to get away from Yahweh was futile, he frankly told the mariners that he was responsible for their plight. At the cost of dire peril to himself he told them to cast him into the sea; and when he was back on *terra firma* after his maritime adventure, he proceeded to Nineveh and proclaimed its impending doom regardless of the probable consequences for him. Impetuous he certainly was. His precipitous effort to run away from God evinces that fact, and his bitter complaint at the disappointing success of his mission does not suggest that he thought much before he spoke. These, however, are incidental traits.

The basic weakness of Jonah's character, as revealed by his behavior, was that he was essentially self-centered, self-righteous, and self-willed. He assumed that he could choose his own mission and message. In his response to the divine commands there is no sign of any sense of unworthiness or any profound dedication to God's will. He could do what he had to do when he could not get out of it, but there is nothing to indicate that he was any more pleased to preach at Nineveh after his briny baptism than he had been before.[18] In brief, he took himself too seriously. He was too much concerned for what in current American parlance would be called his "image." Yahweh, he felt, had made a fool of him by giving him a message to proclaim and then not fulfilling it. Rather than suffer such damage to his professional reputation he would have preferred to see the whole city wiped out, man and beast.

---

[18] Haller, *op. cit.,* supposes that Jonah was converted by his experience at sea and was then willing to undertake his mission (p. 3), but he admits that the prophet's nature has not been transformed; to the end he was still the old Jonah (pp. 32, 34).

Jonah may or may not have been acquainted with Deut. 18:22, but he took for granted, as most people do, its rather jejune criterion of authentic prophecy: "When a prophet speaks in the name of Yahweh, if the word does not come to pass or come true, that is a word which Yahweh has not spoken; the prophet has spoken it presumptuously, you need not be afraid of him." The Ninevites, had they known it, could have quoted this now against Jonah.

Feuillet has a quite different interpretation of all this. He sees a qualification of the deuteronomic criterion in Jer. 28:8-9, which he takes to mean that since the false prophets predict happiness, and the true prophets proclaim judgment, a prophet of peace is not to be believed until his prediction comes true, but a prophet of misfortune may be believed a priori. But predictions of doom may be canceled, because their purpose is to induce repentance; hence the author of the book of Jonah has to show that Jonah's prediction, even though belied by the event, was nonetheless truly from Yahweh ("Sens," p. 345; cf. "Livre," p. 20). Surely this reads too much into the text, both of Jeremiah and of Jonah, and in the case of Jonah it disguises the real issue. The question whether Jonah's message had come from God does not arise here, except as it is involved in what Jonah fears people will think about him.

After the event he claimed that he had known what would happen. That, he said, was why he had rebelled against going to Nineveh in the first place (4:2). Feuillet disposes of this too lightly by calling it an ex post facto rationalization, expressing the prophet's thought after his disappointment but not what the author meant to say at the beginning of the book, where no reason is given for Jonah's refusal (p. 347). According to Feuillet the real reason for the account of Jonah's futile effort to evade his mission was to stress the divine origin of his message. An Israelite of that time might have desired the destruction of a pagan city like Nineveh, says Feuillet, but Jonah did not want to make such a proclamation (p. 344). In chaps. 1–3 Jonah is presented as a prophet; in chap. 4 as a man (p. 347). Here surely Feuillet has made a distinction not justified by anything in the story itself. Jonah's human limitations are all too apparent from the outset. What the text clearly states is that Jonah was unwilling to predict what he feared God would not fulfill.

Good likewise considers Jonah's claim in 4:2 merely "a certain rationale" put into his mouth at this late point in the story (p. 42). "The author has purposely left it out before this," he says, "for only now can we comprehend the prophet's viewpoint" (p. 50). Certainly the statement is more effective dramatically at this point. Such an explanation of Jonah's flight in chap. 1 would have precluded the climax in chap. 4. It does not follow, however, that the reference to Exod. 34:6 was merely "a liturgical cliché, a rote theology," or "pious and well-worn words" (*ibid.*). Jonah drew the wrong practical inference from what he knew about God, but at least he took it seriously enough to act on it. Doubtless there is irony in giving such an exalted conception of God's nature to explain a course of conduct quite inconsistent with it; but the author is deeply convinced of this article of Israel's faith and endeavors to show what it really involves.

Whether he meant to imply that Jonah exceeded his commission in so explicitly predicting the destruction of Nineveh is not certain. The possibility is suggested by the fact that at first Jonah was told only to "cry against" the city (1:2). After delivering him from the sea God commanded him to proclaim to Nineveh "the message that I tell you" (3:2), but what that was or would be is not stated. In any case, Jonah did not plead with the Ninevites to repent. He merely told them that the city would soon be overthrown (3:4).

That Yahweh could actually care what happened to such wicked people was beyond the range of Jonah's spiritual vision. Though he knew that Yahweh was tenderhearted and could be induced to change his mind about punishing sinners, Jonah himself had no compassion. "You pity the plant," Yahweh said to him ironically; but Jonah did not really care about the plant; he was concerned only for his own comfort and prestige.[19] He felt no pity for the thousands of ignorant, helpless people in Nineveh, to say nothing of their animals.

His lack of even normal humane feeling is poignantly contrasted with the compassion of God. Unlike Jonah, Yahweh is not anxious to be consistent. He diligently sends his prophets to warn sinners to repent and so avert the doom they must otherwise suffer (Jer. 7:25; 25:4; 35:15); he rejoices not in the death of the wicked, but that they turn from their wicked way and live (Ezek. 18:23; 33:11). Jonah's unconditional prediction of impending judgment was untrue to the real spirit of Hebrew prophecy, as indeed were many of the oracles against foreign nations in the prophetic books.

What he failed to see, and what the author meant to bring out, was what Abraham Heschel calls "the contingency of anger" and "the supremacy of compassion" in God's ways with man. With fine insight Heschel writes, "God's answer to Jonah, stressing the supremacy

[19] Cf. Haller, *op. cit.*, pp. 46-47: Jonah's concern was not for the plant but for its shade; not for Nineveh but for his own dogma.

of compassion, upsets the possibility of looking for a rational co-
herence of God's ways with the world. History would be more intelligible if God's word were the last word, final and unambiguous
like a dogma or an unconditional decree. It would be easier if God's
anger became effective automatically: Once wickedness had reached its
full measure, punishment would destroy it. Yet, beyond justice and
anger lies the mystery of compassion" (pp. 286-87).

Something like this, no doubt, is what Good means by the absurdity
of God. His chapter on the book of Jonah is headed, "Jonah: The
Absurdity of God" (p. 39), and he writes, "Jonah has had to deal
with an absurd God who insists on being what he says he will be"
(p. 52)—that is, presumably, merciful and gracious. But of course it
is only to Jonah (and to those like him) that such a God seems
absurd. The author's basic purpose was indeed, as Good says, "to
expose absurdity by the irony of satire" (p. 54), but the absurdity
he exposed was Jonah's, not God's.

Compassion is not automatic; forgiveness is not an intrinsic, necessary consequence of repentance. Bickermann considers the book of
Jonah a protest against the comfortable idea of prophecy as conditional in that sense (p. 43). Jonah's unconditional prediction of
Nineveh's doom, he maintains, was authentic, but was revoked by a
free, sovereign act of God. "The story of Jonah teaches us that God
is merciful, but He is merciful because He is the Creator" (p. 48).
In other words, both anger and compassion are contingent not only
on man's response but on the sovereign will of God.

That is the first lesson of the book, and the second is like it.
Jonah's reluctance to preach to the Assyrians and his undisguised
displeasure at their repentance and deliverance reflect a limited view
of the divine solicitude. It is worthy of note, to be sure, that the
Ninevites are not condemned on the ground that they are Gentiles.
Nowhere is there any hint that they are or should be treated as on
any different footing from the people of Israel. They appear simply
as wicked human beings, and it is for their wickedness that they
are judged. Even Jonah's own attitude toward them is not clearly
affected by the fact that they are Gentiles. The author's choice of
Assyrians as the object of Jonah's mission, however, must have had
something to do with his purpose in telling the tale, and it is true
that the pagan sailors in chap. 1 as well as the king and people of
Nineveh appear in a more favorable light than the prophet from
Israel.

What the prophets said about God's readiness to forgive repentant sinners and remit the punishment he had threatened was addressed to the people of Israel. In assuming that the same principle applied equally to Israel's enemies the author of the book of Jonah took a very advanced position. Rare indeed in the Old Testament is such a statement as Isa. 19:24-25 or Amos 9:7. Just how far our author meant to go in putting Israel and the nations on the same level is a matter of some difference of opinion. It is commonly supposed, and not only by those who interpret the book allegorically, that Jonah's mission to Nineveh represents Israel's missionary responsibility as a light to the nations (Isa. 49:6). Thus Stinespring says that the author ridicules his people "for their lack of missionary zeal" (p. 728), and Haller maintains that the idea behind the book is not a universalistic conception of salvation but the conversion of the heathen as the goal of the election of Israel (p. 11).

Haller conceives the situation faced by the author in terms not so much of nationalism as of "a narrow, almost pathological form of orthodoxy" (p. 6), at a time when "the flight into orthodoxy had already begun" (p. 14), and the true aim of Israel's election, which had implicitly a missionary meaning (Gen. 12:3; Zech. 10:9) was being obscured. A theological pattern, consistent in itself but contrary to God's purpose, was becoming hard and set; and it needed to be put to shame by an unexpected and incomprehensible intervention of Yahweh (pp. 51-52). All this may be true, but it rests on presuppositions not to be derived from the book of Jonah itself.

Feuillet places the book of Jonah in the universalistic current in post-exilic Judaism. It shows, he says, that there is something better for Israel to do than lament the survival of the hostile nations: They must be converted. He finds the spirit of the book in an extraordinary breadth of views combined with a truly Israelite mentality. In the example of the pagan Ninevites a theology of pardon based only on the conversion of the heart reaches its goal; and at the same time Jonah's mission to Nineveh exhibits Israel's superiority as possessor of the truth which must some day shine on the whole world ("Sens," pp. 357-59; "Livre," pp. 21-23).

This does not mean for Feuillet, however, that Israel is a missionary of the true God. That idea, he declares, is foreign to the Bible. Even the Servant in Isa. 40–55 is only a passive witness who has received the free grace of Yahweh, and whose marvelous restoration causes the conversion of the Gentiles. In the Servant poems there is an active witness, a missionary; but he is an individual, a prophet, and salvation is conceived only as that of the individual ("Sens," p. 359 and note 1). Several points in this interpretation are open to question, but we are not here concerned with the teaching of II Isaiah.

That the author of Jonah had in mind a missionary function is questioned by Good also, who feels that Haller has gone too far on this point (p. 54 and note 24). Haller's interpretation of the book may indeed put too much stress on the purpose of Israel's election. That idea is nowhere clearly reflected in the book, perhaps only because it is taken for granted. Jonah says, "I am a Hebrew, and I fear Yahweh, the God of heaven" (1:9), as though being a Hebrew and being a worshiper of Yahweh were practically synonymous. The sailors, however, immediately pray and sacrifice and make vows to Yahweh (1:14, 16); and from then on, except for the use of the name Yahweh,[20] there is no suggestion of any difference between Israel and the Gentiles in the eyes of God. Israel worships the true God and has the knowledge of his will, but has no monopoly on his concern, his judgment, or his forgiving grace. People of any land or nation may put Israel to shame by believing and acting in accordance with God's will.

The idea that God's care embraces not only men but even animals is practically unique in the Old Testament. There are very ancient laws dealing with domestic animals, but they are concerned chiefly with the rights of the owners and with the animals only as their property. The remarkable law of Deuteronomy 22:6-7 is apparently an exception, going about as far as any modern legislation. Prov. 12:10, "A righteous man has regard for the life of his beast," goes still further, and the prohibition of muzzling an ox when it treads the grain (Deut. 25:4) is so remarkable that the apostle Paul could not believe it was intended for the benefit of the animal (I Cor. 9:9; cf. 1 Tim. 5:18). The whimsical picture of the beasts of Nineveh wearing sackcloth and crying mightily to God, if it stood alone, might be dismissed as only a humorous embellishment of the narrative; but the closing words of the book, "and also much cattle," can be understood only as emphasizing the compassion of God for animals as well as men.

The truth which the story brings home to the reader is thus twofold: Compassion is supreme in God's way with his creatures; and it is a universal compassion, extending to all of them equally. What is satirized in the behavior of Jonah is a self-centered, arrogant attitude which denies or ignores these two basic truths. Such an attitude and

[20] The king of Nineveh says "God" instead of "Yahweh" (3:8-9); so does the author in 3:10 and 4:7-9; but cf. 4:2-4, 6, 10.

such behavior are not limited to any time or people. Is it possible, then, to single out any specific group or situation at which the satire was aimed?

The possibilities are limited, of course, to the period within which the author can be supposed to have lived, for however wide may be the possible applications of his story, he must have had in mind some definite group or type of his own day. If he and his immediate audience had been contemporaries of the historical Jonah, the story would have had an obvious application for them. In I Kings 14:25 Jonah appears as a prophet of national conquest and glory, like the four hundred court prophets of Ahab (II Kings 22:6, 14-15). Our author, however, was not addressing Jonah's contemporaries, for he had to inform his readers, or remind them, that Nineveh had been a very great city (3:3). Evidently it was so no longer. And if Nineveh was a thing of the past, so too was the kingdom of Israel. The Assyrians had put an end to it more than a hundred years before Nineveh fell and was succeeded by Babylon as ruler of the world in which the Israelites lived.

There was a nationalist party in Judah too, and during the final quarter of a century of that kingdom's existence the fervor of the nationalists reached its peak, stimulated by prophets who declared that the Babylonians could not conquer the chosen people or capture the holy city. These were the men whom Jeremiah opposed at the risk of his life. If our author had lived in the time of Jeremiah, he might have used Nineveh as a symbol of the Babylonian power of that time, as later Jewish and Christian writers used Babylon as a symbol of Rome.[21] Jonah would then have represented the nationalistic, optimistic prophets of early sixth-century Judah. This would imply, however, that the Babylonians, whose downfall the prophets were predicting, might be spared and given another chance if they would repent. Under the conditions of those years it is improbable that a book suggesting such a possibility could have been written or would have survived the fall of Jerusalem.

Schmidt calls the book of Jonah "eine Kampfschrift gegen die Unheilsprophetie" (p. 472). It is true that Jonah appears in it as a prophet of doom, but doom for Israel's enemies. The prophets of doom in pre-exilic Israel and Judah pronounced doom on disobedient Israel; it was the false prophets that cried "peace, peace." During

---

[21] Lods assumes such a use of Nineveh in the Greek period: "The author speaks of Nineveh, but doubtless he is thinking of Babylon, spared by Cyrus, Darius, Xerxes, and Alexander successively" (*op. cit.*, p. 335).

and after the exile the situation was different: The exiles and the restored but disappointed and disillusioned community in Palestine then needed and received encouragement and hope. The prophets of doom at that time were those who predicted doom on Babylon, as in some of the prophecies included in the books of Isaiah and Jeremiah (esp. Isa. 13, 14, 21, 46, 47; Jer. 50, 51). In these there is no suggestion of any divine concern for the Babylonians.

For good and sufficient reasons the Persian period is now generally agreed upon as the most probable time for the composition of the book of Jonah. In addition to the evidence of language and literary relations, the book's place in the history of Hebrew religion is decisive. Caution is necessary at this point to avoid the circular reasoning which would infer the time of composition from the teaching of the book, and its teaching from the time of its composition. All that we know of the religious situation in the fifth and fourth centuries, however, agrees with the situation reflected in the book of Jonah. Haller may go too far in regarding the sailors, each crying to his own god, as a mirror of the syncretistic Persian period (p. 18). They suggest rather the opposite of syncretism. He is quite right, however, in noting that the designation of Yahweh as "the God of heaven" (1:9) is characteristic of the literature of that period (p. 21, note).

There were still prophets in Judah at that time. The professional prophets and prophetesses, who for a consideration would say anything desired by their masters or employers (Neh. 6:6-14) were not the objects of our author's ridicule, for Jonah's faults did not include venality or hypocrisy. There were other prophets, however, who could have served as models for the portrait. Some of the prophetic books composed during this period and the anonymous prophecies incorporated in the books of earlier prophets express an attitude toward other peoples much like that of Jonah toward the Assyrians (e.g., Isa. 60:10-14; 61:5-7).

It seems unlikely, however, that the author was thinking of any prophet in particular or of prophets any more than other people. He chose a prophet as the protagonist of his story, and there were prophets more or less like Jonah; but the picture did not represent them alone. Wolff stresses the fact that nowhere in the book is Jonah called a prophet ("Gotteswort," p. 23). By his story, says Wolff, the author hoped to reach Israel, which felt and believed just as Jonah did ("Studien," p. 76). Haller too believes that the whole people of God is here criticized; for what Nineveh does here, Jerusalem never did (p. 35). Almost equally inclusive is the opinion of Theodore H. Robinson that it was the narrow-minded nationalistic way of thinking of the broad mass of the Jewish people that the author wished to expose (p. 118).

To consider the story, however, an indictment of the whole Jewish people in the Persian period is surely mistaken. It is true that the idea of being a light to the Gentiles was not received with general enthusiasm or widely adopted in the restored community, but there were at least enough disciples of II Isaiah to preserve his work. His spirit, if not his direct influence, is evident at many points in the later books of the Old Testament. The general attitude of the Jews in Palestine toward their Persian overlords seems to have been more friendly and tolerant than it had been toward the Babylonians. In Isa. 56:3-8 a decidedly liberal attitude toward proselytes from the Gentiles appears, and the fact of Israel's mixed origin is frankly recognized in the book of Ruth (itself a bit of protest literature).

At the same time, many of the people, especially those who had remained in Palestine after the fall of Jerusalem, cared neither for the salvation of the Gentiles nor for their own pedigrees and traditions, but mingled and intermarried with the now very mixed population of the country (Ezra 9:1-2; Neh. 13:23-24). In reaction against this tendency there were determined and even extreme advocates of zealous conservatism and rigid exclusiveness, dedicated to the preservation of the ways of the fathers and the purity of their own Hebrew descent (Ezra 9–10; Neh. 13:1-3, 25-28). They seem to have consisted largely of returned exiles like Nehemiah and Ezra. It was this third group that in all probability was the immediate object of the gentle but sharp satire of the book of Jonah.

This conclusion does not depend upon recognizing the satirical character of the story. It agrees with the views of many scholars who classify the book in other ways. What then is gained by assigning it to the category of satire? The situation faced by the author and the message he addressed to it remain the same. Several questions of interpretation are still left open. Some current misinterpretations, however, are avoided. At least we are in a better position to enjoy the story, and the author would like that. Perhaps we can also appreciate it better as an admirable vehicle for a lesson still very much needed. Possibly, seeing ourselves more clearly through this tale of poor, self-centered, childish Jonah, we may even feel a little chastened, a little ashamed, and so learn to take ourselves and our opinions and prejudices less seriously.

List of Works Cited

Bentzen, Aage. *Introduction to the Old Testament*. 2nd ed. Copenhagen, 1952.

Bewer, J. A. *A Critical and Exegetical Commentary on Jonah*, International Critical Commentary, vol. XXV. New York, 1912.

Bickermann, Elias. *Four Strange Books of the Bible*. New York, 1967. (The chapter on Jonah is an English version of an article in French previously published in RHPR.)

Budde, Karl. "Vermutungen zum 'Midrasch des Buches der Könige,' " *ZAW* XII (1892), 37-51.

Cheyne, T. K. "Jonah" (Book). *Encyclopedia Biblica*, vol. II. New York, 1901.

Deden, D. "Jonas" (Buch). *Bibel-Lexikon*. Köln, 1965.

Eissfeldt, Otto. *The Old Testament: An Introduction*. Trans. by P. R. Ackroyd. New York & Evanston, 1965.

Feuillet, A. "Le Sens du Livre de Jonas." *RB* LIV (1947), 340-61 (cited as "Sens").

————. "Le Livre de Jonas." *La Sainte Bible*. 2nd ed. Paris, 1957 (cited as "Livre").

Good, E. M. *Irony in the Old Testament*. Philadelphia & London, 1965.

Gottwald, N. K. *A Light to the Nations: An Introduction to the Old Testament*. New York, 1959.

Haller, Eduard. *Die Erzählung von dem Propheten Jona*. Theologische Existenz Heute, NF Nr. LXV. München, 1958.

Heschel, Abraham. *The Prophets*. New York, 1962.

Hylmö, Gunnar. *Gamla testamentets literaturhistoria*. Lund, 1908.

Jerusalem Bible, The. English trans. and rev., ed. by Alexander Jones. Garden City, N. Y., 1966.

Keller, C. A. "Jonas. Le Portrait d'un prophète." *TZ* XXI (1965), 329-40.

Knight, G. A. F. *Ruth and Jonah, Introduction and Commentary*. Torch Bible Commentaries, rev. ed. London, 1966.

König, E. "Jonah." *Hastings' Dictionary of the Bible*, vol. II. New York, 1911.

Lanchester, H. C. O. *Obadiah and Jonah*. Cambridge Bible for Schools and Colleges. Cambridge, 1918.

Lods, A. *The Prophets and the Rise of Judaism*. Trans. by S. H. Hooke. New York, 1937.

Loretz, Oswald. "Herkunft und Sinn der Jona-Erzählung." *BZ* NF V (1961), 18-29.

Luckenbill, D. D. *Ancient Records of Assyria and Babylonia*, vol. II. Chicago, 1927.

Marti, Karl. *Das Dodekapropheton*. Kurzer Hand-Kommentar zum Alten Testament, XIII. Tübingen, 1904.

Oesterley, O. E., and Robinson, Theodore H. *Introduction to the Books of the Old Testament.* New York, 1934.

Olmstead, A .T. *History of Assyria.* Chicago, 1951.

Perowne, T. T. *Obadiah and Jonah.* Cambridge Bible for Schools and Colleges. Cambridge, 1898.

Robinson, Theodore H. *Die Zwölf Kleinen Propheten: Hosea bis Micha.* Handbuch zum Alten Testament, Erste Reihe, XIV. 2nd ed. Tübingen, 1954.

Schmidt, Hans. *Die Grossen Propheten.* Die Schriften des Alten Testaments, Part II, vol. II. Göttingen, 1915.

Sellin, E. & Fohrer, G. *Einleitung in das Alte Testament.* 10th ed. Heidelberg, 1965.

Smart, J. D. Introduction and Exegesis of the Book of Jonah, *Interpreter's Bible,* vol. VI. New York and Nashville, 1956.

Smith, G. A. *The Book of the Twelve Prophets,* vol. II. New York, 1901.

Stinespring, W. F. "Irony and Satire." *Interpreter's Dictionary of the Bible,* vol. E-J, pp. 726-28. New York and Nashville, 1962.

Vaccari, Alberto, S.J. "Il Genere Letterario del Libro di Giona in Recenti Publicazioni." *Divinitas,* VI (1962), 231-52.

——. *Los géneros literarios de la Sagraca Escritura.* Madrid, 1957.

von Rad, G. *Old Testament Theology.* Trans. by D. M. G. Stalker. New York, 1965.

Wade, G. W. *The Books of the Prophets Micah, Obadiah, Joel, and Jonah.* Westminster Commentaries. London, 1925.

Weiser, Artur. *Das Buch der zwölf kleinen Propheten,* I. Das Alte Testament Deutsch, vol. XXIV. 4th ed. Göttingen, 1963.

Wolff, H. W. "Ist die Bibel Gotteswort oder Menschenwort? Darstellung des Problems an einer Auslegung des Jonabuches." Wolff, Moltmann, & Bohren, *Die Bibel—Gotteswort oder Menschenwort?* Neukirchen-Vluyn, 1959 (cited as "Gotteswort").

——. "Jonabuch." *Die Religion in Geschichte und Gegenwart.* 3rd ed., vol. III, cols. 853-56. Tübingen, 1959 (cited as "Jonabuch").

——. *Studien zum Jonabuch.* Biblische Studien, Heft 47. Neukirchen-Vluyn, 1965 (cited as "Studien").

The Settlement of the Israelites in Southern Palestine and the Origins of the Tribe of Judah

ROLAND DE VAUX, O.P.

According to Josh. 10:28-43, the conquest of the south is attributed to Joshua and to "all Israel." But according to Judg. 1:1-20, this conquest is attributed, after Joshua's death (Judg. 1:1), to Judah and Simeon, and also to Calebite and Kenite groups associated with Judah and Simeon. In particular, the conquest of Hebron, which was the principal city of the territory of Judah and which became the first capital of David, is attributed to Caleb, by Judg. 1:20 as well as by Josh. 15:13-19. It is the fulfillment of a promise made to Caleb in the desert (Josh. 14:6-14) at the time of the ill-fated attempt to penetrate from the south starting at Kadesh (Num. 13–14; cf. Deut. 1:19-46). A comparison of these texts indicates that the problem is complex. Except for Josh. 10, which is pan-Israelite, the other texts represent south-Palestinian and mostly Calebite traditions. It is these versions that we must study first.

I

THE EXPLORATION OF CANAAN AND THE ROLE OF CALEB

(Numbers 13–14; Deuteronomy 1:19-46; Joshua 14:6-14; Numbers 32:6-15)

Numbers 13–14 is part of the group of traditions associated with Kadesh. Twelve spies, one per tribe, among whom were Joshua for the tribe of Ephraim and Caleb for the tribe of Judah, are sent into Canaan. They report that the country is good, but that it is inhabited by a powerful people. In spite of the urging of Caleb, then of Joshua and Caleb together, the people refuse to advance and wish to return to Egypt. God decides to punish the rebellious people but he yields to the intercession of Moses. However, none of the men present shall enter the country except Caleb, or Caleb and Joshua. The people repent and begin the attack, but God is not with them and they are decisively repulsed.

This text is composite.[1] It presents a series of doublets with differences between them. According to 13:17 and 22-24, the spies go only to the Negeb and into the region of Hebron. According to 13:21, they go from the Wilderness of Zin to the entrance to Hamath; that is, they cover the Promised Land in its broadest expanse. In 13:30, only Caleb among the spies encourages the people to fight. In 14:6 ff., both Joshua and Caleb do so. While according to 14:24, only Caleb was to enter the country, this is said of both Caleb and Joshua in 14:30. Considering these differences and the style, literary critics agree in distinguishing a priestly revision which includes 13:1-17a, 21, 25-26, 32-33; 14:1-3, 5-10, 26-38. This revision contains the detailed list of the twelve spies, the addition of Joshua in the same role as Caleb and with the same reward, the announcement of a stay of forty years in the desert where all will die except Joshua and Caleb. The rest represents the older story (13:17b-20, 22-24, 27-31; 14:4, 11-25, 39-45). Within this story any precise distribution among the ancient sources J and E, or L, J, and E seems arbitrary. Yet we must set aside 14:11-23a. This intercession by Moses and his dialogue with God, written in a style which foreshadows that of Deuteronomy and with parallels in the book of Exodus, is an addition to the oldest version. The older story had an introduction, now lost and replaced by that of P. It goes on speaking only of an exploration of the Negeb and of the region of Hebron up to the Valley of Eshcol, and only concerning Caleb. I shall set aside for the moment its conclusion, the episode of the defeat at Hormah (14:39-45).

This narrative, still free from the additions of P and from the older addition of 14:11-23a, is utilized in Deut. 1:19-46 in the introductory speech of Moses.[2] The deuteronomic story is less concrete than that in Numbers. It is mainly a dialogue between Moses and the people, and the spies are kept in the background. The intercession of Moses is omitted. Different in theological purpose it nonetheless

[1] S. Wagner, "Die Kundschaftergeschichten im Alten Testament," *ZAW* LXXVI (1964), 255-69.

[2] On the relationship between the two stories, cf. N. Lohfink, "Darstellungskunst und Theologie in Dtn 1,6-3, 29," *Biblica* XLI (1960), 105-34; G. von Rad, *Deuteronomium, ATD* 2nd ed. (1968), *in loco*; J. L. McKenzie, "The Historical Prologue of Deuteronomy," *Fourth World Congress of Jewish Studies, Papers* I (Jerusalem, 1967), 97.

reproduces essentially the older story: rebellion of the people who will be punished, with the exception of Caleb who will receive the land on which he had trod (vs. 37 which I regard as primitive[3]). Vss. 37 and 38 which mention Joshua are additional [4]: Joshua is presented in vs. 38 not as one of the spies but as the servant of Moses, and vs. 37 relates to Moses who is not allowed into the Promised Land either (cf. Deut. 3:26; 4:21). In Deuteronomy this chastisement appears to be a punishment for Moses' acquiescence to the people (vs. 37, "because of you") who demanded the sending out of the spies and thus showed a lack of faith in God (Deut. 1:22). This is peculiar to Deuteronomy. According to P (Num. 13:2), the spies were sent on the order of Yahweh, and this source, in Num. 20:12, 24, and Deut. 32:50-52, gives a different reason for Moses' death (and that of Aaron) before the entry into the Promised Land: their lack of faith at the Waters of Meribah.[5]

A third parallel text is Josh. 14:6-14. At the time of the dividing of the land, Caleb reminds Joshua of the promise that was made to him in the desert that he could have the land he had explored, and he receives Hebron as his share. The story, which is by the deuteronomic redactor, depends on that of Deuteronomy. It concludes: "So Hebron became the inheritance of Caleb the son of Jephunneh the Kenizzite to this day, because he wholly followed the Lord, the God of Israel" (vs. 14). This text gives the reason for this tradition and explains why Hebron, in the heart of Judah, was occupied by the Calebites, who were not of pure Israelite stock.

Still another text recalls the role of Caleb in the desert; namely Num. 32:6-15. This is a late passage which depends upon the priestly redaction of Num. 13–14 (Caleb and Joshua, the forty years in the desert) and, apparently, upon Josh. 14 (Caleb the Kenizzite).

All these literary forms of the Calebite tradition, even the ancient story in Num. 13–14, on which the other texts depend, belong to a stage in which the individual traditions were already amalgamated into a common history of the Twelve Tribes. This history is unified around the traditions of the House of Joseph, who will enter Canaan by way of Transjordan. Thus Caleb will be part of the forty years of wandering in the desert; he will arrive in the Promised Land with

---

[3] Against Steuernagel and von Rad, but with Noth, *Überlieferungsgeschichtliche Studien,* 2nd ed. (1957), pp. 31-32, esp. p. 32, note 1.

[4] With Steuernagel, von Rad, Noth.

[5] Cf. E. Arden, "How Moses Failed God," *JBL* LXXVI (1957), 50-52; with A. S. Kapelrud's additional note, *ibid.,* p. 242.

Joshua and be eighty-five years old when Joshua gives him Hebron as his share (Josh. 14:10).

But one can go back to a preliterary form of the tradition according to which the Calebite group had entered independently and directly from the south. According to Deut. 1:20-21, which perhaps represents the beginning of the ancient story in Num. 13–14 and disappeared in favor of the priestly revision, Moses gives the order to take possession of the hill country God "has given" to his people. According to Num. 14:24 (cf. Deut. 1:36), Caleb is to enter the land he had spied out. In the following verses we would expect to see Caleb do so. Instead, we have the story of the disaster of Hormah (Num. 14:39-45).

This conclusion gives its theological meaning to the present story of the spies.[6] At the moment the people Israel are on the brink of the land of which God had promised them the conquest, they lose faith. Frightened by the spies' report, they renounce combat and want to return to Egypt. Then they attack, against the will of God and without Moses and the Ark. This is an inversion of the themes of exodus and holy war, "an unholy war and an anti-exodus."[7] The result could only be disastrous.[8] At the same time, the account of the failure at this point permits a link between Calebite traditions and the traditions of the House of Joseph. It explains why the people Israel were thrown out into the desert and could penetrate into Canaan only by a long and wide detour. But this picture was obtained only by combining the Calebite tradition with another south-Palestinian tradition which Num. 14:39-46 uses with adaptations. It originally concerned other groups.

II

THE SETTLEMENT OF SIMEONITE AND LEVITE GROUPS

In Num. 14:39-46 the region of Hebron is no longer in question. We have instead the region south of the Judean hill country on the border of the Negeb. This area is inhabited by the Amalekites and the Canaanites. We must link this passage with the story of the victory over the Amalekites in Exod. 17:8-13, which also belongs to

---

[6] Cf. S. J. De Vries, "The Origin of the Murmuring Tradition," *JBL* LXXXVII (1968), 51-58, esp. 55-57.

[7] Following the expression of W. L. Moran, *Biblica* XLIV (1963), 333-42.

[8] De Vries, *op. cit.*, p. 58; S. Lehming, *ZAW* LXXIII (1961), 71-72.

the Kadesh cycle.[9] These accounts concerning the Amalekites originated from Judah, which had to fight against Amalek until the
time of Saul and David (I Sam. 15, 30). But these Judean traditions
unify the memories of the various southern groups, and one can
ask whether the tradition concerning Hormah is not primitively
Simeonite.

Numbers 14:39-45 says that the Israelites were beaten "all the
way to Hormah" (vs. 45). Hormah is very probably Khirbet el-
Meshâsh, east of Beersheba. We are already fifty-three miles north
of Kadesh on the border between the Negeb and the hill country.
Since the Israelites had climbed to the heights of the hill country
(vs. 44), they had penetrated to the north of Hormah, and they
were beaten back southward "all the way to Hormah." They had
thus conquered Hormah. In fact this conquest is recounted in Num.
21:1-3. This note is out of its chronological and geographical context.
The mention of the king of Arad in vs. 1 is an insertion into the
primitive text, which contained only "the Canaanite," a justifiable
insertion since Arad is near Hormah. The conquest proceeded from
the south. The Israelites went up "by the way of Atarim," which
is not identified with certainty. It may be the route marked out
later by small Iron Age forts.[10] If we dissociate the episode from an
immediate link with Kadesh, the route may be the one which rises
from the Dead Sea toward Arad.

This second hypothesis seems to be confirmed by a parallel account
of the seizure of Hormah (Judg. 1:16-17): The Kenites go up with
the sons of Judah from the "city of palm trees" to the Negeb near
Arad and settle there. Judah and Simeon defeat the Canaanites
who inhabit Zephath. They destroy the city which then takes the
name Hormah (*herem*, "destruction"). This "city of palm trees"
cannot here be Jericho, as in other texts.[11] It is the Tamar of I Kings
9:18 and Ezek. 47:19, the present 'Ain Ḥoṣb, sixteen and a half miles
southeast of the Dead Sea, in the Arabah.[12] This is still another
entry into Canaan from the south, which leads to the conquest of
Hormah by Judah and Simeon. But the true conquerer is Simeon,

[9] M. Gronback, "Juda und Amalek. Überlieferungsgeschichtliche Erwägungen
zu Exodus 17:8-16," *ST* XVIII (1964), 26-45; the passage from Num. 14:39-45
is studied on pp. 35-37.

[10] Y. Aharoni, *IEJ* X (1960), 109.

[11] Cf. however B. Mazar, *JNES* XXIV (1965), 300 and note 17; R. Schmid, *TZ*
XXI (1965), 263; V. Fritz, *ZDPV* LXXXII (1966), 331.

[12] Y. Aharoni, "Tamar and the Roads to Elath," *IEJ* XIII (1963), 30-42. It has
even been proposed that *ha'atarim* of Num. 21:1 is a corruption of *hattemarim*
of Judg. 1:16.

for it is to Simeon that Hormah belongs, according to Josh. 19:4 and I Chron. 4:30. However, since Simeon had been absorbed by Judah and was established "in the midst of" Judah (Josh. 19:1), the conquest is attributed to Judah and Simeon, and Hormah is also counted among the cities of Judah (Josh. 15:30).

In the two accounts of Num. 21:1-3 and Judg. 1:17, the name Hormah is explained by the "destruction" (*ḥerem*) exercised against the city. This is a popular explanation, since the city was probably already mentioned in the Egyptian Execration Texts from the nineteenth century B.C., and in the inscriptions of Amenhemet III in Sinai.[13] But this popular explanation does not suppress the reality of the fact, for Num. 21:1-3 comes from the Yahwist source and Judg. 1:17 is part of the picture of the conquest following the Yahwist tradition.[14] The two texts preserve the memory of a penetration by Simeonite elements from the south. In fact it is in the south that we find the tribe of Simeon settled, according to the geographical section of the book of Joshua. It does not describe the borders of the territory because this territory was included under the tribe of Judah. However, Josh. 15:21-32 gives a list of the cities of Judah in the Negeb whose second part (26b-32) is parallel to a list of Simeonite cities in Josh. 19:2-8 and I Chron. 4:28-32.

A comparison of these lists has led to different conclusions. Alt dates the lists in Josh. 15–19 from the time of Josiah but thinks that the people of the Negeb still remembered a primitive settlement by the Simeonites.[15] Noth, who accepts the same date for the lists of cities of Joshua, considers Josh. 19:2-8 an artificial reconstruction by an editor who, from Josh. 15 on, wanted to draw up a list of "Simeonite" cities.[16] Cross and Wright put the lists at the time of Jehoshaphat and think that Josh. 19:2-8 and I Chron. 4:28-32 are not derivative from Josh. 15 but go back to an independent list of Simeonite cities.[17] Kallai has this list go back to the era of David, with a revision under Hezekiah.[18] Aharoni, who attributes the revised

---

[13] Mazar, *op. cit.*, p. 298 with references.

[14] S. Mowinckel, *Tetrateuch—Pentateuch—Hexateuch*, BZAW XC (1964), 17-33.

[15] A. Alt, "Judas Gaue unter Josia," *PJB* XXI (1925), 100-116=*Kleine Schriften*, II (1953), 276, 288, esp. pp. 285-86.

[16] M. Noth, *Josua*, HAT 2nd ed. (1953), p. 113; *The History of Israel* (1960), p. 58.

[17] F. M. Cross and G. E. Wright, "The Boundary and Province Lists of the Kingdom of Judah," *JBL* LXXV (1956), 202-26, esp. p. 209 and pp. 214-15.

[18] Z. Kallai, "The Town Lists of Judah, Simeon, Benjamin, and Dan," *VT* VIII (1958), 134-60, esp. pp. 156-59; *idem, The Tribes of Israel* (Hebrew), (1967), pp. 295-303.

lists to the reign of Uzziah, thinks that the territory attributed to Simeon represents what at the time of David was called the Negeb of Judah (I Sam. 27:10; 30:14; II Sam. 24:7) with Beersheba at its center.[19] Finally, Talmon feels that the list of the cities of Simeon is no later than the reign of David.[20] This opinion is based on an indication in I Chron. 4:31*b* ("These were their cities until David reigned."). It is under his reign that the integration of Simeon into Judah would have been made. In fact, the Simeonites disappear from history from David's time on.

Whatever the case, the problem remains that of finding out when the Simeonites settled in the far south of Palestine. According to biblical tradition, their history is parallel to that of the Levites. Simeon and Levi are both sons of Leah. According to Gen. 34 the two groups stayed in central Palestine until they were forced to leave because of a conflict with the permanent residents of Shechem. The episode is linked to the prehistory of Israel, long before the Exodus and the Conquest. Simeon and Levi are also mentioned together in the "Testament of Jacob" (Gen. 49:5-7). They are cursed for their violence and dispersed into Israel.[21] They had, according to the text, suffered a catastrophe which is not made clear but which is not the conflict at Shechem. It is told in different terms, and from it they escaped unscathed, according to Gen. 35:5.[22] At the time Gen. 49:5-7 was written the two tribes have no longer any territory of their own. Simeon, we have seen, is integrated or just about to be integrated (if we take I Chron. 4:31*b* literally) to Judah in the Negeb.

As for Levi, Gen. 49:5-7 may still be referring to the profane group of Levites as in Gen. 34, or already to the priestly tribe of Levi. In any case, we have evidence that Levi too has very ancient connections with the south and that it is probably there that it was transformed into a priestly tribe, if we accept a continuity between the two groups. Beside the canonical division of the Levites into three families descending from the three sons of Levi, Gershon, Kohath, and Merari, the note in Num. 26:58*a* divides the Levites into five clans: the Libnite, Hebronite, Mahlite, Mushite, and Korahite.[23] The first two clans

---

[19] Y. Aharoni, "The Negeb of Judah," *IEJ* VIII (1958), 26-38.

[20] S. Talmon, "The Town Lists of Simeon," *IEJ* XV (1965), 235-41.

[21] Finally, H. J. Zobel, *Stammesspruch und Geschichte* (1965), pp. 65-72; A. H. S. Gunneweg, *Leviten und Priester* (1965), pp. 44-52.

[22] This point must be considered as established; cf. in particular S. Lehming, "Zur Überlieferungsgeschichte von Gen. 34," *ZAW* LXX (1958); A. de Pury, "Genèse XXXIV et l'histoire," *RB* LXXVI (1969), pp. 5-49.

[23] R. de Vaux, *Les Institutions de l'Ancien Testament*, II 2nd ed. (1967), 230; M. Noth, *Das Vierte Buch Mose, Numeri, ATD* (1966), *in loco*.

are obviously the inhabitants of Libnah and Hebron. The Korahite clan is related to Korah, which appears in I Chron. 2:43, in a list of "sons" of Caleb which are mainly place names and where Korah is a neighbor of Hebron. The other two names are unclear. This aberrant list is certainly very ancient. It localizes, and seems to limit, the original habitat of the Levites in the southern part of the land of Judah. Already at the time of the Judges, they were moving toward the north (Judg. 17–18; 19:1-2). One can add that a tradition, evidently originating in southern Palestine, gives as Moses' father-in-law the Kenite Hobab, whose family settled near Arad.[24] This presupposes the presence of Levites in the region in ancient times.

This settlement by the groups of Levites in southern Judah is perhaps confirmed by the list of Levitical cities (Josh. 21:1-42; I Chron. 6:39-66). This list rests on an ancient document which describes the populating of the Levitical lands either just after the schism,[25] or under David,[26] or under Solomon.[27] But the Levites did not settle these cities at any of these times. They were already established there.[28] It is worthy of note that these cities are not equally spaced. They are in groups separated by unsettled areas. In the Judean hill country, there is not a single Levitical city between Hebron and Jerusalem. They are all in the south: Hebron and Libnah, of which two Levitical clans of Num. 26:58 bear the names, and farther south Debir, Juttah, Eshtemoa, Jattir, which can be exactly pinpointed, plus Holon (Hilen?) and Ain (Ashan?) which have not been identified but must also be situated in the south.[29]

The relations between the Levites and Kadesh are often emphasized. In Moses' blessing (Deut. 33:8) Levi receives the Urim and Thummim, sacred lots which are the privilege of his priesthood,

---

[24] On the relation between the traditions about Moses' Kenite marriage and those concerning his Midianite marriage, cf. R. de Vaux, "Sur l'origine kénite ou madianite du Yahvisme," *Eretz-Israel, Albright Volume,* IX (1969), 28-32.

[25] de Vaux, *op. cit., Les Institutions,* pp. 224-26.

[26] W. F. Albright, "The List of Levitic Cities," *Louis Ginsberg Jubilee Volume,* I (1945), 49-73.

[27] B. Mazar, "The Cities of the Priests and Levites," *Congress Volume, Oxford,* SVT VII (1960), 193-205.

[28] M. Haran, "Studies in the Account of the Levitical Cities," *JBL* LXXX (1961), 45-54, 156-65.

[29] Y. Aharoni, *The Land of the Bible* (1967), pp. 268-73. Evidence of a Levitical settlement in the Negeb has been sought in the Egyptian geographical lists: in a list of Ramses III *w rwy* "territory of Levi" (J. Simons, *The Geographical and Topographical Texts of the Old Testament* [1959], p. 165, notes 30 and 94); in the list of Shishak *ngb rwy* "Negeb of Levi" (*ibid.,* p. 180, note 74); cf. S. Yeivin, "The Exodus," *Tarbiz* XXX (1960-61), 6. Accepted by S. Mowinckel, *Israels opphav og eldste historie* (1967), p. 146.

after having been tested at Massah and having striven with God at the Waters of Meribah.[30] Massah and Meribah are found in Exod. 17:1-7 as one name, Massah-Meribah, the setting of the water miracle, which is here placed at Rephidim on the road to Sinai (vs. 1), or at Horeb (vs. 6). But a doublet of this story is given in Num. 20:1-13 where the miracle of the Waters of Meribah is set at Kadesh. This text of Num. 20, which for the most part is priestly, comes from the same ancient source as Exod. 17 but differs from it in the placing of the episode at Kadesh and in the absence of the name Massah. This is perhaps the preferable version. Consequently Meribah is called Meribath-Kadesh in the later texts (Num. 27:14; Deut. 32:51; Ezek. 48:28).

But this legend of the Waters of Meribah is difficult to use as proof of a link between the Levites and Kadesh. In effect, the miracle is brought about by the lack of water from which the people are suffering (Exod. 17:1; Num. 20:2). But the region around Kadesh is the best supplied with water in the whole Sinai peninsula. One could answer that tradition said that it was precisely the miracle of Moses which originally furnished the water at Kadesh. However, the tradition does not say so. Furthermore, neither Exod. 17 nor Num. 20 speaks of the Levites; it is the people who test (*massah*) God who enter into strife (*meribah*) with him. This is a popular etiology, a traditionally accepted etymology. The name "Meribah" was given to a spring near which trials (*rîb*) were held and it must also have had a sacred character (this is the meaning of the name Kadesh). Moreover, one can point out that in Gen. 14:7 the ancient name of Kadesh is given as "Enmishpat," the "spring of judgment." Inversely, Deut. 33:8, which speaks of the Levites, makes no allusion to the miracle of Exod. 17 and Num. 20. It refers to an episode unknown to us otherwise. It is even possible that this text does not contain any geographical name at all and that we should translate, using the etymologies mentioned above: "Thy Urim and thy Thummim (thou givest) to thy godly one, whom thou didst test by the trial, with whom thou didst strive *on the day* (reading *lᵉyom* in place of *'al mê*) of the strife." [31] It remains clear that Deut. 33:8 has been

---

[30] On this text and its connections with Exod. 17 and Num. 20, other than the commentary of G. von Rad, *Deuteronomium ATD* 2nd ed. (1968), *in loco*, cf. S. Lehming, "Massa und Meriba," *ZAW* LXXIII (1961), 71-77; J. Koenig, "Sourciers, thaumaturges et scribes," *RHR* CLXIV (1963-B), 17-38, 165-80; H. J. Zobel, *Stammesspruch und Geschichte*, pp. 32-34; H. Schmid, *Mose. Überlieferung und Geschichte* (1968), pp. 91-93.

[31] Thus Lehming, *op. cit.,* "Massa."

geographically interpreted by tradition, and it is from this source that Massah entered into Exod. 17. If one combines these two texts with that of Num. 20, one can say that there has been a tradition which put Levi in a special relation to Kadesh. But what I have said shows that this tradition is perhaps not a primitive one. The tendency to associate all the religious and civil organization of Israel with Kadesh, especially the Levitical institutions, is probably exaggerated.

The fact remains that there were Simeonite groups in the far southern part of Palestine and Levitical groups in Judah and perhaps at Kadesh. The problem is to find out when they settled there. According to Judg. 1:1-2 the seizure of Hormah by the Simeonites (Judg. 1:17) should have taken place after the death of Joshua, thus during the Period of the Judges. But Judg. 1:1–2:5 is a collection of information not included in the book of Joshua because it did not fit into the scheme or theological intent of that book; it must spring from a Yahwist account of the conquest.[32] The introduction, "After the death of Joshua," is editorial and is related to Josh. 24:29-31, verses which are themselves an addition taken from Judg. 2:8-10 where they are found word for word. Josh. 24:28 was primitively continued by Judg. 2:6. The settlement of the Simeonites in the south is earlier than the time of the Judges.

This settlement and that of Levi are sometimes connected with Gen. 34. Following the episode at Shechem the two tribes would have emigrated toward the south. They would have settled there long before the Exodus and would not have gone down into Egypt. However, the texts do not permit such conclusions. Gen. 34 shows the two groups obliged to leave central Palestine during the Patriarchal Age but does not indicate where their migration ended. The other texts place them in southern Palestine at the time of the Conquest but do not say what happened to them in the meantime. In addition, recent studies seem to have proved that Simeon and Levi, who appear only in vs. 25 and in the conclusion (vss. 30-31), were secondarily added to the story in Gen. 34, which at first concerned only the "sons of Jacob."[33] Finally, according to Num. 21:1-3 and Judg. 1:16-17, the Simeonites, at least, reached their territory from the south.

This entry into Canaan from the south, in which Judg. 1:16-17 associates Simeon and Judah and with the Calebites, is not connected

[32] S. Mowinckel, *op. cit.*, *Tetrateuch*.

[33] S. Lehming and A. de Pury cited above in note 22. It is very doubtful that these "sons of Jacob" would have replaced here a clan of "sons of David" which had nothing in common with Jacob as A. de Pury would have it.

with the conquest attributed to Joshua.[34] However, according to Num. 21:1-3 and 14:39-45, the taking of Hormah and the ill-fated attempt to advance farther to the north are linked with the history of the group which came out of Egypt with Moses. This link may be secondary; yet it may also have some historical basis. The mention of Simeon retained as a hostage in the story of Joseph (Gen. 42:26; why specifically Simeon?) may cover a memory of the Simeonites' possible sojourn in Egypt. More directly, in dealing with Levi we must keep in mind the relations between Moses and this tribe. The Egyptian name of Moses himself and of several "sons of Levi"—at least Phinehas, Hophni, and Merari—are Egyptian.

When it became common to all the people, the tradition expanded and simplified the individual traditions it kept. Under normal circumstances relations among Palestine, Sinai, and Egypt were easy. Semi-nomadic groups came and went frequently. The stories of Abraham, of Joseph and his brothers, and of Moses in Midian give evidence which is confirmed by extra-biblical sources. There were several "descents into Egypt," and Simeon and Levi could have gone down at any time. There were also several "departures from Egypt." The stories of the Exodus combine two versions, one where the Israelites are expelled from Egypt and the other where they flee from Egypt. Two different routes are also included: one toward the north, the other to the east. The expulsion-exodus occurs by the northern route. The flight-exodus takes place on the route to the east. One can suppose that the groups under Simeon (and Judah?) and part of the group under Levi participated in the expulsion-exodus and stopped in the region of Kadesh, in the neighborhood of the Calebites, the Kenites, *etc.* The group in the flight-exodus, under the leadership of Moses, came first to Sinai, then entered into contact, or renewed contact, with the other groups at Kadesh. Biblical tradition is, in fact, emphatic about a stay in Kadesh, and it is difficult to explain otherwise that Yahwism, the religion of Moses, should be so firmly implanted in the tribes of southern Palestine. But the groups of Simeon and Levi (and Judah?) continued to have their own history and, with the Calebites, settled in their territories by coming up directly from the south. This hypothesis seems to take sufficiently into account the biblical texts, the traditions they use, and the possibilities from general history.

[34] H. Haag, "Von Jahwe geführt. Auslegung von Richter 1, 1-20," *Bibel und Leben* IV (1963), 103-15.

III

THE SETTLEMENT OF CALEBITE GROUPS IN THE REGION OF HEBRON

1. *Caleb.*

We have seen that, according to a tradition, the region of Hebron had been promised to Caleb (Num. 13–14; Deut. 1:19-46; Josh. 14:6-14), and that very probably the primitive tradition of Num. 13–14 was completed by the story of the taking of Hebron by the Calebite groups.[35] This is precisely what is recounted by Josh. 15:13-19 and Judg. 1:10-15, two parallel passages. According to Josh. 15:13-14 Caleb takes possession of Hebron, and vs. 13 establishes the link with Josh. 14:13, where Hebron is given to Caleb as an inheritance. Judg. 1:20 mentions again this taking of Hebron by Caleb, but it is attributed to Judah in Judg. 1:10 and to Joshua in Josh. 10:36-37. What we have are three stages in the evolution of the tradition.

The Calebite occupation spread out to the south of Hebron. According to I Sam. 25:1-3 Nabal the Calebite had his flocks at Carmel (Khirbet Kirmil), and he lived in Ma'ôn (Khirbet Ma'în) respectively seven and a half and nine and a half miles south of Hebron. According to I Sam. 30:14, there was a Negeb of Caleb, which designates perhaps the same region, or an area south of the Judean hill country. One can complete this picture with the genealogical lists of Judah in I Chron. 2 and 4, which we have already used for the Simeonites.[36] They assemble diverse information of different dates, and mix names of places with names of people. There are three lists of the line of Caleb: I Chron. 2:18-24, 42-50; 4:11-20. The most homogeneous is that in I Chron. 2:42-50. To Hebron and Ma'ôn which we have already cited it adds Ziph (between Hebron and Carmel); Tappuah, otherwise known as Beit Tappuah (Taffuḥ, west of Hebron); Beth-zur (about four miles north of Hebron); Madmannah, which reappears as a southern Judean city in Josh. 15:31 (Umm Deimneh, twelve and a half miles northeast of Beersheba); plus other unidentifiable places. This list is ancient and retains the memory of the Calebite occupation before the integration of Caleb into the Judean group. This occupation thus spread out a little to the north of

---

[35] R. Schmid, *TZ* XXI (1965), 263-64.
[36] On these lists, cf. M. Noth, "Eine siedlungsgeographische Liste in Chron. 2 und 4," *ZDPV* LV (1932), 97-124; J. Myers, *I Chronicles, Anchor Bible* (1965), *in loco;* Y. Aharoni, *op. cit., Land*, pp. 224-27.

Hebron (to Beth-zur) and down to the edge of the Judean hill country north of Beersheba (to Madmannah).

According to I Chron. 2:24 Caleb married Ephratah, who bore his son Ashur, father of Tekoa. Ephratah is a Judean clan from which David is descended and which was settled in Bethlehem (Ruth 1:2; I Sam. 17:12). Bethlehem is also called Ephratah in Ruth 4:11, Josh. 15:59 (LXX), and Mic. 5:1 (Heb.). This marriage and the birth of Tekoa (Khirbet Tequ‘, five miles south of Bethlehem) indicate a peaceful melting together of Calebite and Judean elements in the region between Bethlehem and Hebron.

2. Othniel.

Caleb was eventually absorbed into the genealogies of Judah. However, certain texts retain the memory that Caleb was a Kenizzite (Josh. 14:6, 14; from which Num. 32:12 is derived). These Kenizzites are related to the Edomites according to Gen. 36:11, 15, and 42. According to Josh. 15:17 Kenaz is the brother of Caleb, and Judg. 1:13 and 3:9 say he was a younger brother. It is the son of this Kenaz, Othniel, Caleb's nephew, to whom the conquest of Debir, originally called Kiriath-sepher, is attributed. The story, with minor differences, is found in Josh. 15:16-19 and Judg. 1:12-15. Tell Beit-Mirsim, twelve and a half miles southwest of Hebron on the border of the Shephelah, is identified by its excavator, Albright, as Debir. This has been seriously questioned, and Khirbet Rabuḍ, about eight miles from Hebron east of the Hebron-Beersheba road, has been proposed as an alternative.[37] In the biblical story, Caleb had promised his daughter Achsah to the conquerer of Debir. Thus married to Othniel, Achsah asks her father for *gullôt* of water, basins, and he gives her "the upper basins and the lower basins" (Josh. 15:19; Judg. 1:15), the region of the springs of Seil ed-Dilbe on the present road, five miles south of Hebron.[38]

We know nothing more about the expansion of Othniel's group. But this same Othniel, son of Kenaz, younger brother of Caleb,

[37] K. Galling, "Zur Lokalisierung von Debir," *ZDPV* LXX (1964), 135-41; M. Noth, *ZDPV* LXXII (1956), 35 ff.; H. J. Stoebe, *ZDPV* LXXX (1964), 13; H. Donner, *ZDPV* LXXXI (1965), 24-25; ceramics of the Late Bronze Age and Iron I is now the opinion of Y. Aharoni (verbally). W. F. Albright firmly maintains the identification with Tell Beit-Mirsim, more recently in *Archaeology and Old Testament Study,* D. Winton Thomas, ed. (1967), p. 209.

[38] Albright, *ibid.*, pp. 207-8, explains that *gullôts* are underground basins augmented by springs, as one finds around Tell Beit-Mirsim.

reappears as the first "judge" of Israel in Judg. 3:7-11. He delivers Israel from the oppression of Cushan-rishathaim, king of Aram Naharaim. But this is a strange story. The name of the oppressor, "Cushan of the doubly evil," is either made up or deformed; his country Aram Naharaim is Upper Mesopotamia. Some scholars have contended for the historicity of the story by seeing in Cushan-rishathaim a certain Syrian, Irshu, who usurped the power in Egypt about 1200 B.C. and who was overthrown by the first Pharaoh in the Twentieth Dynasty, the father of Ramses III.[39] But this solution is very conjectural. The identity of this Irshu is just as uncertain in the Egyptian documents as that of the "king of Aram" in the Bible. The answer by recent commentators on Judges[40] is, on the whole, preferable: They correct "Aram" to read "Edom" and consider "Naharaim" in vs. 8 as an addition (the word does not reappear in vs. 10). It is possible that Edomite elements, to whom the Kenizzites were related according to Gen. 36:11, 15, and 42 could also have tried to settle in southern Palestine. It has even been suggested that this Cushan-rishathaim is Husham of the land of the Temanites, the third king of Edom in the list in Gen. 36:34.[41] In any case, it seems that the deuteronomist must have used a Kenizzite tradition about Othniel in order to include the tribe of Judah in his picture of the liberating judges.

3. Jerahmeel.

Another group related to the Calebites is that of Jerahmeel, who is called the brother of Caleb in I Chron. 2:42, his older brother according to I Chron. 2:9. The list of his descendants (I Chron. 2:25-33) contains, apparently, only names of people, which could mean that the Jerahmeelites stayed nomadic but which does not allow us to identify their territory. However, I Sam. 27:10 mentions the Negeb of the Jerahmeelites along with that of Judah and that of the Kenites, and I Sam. 30:29 cites the "cities" of the Yerahmeelites along with those of the Kenites among the places to which David sent part of the spoils from the Amalekites. All this indicates that their territory extended in the south. The geographical list of Shishak mentions several forts of the Negeb among which are those of

---

[39] A. Malamat, "Cushan Rishataim and the Decline of the Near East around 1200 B.C.," *JNES* XIII (1954), 231-42.

[40] R. Tamisier, 1949; A. Vincent, 1952; H. W. Hertzberg, 1953; J. Gray, 1967.

[41] Previously Klostermann, and more recently A. Vincent and J. Gray in their commentaries: *husam ro's hattemanim* would have become *kusan rišatayim*.

'rd rbt and 'rd n bt yrhm; that is, "Arad the Great" and "Arad of the House of Yerahm." The first must be the recently excavated fortress at Tell Arad. The second could be the ancient city of Arad, which is now identified at Tell el-Milḥ, and the name would be reminiscent of the settlement of the Jerahmeelites in the area.[42] That would give us at least one fixed point in their territory.

4. Kenites.[43]

The Kenites were the neighbors of the Jerahmeelites according to I Sam. 27:10; 30:29. Judg. 1:16 says they came up from Tamar, in the Arabah, and that they settled in the Negeb of Arad. Their name, which in Arabic means "smiths," marks them as metal workers, and this goes along with their having come from the Arabah where there were copper mines. They seem to have remained semi-nomadic for a long time. In Judg. 4:11; 5:24, Heber the Kenite camps in Galilee; in I Sam. 15:6 the Kenites mingle with the Amalekite nomads. But those who settle in the Arad region become more stable. I Sam. 30:29 speaks of their "cities"; Josh. 15:56-57 mentions a city of Zanoah the Kenite[44] in the region of Ma'ôn. The Kenites must thus have settled southwest of Hebron on the border of cultivated land. In one tradition these Kenites had family ties with Israel: Moses married a Kenite woman (Judg. 1:16; 4:11).

SUMMARY

Let us sum up the results of the first part of our examination of the settling in southern Palestine. Up to a little north of Hebron, the whole Judean hill country was occupied by diverse groups mostly of non-Israelite stock. The most important was that of Caleb, around Hebron, flanked in the southwest by the Kenizzites of Othniel at Debir and in the southwest by the Kenites between Tell Arad and Ma'ôn. There were Levite groups scattered through the hill country.

---

[42] Y. Aharoni, in *op. cit., Archaeology and Old Testament Study*, p. 401, and *op. cit., Land*, p. 289. On Arad, cf. also M. Weippert, *ZDPV* LXXX (1964), 185; V. Fritz, "Arad in der biblischen Überlieferung und in der Liste Schoschenks I," *ZDPV* LXXXII (1966), 331-42; M. Naor, "Arad and Horma in the Conquest Narrative" (Hebrew), *BIES* XXXI (1967), 157-64.

[43] On the Kenites, cf. recently N. Glueck, *Rivers in the Desert*, 2nd ed. (1968), esp. pp. 132-34; F. C. Fensham, "Did a Treaty Between the Israelites and the Kenites Exist?" *BASOR* CLXXV (Oct., 1964), 51-54; B. Mazar, "Arad and the Family of Hobab the Kenite," *JNES* XXIV (1965), 297-303.

[44] M. Noth, *op. cit., Joshua, in loco*; A. Alt, *op. cit., Kleine Schriften*, p. 286.

In the Negeb Simeonites were in the region of Beersheba (Hormah), and the Jerahmeelites wandered around the far south with perhaps a fixed point at Tell el-Milḥ. Their territories partly overlapped, as is suggested by the geographical proximity of Tell Arad (Kenites), Hormah=Khirbet el-Meshâsh (Simeon), and Tell el-Milḥ (Jerahmeel). This occupation was not the result of a merely peaceful infiltration. Tradition preserves the record of warlike conquests (Hebron, Debir, and Hormah) and also certain defeats (like that north of Hormah). These groups came from the south. The Calebite occupation is linked to the story of the spies in Num. 13–14. The Simeonites and the Kenites came up from the Arabah (Judg. 1:16-17).

Such are the data of the tradition. At present archaeological research neither confirms the fact of these conquests nor specifies the date of the occupation. The excavations which have been started on the former site of Hebron have yielded nothing between the Middle Bronze Age and a relatively late period of Iron I.[45] The excavations at Tell Beit-Mirsim are often used to establish the fact of the Conquest and to date it around 1234-1250 B.C.[46] The site actually was destroyed about this time, but we have seen that its identification with Debir is debatable and thus archaeology cannot confirm biblical tradition on this precise point. Tell Arad was not occupied between the Early Bronze Age and the end of the eleventh century B.C. At Tell el-Milḥ, the possible site of the former Canaanite city of Arad, the occupation of the tenth-ninth century B.C. lies just above the ruins from the Middle Bronze Age.[47] Khirbet el-Meshâsh, which has been proposed as a possible site for Hormah, has Middle and perhaps Late Bronze potsherds on the surface, but the site has not been excavated. These two sites are in the valley east of Beersheba which was on the edge of the non-nomadic Canaanite settlement. Farther south, in the Negeb, permanent settlement does not seem to have begun before the eleventh century B.C.[48] In particular, a small dig has uncovered at Tell Esdar, halfway between Beersheba and Aroer, a village founded in that century.[49] This may be one of the cities of which I Sam. 30:29 speaks.

[45] Preliminary reports of P. C. Hammond, *RB* LXXII (1965), 267-70; LXXIII (1966), 566-69; LXXV (1968), 253-58.

[46] Since the beginning of the excavations it has been the opinion of W. F. Albright who has stated it on many occasions, most recently in *op. cit., Archaeology and Old Testament Study*, pp. 207-19, with the precise date (p. 218).

[47] On the excavations at Tell el-Milḥ, cf. provisionally M. Kochavi, *RB* LXXV (1968), 392-95.

[48] Y. Aharoni, *op. cit., Archaeology and Old Testament Study*, pp. 389-90.

[49] M. Kochavi, *IEJ* XIV (1964), 112.

It would be imprudent, however, to use the present lack of substantiation from archaeology to deny any historical basis to the biblical tradition. A penetration from the south by groups, we have enumerated corresponds to economic geography and to a general law of history; namely, the entry into a cultivable region by land-hungry shepherds. It is likely that their migration was facilitated by a disappearing or decadent society inhabiting this region, but it is equally possible that they encountered certain armed resistance. It is significant that biblical tradition puts the first facts about the "conquest" at the time when the immigrants were reaching the edges (postulated by modern archaeologists) of the sedentary civilization. As for the date of the settlement of the groups of Simeon and Levi and their associates in the Judean hill country or on its southern fringe, we can only give an approximation. If one accepts, as we have done, the fact that these groups had been, before their entry into this region, in contact with the group coming out of Egypt with Moses, and if one dates, as is generally done, the Exodus around the middle of the thirteenth century B.C., the settlement occurred later than this date. It is earlier than the eleventh century, when these groups appear established in their territories in the story of Saul and David, and when, according to archaeological findings, the towns in the hill country were repopulated and villages were being built down to the Negeb. The settlement of Simeon and Levi in southern Palestine must thus be approximately contemporary to the entry into Canaan, by way of Transjordan, of the group Moses had led out of Egypt.

IV

THE SETTLEMENT OF THE JUDEAN GROUPS

The marriage of Caleb and Ephrathah (I Chron. 2:24) represents, as we have said, a peaceful expansion of the Calebites toward the north, where they mingle with the Ephratheans, whose center is Bethlehem. We are told that Ephrathah had first been the wife of Hezron, son of Perez, who was the son of Judah (Num. 26:21; Ruth 4:18; I Chron. 2:4-5; Gen. 46:12). Thus we have here a truly Judean lineage.

In the lists in I Chron. 2 and 4 the line of Hezron-Ephrathah is obscured by literary manipulations, but it seems[50] to be from Eph-

---

[50] According to the reconstruction by M. Noth, *op. cit., Josua*, note 36, which is accepted by J. M. Myers and Y. Aharoni, but rejected by W. Rudolph, *Chronik-bücher, HAT*, 1955.

rathah's first marriage with Hezron and not her marriage with Caleb that Hur was born. This Hur has as "descendants" (I Chron. 2:50-55; 4:2-4, 16-19) a list of places located between Bethlehem and Beth-zur (Etam, Gedor), then to the north and northwest of Bethlehem (Nephtoah, Kiriath-jearim, the Valley of Sorek, Eshtaol, Zorah), and in the Shephelah (Soco, Qeila).

Another Judean line is the lineage of Shelah, son of Judah (I Chron. 4:21-23). The only place that has been positively identified is Mareshah (Tell Sandaḥanna) in the Shephelah northwest of Lachish.

This list of the peopling of Judah taken from Chronicles, even if one dates it with Noth as early as the ninth century B.C., represents the result of a slow westward progression from the region of Bethlehem. Thus Kiriath-jearim at first was part of the Gibeonite tetrapolis (Josh. 9:17) which had made an alliance with the House of Joseph (Benjamin?). Thus again, Eshtaol and Zorah could not have been occupied by the Judeans until after the Danite migration (Judg. 18) and they are attributed to the tribe of Dan by Josh. 19:41.

In fact, the Judeans could only expand toward the west. To the north they were hemmed in by a line of Canaanite cities (Jerusalem, Aijalon, and Gezer); in the south by the Calebites at Hebron.

The settlement of Judah in its primitive territory, the region around Bethlehem, seems to have been accomplished peacefully. There was no conquest of Bethlehem, and it was not a Canaanite stronghold. In the Amarna Letters it is only a dependency of the king of Jerusalem.[51] Jerusalem itself was conquered only by David (II Sam. 5:6-9). The story in Judg. 19:11-12 proves that it did not belong to Israel at the time of the Judges. In fact, the outline of the tribal frontiers puts it outside the territory of Judah (Josh. 15:8; 18:16). When it was integrated into the administrative system of the monarchy it was counted among the cities of Benjamin (Josh. 18:28). But one knew that it had not been conquered. The Benjaminites could not drive out the Jebusites who lived there with them "to this day" (Judg. 1:21). An interpolator substituted the Judeans for the Benjaminites in a note added to the list of the cities of Judah in Josh. 15:63. All these texts force us to reject the affirmation in Judg. 1:8 according to which the Judeans took Jerusalem and set it on fire. Some have tried to preserve the historical validity of this text by saying that the Judeans took and destroyed Jerusalem but could not keep it,[52] or that the text refers to a victory won under the wall of Jerusalem

---

[51] Letter 290, 15-16, in *ANET* 2nd ed., p. 489a.
[52] Y. Aharoni, *op. cit., Land*, p. 197.

which assured the possession of the land belonging to the city.[53] These two solutions are arbitrary.

In reality, Judg. 1:8 is a gloss occasioned by the strange story of the preceding verses (Judg. 1:4-7) according to which Judah and Simeon wage a battle at Bezeq with the Canaanites and Perizzites who are defeated. King Adoni-bezeq is captured and wounded. Then "they" (his own men or the Israelites?) take him to Jerusalem where he dies. The reference to Jerusalem, misunderstood, brought about the gloss in vs. 8. But in the story in vss. 4-7 the name of Jerusalem was included because this Adoni-bezeq was confused with the king of Jerusalem, Adoni-zedeq (Josh. 10) who intervenes in a completely different context. Consequently certain commentators correct Adoni-bezeq to read Adoni-zedeq without any basis in the versions. But we know of only one Bezeq in the Old Testament (I Sam. 11:8). It is located at Khirbet Ibziq on the road between Shechem and Beth-shan.[54] Furthermore, the Perizzites are situated by the Bible in the hill country of Ephraim (Josh. 17:15), in the region of Shechem (Gen. 34:30). We are far away from Jerusalem. It has been supposed that Judah and Simeon, who would have arrived with Joshua's group, must have waged war in the hill country of Ephraim before going down to the south.[55] But, as we have seen, Simeon approached from the south. It is more likely that we have here a recollection of Simeonite prehistory; the tribe having seemingly stayed in central Palestine in the Patriarchal Age.[56] The same recollection of the distant past may also be responsible for the insertion of Simeon (and Levi) into the story in Gen. 34.[57]

On the other hand, there is a tradition concerning Judah which is associated with the Patriarchal period but which is much more likely to be from the time of the tribal settlement. It is the story of Judah and Tamar recorded by the Yahwist in Gen. 38. It gives an example of the levirate marriage law, but it also explains the development of the tribe of Judah through a personal adventure of its ancestor. Judah was separated from his brothers, went down to

---

[53] H. W. Hertzberg, *Josua, Richter, Ruth, ATD* (1953), p. 150; J. Gray, *Joshua, Judges, and Ruth* (1967), p. 247.

[54] P. Welten, "Bezeq," *ZDPV* LXXXI (1965), 138-65, esp. pp. 140-41.

[55] Y. Aharoni, *op. cit., Land*, p. 197.

[56] Thus H. W. Hertzberg, "Adonibezek," *JPOS* VI (1926), 213-31=*Beiträge zur Traditionsgeschichte und Theologie des Alten Testaments* (1962), pp. 28-35; *idem, Josua*, p. 149; J. Gray, *op. cit., Joshua*, pp. 246-47. Welten, *op. cit.*, using vs. 7b postulates a powerful Canaanite kingdom in the region of Shechem, heir of that of Labaya of Amarna times. This is not borne out by the evidence.

[57] Cf. above, p. 114.

Adullam (esh-Sheikh Madhkur) in the Shephelah, three miles south-west of Soco. He kept his flocks at Timnah, four miles northeast of Adullam. The other places in the story, Chezib and Enaim, have not been identified but must be located in the same area. Judah married the daughter of a Canaanite named Shua, who bore him three sons, Er, Onan, and Shelah. Er married Tamar, another Canaanite in all likelihood. Tamar having become the widow of Er, disappointed by the application of the levirate law, by Onan's failure, and then by Judah's refusal to give her Shelah, succeeded by a trick in sleeping with her father-in-law and bore twins, Perez and Zerah. This story illustrates the expansion of Judean groups toward the plain, their family union with the Canaanites, the formation of clans soon extinct, those of Er and Onan, and of the three Judean clans enumerated in Num. 26:20: the Shelanites, the Perezites, and the Zerahites. This peaceful penetration into the Low Country goes along with the conclusions we have drawn from the study of the lists of settlement in I Chron. 2 and 4.

There is thus nothing in the traditions which justifies the sweeping affirmation in Judg. 1:9: "And afterward the men of Judah went down to fight against the Canaanites who dwelt in the hill country, in the Negeb, and in the lowland." It is merely an editorial introduction to the diverse traditions of Judg. 1:1-19, which were attributed to Judah and which we have restored to the groups that were eventually absorbed into Judah: vs. 10, the taking of Hebron by Caleb (cf. vs. 20); vss. 11-15, the taking of Debir by Othniel; vss. 16-17, the occupation of the Negeb of Arad by the Kenites and the taking of Hormah by Simeon.

Vs. 18 remains: Judah conquered Gaza, Askelon, and Ekron; and the Septuagint adds Ashdod. But this affirmation contradicts several texts. Vs. 19 says that Judah was unable to drive away the inhabitants of the plain. Josh. 13:2-3 and Judg. 3:3 say that the whole of the Philistine territory was still left to be conquered. In reality, this region had never belonged to Israel, except perhaps partially for a short period under Josiah.[58] Finally, the presumed site of Ekron does not seem to have been occupied before the Philistines.[59] In

---

[58] The only testimony we have about it is the fortress of the Meṣad Ḥashavyahu, sixteen miles south of Haifa, where a brief Israelite occupation followed a Greek commercial establishment, J. Naveh, "A Hebrew Letter from the Seventh Century B.C.," *IEJ* X (1960), 129-39; *idem*, "The Excavations at Meṣad Ḥashavyahu," *IEJ* XII (1962), 89-113.

[59] J. Naveh, "Khirbet al-Muqqanna'-Ekron. An Archaeological Survey," *IEJ* VIII (1958), 87-100, 165-70.

support of Judg. 1:18 one can only cite Josh. 15:45-47, which counts Ekron, Ashdod, and Gaza among the cities of Judah. However, this text is clearly an addition.[60] Some have tried to preserve Judg. 1:18 by saying that the outlying cities really were conquered but were soon abandoned by Judah under the pressure of the Philistines.[61] In turn, the Septuagint resolved the contradiction between Judg. 1:18 and the other texts by adding a negative: Judah did *not* conquer Gaza, Askelon, Ekron, and Ashdod.[62] These subterfuges must be renounced. Vs. 18 is, like vs. 8, an addition intended to raise still higher the prestige of Judah, for the greater glory of which Judg. 1:2-19 was written. Yahweh delivered the land into its hands (vs. 2). Yahweh was with them and they took the hill country (vs. 19). These successes are placed in opposition to Benjamin's failures (vs. 21) and those of the other tribes (vss. 27-34).

It is not to Judah but to Joshua and to all Israel that Josh. 10:28-39 attributes the conquest of a series of cities which will be counted in the territory of Judah: Makkedah, Libnah, Lachish, Eglon, Hebron, and Debir. G. E. Wright has tried to reconcile this account with that of Judg. 1. According to him a lightning campaign by Joshua against the royal Canaanite cities, which were key cities, would have been followed by a period of strife after Joshua's death (Judg. 1:1).[63] K. Elliger considers the taking of Makkedah as an appendix to the story of the battle of Gibeon (Josh. 10:1-15) and suggests that the destruction of Libnah, Lachish, and Eglon be attributed to the Calebites and the Kenizzites, who could not hold their own there and went up from there to Hebron and Debir, where they settled.[64] M. Noth, on the other hand, thinks that these cities are those of the kings of the cave of Makkedah, which would be distinct from

---

[60] Thus Cross and Wright, *op. cit.*, p. 204; Y. Aharoni, *VT* IX (1959), 240.

[61] Admitted as a possibility by G. E. Wright, *JNES* V (1946), 109, and more emphatically by Y. Kaufmann in his Hebrew commentary on Judges (Jerusalem, 1962), pp. 82-83. The excavations at Ashdod, which showed that the city had been destroyed in the second half of the thirteen century then remained abandoned until it was occupied by the Philistines, have been used to favor this hypothesis. D. N. Freedman, *BA* XXVI (1963), 136; M. Dothan, *IEJ* XIV (1964), 84=*Archaeological Discoveries in the Holy Land* (1967), p. 132; M. Dothan and D. N. Freedman, *Ashdod I* (1967 [='Atiqot VII]), p. 9; T. C. Mitchell, in *op. cit., Archaeology and Old Testament Study*, pp. 411-12.

[62] Certain exegetes prefer this text to the Hebrew one and insert vs. 18 between vss. 19*a* and 19*b*. But the Septuagint is suspected of having changed vs. 18 to agree with vs. 19.

[63] G. E. Wright, "The Literary and Historical Problem of Joshua 10 and Judges 1," *JNES* VI (1946), 105-14; *idem, Biblical Archaeology* (1957), pp. 69-70, 81-83.

[64] K. Elliger, "Josua in Judea," *PJB* XXX (1934), 47-71.

the five kings of the Gibeonite campaign.[65] In any case, the historian cannot benefit much from these schematic notes. It does not seem possible to attribute to Joshua and to all Israel this southern campaign. According to the Bible itself we have restored the taking of Hebron and Debir to Caleb and Othniel. Can one at least give Judah credit for the conquest of the other cities of the Shephelah (Libnah, Lachish, and Eglon), and date this conquest at the time of the settlement? What we have said about the peaceful infiltration of Judah into the Shephelah, especially with respect to Gen. 38, makes this doubtful.

What light does archaeology shed on this? Libnah, long identified as Tell eṣ-Ṣafi, is now generally placed at Tell Bornat, five and a half miles farther south. According to a surface exploration the site was occupied at the end of the Late Bronze and the beginning of the Iron Ages, but it has not been excavated. Eglon is located at Tell el-Ḥesi by recent authors. The site was excavated in 1890-93 by Petrie and Bliss.[66] It appears that the city was destroyed at the end of the Late Bronze Age, but that it was deserted during most of the Period of the Judges. Lachish must be at Tell ed-Duweir, which has been incompletely but very well excavated. The city was destroyed at the end of the Late Bronze Age, but the date is not certain. An Egyptian inscription on a bowl bears the date of the fourth year of an unidentified Pharaoh. If, as is likely, it refers to Merneptah, the date would be *ca.* 1220 B.C. in our chronology. But this date is not that of the destruction. It gives only a *terminus post quem* and we must take into account a scarab from Ramses III found in the ruined layer.[67] This would bring the date of the destruction down to the first decades of the twelfth century,[68] after Joshua and at the beginning of the Philistine era. Neither can one be sure of the identity of the aggressors. They could have been the Israelites, the Egyptians, the Sea People (Philistines), or other Canaanites. In any case, the site remained abandoned afterward for over a century; that is, during the whole Period of the Judges. This archaeological evidence makes it possible that the mention of Libnah, Eglon, and Lachish in Josh. 10 represents an increase in the territory of Judah under David or Solomon. Furthermore, it

[65] M. Noth, "Die fünf Könige in der Höhle von Makkeda," *PJB* XXXIII (1937), 22-36, and *op. cit. Josua, in loco.*

[66] F. J. Bliss, *A Mound of Many Cities, or Tell el-Hesy Excavated,* 1894.

[67] This is the latest judgment of O. Tufnell, *Lachish IV. The Bronze Age* (1958), pp. 37, 98.

[68] O. Tufnell, in *op. cit., Archaeology and Old Testament Study,* p. 302.

must be noted that Eglon never appears outside the book of Joshua and that Libnah and Lachish are mentioned elsewhere only late in the time of the monarchy: Libnah in II Kings 8:22 under Joram, and Lachish in II Kings 14:19 under Amaziah.

There is thus no really ancient tradition which allows us to attribute to the tribe of Judah any conquest whatsoever. These traditions only give us the picture of their peaceful settlement around Bethlehem, their intermingling with the Calebites established at Hebron, and their peaceful infiltration into the Shephelah.

It is difficult to determine how these groups came to be in the region around Bethlehem. They might have come up from the south like the Simeonites with whom they fused, and Judg. 1:16, which says that the Judeans came up with the Kenites, could be taken literally. In addition, the line formed by the Canaanite cities of Jerusalem, Aijalon, and Gezer, would have obstructed their descent from the north. On the other hand, when Gen. 38:1 says that Judah "went down from his brothers," it may be an exact recollection that Judah had left the other tribes after the crossing of the Jordan. In this case, the Judeans would have reached Bethlehem by the way of the desert, between Jerusalem and the Dead Sea.

As a matter of fact, there was, in this region, a tradition which connected Judah with Joshua's conquest of Jericho and Ai. It is the story of Achan (Josh. 7:1-26). Achan belonged to the Judean clan of Zerah. He transgressed the ban (*herem*) pronounced against Jericho, and this brought about the failure of the first attack against Ai. As punishment he was burned with his family and his possessions, and a pile of stones was raised over him. The place was called the "Valley of Achor" which means "Valley of Misfortune," because he had brought misfortune to Israel. This valley marks the border between Benjamin and Judah, but it is in Judean territory. It is incontrovertibly identified as the Buqe'a, the plain which extends west of the Qumran cliff.[69]

This narrative is a local tradition which first existed independently. It could be of Judean origin, but is more probably Benjaminite, since it speaks derogatorily of Judah. A Benjaminite origin would better explain the fact that the story was attached—and artificially at that[70]—to the accounts of Jericho and Ai, which are Benjaminite traditions. The only thing this story teaches us is that the Judean

[69] M. Noth, *ZDPV* LXXI (1955), 42-55.

[70] M. Noth, *op. cit., Josua*, pp. 43-46; Hertzberg, *op. cit., Josua*, pp. 48-49; Gray, *op. cit., Joshua*, pp. 80-81.

clan Zerah owned this region. This completes the picture of the settlement of Judah we have taken from I Chron. 2 and 4 and Gen.
38. But it does not tell us where this Zerahite group came from, or
how it got into its territory to the east and northeast of Bethlehem.
If Judah entered Canaan by crossing the Jordan, the clan of Zerah
could have stopped in the Valley of Achor while the rest of the
group continued toward Bethlehem. If Judah came in from the
south with the Simeonites and other groups, and if the center of
settlement was the area around Bethlehem, where the clan of Ephrathah[71] lived, this Zerahite occupation would be a secondary expansion of Ta'amri Bedouins from Bethlehem. This secondary
character is confirmed by the genealogy of Zerah: He was born of a
Canaanite mother in the Shephelah (Gen. 38:40). All things considered, it is more likely that the Judeans entered Canaan from
the south, at the same time as the Simeonites with whom tradition
closely associates them.

V

THE ORIGINS OF THE TRIBE OF JUDAH

This uncertainty about the immigration route is part of the mystery
which surrounds the origins of the tribe of Judah. The etymology of
the name is unknown. Some scholars think it was the name of a
person.[72] However, it seems more likely that it was a geographical
name, that of a region (like Ephraim or Naphtali).[73] Traces remain
of this primitive usage. Judg. 17 speaks of Bethlehem of Judah
several times, as does Judg. 19, just as one speaks of Jabesh-gilead
in Judg. 21:8-9, or of Kedesh of Galilee in Josh. 20:7 and 21:32.
In I Sam. 23:3 David's men say to him: "Behold, we are afraid here
in Judah; how much more then if we go to Keilah," but Keilah is
inhabited by "Judeans." One speaks of the hill country of Judah
beside that of Ephraim and that of Naphtali (Josh. 20:7); of the
desert of Judah (Judg. 1:16) as of the desert of Ziph (I Sam. 26:2),
or of Ma'ôn (I Sam. 23:25), or of Tekoa (II Chron. 20:20). Judah
is the hill country region which stretches from the area north of
Bethlehem to that south of Hebron. It is not the tribe that gave its

---

[71] Cf. above, p. 120.

[72] Particularly W. F. Albright, "The Names 'Israel' and 'Judah,'" *JBL* XLVI
(1927), 151-85, esp. pp. 168-78.

[73] L. Waterman, *AJSL* LV (1938), 29-31; M. Noth, *Die Welt des Alten Testaments,* 4th ed. (1962), pp. 50-52; *idem, The History of Israel* (1960), p. 56.

name to the region. It is the region which gave its name to the tribe that lived there, which found for itself an eponymous ancestor with the same name: Judah son of Jacob.

Indeed, in all of Genesis, Judah plays a personal part in only two stories: once in Gen. 38, where Judah personifies a group of men in an account which, as we have seen, comes from the period following the settlement and not from Patriarchal times; and again in the story of Joseph, where Judah fills the place of Reuben in the south-Palestinian version of the story.

The Song of Deborah (Judg. 5), which may date from the third quarter of the twelfth century B.C., makes no reference either to Judah or to Simeon. This could mean that these tribes, living isolated in the south, were not concerned in this war and did not have to decide whether or not to participate in it. On the other hand, it may indicate that they were not yet a part of Israel. This lack of mention prevents us from determining whether Judah already existed as a tribal entity with its own name. But Judah and Simeon are mentioned as tribes in the Testament of Jacob (Gen. 49), and Judah alone in the Blessing of Moses (Deut. 33). The language and poetic style of these two compositions have led several authors to date them before the monarchical period.[74] However, a study of the literary forms indicates that these poems contain elements from different periods.[75] If we try to date the passages about Judah and Simeon according to the historical situations they imply, we run into a vicious circle since it is precisely that history we are trying to determine. Yet we can say that the passage about Simeon (and Levi) in Gen. 49:5-7 indicates that Simeon, scattered into Israel, had already lost its individuality. Furthermore, the passage in Gen. 49:8-12, about Judah before whom his brothers bow down and who will not see the scepter depart from him, presupposes a domination by Judah which did not start until the time of David. The absence of Simeon from Deut. 33 can be explained only if the tribe had already been absorbed by Judah. The passage about Judah (Deut. 33:7) is a hope that he be brought back to his people. That may be an allusion to a breaking away of Judah at the time of the settlement (cf. Judg. 1). But it may also describe the situation created by the political

---

[74] W. F. Albright in his latest book, *Yahweh and the Gods of Canaan* (1968), p. 15 (Deut. 33 before the destruction of Shiloh), p. 17 (Gen. 49 after the destruction); F. M. Cross and D. N. Freedman, "The Blessings of Moses," *JBL* LXVII (1948), 191-209 (Deut. 33 toward the end of the eleventh century).

[75] Zobel, *op. cit.*; A. H. J. Gunneweg, "Über den Sitz im Leben der sog. Stammessprüche (Gen. 49; Deut. 33; Judg. 5)," *ZAW* LXXVI (1964), 245-55.

schism following the death of Solomon. Thus all these old texts teach us nothing certain about the tribe of Judah before David.

Recent authors have concluded that the tribe of Judah was not formed until the time of David.[76] One can object that Judah is one of the twelve tribes and that its territory is thus described in the map of the tribes in Josh. 13–19. This delineation of tribal frontiers (not the lists of cities) would go back to the premonarchical era.[77] But the theory of an "amphictyony" at the time of the Judges is seriously questioned today. Besides, admitting the existence of an ancient document on which Joshua 13–19 is based, it is now recognized that the borders given to the tribes do not all come from the same period. In particular, the southern, eastern, and western borders of the tribe of Judah are only the ideal borders of the land of Canaan, while the northern boundary, the only one described in detail, is that of Judah under the reign of David.[78]

On the other hand, it appears that as early as the time of Saul Judah was no longer just the name of a territory but had become the name of the tribe which occupied it and that this tribe was part of the kingdom of Saul.[79] But this integration of Judah into Israel was then perhaps rather recent, which would explain its absence from the Song of Deborah. Besides, we do not know what this tribe of Judah stood for at the time of Saul, and we know even less about preceding times. The existence of an "amphictyony" in the south with six members, which would have included Judah, Caleb, Othniel, Jerahmeel, Simeon, and the Kenites around the sanctuary at Hebron is an unfounded hypothesis. It would confirm the fact that Judah achieved dominance at a late date. It seems to have been under and by David that the tribe of Judah found its true identity. It was composed of heterogeneous elements: the Calebites, Kenizzites, and Jerahmeelites are included in its genealogy, and it absorbed Simeon. The three main clans of Judah are the result of a fusion with the Canaanites: the clan of Shelah from the marriage of Judah with a

[76] Particularly S. Mowinckel, in *Von Ugarit nach Qumran*, BZAW LXXVII, 2nd ed. (1958, 1961), 137-38; *op. cit., Tetrateuch*, p. 66; and *op. cit., Israel*, pp. 139-40; cf. also M. A. Cohen, *HUCA* XXXVI (1965), 94-98.

[77] Cf. fundamentally, A. Alt, "Das System der Stammesgrenzen," in *Sellin Festschrift* (1927), pp. 13-24=*Kleine Schriften*, I (1953), 193-202.

[78] The two most recent works on tribal geography agree at least on this point: Y. Aharoni, *op. cit., Land*, pp. 227-35; Z. Kallai, *op. cit., The Tribes of Israel*, and previously *The Northern Boundaries of Judah* (Hebrew), 1960.

[79] K.-D. Schunck, *Benjamin*, BZAW LXXXVI (1963), 124-26; *Volume du Congrès. Genève*, SVT XV (1966), 257, note 6; R. Smend, "Gehörte Juda zum vorstaatlichen Israel?" *op. cit., Fourth World Congress of Jewish Studies*, pp. 57-62.

Canaanite, the clans of Perez and Zerah from his incest with Tamar. The only pure clan is that of Ephrathah settled in Bethlehem. It is David, the Judean of Bethlehem, who leads the way to a union of all these elements by his victory over a common enemy, the Amalekites, and by the gifts he gives to "his friends" (I Sam. 30:26).[80] The list which follows (I Sam. 30:27-31) enumerates indeed the various groups he will unite under his scepter. It is significant that right after Saul's death David settles not at Bethlehem, the city of his birth, but at Hebron, the Calebite city,[81] and that it is there that he is recognized as king over the "house of Judah"; it is the first occurrence of this expression. The constituted tribe of Judah is to be identified with the first kingdom of David at Hebron.

[80] Following the Greek (plural) as opposed to the Hebrew (singular); it is arbitrary to correct the Hebrew (and Greek) from "according to their cities"; "the ancients of Judah" which precedes without grammatical transition is an obvious gloss.

[81] It is interesting to note but imprudent to accept the hypothesis of H. Winckler, *Geschichte Israels* (1905), p. 25, who, in II Sam. 3:8 has Abner say, "Am I prince of Caleb?" (*rôš kâléb*), with an allusion to David at Hebron. The hypothesis is, however, maintained by S. Mowinckel in the three passages cited above in note 76.

Israel: Amphictyony: 'AM; ḲĀHĀL; 'ĒḌÂH

GEORGE W. ANDERSON

In his recently published book, *The Knowledge of God in Ancient Israel,* Professor R. C. Dentan surveys one basic aspect of Old Testament theology, the doctrine of God, which he describes as "the pole around which all other topics normally included in treatises on the theology of the Old Testament—ideas about the nature of man, sin, salvation, ethics, and cultus—should properly be organized." [1] The book contains a persuasive and balanced exposition of the implications of that statement. It is, nevertheless, remarkable that Dentan finds it necessary to preface his treatment of his chosen theme with an introductory chapter entitled "The Mystery of Israel." "The central figure of the Bible," writes Dentan, "is a community called Israel. The Bible is also, of course, a book about God, and one might accurately say that God is its hero; but in fact we know and see the God of the Bible only through the mind and eyes of Israel" [2]; and again, "There can be no comprehension of biblical religion, faith, theology—or whatever one chooses to call it—without the idea of 'Israel,' for at every stage that idea stands at the very center, and biblical faith is inconceivable without it." [3] It is not easy to understand why those scholars who have attempted to construct Old Testament theologies around one central dominating idea have given so little attention to the thought of Israel as the people of God. But even if that particular theological enterprise is held to be doomed to failure, the subject is so pervasive in the Old Testament that the student of the history of the religion of ancient Israel can-

[1] R. C. Dentan, *The Knowledge of God in Ancient Israel* (New York, 1968), p. vii.
[2] *Ibid.,* p. 3.
[3] *Ibid.,* p. 32.

not safely disregard the double question, what Israel was, historically and empirically, and what was the nature of Israel's self-understanding.

The present essay is part of an attempt to reexamine that self-understanding. It primarily deals with a reconsideration of a hypothesis concerning both the empirical nature of ancient Israel at a particular period and also the impact of that phase in her corporate experience on a wide area of her faith and practice. I refer to the view that in the early period the Israelite tribes constituted an amphictyony. This hypothesis is associated to some extent with the name of Alt,[4] and more particularly with that of Noth.[5] But, as G. Fohrer has pointed out,[6] there are at least five different forms of the hypothesis.

(1) An amphictyonic arrangement was ascribed to Israel's pre-mosaic period (*"schon vor der Entstehung eines Volkes Israel"*) by Ewald.[7] He did not, indeed, use the word "amphictyony"; but he drew attention to the importance of the number twelve, and to the way in which the twelvefold division could serve as a basis for the orderly registering of opinions (voting) and for the arrangement of the clans in camp and their mustering for war (cf. Num.1–2; 7). Moreover, he noted possible parallels in ancient Greco-Italian literature and history: Etruscans, Livy, i,8; twelve princes of the Phaeacians, Homer, Od. viii. 390-91; the Thracians, Homer, Il. x. 488-95, a singularly doubtful instance; Ionians and Aeolians, Herodotus i. 145-46, 149; and the alleged duodecimal division of ancient Attica, Philochorus, *ap.* Strabo, ix, p. 396. Ewald also referred to parallels among the Bornu of Africa and in America. A similar observation was made by Gunkel in an extended discussion of the narrative of the birth of Jacob's children in Gen. 29:31–30-24 [8] with reference to some of the Greco-Italian parallels; the children of Aeolus, Homer, Od. x. 5; the amphictyonies of Delphi, Ionia, and of the Ionian Achaeans, and the Etruscan league.[9]

---

[4] *Der Gott der Väter, BWANT* III, 12 (1929), 58-59=*Kleine Schriften,* I (1953), 54-55=*Essays on Old Testament History and Religion* (1967), pp. 53-54; *Die Staatenbildung der Israeliten in Palästina* (1930), pp. 9 ff., 26-27=*Kleine Schriften,* II (1953), 7-8, 21-22=*Essays on Old Testament History and Religion* (1967), pp. 179-80, 192-93.

[5] *Das System der zwölf Stämme Israels, BWANT* IV, 1 (1930).

[6] *TLZ,* XCI (1966), cols. 802-3.

[7] *Einleitung in die Geschichte des Volkes Israel,* I, 3rd ed. (1864), 519 ff., esp. p. 530 with n. 2, and p. 531, n. 1.

[8] *Genesis,* 3rd ed. (1910), p. 332.

[9] Cf. B. Luther in E. Meyer, *Die Israeliten und ihre Nachbarstämme* (1906), p. 148 and n. 1, and E. Meyer's own observations, *op. cit.,* pp. 233-34; E. Szanto "Die griechischen Phylen," *Sitzungsber. der Wiener Akad.,* phil-hist. Klasse, Vol. CXLIV (1901).

(2) The term "warlike confederacy" (*kriegerische Eidgenossenschaft*) was used of Israel as it came into existence in the *mosaic* period by Wellhausen: "*Jahwe war das Feldgeschrei dieser kriegerischen Eidgenossenschaft, der kürzeste Ausdruck dessen, was sie unter sich einigte und gegen aussen schied.*" [10] It fitly expresses the view of Israel in the period of the judges which was expounded by Max Weber.[11] The composition of the confederacy varied from time to time both in the identity and in the total number of its members.[12] Its character was thus described by Weber: "The Israelite confederacy itself, according to unambiguous tradition, represented a war confederation under and with Yahwe as the war god of the union, guaranteeing its social order and creator of the material prosperity of the confederates, especially of the requisite rain. This is brought to expression by the name 'Israel' which was meant to designate directly 'the people of the fighting god' . . . . In any case, 'Israel' was no tribal name but the name of an association, at that, of a cult league." [13] Weber's emphasis on the martial character of the confederacy is closely linked with his view that it had much to do with the development of law. The charismatic "war hero or war prophet" [14] was also recognized beyond the boundaries of his own tribe as a source of legal decision, and of ritual and moral instruction. Asserting that '*ēdâh* is the term appropriate to the army assembly of Israel, and equating '*ēdäh* = assembly with '*edah* = testimony or decree, Weber finds it possible to conclude that the army issued general decrees.[15] Thus his emphasis lies on the military and legal functions of the confederacy. Concerning cultic activities he is vague, and concerning any possible central sanctuary even less precise. He says that there were "perhaps, also some periodic amphictyonic ritualistic acts such as are possibly represented by the Shechemite curse and prayer ceremony and the repeatedly mentioned annual Yahweh festivals in Shiloh (Judg. 21:19 and I Sam. 1:3)." [16]

(3) The best-known and most influential of amphictyonic theories is that presented by Martin Noth, originally in *Das System der zwölf Stämme Israels* (*BWANT* IV, 1 [1930]), and later in his *Geschichte*

---

[10] *Israelitische und jüdische Geschichte*, 7th ed. (1914), 9th ed. (1958), p. 23.
[11] *Gesammelte Aufsätze zur Religionssoziologie*, III, 2nd ed. (1923), 81 ff.= *Ancient Judaism* (1952), pp. 75 ff.
[12] Weber, *Ancient Judaism*, p. 82.
[13] *Ibid.*, p. 81.
[14] *Ibid.*, p. 83.
[15] *Ibid.*, p. 90.
[16] *Ibid.*

Israels (1950, 2nd ed., 1954; E.T. *History of Israel,* 2nd ed., 1960).
Noth's argument is based on a thorough examination of the varying
forms of the list of the sons of Israel who are represented as the
eponymous ancestors of the Israelite tribes. It proceeds, by way of
a comparison with amphictyonic leagues in ancient Greece and
Italy, to the conclusion that during the period of the Judges (i.e.,
before the establishment of an Israelite state with centralized organization) the Israelite tribes were united in a sacral confederacy, united
not so much, as on Weber's hypothesis, by common military activity
(except in the rare event of war against an offending member of
the amphictyony) as by worship at a central sanctuary which was
the source of an amphictyonic law by which the relations of the
members were regulated. Noth held that the group of six "Leah"
tribes formed an earlier confederacy which was already settled in the
land at the time when "the House of Joseph" under Joshua's leadership occupied territory in the central hill country; and it was the
stimulus of this event which led to the establishment of the twelve-
tribe confederacy consisting of the newcomers, the "Leah" group,
and the other groups which were already resident in the land.

Before considering this hypothesis in greater detail, we may note
briefly (following Fohrer's classification) two types of variation
upon it:

(4) Those views in which the total number of the members of
the confederacy is reduced to ten, or great emphasis is laid on the
Holy War as a characteristically important activity of the amphictyony, or its legal and administrative functions are elaborated and
held to have been concentrated in a leader and a college of elders.[17]

(5) Theories of a series of smaller Israelite amphictyonies, earlier
than, or contemporaneous with, the twelve-tribe confederacy.[18] Noth's
hypothesis has been widely accepted and its implications, real or
supposed, have produced far-reaching results in many books and
articles about the development of early Israelite society, law, and
worship. It may be doubted whether Noth himself would have accepted all the inferences which have been made from his own
conclusions. Indeed, one might hazard the guess that at least as

---

[17] J. Dus, "Die 'Ältesten Israels,' " *Communio Viatorum,* III (1960), 232 ff.;
"Die 'Sufeten Israels,' " *Archiv. Orientálni,* XXXI (1963), 444 ff.

[18] E.g., in Hebron—A. H. Sayce, "The Cuneiform Tablets of Tel El-Amarna
. . . ," *PSBA* XI (1888/89), 347; at Mamre—A. Alt, *Der Gott der Väter,* pp. 58-59
=*Kleine Schriften,* I, 54-55=*Essays on Old Testament History and Religion,* pp.
53-54; M. Noth, *System,* pp. 107-8; at Kadesh—S. Mowinckel, "Kadesh, Sinaj, og
Jahve," *Norsk Geografisk Tidsskrift* IX (1942), 13-14.

many students of the Old Testament have accepted the amphictyonic theory without reading *Das System der zwölf Stämme Israels* as have rejected Mowinckel's hypothesis of an enthronement festival without reading the second volume of *Psalmenstudien*. But during the past few years there have been sporadic indications of an increasingly skeptical attitude toward the amphictyonic theory. There may, therefore, be some point in reconsidering the basis and scope of the theory as originally propounded by Noth, the validity of the more notable criticisms which have been offered, and what, if anything, remains after the completion of the exercise.

The various ramifications of the theory which have been developed since Noth published his treatise are so numerous that a complete reappraisal of the situation would require a substantial monograph rather than a paper.

1. There is first the question of the nature and number of the tribal systems in ancient Israel and the relation of the lists of eponyms and of tribes to historical reality at various periods.

2. Second, and closely connected with part of the above inquiry, there is the vexing question of the nature of the Israelite settlement in the land of Canaan, a question on which there is still a bewildering variety of viewpoints.[19]

3. Granted that there was an Israelite amphictyony or confederacy, what was its principal function? (a) Was it primarily cultic—the care of a central sanctuary and the celebration of one or more annual festivals at that sanctuary? (b) Was a military activity, the prosecution of the Holy War, an important function? (c) Were legal and administrative enactments prominent among the activities of the representatives of the tribes when they assembled at the central sanctuary?

4. Various questions arise concerning the alleged central sanctuary: (a) Is there adequate evidence that in the period of the judges the communal and cultic life of "all Israel" had its focal point in a central sanctuary? (b) Was there more than one central sanctuary during successive phases of the period of the judges? (c) Was the sanctuary in effect not a place but the Ark, so that the location of amphictyonic worship depended on the location for the time being of the Ark?

5. What, if any, were the officers of the amphictyony and what their functions?

[19] An admirable survey and appraisal of recent discussions of this problem up to 1966 is given by Manfred Weippert in *Die Landnahme der israelitischen Stämme in der neueren wissenschaftlichen Diskussion, FRLANT* XCII (1967).

Most, if not all, of the above problems embarrass the inquirer by the paucity of evidence available for their solution and the wealth of ingenious speculation to which they have given rise. I, therefore, propose to select only a few points which I take to have been basic to Noth's original thesis, and to consider them and, with them, some of the objections which have been offered by Noth's recent critics.

I. The basis of Noth's entire hypothesis is his examination of the varying forms of the twelve-tribe system. The principal passages which he discussed were (a) the Blessing of Jacob (Gen. 49), the narratives of the births of the sons of Israel (Gen. 29:31–30:24); and the lists derived from them in Deut. 27:12-13; Gen. 25:23-26; Exod. 1:2-4; Gen. 46:8-25; I Chron. 2:1-2; Ezek. 48:31-35—all of which are characterized by the inclusion of Levi, and secondly (b) those passages which exclude Levi but retain the number twelve by re-placing Joseph by Manasseh and Ephraim, of which the most im-portant is Num. 26:5-51 (cf. also Num. 1:1-15; 2:3-31; 10:14-28; 7:12-83).[20] The first outcome of his examination was the conclusion that the twelve-tribe system is an independent element in the Old Testament tradition, already established before the rise of the mon-archy. Thus he was able to reject the view of B. Luther[21] and Ed. Meyer[22] that II Sam. 19:44 attests an earlier phase in the tradition, according to which Israel and Judah were originally represented as the two sons of Jacob, and also the contention of B. Luther[23] that the twelve-tribe list was a secondary construction based on Solomon's administrative division of the land of Israel into twelve administrative districts. His comparison of the varying forms of the list provided strong grounds for the inference that at some stage the six "Leah" tribes formed a recognizable group existing before the group of twelve tribes took shape.

If Noth's literary argument is accepted, the earliest literary form of the list (Gen. 49) dates from the time of either David or Solomon, though its component oracles are doubtless of earlier date. Further, since the origin of the twelve-tribe system is understandable only in a period when the tribes were conscious of their individual existence, the formation of the Israelite state under David is the latest date before which the system may be inferred to have come into existence. That the system is older than David's reign is evident from the

---

[20] He rejected the Song of Deborah as evidence for an alternative form of the list, containing only ten tribes. *System*, pp. 5-6, 36.

[21] *ZAW* XXI (1901), 29 ff.

[22] *Die Israeliten und ihre Nachbarstämme*, pp. 230-31.

[23] *ZAW* XXI (1901), 34-35.

fact that it includes tribes which had ceased to exist as such by David's reign. Indeed, the very fact that the system appears in varying forms shows that it is not merely an artificial construction but comes from a time when the tribes had a separate existence.

This conclusion, that the twelve-tribe system existed at so early a date, is of prime importance for our understanding of the nature of Israel and of Israel's self-understanding in the early period.

II. But if Noth's fixing of the *terminus ad quem* is based on literary and form-critical evidence, his suggestion for the *terminus a quo* is based on what he holds to be general probability, and that in two senses.

(a) It is his view that the formation of such a confederacy would most naturally be promoted by some historical experience which the members had undergone, such as the simultaneous occupation of neighboring territory.

(b) He further suggests that the appropriate experience was the invasion of the land by the "house of Joseph" and that the appropriate occasion in the history of the Israelite tribes for the formation of the twelve-tribe confederacy was the assembly at Shechem described in Josh. 24; it was at Shechem, Noth argues, that the six-tribe "Leah" confederacy combined with the "house of Joseph" and with other elements to form the familiar twelve-tribe system. These contentions are not in themselves inherently improbable, but they seem to me to carry a somewhat diminished degree of probability as compared with the conclusions reached in the earlier part of his study.

Here let me interject that if in this paper I agree with some of the criticisms of Noth's position which others have made, or myself express doubt about the strength of some of his conclusions, this should in no way be taken to imply disrespect for Noth's work. A return to his creative study has impressed me afresh with the thoroughness with which he carried out his inquiry and the fairness with which he expressed his conclusions. He himself admitted that his hypothesis of an early Israelite amphictyony did not admit of mathematical proof. What I am concerned to discover is whether particular elements in the hypothesis are further removed from certainty than others and how that variable degree of probability affects the hypothesis as a whole. In the present instance, then, we should note that the suggestion that the amphictyony was brought into existence as the result of some historical happening which affected the lives of its constituent members is in itself reasonable, but not definitely proven of the Israelite amphictyony, and further, that the view that the formal union of the members into a sacral confederacy on the occasion of the assembly at Shechem depends on an interpretation of Josh. 24 which, while not in itself unreasonable, is open to question.

III. But, granted the validity of Noth's conclusions about the ancient origin of the fixed twelve-tribe system, and even accepting provisionally his conjecture that the twelve tribes were formally linked in the manner described at the assembly at Shechem, may the resultant "confederacy" be fitly described as an "amphictyony"?

(a) It has been objected that there is in fact no Hebrew expression corresponding to "amphictyony" (ἀμφικτυονία). It is, of course, possible to have the reality without the name. But when we consider the range of words describing family, social, and national groups in the Old Testament, it would indeed be strange if an institution allegedly so fundamental to the early constitution of Israel was in fact anonymous, or else had a name which is now lost without trace.[24] It might, indeed, be claimed that the word "Israel" itself is the required term. Against this suggestion Fohrer has objected that a name compounded with "El" and not "Yahweh" is a quite inappropriate label for a confederacy whose chief bond of union was the worship of Yahweh.[25]

This argument seems to me to be of dubious force, since the name "Israel" is, on the Old Testament evidence, closely linked with the worship of Yahweh. The decisive argument against accepting "Israel" as the Hebrew counterpart of "amphictyony" is simply that "Israel" is a proper noun, whereas what we are looking for is a common noun. To take a parallel from ancient Greece, what we require is not a counterpart to "Pylae-Delphi" or to "Calaurea" or to "Panionium" (which is what "Israel" gives us), but a counterpart to the word "amphictyony" (ἀμφικτυονία). So far as I have been able to discover, there are only three possible candidates: 'am, ḳāhāl, and 'ēḏâh. Whether they, or any other Old Testament terms which might be suggested, are appropriate terms to apply to an Israelite amphictyony is another matter.[26]

(b) But, even if there is not a legitimate Hebrew counterpart to

[24] Fohrer, *op. cit.*, cols. 806-7.

[25] *Ibid.*, col. 807.

[26] When part of the present study was read at the 44th Winter Meeting of the British Society for Old Testament Study (January 1969), the suggestion was made in the ensuing discussion that the Hebrew equivalent of "amphictyony" is šiḇṭê Yiśrāēl. But this does not convey the specific sense of "amphictyony" and is open to the objection advanced above against "Israel." None of the terms used to describe Israel as the wife, son, vine, or vineyard of Yahweh is relevant to the present discussion.

"amphictyony," the crucial question is, "Was there *in fact* an Israelite amphictyony during the period of the judges, or at any earlier period (since, by definition, the amphictyony ceased to have an independent existence after the creation of the Israelite monarchical state)? Do the Israelite tribes, in their mutual relations and in their cult and organization, display the characteristics of an amphictyony?"

Noth applied the term "amphictyony" to the league of Israelite tribes by direct analogy with the amphictyonies of the ancient Greco-Italian world. Of these the most notable was the amphictyony of Pylae-Delphi which, corresponding to its double name, had not one but two sanctuaries—the temple of Demeter at Pylae and the temple of Apollo at Delphi. It consisted, at least as a concept, of twelve *ethne,* not *cities,* from which were drawn the representatives who met in the amphictyonic council. Others in the Greek world were that of Delos (temple of Apollo), that of Onchestus in Boeotia (temple of Poseidon), that of Calaurea (temple of Poseidon), the Panionium, a league of twelve Ionian cities on the coast of Asia Minor (temple of Poseidon at Mycale), the league of six Dorian cities (temple of Apollo at Cnidus), and the six Triphylian cities (temple of Poseidon). In Italy there was the Etruscan league of *duodecim populi,* serving the temple of Voltumna and celebrating a cultic festival in the spring (Livy, I, 8, 3), and the Bruttian league of *duodecim populi* (Livy, XXV, 1, 2).

It will be noted that the numbers twelve and six recur in several of these confederacies. The parallel with biblical groups of twelve and six has been noticed, as we have seen, by Ewald. Noth took further what he believed to be the implications of the similarity, transferring, as Weber had done, the term "amphictyony" to the Hebraic situation. It was the occurrence of the numerical similarity which was the basis of his further deductions. But it has been questioned whether the similarity was as close as he held and also whether the deductions were valid.

(c) The existence of the twelve-tribe system with its six-tribe kernel was, as we have seen above, the clearest outcome of Noth's basic investigation. But it is not clear that in the Greco-Italian world the existence of an amphictyony was characterized by any specific number. The Calaurian league had seven members. The Boeotian league (776-387 B.C.) is variously reported as having had ten, eleven, and twelve members. It seems that Noth's insistence on the importance of the numbers twelve and six was exaggerated.

(d) It has, moreover, been questioned whether the inference

that a social and religious phenomenon found in the Greco-Italian world also existed in the very different milieu of the ancient Near East. It is a hazardous assumption in default of more definite evidence than is available. There are, it is true, in the Old Testament twelvefold lists of the ancestors of peoples other than Israelites: the Aramaeans (Gen. 22:20-24), the Ishmaelites (Gen. 26:13-16), the Edomites (Gen. 26:10-14), and the Arabians (Gen. 25:2). But these lists are not accompanied by any reference to any of the characteristics and activities of amphictyonies. They are simply lists of names, with no allusion to a common sanctuary or to cultic, administrative, or military functions. There does not appear to be any evidence of the existence of an amphictyony in any ancient Near Eastern community outside Israel (*pace* W. W. Hallo, "A Sumerian Amphictyony," *JCS* XIV (1960), 88-114) either as a borrowing or as an independent development.[27] Indeed, it has been argued by B. D. Rahtjen that the only phenomenon resembling an amphictyony of which we have evidence on Canaanite soil is the Philistine Pentapolis. Like practically all the Greek amphictyonies, it consisted of *cities,* not tribes. Its central sanctuary (so Rahtjen alleges) was a temple (at Ashdod, and, earlier, at Gaza), not, like the Israelite one, on Noth's view, an object such as the Ark. Even if not all of Rahtjen's contentions about the nature of the presumed Philistine amphictyony are acceptable, he has presented a strong *prima facie* case for the view that the Philistine pattern resembles that found in the amphictyonies of ancient Greece and Italy much more closely than anything for which we have evidence in ancient Israel. He may not have conclusively demonstrated that the Philistine cities formed an amphictyony. But his arguments underline the fact that much of the supposed case for the existence in ancient Israel of an amphictyony is in the nature of deductive inference and even of speculation. What might seem to be a secure point of similarity with the Greek and Italian amphictyonies (the occurrence of the numbers twelve and six) is, as we have seen, of dubious validity.

IV. The existence of a central sanctuary was vital for the ancient amphictyonies. The duties of the members of an amphictyony included the care, in due rotation, of such a sanctuary, which formed the cultic and administrative or legal center of its life. There the annual festivals were held. There the representatives (ἱερομνήμονες) of the members assembled. There the amphictyonic law was promulgated. According to Noth, the central sanctuary was where the

---

[27] Cf. Fohrer, *op. cit.,* cols. 807-8.

Ark was (indeed, the Ark itself was the central sanctuary), the *neśi'im* (Num. 1:5-15) were the amphictyonic representatives; and parts of the Book of the Covenant (cultic and moral stipulations) formed the amphictyonic law.[28] The central shrine was originally at Shechem, where, if the interpretation of Josh. 24 mentioned above is correct, the amphictyony came into being. Later it was transferred to Bethel (Judg. 20:18, 26-27; 21:2), then to Gilgal, and finally to Shiloh (I Sam. 3:3).

A vigorous assault on the idea that there was any cultic, legal, or administrative centralization in the period of the judges has been launched by H. Orlinsky.[29] He claims that in the book of Judges, which refers to the period in which the amphictyony is presumed to have existed, we hear of judges who were local, whose activity was evoked by outer pressures and not by internal and domestic needs, and who do not appear to have been associated with a central shrine (they were not amphictyons). There is no mention of an amphictyonic meeting at a central sanctuary: In Judg. 19–21 the avengers take counsel at Mizpah, though the Ark was at Bethel (20:27). In the account of the rallying of the various contingents in Judg. 4–5, there is no mention of either central shrine or Ark.[30] In general, he holds that conditions in the period of the judges made for local independence rather than even partial centralization implied by an amphictyonic arrangement, and further, that the early Israelite conception of God was incompatible with the exclusive centralization of worship at a single shrine. In the patriarchal period God made his presence known in different localities; and in the period of the judges worship was offered at a number of places. Hence, Orlinsky argues, an amphictyonic arrangement was inappropriate for Israel.

This last contention appears to be based on a misunderstanding of Noth's position. Noth did not hold that worship was offered solely at a central sanctuary. Indeed, he expressly stated that the law requiring all males to "see the face of Yahweh" three times in the year, at the annual agricultural festivals, referred to the local shrines and not to the central shrine.[31] But that apart, the indictment is indeed a formidable one. Even if Orlinsky's picture of conditions during

---

[28] *System*, pp. 94-95, 97 ff.

[29] "The Tribal System of Israel and Related Groups in the Period of the Judges," *Studies and Essays in Honor of Abraham A. Neuman* (1962), pp. 375 ff.

[30] It should be remembered that Noth rejected the Song of Deborah as a source of knowledge about the tribal system (*System*, pp. 5-6, 36).

[31] *System*, pp. 97-98; *History*, pp. 97-98.

the period is unduly dark, suggesting almost disintegration rather than the mere absence of centralization, it is not easy to discern the amount of cultic and organizational centralization required by the amphictyonic theory. As has been noted above, Noth held that the true central shrine was the Ark, and that the place where it was for the time being became the central point for the life of the amphictyony. There is, however, no explicit reference to the presence of the Ark at Shechem, the center where, according to Noth, the amphictyony was established. We hear of it at Gilgal (Josh. 3–4; 7:6); and the reference to the celebration of the Passover there (Josh. 6:10-12) and to the circumcising of the people (Josh. 5:2-9) may well point to a close connection between Gilgal and the covenant. There is also mention of the Ark's having been at Bethel (Judg. 20:27-28). But it is principally at Shiloh and its temple that we hear of the presence of the Ark (I Sam. 3–4; cf. Josh. 18:1; Judg. 18:31; Jer. 7:12).

Any indications that there may be in the book of Judges of a possible series of central sanctuaries at different times are at best slight and inconclusive. The question has been subjected to a thorough and judicious investigation by W. H. Irwin.[32] At the outset he rightly emphasizes the cardinal importance for the amphictyonic hypothesis of a common central sanctuary, and not unfairly comments that on this matter Noth's argument is *"grandement déductive."* [33] Irwin's cautious conclusion is that the evidence that such a sanctuary existed is at best fragmentary, but that, on the other hand, it is impossible to demonstrate that such a sanctuary did *not* exist. What is abundantly clear is that precisely at this point of cardinal importance the analogy with the Greek and Italian parallels is seen to be ominously weak. There is no adequate evidence of a simple chronological succession in the traditions about the various sanctuaries. Furthermore, the traditions which describe the period of the judges and the religious conditions then prevailing do not support the hypothesis that the Israelite tribes had a common central sanctuary.[34]

[32] "Le sanctuaire central israélite avant l'établissement de la monarchie," *RB* LXXII (1965), 161-84.

[33] *Ibid.*, pp. 161-62.

[34] *Ibid.*, pp. 182-83. Out of the extensive literature about the alleged central sanctuary and the relation to it of the Ark (a literature too voluminous to be adequately reviewed here), reference may be made to the important and stimulating discussion given by R. Smend in *Jahwekrieg und Stämmebund; Erwägungen zur ältesten Geschichte Israels, FRLANT* LXXXIX (2nd ed., 1966), 56 ff., where

Even more exiguous is the evidence that in the period of the judges tribal representatives met at the central sanctuary. Noth held that the appropriate Hebrew term for such a representative was *nāśî'*, and his discussion of it is closely linked with his comments on the use of *ḳāhāl* and *'ēḏāh* to which we shall return. *nāśî'* can have the quite general sense of "leader," "prince" (e.g., Gen. 34:2). Noth's discussion of the term centers on the frequent and particular use of it in Ezekiel and in passages usually attributed to P. In Ezekiel it is applied to rulers of whom it is not thought appropriate to use the term *meleḵ*, which in Ezekiel is reserved almost exclusively for the Egyptian Pharaoh and the great kings of Mesopotamia. Noth argues that this application of the word is later than and derived from its use in P, and that in the majority of the P passages (particularly Num. 1:5-15; 2; 7) the word denotes a tribal representative who had consultative and sacral responsibilities. There is nothing inherently improbable in Noth's contention that these passages embody ancient tradition, and that the word *nāśî'* in this sense reflects not simply exilic or post-exilic usage but something considerably more ancient. But his claim that the more general sense of the word in Ezekiel is secondary to its alleged sense in the P passages is not self-evidently true. Indeed, one may question whether the application of the term in P is quite as specific as Noth maintains. The persons referred to do indeed represent the twelve tribes and do carry out a sacral function in that they present offerings from their respective tribes (Num. 7). If it is assumed or proved that early Israel was an amphictyony, then these representatives will fit into the amphictyonic pattern. But if, as has been argued above, the amphictyonic hypothesis is open to question because the case for it rests in part on unproven assumptions and parallels which are of doubtful validity, then the references to these representatives add little or nothing to the supporting arguments. Indeed, one may go further and take note of Orlinsky's trenchant observation[35] that the term *nāśî'* occurs nowhere in the book of Judges, "the book that is alleged to have sprung from an amphictyonic society." The no-

---

it is argued that the central sanctuary was independent of the presence of the Ark. The associated problem of the Holy War, with which Smend's work also deals, is not discussed above, since the aim of the present study is to examine what appear to be the essential features in Noth's hypothesis and not the ramifications of derivative and kindred hypotheses.

[35] Orlinsky, *op. cit.*, pp. 378-79, n. 2. On the term *nāśî'*, see further H. Cazelles, *Études sur le code de l'alliance* (1946), pp. 81-82, 137-38; W. H. Irwin, *op. cit.*, p. 169; E. A. Speiser, "Background and Function of the Biblical Nāśî'," *CBQ* XXV (1963), 111 ff.

toriously inconclusive argument from silence must here be allowed to carry considerable weight.

The same argument cannot be brought with equal force against Noth's theory that the term "judge of Israel" points to an institutional office in the amphictyony of the premonarchic period.[36] The expression occurs in the Old Testament only once, viz., in Mic. 4:14 (*EVV* v.1), where, so Noth holds, it probably refers not to the king but to the holder of an ancient office which had survived from the time of the judges through the monarchic period. Noth suggests that the so-called "minor judges" of Judges 10:1-5; 12:7-15 were "judges of Israel" in this sense. Though they are not exactly so described, they are said to have "judged Israel." The fact that the references to them are not couched in deuteronomistic style and do not conform to the deuteronomistic chronological pattern suggests that they are independent, and possibly ancient, historical fragments. But it remains open to question whether the statement that these men "judged Israel" means that each of them held an amphictyonic office relating to the whole Israelite confederacy, and that this does not apply to others who in the book of Judges are said to have "judged Israel" (Othniel, 3:10; Deborah, 4:4; Samson, 15:20). Even if these questions are answered in terms favorable to Noth's theory of the nature of the office, the office itself fits into an amphictyonic system only if the latter is presupposed on those other grounds which, if the general argument above is sound, are less than convincing.[37]

Orlinsky has protested [38] against the anachronistic misuse of the term "charisma" in connection with the period of the judges. It might further be claimed that the term "amphictyony" has come to exercise its own peculiar "charismatic" influence in scholarly discussion about the organization of early Israel, inhibiting critical scrutiny of inferences drawn from Noth's original hypothesis. As a technical term drawn from environments very different from those of ancient Israel, its use in relation to Israel begs questions rather than answers them.[39] Noth did indeed adduce good grounds for the view that a twelve-tribe system existed in the premonarchic period.

[36] "Das Amt des 'Richters Israels,'" *Festschrift Alfred Bertholet* (1950), pp. 404-17.

[37] On the presumed office of judge of Israel, see further, K.-D. Schunck, "Die Richter Israels und ihr Amt," *Supplements to VT* XV, *Volume du Congrès Genève* (1965, 1966), 252 ff.; D. A. McKenzie, "The Judge of Israel," *VT* XVII (1967), 118 ff.

[38] *Op. cit.,* p. 377, n. 1.

[39] Cf. G. Buccellati, *Cities and Nations of Ancient Syria* (1967), pp. 114-16.

But there appears to be little evidence of the distinctive features of an amphictyony. Centralization was a problem or an elusive ideal during the period of the judges rather than a dominant factor in the life of the Israelite tribes. That the Ark conferred a special status on any place in which it was located is by no means an implausible theory which accords well with its later history and, in particular, with its relation to Jerusalem and its Temple. But of its locations in the period from Joshua to Samuel, we have only scraps of evidence; nor have we anything more substantial concerning a central sanctuary or a succession of sanctuaries. The indications are not so much of centralization and unity as of the fragments of a unity not yet realized, or rather of a lost unity surviving as an ideal. A unity which survived the adverse conditions of the period of the judges was as old as, or older than, the settlement. Noth's view that the Israelite confederacy (a term which may be used in preference to "amphictyony") came into existence as an aftermath of the invasion of the land by "the house of Joseph" under Joshua is an inference drawn in part from general considerations and in part from one interpretation of the highly problematical last chapter of Joshua. The indications, however, are that there was little or no effective centralization during the period from Joshua to Saul. Further, the narratives about the rise and early history of the monarchy presuppose an already existing consciousness of Israelite unity. It seems natural, therefore, to look for the establishment of this unity, not in the emergence of an amphictyony on Canaanite soil in the wake of the invasion, but rather, where so much ancient Israelite tradition would lead us to expect to find it, in the period before the settlement, and, more specifically, in the establishment of the Sinai covenant between Yahweh and the Israelite tribes. Such an assertion, thus briefly made, bypasses much elaborate argument about the early history and relationships of the tribes.[40]

[40] A cogently argued and fully documented survey of the problems involved, leading to conclusions similar to those advanced above, is to be found in A. D. H. Mayes, *Amphictyony and Covenant: A Study of Israel in the Pre-Monarchy Period* (1969 [Edinburgh doctoral thesis, hitherto unpublished]). A key question is whether Judah formed part of Israel at any time before the establishment of the monarchy. My own view, which cannot here be argued in detail, is that it did, in spite of the indications in parts of Judges (and esp. chaps. 4 and 5) that any connection which Judah may have had during that period with the tribes of the center and north was at best tenuous. This state of affairs following a settlement by Judah in the south of the country independently of the invasion under Joshua, is compatible with an earlier association of Judah with the "Joseph" tribes during the wilderness period. The case is argued by Mayes. See also R. Smend, "Gehörte Juda zum vorstaatlichen Israel?" *Fourth World Congress of Jewish Studies*, I (1967), 57 ff. and the literature there cited.

But it is not the purpose of the present study to investigate tribal origins or to trace tribal history. Its aim is, rather, to inquire whether the theory of an amphictyony in the period before the monarchy adequately accounts for Israel's self-consciousness. If the arguments advanced are sound, and if Israel's consciousness of itself as a unity (a union of tribes) dates from the period before the settlement, then to look for the establishment of that unity elsewhere than in the institution of the Sinai covenant is to disregard the testimony of tradition in the interests of airborne guesswork. But to find the origins of Israelite unity in the Sinai covenant is not to exclude the admission to it, after the invasion, of diverse elements, tribal and other. Of this, Josh. 24 may well contain a record.

It remains to consider briefly the relevant terminology. It has been argued above that no word or phrase applied to Israel in the Old Testament may fairly be regarded as corresponding to ἀμφικτυονία. The three principal terms which call for consideration are ʿam, ḳāhāl, and ʿēḏâh. All three have been the subject of studies by L. Rost [41] to which reference may be made for details.

ʿam may be applied to an individual as a term of kinship (Gen. 19:38), or to a community as a *"kollektiver Verwandtschaftsbegriff"* (so Rost), though it would be idle to claim that the idea of kinship is present in every collective application of the term. It may be applied to the men of the community who are capable of bearing arms (1 Kings 20:15), or to the community assembled for juridical (Jer. 26:9) or cultic purposes (Judg. 21:4; 1 Kings 21:9; Jer. 36:9). It is not applied exclusively to Israel (cf. Num. 21:29; Amos 1:5). But it is applied to Israel with great frequency and in phrases which express Israel's special relationship to Yahweh: ʿam sᵉgullâh (Deut. 7:6; 14:2; 26:18); ʿam naḥᵃlâh (Deut. 4:20; 9:26, 29; Ps. 28:9); ʿam ḳāḏôš (Deut. 7:6). Thus it may fairly be regarded as a term applied to Israel par excellence and as expressing in many contexts Israel's special relationship to Yahweh. It may, but need not, have a cultic reference. There is nothing to suggest that the term carries any "amphictyonic" implication.

Noth argued [42] that although the words ḳāhāl and ʿēḏâh occur for the most part in later passages, in their technical sense of congregation or assembly as applied to Israel they are survivals of the usage of the ancient Israelite amphictyony. Although both terms may be used in

[41] "Die Bezeichnungen für Land und Volk im Alten Testament," in *Festschrift Otto Procksch* (1934), pp. 125 ff., esp. pp. 141 ff.; *Die Vorstufen von Kirche und Synagoge im Alten Testament, BWANT* IV, 24 (1938).
[42] *System*, pp. 102-3, n. 2.

a more general, and even in a pejorative, sense (e.g., *ḳāhāl* in Gen. 49:6; *'ēḏâh* in Ps. 22:17; *EVV* 16), they refer predominantly to Israel. From his exhaustive survey of the occurrences, Rost concludes that both terms are applied to Israel when assembled for cultic or juridical purposes; but, whereas *ḳāhāl* may also be used of Israel assembled for war, in P the word *'ēḏâh* is avoided in such context and replaced by *'am*. His analysis of the applications of *'ēḏâh* to Israel in P indicate a religious assembly, gathered around the tent of meeting, and divided into tribes and fathers' houses, with Moses presiding over the entire gathering, and with a *nāśî'* at the head of each tribe and a *rō'š* at the head of each father's house. It must be admitted that in this picture there are features which are appropriate to the amphictyonic hypothesis as presented by Noth. But (a) the picture does not *require* the amphictyonic hypothesis, and (b) while it is *possible* that P here reflects ancient usage of the word *'ēḏâh*, it is far from proven; and whether it is held to be *probable* depends on one's general attitude to the amphictyonic hypothesis. For *ḳāhāl* no similar case can be made.

All three terms (*'am, ḳāhāl, 'ēḏâh*) merit much fuller discussion as expressions of Israel's self-understanding as the people of Yahweh. My present purpose is not to draw out their full meaning, but simply to argue that, as applied to Israel, they have no necessary reference to an amphictyony. Seen in historical perspective, none of them is incompatible with the view maintained above; namely, that the ideal unity of Israel, which survived the divisive influence of the period of the judges, the disruption of the kingdom, and the dispersion, was based on the Sinai covenant.

I have great pleasure in offering this short study, such as it is, as a tribute to Professor Herbert G. May, in respect for his scholarship and in gratitude for his friendship.

Were There an Ancient Historical Credo in Israel and an Independent Sinai Tradition?

J. PHILIP HYATT

Gerhard von Rad published in 1938 a monograph which has had great influence on Old Testament scholarship, especially in the study of the origins of the Hexateuch and of the relationship of the Israelite cult to the origin and preservation of Israel's traditions. This monograph had the title, *Das formgeschichtliche Problem des Hexateuch* [1]; it was reprinted in von Rad's *Gesammelte Studien zum Alten Testament* in 1958,[2] and an English translation appeared in 1966.[3] The views developed in that monograph form the basis of many of his views in the first volume of his *Old Testament Theology*.[4]

Closely related to the theories of von Rad are those of Martin Noth, presented especially in his *Überlieferungsgeschichte des Pentateuch*,[5] the historical implications of which are developed in his *History of Israel*.[6] The views of these two scholars are not identical, but they are similar, the differences being of minimal importance.

Von Rad begins his monograph with a consideration of the nature

---

[1] *BWANT*, 4. Folge, Heft 26. Stuttgart, 1938.

[2] Theologische Bücherei: Neudrucke und Berichte aus dem 20. Jahrhundert, Vol. VIII, *Altes Testament* (Munich, 1958), pp. 9-86.

[3] "The Form-Critical Problem of the Hexateuch," in *The Problem of the Hexateuch and Other Essays*. Trans. by E. W. Trueman Dicken (Edinburgh and London, 1966), pp. 1-78. This is referred to in the following pages as *Problem*, with the page numbers of this English translation. In some instances, however, I quote the German used by von Rad.

[4] Trans. by D. M. G. Stalker (New York, 1962 [based on the first German ed. of 1957 and including revisions for the 2nd German ed.]). See esp. pp. 121-25.

[5] Stuttgart, 1948.

[6] New York, 1958 (based on the 2nd German ed.). A 2nd English ed. appeared in 1960.

of the cultic prayer in Deut. 26:5b-9. This purports to be the words which were to be spoken by an individual as he brought his firstfruits of the ground to the temple; it immediately precedes a statement about the paying of the tithes of the third year. This prayer is really a confession of faith,[7] or rather "an enumeration of the saving facts [*Heilstatsachen*] which were the constitutive element of the religious community."[8] It is in fact a Credo, and "probably the earliest recognizable example." The designation "short historical Credo" used by von Rad is the name by which this section of Deuteronomy has often been referred to since his monograph appeared.

Von Rad then finds this same literary type (*Gattung*) in two other places: Deut. 6:20-24 and Joshua's speech to the gathering at Shechem in Josh. 24:2b-13, which he says "may be described as already a Hexateuch in miniature."[9] In these he finds the major features of the *Heilsgeschichte* from the Patriarchal period to the entrance into the Promised Land. The minor accretions are of small significance.

Von Rad next studies a group of passages in which he finds free adaptations of the historical Credo, especially in cult lyrics. These are 1 Sam. 12:8; Ps. 136; the Song of the Red Sea in Exod. 15; Pss. 105, 78, 135, and 106. In the last four the poems become wider in scope and are less tied to the traditional pattern. Ps. 106 is exilic or possibly even post-exilic. As he says in his *Old Testament Theology*, these later passages show a tendency toward epic elaboration and reflection.[10]

There is one fact which stands out in these historical creeds or summaries: the absence of any mention of the events at Sinai, except in Ps. 106. Von Rad believes that the earliest example in the Old Testament of the working of the Sinai story into the canonical *Heilsgeschichte* is the great prayer of Neh. 9:6-37. The revelation at Sinai is referred to in vss. 13-14. At this stage the *Gattung* of the historical Credo falls apart, for the historical summary begins with creation and goes down to post-exilic times.

Von Rad sees the Sinai pericope as a tradition that developed independently of the other Hexateuchal traditions. One reason for this is the omission of the Sinai tradition from the historical Credo and summaries to which we have just referred. But there are other reasons. He points to the view held long ago by Wellhausen that one form of

[7] Justification for translating *Thodah* as "confession of faith," rather than as "thanksgiving" is given in von Rad, *Old Testament Theology*, I, 357.

[8] *Problem*, pp. 4-5.

[9] *Ibid.*, p. 8.

[10] P. 123.

the tradition preserved in Exodus had the Israelites going directly from the Red Sea to Kadesh, without an expedition to Sinai (see esp. Exod. 15:22b, 25b). Furthermore, following Gressmann, he thinks that the cycle of Sinai narratives in Exod. 19–24, 32–34 is both preceded and followed by Kadesh narratives (Exod. 17–18; Num. 10–15). The Sinai pericope has been worked into the longer narrative only by editorial manipulation in Num. 10:29 ff. Also, von Rad points to the well-known difficulty in analyzing the sources of the Sinai pericope. In his opinion the Sinai tradition existed independently until it was worked into the scheme of the Hexateuch by the Yahwist, probably in the time of Solomon. The Sinai tradition was originally, in his opinion, the festival legend used at Shechem in the ceremony of covenant renewal in the autumn, at the time of the festival of Booths. The settlement tradition, on the other hand, was the cult legend of the festival of Weeks, originating at the Gilgal sanctuary.

Martin Noth expanded the work of von Rad, to which he refers generally with approval, in his *Überlieferungsgeschichte des Pentateuch*. In his view there were five main themes in the traditions which were combined to make the Pentateuch: the Exodus from Egypt, the leading into Canaan, the promise to the Patriarchs, the leading in the wilderness, and the revelation at Sinai. These main themes were filled out and linked together by various individual traditions, such as those of the Egyptian plagues, the encounter with Midianites, the apostasy in making the golden calf, the story of Caleb at Hebron, and others. The tradition concerning the Exodus is the oldest of all, and the kernel about which the Pentateuchal narratives were formed; the revelation at Sinai was the latest. Noth thinks the story of the revelation at Sinai is basically historical but originally concerned a group different from those who came out of Egypt. On the basis of Nabataean inscriptions found in the southern part of the Sinai peninsula, especially at the entrances to the massif of the Jebel Serbal, deriving from Nabataean pilgrims of the second and third centuries A.D., he conjectures that in this district there had been a sacred mountain "from time immemorial" that may have been the Sinai of the ancient Israelite tradition.[11] Yet, Moses was not connected with the Sinai tradition in its original form. According to Noth, he is to be associated only with the phase of the preparations for the occupation of Canaan by the tribes of central Palestine. In the view of von Rad, it was the Yahwist who first worked the Sinai traditions into the over-

[11] *History of Israel,* pp. 126-37.

all scheme of the Hexateuch. Noth, on the other hand, posits the existence of a *Grundlage* (G) before the time of J and E. This *Grundlage* contained the traditions common to J and E, but Noth is uncertain whether it existed in oral or in written form. In either case it contained the essentials of the Sinai story.

The year 1938 was not an auspicious year for a German scholar to publish a monograph breaking new ground in the study of the Hexateuch; one has only to recall the international situation at that time. It is not surprising that von Rad's monograph apparently remained largely unknown outside Germany for several years. In 1950, G. Ernest Wright published a paper entitled "Recent European Study in the Pentateuch" in *The Journal of Bible and Religion*,[12] devoted to a survey and brief critique of four books by von Rad and Noth. At that time he depended upon von Rad's German commentary on Gen. 1–12:9 (published in 1949) for information concerning von Rad's views on the composition of the Hexateuch, saying that von Rad's earlier book, *Das formgeschichtliche Problem des Hexateuch,* was not available to him. However, with the clearing of the international situation after World War II and the publication of further work by von Rad and Noth, their views became well known. Those of von Rad which we have sketched above appear to have been rather widely accepted in this country, but perhaps not so widely on the European continent and in Britain. They have not always been accepted as a whole. The view that Deut. 26:5b-9 constitutes an ancient historical Credo that was the nucleus of the Hexateuch has been more widely embraced than the view that the Sinai tradition was originally an independent tradition which was only later worked into the whole.

G. Ernest Wright, in the article cited above, expressed general approval of von Rad's thesis concerning the brief historical Credo in Deut. 26, but expressed reservations concerning the complete independence of the Sinai tradition. In subsequent writings he has taken the same position.[13] Von Rad's view regarding Deut. 26:5-9 and related passages has been adopted in two books which are frequently used as textbooks by college and seminary classes.[14] The extent to

---

[12] XVIII (1950), 216-25.

[13] E.g., "The Faith of Israel," *IB* I, 350-51, *Exegesis of Deuteronomy, IB* II, 483-85.

[14] B. W. Anderson, *Understanding the Old Testament*, 2nd ed. (Englewood Cliffs, 1966), pp. 9-11; Walter Harrelson, *Interpreting the Old Testament* (New York, 1964), pp. 9, 36. See also B. D. Napier, *Song of the Vineyard* (New York, 1962), p. 4, and G. W. Anderson, *A Critical Introduction to the Old Testament* (London, 1959), p. 56.

which this view has been popularized in some quarters may be illustrated by the following quotation from the brief introduction to the Pentateuch in *The Oxford Annotated Bible:*

> The Pentateuch embraces a great diversity of material which reflects Israel's pilgrimage from the time of Abraham to the Exile. The whole tradition, however, has been shaped by basic themes found essentially in the confession of faith preserved in Dt. 26:5-10 (compare Josh. ch. 24). The Pentateuch may be regarded as an elaboration of this creedal statement, according to the interests and insights of various circles of tradition.[15]

The views of von Rad and Noth have been attractively presented, and to some extent they have much inherent plausibility. However, they have not been adopted by many scholars and have been subjected to careful criticism by some. It is the purpose of the present paper to present in summary form the criticisms which have been made of the views sketched above, by Artur Weiser,[16] C. H. W. Brekelmans,[17] Leonhard Rost,[18] and Georg Fohrer[19] (listed in order of their publication), together with some criticisms of my own. I hope that this essay may contribute something to the continuing debate over the important questions raised by the views of von Rad and Noth.

I.

One of the basic foundations of von Rad's view is the great antiquity of the confessional statement in Deut. 26:5-9. His view requires that the confession originate before the time of the Yahwist, whom he assigns to the period of Solomon, and in all likelihood in the period of the settlement in Canaan or, as it is often called, the time of the amphictyony. Von Rad's statement is as follows: "All the evidence points to the fact that this prayer is very much older, both in form

---

[15] P. xxiv (written by B. W. Anderson).

[16] *The Old Testament: Its Formation and Development* (New York, 1961 [based on the 4th German ed., 1957]), pp. 83-90. (Cf. 6th German ed., 1966, pp. 81-88.)

[17] "Het 'historische Credo' van Israël," *TvT* III (1963), 1-11.

[18] *Das kleine Credo und andere Studien zum Alten Testament* (Heidelberg, 1965), pp. 11-25. The lead essay in this volume is published here for the first time; the other essays are reprints of previously published articles.

[19] *Introduction to the Old Testament.* Initiated by Ernst Sellin. Completely revised and rewritten by Georg Fohrer. Trans. by David E. Green (Nashville, 1968 [based on the 10th German ed., 1965]). Because this volume has been so completely revised and rewritten by Fohrer, it must be considered as his work.

and content, than the literary context into which it has since been inserted." [20] A footnote to this sentence says, "The rhythmical and alliterative character of the opening phrases in particular reveals its antiquity." Here the reference is to the opening phrases in the Hebrew: *'arammî 'ōbhēdh 'ābhî wayyēredh miṣráyemâ wayyāghār shām bimethê mecāṭ.* Von Rad recognizes clearly that there is deuteronomic phraseology in vss. 5-9, especially in the latter half of the prayer. But he speaks of this as being only *deuteronomische Über-malung* ("the deuteronomic editor's retouching"). He remarks that one might "even be so bold as to remove the traces of the deuteronomic editor's retouching and to attempt a reconstruction of the original formula," but he does not make such an attempt himself. It is more important in his opinion to "determine whether the present association of the prayer with the presentation of the first-fruits is original or whether it was effected only at a later stage," and he chooses the former alternative.

The question of the extent and significance of the deuteronomic phraseology in this passage is taken up in detail by Rost.[21] He submits the language of the passage to careful study and is able to show that many words and phrases occur only, or frequently and most characteristically, in late texts (that is, approximately of the seventh century and later). Rost discusses seventeen words and phrases, of which the following are the more significant [22]:

(1) *bimethê mecāṭ* "few in number" occurs elsewhere only in Deut. 28:62. (Other phrases with similar meaning do occur; e.g., *methê mispār* in Gen. 34:30 [J]; Deut. 4:27; Jer. 44:28; Ps. 105:12; 1 Chron. 16:19.)

(2) "a nation, great, mighty, and populous" occurs only here in its "baroque" form, with piling up of adjectives. Shorter phrases with various combinations occur elsewhere, as early as J.

(3) *rc* in the hifil is construed with the accusative (here *'ōthānû*) only here and in 1 Sam. 25:34; it is construed with *le* in Num. 20:15; Josh. 24:20.

(4) "hard bondage" occurs, with the exception of 1 Kings 12:4, only in P (Exod. 1:14; 6:9).

---

[20] *Problem,* p. 4. Cf. G. von Rad, *Deuteronomy: A Commentary* (Philadelphia, 1966), pp. 157-59.

[21] *Das kleine Credo,* pp. 12-14.

[22] The English renderings are from RSV; the Hebrew is given only when it is significant. I follow Rost's practice of giving the word or phrase as it appears in Deut. 26:5-9, although of course there are sometimes slight variations in parallel passages. Unfortunately there is a small number of errors in Rost's references which I am not able to rectify.

(5) "and sojourned there" occurs in the Old Testament a total of fifteen times; of that total, eight occurrences are here, Deut. 18:6 and in the Baruch biography of Jeremiah (Jer. 35:7; 42:15, 17, 22; 43:2; 44:8, 12, 14).

(6) "the God of our fathers" occurs in J and E four times but with special frequency in the introductory and concluding speeches of Deuteronomy, and otherwise in deuteronomistic or post-exilic passages, particularly in the work of the Chronicler.

(7) J says that God sees the suffering of men, but the nouns $^{c}\bar{a}ni$ and $^{c}\bar{a}m\bar{a}l$ occur together only in Ps. 25:18; $^{c}\bar{a}m\bar{a}l$ and $lahas$ occur only in Ps. 44:25 and the three together only here.

(8) The leading out of Egypt is common to all the Pentateuchal sources, but it is a theologoumenon that occurs with special frequency in the introductory speeches of Deuteronomy (chaps. 1-11).

(9) "with a mighty hand and an outstretched arm" occurs four times in the introductory speeches of Deuteronomy (4:34; 5:15; 7:19; 11:2), and frequently in Jeremiah and Ezekiel, and in Ps. 136:12; 2 Chron. 6:32.

(10) "with great terror" is otherwise only in Deut. 4:34; Jer. 32:21.

(11) "with signs and wonders" occurs six times in the framework speeches (*Rahmenreden*) of Deuteronomy, otherwise seldom (Deut. 4:34; 6:22; 7:19; 13:2, 3; 28:46; 29:2; 34:11).

(12) That Yahweh brings the people into "this place" (or, more often the "land") is said by J (Exod. 13:5; 23:20; Num. 14:3, 8, 16, 24; 16:14), but it is particularly frequent in the *Rahmenreden* (Deut. 6:10; 7:1; 8:7; 9:28; 11:29; 30:5; 31:20, 21, 23; cf. 14:23, 25; 17:8, 10, etc.).

(13) Likewise, the phrase "flowing with milk and honey" appears in J, but with special frequency in the *Rahmenreden* (Deut. 6:3; 11:9; 26:15; 27:3; 31:20).

The cumulative evidence of Rost's study is impressive. He concludes that the closest parallels to the language of Deut. 26:5-9 are found in the *Rahmenreden* of Deuteronomy and what he calls the Baruch biography of Jeremiah; not with *Urdeuteronomium* or the deuteronomic laws. The date suggested by these literary parallels is shortly before the beginning of the Exile, or in the early years of the Exile. Rost himself prefers the view that the passage originated in the time of Josiah. He sees the reign of Josiah as a time of restoration of old religious practices and strict Yahweh worship after a long period of political submission to foreign powers and adoption of foreign religious practices, beginning about 732 B.C., with a brief interlude in the time of Hezekiah. The reformers under Josiah were influenced by Hosea's polemic against the kingship and idealization of the wilderness period. In such a situation the introduction of Deut. 26:5-10, with its idealization of the older period of the Exodus and wilderness, was natural. He sees this passage as being not so much a confession as a constant reminder of the saving activity of Yahweh and an injunction to the people of Judah not to forget the mighty acts of Yahweh, as generations following the time of Joshua had done.

Rost thinks there may have been a very old formula which consisted only of the following: "An Aramean about to perish was my father, but now I have brought the firstfruits of the ground, which thou, O Yahweh, hast given me." In this offering formula there is a contrast between the Aramean father who was landless, nomadic, and constantly near to catastrophe on the one hand, and the farmer who has come into possession of land, on the other. Rost sees the intervening verses as built up mainly out of the traditions which lie behind passages such as Gen. 15:13-16; Judg. 2:6 ff.; and Deut. 6:20-24.

Whether we agree with all the details of Rost's view or not, his study of the language of the so-called "ancient short historical Credo" should make it extremely doubtful that it is really ancient. It appears rather to be largely a product of the seventh century or early sixth century B.C. Rost may be correct in seeing an old offering formula in part of vss. 5 and 10, but what is left is not a "historical Credo" which could have formed the nucleus of the Hexateuch. Deut. 26:5-9 is a late summary of traditions rather than a very early nucleus of traditions. The evidence which von Rad gives for the antiquity of this passage is meager indeed. The "rhythmical and alliterative character of the opening phrases" surely does not prove the antiquity of the whole passage! Neither alliteration nor rhythm is in itself a guarantee of antiquity. As for the alliteration, it involves only three words (see above) and could be fortuitous rather than intentional.

Von Rad's thesis demands the antiquity of the "Credo" in Deut. 26, as we have seen. It is not clear, however, that his thesis demands equal antiquity for related passages such as Deut. 6:20-24 and Josh. 24:2b-13. As for the latter, he says: "Here too, the text is shot through with all kinds of accretions and embellishments (*allerlei Floskeln und Zutaten*) which are immediately recognizable as deriving from the hexateuchal presentation of history." [23] Yet he insists that Joshua's speech here is not an *ad hoc* composition, but that it uses "a form

[23] *Problem,* p. 22.

which is basically unchangeable and allows liberty of adjustment only in insignificant ways."

A careful reading of Josh. 24:2-13 and Deut. 6:20-24 will show that both are filled with phraseology and ideas characteristic of Deuteronomy and the deuteronomistic histories.[24] The latter in particular must be read in its context (as will be discussed more fully below). The details of the history which are added in Josh. 24:2-13 are hardly as minor and insignificant as von Rad's words suggest.

II.

The German title of von Rad's monograph indicates that it is a study in *Formgeschichte* or, as the term is usually rendered in English, "form-criticism" (it has often been noted that this rendering is not quite accurate, since the German means literally "form history" and the method involves the history of the literary forms as well as their origin and *Sitz im Leben*). His overall purpose is to attempt to show how the Hexateuch reached its present shape. He accepts the classical literary analysis of the Hexateuch and indeed emphasizes the creative genius of the Yahwist (J). His main objective, however, is to get behind the usual literary sources and show some of the steps by which the traditions developed before they were incorporated into the work of J and E. A fundamental part of his thesis is the claim that he has recognized a distinct literary type (*Gattung*) in the "historical Credo." The *Gattung* includes Deut. 26:5b-9; 6:20-24; and Josh. 24:2b-13, and the Psalms and other cult lyrics which he discusses are adaptations of this *Gattung*. He says that the *Gattung* finally breaks down in the late passages (Ps. 106 and Neh. 9:6 ff.)

This aspect of von Rad's thesis has been criticized especially by C. H. W. Brekelmans in the article cited above (note 17). Brekelmans presents various arguments against von Rad's thesis. He too has noted that the vocabulary of the passages in Deut. 6 and 26, and Josh. 24, are strongly deuteronomic or deuteronomistic, but his study of this problem is not so full as Rost's. His principal criticism is that von Rad has not proved the existence of the historical Credo as an independent *Gattung*. Von Rad has, in the opinion of Brekelmans, taken the passages to which he gives this name out of their context. When put into context, the passages must be considered as belonging to other *Gattungen*.

---

[24] On Josh. 24, see esp. Martin Noth, *Das Buch Josua*, 2nd ed. Handbuch zum Alten Testament, I/7 (Tübingen, 1953), 135-41, and John Gray, *Joshua, Judges, and Ruth*. The Century Bible (New York and London, 1967), pp. 32-7, 191-200.

Brekelmans begins with a form-critical study of Deut. 6:20-25. In form this pericope resembles four other passages: Exod. 12:26-27; 13:14-15; Josh. 4:6-7, 21-24. All have a question-and-answer form that he sets out in the following manner[25]:

Exod.	13:14a	And when in time to come your son asks you, "What (means) this?"
	14b	then you shall say to him . . .
	15b	Therefore, I sacrifice to Yahweh . . .
Josh.	4:6b	When your sons ask in time to come, "What (mean) these stones?"
	7a	Then you shall tell them . . .
	7b	And these stones shall be a memorial . . .
Exod.	12:26	And when your sons say to you, "What (means) this service?"
	27a	Then you shall say . . .
Josh.	4:21	When your sons shall ask their fathers in time to come, "What (mean) these stones?"
	22	then you shall inform your sons . . .
Deut.	6:20	When your son shall ask you in time to come, "What (mean) the testimonies and the statutes and the ordinances . . . ?"
	21	Then you shall say to your son . . .
	24	Therefore, Yahweh commanded us to do all these statutes . . .

The similarity of these five passages in form is immediately evident. There are slight variations that are of little significance; e.g. between the singular and plural, "son" or "sons"; and between the use of the verb *shā'al* and the verb *'āmar*. The complete form is as follows: (1) the son(s) ask(s) a question of the father(s); (2) the father(s) replies (reply) with a statement of a historical fact (or facts), and (3) the conclusion shows the relevance of the answer given to the question that was asked.[26] But there is also a great similarity in con-

[25] I follow Brekelmans' order, but the translation is not RSV. I have made a translation that shows more clearly the similarities in form in the Hebrew.

[26] Brekelmans acknowledges his dependence upon J. Alberto Soggin, "Kult-ätiologische Sagen und Katechese im Hexateuch," *VT* X (1960), 341-47. Soggin discusses all the passages, and his conclusions are similar to those of Brekelmans. However, he apparently accepts von Rad's thesis that there was an ancient historical Credo form, and does not see that his study may contribute to the denial of the existence of that form. He points out that Josh. 22:24 begins in the same manner but does not continue with the other elements.

tent. Each passage has to do with the origin or meaning of a cultic practice or place. Exod. 12:26-27 concerns the meaning of the sacrifice of the passover lamb; Exod. 13:14-15 concerns the offering of firstlings (here connected with the passover, probably erroneously); Josh. 4:6-7 concerns the meaning of the stones erected in the Jordan river; Josh. 4:21-22 concerns the stones in the sanctuary at Gilgal; and Deut. 6:20-25 concerns the very origin and meaning of the law. It is possible that these passages originated in the cult. Soggin thinks that these are fragments of an old catechesis (*Katechese*) in which the questions and answers are presented liturgically, since they are not questions which would have originated in normal childish curiosity.[27] He points out, however, that these passages are deuteronomic or in deuteronomistic contexts.[28] This may not be without significance, for while such contexts may preserve old liturgical elements, it is also possible that the liturgical form is of late origin. Deuteronomy lays emphasis upon the teaching of children by the fathers (4:10; 6:7; 11:19). We know too little in detail about the pre-exilic liturgy to be dogmatic on this subject.

In the light of the similarities between Deut. 6:20-25 and the four passages cited, Brekelmans insists that we must consider vss. 21-23 (which contain the so-called historical Credo) as a part of the greater whole, and that those verses must not be separated from the question in vs. 20 and the conclusion set forth in vss. 24-25. Also, we are justified in following him and Soggin in denominating the *Gattung* to which these five passages belong as catechesis or catechetical instruction rather than as historical Credo.

Brekelmans turns next to a consideration of Josh. 24:2b-13. He insists that this passage must be considered within its context of the whole chapter, which describes the ceremony of covenant renewal at Shechem.

As others have done, Brekelmans compares the account here with the form of the vassal treaties which were known in various nations of the ancient Near East, particularly among the Hittites. He says that of the four constituent parts usually found in those treaties, two are clearly found in Josh. 24: the Introduction which consists of (a) the name and title of the "great king" (vs. 2a), and (b) the historical prologue, which recounts the relationships previously existing between the king and the vassal and his ancestors (vss. 2b-13); and the

[27] *Ibid.*, X, 345.
[28] *Ibid.*, X, 343-44. My own studies in Exodus, to be presented in a forthcoming commentary, have persuaded me that Exod. 12:24-27a; 13:3-16 are the result of deuteronomistic redaction.

Stipulations, containing here only the general stipulation in vs. 14. In place of the two additional elements (the Invocation of the Gods as Witnesses and the List of Blessings and Curses), Josh. 24 contains the account of the covenant ceremony. In Israel an invocation of gods other than Yahweh would not have been possible. However, we may point out that in vs. 22 the people themselves, and in vs. 26 the great stone of Shechem, are designated as witnesses (cf. Isa. 43:10); and that vss. 19-20 imply, if they do not definitely state, a curse for disobedience to the covenant on the part of the people.

Brekelmans very properly insists that one should not separate vss. 2b-13 from what precedes and what follows; particularly from vs. 2a containing the name of God, and vs. 14, which begins with *we^cattāh*, "and now." This connects vss. 14 ff. with the verses that precede. The *Gattung* to which the whole chapter belongs is that of a covenant formulary; specifically, vss. 2b-13 are the "historical prologue" in such a formulary, to use the name adopted for the Near Eastern treaties.

The form in which vss. 2b-13 are cast is that of a *Gottesrede*, a speech of Yahweh to the Israelites. This fact was observed by von Rad, but he nevertheless said that the retrospect of history given here is closely allied to Deut. 26:5 ff.[29] But it is not at all probable, as Brekelmans observes, that an original "historical Credo" developed into a covenant formulary. Such a form-critical development is not likely. Like the catechesis, the covenant formulary must be considered as an independent literary type. The fact that the actual saving deeds (*Heilsdaden*), which occur in both, correspond more or less in detail arises from the fact that such saving deeds touch the essence of Israel's religion.

I believe that this judgment concerning Josh. 24, and the comparison with the Near Eastern treaties, are quite valid. Much work has been done on those treaties, and many speculations concerning their relationship to covenant formulas or ceremonies of the Old Testament have been made. Too much is sometimes claimed for them. But it is precisely in the later literature, specifically Deuteronomy and deuteronomistic passages, that the most probable influence on the Old Testament can be seen.[30] I do not think their influence can

[29] *Old Testament Theology,* I, 122-23.

[30] There is a large bibliography of materials dealing with this subject, some of which is given by Brekelmans. One of the most useful, as well as most sane, treatments of the whole subject is D. J. McCarthy, *Treaty Covenant: A Study in Form in the Ancient Oriental Documents and in the Old Testament. Analecta Biblica,* XXI (Rome, 1963). He shows that the treaty form was very widespread in the ancient Near East, beginning in Mesopotamia in the third millennium. He argues for the basic unity of the treaty form, with some variations in detail

be seen in the early (J, E) accounts of the events at Sinai, although the present full account of the events of Sinai, Exod. 19–23, may show such influence.

Brekelmans turns finally to a form-critical consideration of Deut. 26:5-9 in the light of his conclusions regarding the above passages. Here he insists that one must not separate vs. 10 from vss. 5-9 as von Rad has done. Vs. 10 is closely related to the preceding verses by the opening word, $w^e{}^catta$, "And now," just as Josh. 24:14 is related to the preceding section by the same word. Thus, vss. 5-9, which von Rad calls the short historical Credo, constitute rather the introductory historical prologue and motivation for the offering of the firstfruits before Yahweh. One does violence to the text by separating vss. 5-9 from vs. 10. Brekelmans thinks it is not impossible that the literary form of Deut. 26:5-11 has been strongly influenced by that of the covenant formulary as found in Josh. 24.

These criticisms of von Rad on form-critical grounds seem to me to be valid. We must agree with Brekelmans that von Rad has not successfully isolated a *Gattung* that can be correctly called "historical Credo." What he calls by this name are in fact historical summaries, short or long, embedded within *Gattungen* that should be designated as catechesis, covenant formulary (or more fully: the form for ceremony of covenant making or renewal), or prayer to be made with the offering of firstfruits.

It is worth noting that historical summaries similar to those found in the above passages occur in other books of the Old Testament which are not discussed by von Rad. A good example is the long prayer in Jer. 32:16-25. This is undoubtedly a deuteronomistic passage.[31] It refers to Creation (vs. 17), the showing of signs and wonders in Egypt (vs. 20), the Exodus from Egypt (vs. 21), and the gift of the land (vss. 22-23). This prayer has similarities to the much longer prayer in Neh. 9:6 ff. Both prayers emphasize the fact that Yahweh, who created the world, has been active in the history of the people of Israel even up to the very time in which the person is praying.

Perhaps it is worth pointing out also that in four other deuteronomistic passages in Jeremiah we have a question-and-answer form that is somewhat similar to the question-and-answer form of the catecheses

---

naturally occurring. He thinks that the core of Deuteronomy provides the best example in the Old Testament of the full covenant form that is comparable to the treaty form, and sees its influence also in chapters such as 1 Sam. 12 and Josh. 24. See further H.-J. Kraus, *Worship in Israel* (Richmond, 1966), pp. 136-41; and John Gray, *Joshua, Judges, and Ruth*, pp. 32-37, 191-98.

[31] J. P. Hyatt, *Introduction and Exegesis of Jeremiah, IB* V, 789, 1042, 1049.

discussed above—5:18-19; 9:12-16; 16:10-13; 23:8-9 (cf. Deut. 29:22-28; I Kings 9:8-9).[32] The content is different, for the passages give a convenient explanation of the Exile for questioners in the future.

III.

One feature of the so-called historical Credos and their development in cult lyrics which von Rad has noticed and emphasized is the almost complete absence of reference to the revelation at Sinai. He sees it first in Neh. 9:6 ff. and Ps. 106. From this he deduces that the Sinai tradition developed in isolation from the other themes of the Hexateuch. As we have noted above, Martin Noth has expanded this view in his work on the tradition history of the Pentateuch, considering the Sinai tradition as the latest of five separate "themes" to be developed and considering Moses as an insertion into that tradition and not an original figure in it.

If the arguments given above against the antiquity of the so-called historical Credo are valid, then the omission of the Sinai tradition from the Credos cannot be used as evidence for the isolation of that tradition from the others. Indeed, Noth's attempt to isolate five separate themes in the Pentateuch, handed down separately and first combined in the *Grundlage* which lay back of J and E, is not convincing, and relatively few scholars have accepted his theory in full. Many who subscribe to von Rad's thesis regarding the historical Credos either do not go on to mention Noth's thesis, or they do not consider it valid.

Nevertheless, a good explanation for the absence of the Sinai revelation in the historical summaries with which we are here concerned was offered long ago by A. Weiser.[33] He maintained that the subject of the Sinai tradition is not a historical event in the same sense as the events of the Exodus from Egypt and entry into Canaan. The Sinai tradition tells of an encounter with Yahweh which leads up to the acceptance by the people of the will of God proclaimed in the commandments. Consequently it was not natural to mention it in the same breath with God's acts of salvation in those texts which are concerned with the latter. Thus the failure to mention the Sinai tra-

---

[32] *Ibid.*, p. 789 and *ad loc.*

[33] *The Old Testament: Its Formation and Development*, pp. 83-88. The first German ed. of this work appeared in 1948. According to Weiser, all the traditions were developed at the covenant festival which occurred annually, probably in the autumn, and were produced for use in the cult. He thinks that the sacral union continued even after the monarchy was founded.

dition beside the saving acts of Yahweh does not spring from ignorance of the tradition. Weiser says that "history" and "law" existed side by side as the two fundamental pillars of the tradition from early times.

Furthermore, as Brekelmans observes, the various passages which von Rad calls historical Credos imply, or involve in some manner, the revelation of the law. In Deut. 6:20-25 the son inquires about the law which Yahweh has commanded; in the reply, the motivation for keeping the law is derived from the saving acts of Yahweh in the Exodus and the gift of the land. In Josh. 24, the historical prologue of vss. 2-13 leads up to the formation (or renewal) of the covenant and Joshua's making of statutes and ordinances (vs. 25). In Deut. 26:5-11 the offering of firstfruits, as commanded in the law (cf. Exod. 23:19; 34:26) is motivated also by what Yahweh has done in the past history. Thus these various texts, taken as a whole, cannot be used as evidence for the separation of the traditions.

Writing in his *Old Testament Theology,* von Rad appears to express in a footnote some misgiving over the separation of the five themes of the Pentateuch. He says that the literary material seems to justify Noth in holding to the original cultic independence of the various themes, for in the majority of cases the themes do seem to be independent. But then von Rad says: "Nevertheless these single themes themselves always presuppose an idea of the whole. Guidance in the wilderness cannot be thought of apart from the deliverance from Egypt and vice versa. Again, the promise to the patriarchs, after it passed over from the cultic communities of the people belonging to Abraham and Jacob to Israel, was immediately referred to the deliverance from Egypt, etc. . . . There is much to be said for the assumption that the Credo itself presupposes the combination of an originally independent set of traditions with the central Exodus tradition." [34]

If we look at the materials in the Pentateuch regarding the Sinai events, we cannot easily isolate the Sinai tradition from the Exodus that preceded it and the events that followed. There are indeed serious difficulties in the literary analysis of the JE material of Exod. 19–24 and 32–34, and problems are raised by the occurrence of wilderness narratives both before and after the Sinai narratives, but the early chapters in Exodus look forward to Israel's being at Sinai (see Exod. 3:12, 18; 5:3; 7:16; 8:27). There are other passages or verses in the early sources that provide connections between the

[34] I, 122, note 21.

themes, looking forward or backward (see e.g. Gen. 12:1-3; 15:13-16; Exod. 13:19; 14:11; 16:3; 17:3; Num. 14:22). Furthermore, Moses plays such an outstanding role in the traditions of Sinai, as well as in those of the Exodus and later events, and he is so well integrated into all of them, that we should not under any circumstance consider him as only a secondary insertion into those narratives. His presence is required as a historical figure, not simply as a literary figure to bind the various traditions together.[35] This is not to deny, of course, that the figure and the office of Moses were subject to considerable growth and change as the traditions developed.

IV.

The above arguments have successfully shown, I believe, that (1) the passages which von Rad designates as "ancient historical Credos" are not really ancient; that is, they did not originate in the period before J, or before the *Grundlage* that lay behind J and E; (2) the "historical Credo" did not exist as an independent *Gattung*; and (3) omission of the Sinai tradition from the "historical Credos" does not prove that the Sinai tradition developed in isolation from the other traditions, and indeed there are reasons for believing that it developed along with those traditions.

We have not sought to consider in detail the passages which von Rad terms cult lyrics in which the historical Credos were adapted and developed. It has seemed sufficient to demonstrate that the primary passages from which these are supposed to have developed were not early. Careful consideration of all these would require more space than is here available, and most of them are very difficult or impossible to date with precision. We consider them to be forms in which historical summaries were used, just as historical summaries were used in the forms we have designated as catechesis, covenant formulary, and offering prayer. Some of them are probably post-exilic, showing dependence upon the Hexateuch in its completed form (e.g., Pss. 105, 106, 136). Von Rad apparently considers them to be relatively late in their present form.

---

[35] Von Rad is less precise than Noth regarding the probable role that Moses played in the actual history, but he does not attempt to give a sketch of the "historical" Moses; see his *Old Testament Theology*, I, 13-14, 289-96; and *Moses* (World Christian Books No. 32, 2nd Series [New York, n.d.]). For general discussions of the problem, see Rudolf Smend, *Das Mosebild von Heinrich Ewald bis Martin Noth*, Beiträge zur Geschichte der biblischen Exegese, III (Tübingen, 1959), and Herbert Schmid, *Mose: Überlieferung und Geschichte*, BZAW CX (Berlin, 1968).

It may be somewhat misleading to refer to the primary passages under consideration as "Credos"; that is, as creeds or confessional statements. This is, of course, of fundamental importance to von Rad, who interprets much of the Old Testament from a confessional, or kerygmatic, standpoint. There can be no doubt that the ancient Israelites believed in a God who manifested his power and grace in the history of his chosen people, performing on their behalf saving acts (*sᵉdhāqôth*). Yet, there must be a question as to whether this belief arose at so early a time and whether it was sufficient to express the "creed" of ancient Israel, if indeed we may refer to Israelite religion as a creedalistic religion. It is perhaps significant that Judaism came to consider its confession of faith as being embodied in the *Shemaᶜ*, Deut. 6:4-9 (to which were often added Deut. 11:13-21; Num. 15:37-41), rather than in any of the so-called historical Credos.[36] The *Shemaᶜ* emphasizes (1) the oneness and sovereignty of Yahweh,[37] (2) the obligation to serve and obey him through love, and (3) the obligation to remember his commandments and teach them to the children. The *Shemaᶜ* in the narrow sense says nothing about a saving act in history; only in Num. 15:41 is there a reference to the Exodus from Egypt.

It is probably better, therefore, to use a neutral term for the passages under consideration and call them simply historical summaries.

The date of many of these historical summaries is the seventh or sixth century B.C. Two of the primary passages are in that part of Deuteronomy which we should probably call proto-Deuteronomy: Deut. 6:20-25; 26:5-11. The date of proto-Deuteronomy is most likely the seventh century, possibly the latter part of the eighth century in the reign of Hezekiah. At least three of the passages we have considered are deuteronomistic, being in texts that were edited or compiled by deuteronomistic redactors: Josh. 24:2-13; I Sam. 12:6 ff.; and Jer. 32:16-25. The date of the deuteronomistic histories is within the half century from around 600 B.C. to around 550 B.C.[38] The deuteronomistic

---

[36] Ismar Elbogen, *Der jüdische Gottesdienst in seiner geschichtlichen Entwicklung*, 4th ed. (Frankfurt-am-Main, 1931), pp. 15-26; G. F. Moore, *Judaism*, I (Cambridge, 1927), 291, 465.

[37] In rabbinic Judaism, Deut. 6:4 was interpreted as confessing primarily the sovereignty of Yahweh. It was not until the mediaeval period, under the influence of Christian speculative theology, that it was interpreted as proclaiming primarily the oneness of God. See L. H. Silberman, "God and Man," in *Great Jewish Ideas*, ed. A. E. Millgram (New York, 1964), pp. 151-63, esp. pp. 151-53.

[38] According to Noth, *Überlieferungsgeschichtliche Studien*, I (Halle, 1943), 1-110, *das deuteronomistische Geschichtswerk*, consisting of Joshua–Kings, was compiled by a single "author" living around 550 B.C., although rather numerous

editor of Jeremiah lived in the middle of the sixth century B.C.[39] Such historical summaries are consonant with the strong consciousness of history found in the deuteronomic-deuteronomistic writers, as well as their deep belief in the providential control by Yahweh of Israel's history. In every case the historical summary, or historical data, are referred to, not for their own sake, but in order to show or imply that the God of Israel's past is still active in the present in judgment, in commandment, or in saving grace. It would be a mistake to suppose that such ideas originated in the seventh-sixth centuries, but they became especially strong at that time.

It should be obvious that our denial of the antiquity of the historical summaries and our questioning whether they should be viewed as confessional statements do not imply a denial of the importance in ancient Israel of belief in Yahweh's control of history. This point is strongly emphasized by most Old Testament scholars today. Such an emphasis was characteristic of ancient Israel, but it was not unique in Israel. Bertil Albrektson in his recent work, *History and the Gods: An Essay on the Idea of Historical Events as Divine Manifestations in the Ancient Near East and in Israel*,[40] has amply demonstrated that in the various religions of the ancient Near East from the third millennium on, there was belief in the divine control of history (as well as of nature) and in revelation of the deity through historical events. He is able to show even that the other religions knew the idea of the divine control of events through the divine "word," and the idea that the gods worked in history according to their own plan or purpose. The religion of the Israelites had its unique features, but they cannot be simply stated as a contrast between Israelite belief in revelation through history and pagan belief in revelation through nature, or through the word. The uniqueness is more likely to be found in the unusual course of Israelite history, its long perspective, and Israelite insistence upon unitary control of historical events.

Addendum.—Since the completion of this essay, the following article has appeared: Calum Carmichael, "A New View of the Origin of the Deuteronomic Credo," *VT* XIX (1969), 273-89. Carmichael thinks that the Credo in Deut. 26 is of deuteronomic origin; it results

---

additions were made to it later. For other points of view, see O. Eissfeldt, *The Old Testament: An Introduction* (New York and Evanston, 1965), pp. 242-48; Fohrer, *Introduction*, pp. 192-95.

[39] J. P. Hyatt, "The Deuteronomic Edition of Jeremiah," in *Vanderbilt Studies in the Humanities*, I (Nashville, 1951), 71-95, esp. pp. 89-91.

[40] *Coniectanea Biblica*, Old Testament Series I. Lund, 1967.

from Deuteronomy's attempt to "historicize" the ancient practice of offering firstfruits. It makes use of early traditions, such as the tradition in Num. 13 concerning the spies who brought some of the fruit of the land of Canaan back to Kadesh, and the message of Moses to the king of Edom in Num. 20:14-16, sent from Kadesh. There is no problem over the non-mention of Sinai because of the importance of Kadesh in those events. While Carmichael's thesis is suggestive, I find his view of the relationship between the Credo and Num. 13 and 20:14 unconvincing. However, the parallel to Num. 20:15-16 is striking. Dennis J. McCarthy, "What Was Israel's Creed?" *Lexington Theological Quarterly,* IV (April 1969), 46-53, accepts von Rad's view of the antiquity of the short historical Credo, but he sees it as being a plea for faith rather than an affirmation of faith, and thinks it was used in several different ways in later Old Testament passages. He thinks a better term than Credo is "commonplace," the word used by Renaissance rhetoricians to translate Greek *topos;* it is something like a text used for several different sermons. J. A. Thompson, "The Cultic Credo and the Sinai Tradition," *The Reformed Theological Review,* XXVII (May/August 1968), 53-64, also accepts the antiquity of the Credo, but says that the Sinai tradition is absent from it because the worshiper who used it was not concerned with the Sinai event; he was concerned to express thanks to Yahweh that he had been able to reap his harvest in the land. Thompson emphasizes the importance of the Near Eastern treaty form, especially the historical prologue, in the Credo and various related passages. (I am indebted to my colleague, J. L. Crenshaw, for calling my attention to the last two articles.)

It is a great pleasure to contribute this essay to the *Festschrift* which honors my colleague and longtime friend, Herbert May. We have been friends for more than thirty years, and we have worked together closely on the Standard Bible Committee, of which he is now Chairman. I have great affection for him, and deep admiration for his many contributions to biblical scholarship in a variety of ways. It is an honor to salute him on the occasion of his retirement from the faculties of Oberlin College and Vanderbilt University.

The Arabian Genealogies
in the Book of Genesis
FRED V. WINNETT

The book of Genesis contains four genealogies which have to do with Arabia and the Arabs. They are as follows:

    I. The sons of Cush, 10:6-7.
    II. The sons of Joktan, 10:26-30.
    III. The sons of Keturah, 25:1-4.
    IV. The sons of Ishmael, 25:12-16.

In view of the fact that ancient traditionists frequently employed genealogies as a way of presenting the basic facts of family, tribal, and even national history in easily remembered form,[1] the student of ancient Arabia cannot help eyeing the above-mentioned genealogies with considerable interest. If they are based ultimately on Arabian sources, which would seem to be a reasonable assumption in the case of some of them at least, they should contain information of considerable value for the reconstruction of early Arabian history. It may be possible to learn from them which Arabian kingdoms were flourishing and which nomadic tribes were most powerful, at the time the genealogies were compiled. They may even reveal the traditions that were current among the Arabs themselves regarding their origin. If we succeed in eliciting such information, it will be of comparatively little use to us, however, unless the age of the genealogies can be determined and thus the historical period, or periods, to which the information pertains. Our first aim, therefore, must be to ascertain the date of the genealogies, if that is at all possible. Do they come from one hand and one period, or from several hands and several periods?

We may begin with the observation that the first two genealogies, those of the sons of Cush and the sons of Joktan, form part of the

[1] See S. A. Cook, "Genealogies," *EB*, and R. A. Bowman, "Genealogy," *IDB*.

Table of Nations in Gen. 10. This Table is generally recognized to be composite in character, a mixture of J and P elements, with the Cushite genealogy being assigned to P and the Joktanid to J. In my opinion there is no reason why both genealogies cannot be assigned to J. If the J writer be dated to the ninth or tenth century B.C., as is commonly done, the genealogies present us with a picture of Arabia at a period earlier than any that can be obtained from native Arabian sources. This would be very welcome indeed, but it is by no means certain that the J writer responsible for the genealogies can be dated so early. I have elsewhere[2] given reasons for believing that the Primeval History, of which the Table of Nations forms an integral part, was composed by a late J writer, J2, who must be dated to the sixth century B.C.

The third and fourth genealogies in the above list, those giving the sons of Keturah and the sons of Ishmael, form part of the conclusion to the Abraham story in the first part of Gen. 25. It is generally agreed that the Ishmaelite genealogy comes from the hand of P, a fifth-century B.C. editor, but reasons will be given below for believing that the genealogy is based on one that once stood in J2's narrative.[3] With regard to the Keturah genealogy opinions differ, although critics agree that it comes from a non-P source. Due to limitations of space it is impossible to enter into a full-scale discussion of the matter here. I can only state my own view that the genealogy is the work of J2.[4] The earlier J1 narrative, beginning with Gen. 12, contains no genealogies.[5] J2, on the other hand, makes frequent use of such, as does P. Since the Keturah genealogy contains no marks of P authorship, it may be attributed with some confidence to J2. All four genealogies are then, I believe, the work of J2.

Objection to a theory of common authorship will be raised on the ground that the genealogies contain at least one glaring inconsistency:

---

[2] *JBL* LXXXIV (1965); see esp. pp. 1-5. My own view of the literary structure of Gen. 10 is as follows: to J2 belongs the list of the sons of Japheth (vss. 2-4), the sons of Ham (vss. 6-19), and the sons of Shem (vss. 21-30). P provided the Table with an introduction (vs. 1) and conclusion (vs. 32), and with a dividing formula between the sections (vss. 5, 20, and 31). The traditions which J2 brought together are not entirely consistent but these inconsistencies are not, in my opinion, sufficient basis for the complex analyses of the chapter with which we are usually presented. For a critical review of these, see C. J. de Catanzaro, *A Literary Analysis of Genesis 1–11* (Ph.D. thesis, Toronto, 1957), pp. 181-202.

[3] See below, p. 194.

[4] For a detailed discussion of the matter, see N. E. Wagner, *A Literary Analysis of Genesis 12–36* (Ph.D. thesis, Toronto, 1965).

[5] The story of the birth of Jacob's children in chaps. 29 and 30 can scarcely be regarded as such.

In the first genealogy, Sheba and Dedan are given as the sons of Raamah, in the second, Sheba is a son of Joktan, and in the third, Sheba and Dedan are sons of Jokshan. It must be remembered, however, that the presence of different, even conflicting, traditions does not necessarily mean that we are faced with the work of different Hebrew writers. The same writer, unable to choose between them, may have decided to preserve both.

If the genealogies are of common J2 authorship, they doubtless reflect the political and tribal situation in Arabia in his day, i.e. the sixth century B.C., not in the tenth or some earlier century as is usually assumed. This means that they come from a period for which indigenous Arabian sources in the form of inscriptions are available. The genealogies and the inscriptions should, therefore, complement one another, and there should be no marked discrepancy between them. The correctness or incorrectness of the theory here proposed should become apparent as the genealogies are subjected to close examination.

I.

THE SONS OF CUSH

The sons of Cush: Seba, Havilah, Sabtah, Raamah, and Sabteca. The sons of Raamah: Sheba and Dedan. (Gen. 10:7; I Chron. 1:9.)

The justification for including this genealogy in a discussion of the Arabian genealogies is that it contains the names of at least two Arabian kingdoms, Sheba and Dedan. These names, however, constitute an extension of the basic genealogy of five sons. The real problem is to determine whether any of the names in the basic list are Arabian. Whatever conclusion may be arrived at, it is clear that J2 regarded them all as African, or at least as ultimately of African origin, for "Cush" (Heb. *Kûsh*), the name applied to the ancestor of the group, was used in Hebrew as "a vague term connoting the entire Nile Valley, south of Egypt, including Nubia and Abyssinia." [6]

1. Seba (Heb. *Sᵉbā'*).

It is often assumed that this name is the South Arabian form *SB'* (classical Arabic *Saba'*) and hence a mere variant of Sheba (Heb.

---

[6] E. Ullendorff, *Ethiopia and the Bible*, Schweich Lectures, 1967 (London, 1968), p. 5. The *Kûsh* of Gen. 10:8 may be a corruption of *Kish*, the place where, according to Sumerian tradition, civilized life was resumed after the Flood (see *ANET*, p. 265).

Sheḇā'), but the association of Seba with Egypt and Cush in Isa. 43:3 suggests that it was a comparable African, rather than an Arabian, entity. In Isa. 45:14 the three names are again linked except that, instead of using the place-name Seba, the author employs the gentilic form "Sebeans" (*sb'ym*).[7] The mention of Seba along with Sheba in Ps. 72:10 is further evidence that the names denote two different entities. Their association here is probably due to the author's desire to achieve alliterative effect.

According to Isa. 45:14 the Sebeans were "men of stature." If the ancient South Arabians were anything like their modern descendants,[8] they cannot have been noted for their stature, whereas the Ethiopians were so noted (see Isa. 18:2). Such evidence, then, as we possess regarding Seba and the Sebeans points to their being an African region and people.[9]

A more precise identification of Seba is made possible by traditions preserved in Herodotus and Josephus. Herodotus (vii. 70), writing about 430 B.C., speaks of a kingdom of Ethiopia centered at the city of Meroë, while Josephus (*Antiq.*, ii. 249) knew of a tradition that the ancient name of Meroë was Saba. He says that it was given the name of Meroë by Cambyses following the latter's capture of the city (in 525 B.C.). S. R. Driver (*Genesis*, 2nd ed., p. 119) says that "there is . . . no evidence that Meroë was ever called Seba; and it is better . . . to understand by Seba a branch of the Cushites settled on the W. coast of the Red Sea." It is doubtful if the testimony of Josephus can be disposed of so readily. There would be no point in Josephus inventing such a tradition. Furthermore, no other identification meets so well the requirements of the contexts in which Seba is mentioned. A kingdom centered at the site of Meroë makes a far more natural associate of Egypt and Cush than does the little town of Saba on the Red Sea coast to which commentators usually refer.

As noted above, Deutero-Isaiah speaks of Seba and Cush as separate entities. This suggests that in his day, the sixth century B.C., there were two kingdoms on the upper Nile: a Nubian kingdom centered at Napata and an Ethiopian kingdom centered at Saba (Meroë).[10]

---

[7] The rendering of this word in both the AV and RSV by "Sabeans" is misleading. The Hebrew word for "Sabeans" was *šb'ym* (cf. Joel 3:8).

[8] For statistics regarding the stature of some modern Southern Arabs, see Bertram Thomas, *Arabia Felix* (New York, 1932), pp. 323-25.

[9] This is also the view of G. Van Beek, "Sabeans" (*IDB*).

[10] For the theory that these kingdoms may have owed something to South Arabia, see the references given in W. H. Schoff, *The Periplus of the Erythraean Sea* (New York, 1912), pp. 59-60.

2. Havilah.

Apart from the Cushite genealogy, this name occurs elsewhere only in Gen. 2:11; 25:18, and I Sam. 15:7.[11] According to Gen. 25:18 the Arab descendants of Abraham "dwelt from Havilah to Shur, which is opposite Egypt, as far as Asshur," i.e., from Havilah in the east to that part of Sinai lying next to Egypt on the west, and as far north as Assyria (or Syria).[12] The verse is preceded by a list of the sons of Ishmael, and this has led scholars to seek an identification of Havilah with some region in North Arabia, a region which by its very character would form a natural eastern limit to Ishmaelite settlement. Hence Skinner[13] suggested an identification with the great expanse of sand dunes in North Arabia known today as the Nafūd.

A literary analysis of Gen. 25:1-18 shows, however, that vss. 7-17 come from P, and that vss. 1-6 and 18 come from some form of J (in the present writer's opinion from J2).[14] Vs. 18 forms the natural sequel to vs. 6. The plural "they dwelt" at the beginning of vs. 18 is then explained.[15] If vs. 18 was the original sequel of vs. 6, Havilah marked the eastern limit of the region occupied by the sons of Keturah as well as the sons of Ishmael. It is more natural, then, to regard it as denoting some part of eastern or southeastern Arabia. The Nafūd lies too far north and not far enough east to meet the requirements of the narrative. There is, however, another, even vaster expanse of sand dunes which would fit the context admirably; that is "the Empty Quarter" (*ar-rubʻ al-ḥāli*).[16] This great desert forms a natural barrier to further settlement in an easterly direction until the regions of Zufār (Dhufar) and Oman are reached.

[11]The reference in I Sam. 15:7 may be at once ruled out of consideration since it seems to be a quotation, very inappropriate in its present context, from Gen. 25:18.

[12] The assertion of S. R. Driver (*op. cit.*, p. 243) that " 'Assyria' can hardly be meant, as it would be in the wrong direction altogether," is unwarranted since "Asshur" here denotes the northern border of Arab settlement. Hence either "Assyria" or "Syria" is meant. For a further discussion of this term, see below, p. 190.

[13] Driver, *ibid.*, p. 202. Glaser, *Skizze der Geschichte und Geographie Arabiens*, II (Berlin, 1890), 323-26, 341-43, would locate Havilah in central Arabia. Driver (*op. cit.*, p. 39) prefers a location "in the N. E. of Arabia, on the W. coast of the Persian Gulf."

[14] See pp. 172-73.

[15] Vs. 18b, with its employment of a verb in the singular and its implied reference to Ishmael (see 16:12), supports the usual interpretation of 18a as referring to the Ishmaelite tribes only. I believe, however, that 18b was added by P, who had 16:12 in mind. P was also responsible for vss. 16-17 and 19-20.

[16] See the *Oxford Bible Atlas*, ed. by Herbert G. May with the assistance of R. W. Hamilton and G. N. S. Hunt (Oxford, 1962), pp. 52-53.

Havilah (Heb. *ḥᵃwîlāh*) has usually been explained from Hebrew *ḥôl*, "sand," and said to mean "sandy" or "sandland." [17] The name must, however, be Arabic, and there is as yet no evidence that *ḥôl* was used in ancient Arabic, although the existence of many links between Hebrew and Old South Arabic[18] makes it unwise to rule out this possibility entirely. If Havilah be indeed the Empty Quarter, it is natural to seek to equate *ḥᵃwîlāh* with *al-ḥāli*, "the empty." This, however, is difficult since the latter comes from the root *ḥalā* (with final *w*) whereas *ḥᵃwîlāh* is manifestly derived from either *ḥāla* or *ḥāla* (with medial *w*). Arabic *ḥāla*, meaning "to manage," does not offer a suitable etymology, but *ḥāla*, "to change, shift, prevent, interpose," offers several appropriate meanings. *Ḥᵃwîlāh* could mean "(the) changing, shifting (region)," with reference to the ever-shifting position of the sands of the Empty Quarter, or "obstacle, barrier" (cf. Ar. *ḥiwāl*, "obstacle, partition," and *ḥāla baina fulān wabaina al-'amr*, "to bar, obstruct someone's way to something").[19] Such a name would be appropriate since this vast desert interposes a very formidable barrier between Southern and Central Arabia. The theory, however, makes it necessary to assume that the ancient name, derived from *ḥāla* and meaning either "shifting" or "barrier," was later reinterpreted to mean "empty" (derived from *ḥalā*), and this seems highly unlikely. It is far more probable that the great desert of South Arabia has always been known as *al-ḥāli*, "the empty," and that this name became confused, either in J2's mind or in the mind of his informant, with the name *Ḥᵃwîlāh*, another remote region which will be discussed below. Other instances of what appears to be faulty transmission of South Arabian names will be encountered below.

The other reference to Havilah, that in Gen. 2:11, occurs in a passage (vss. 10-14), mythological in character, which refers to four great rivers (Pishon, Gihon, Tigris, and Euphrates) which took their rise in the Garden of Eden. The first two names have an air of unreality in this context since Gihon is elsewhere the name of the spring which furnished ancient Jerusalem with its only perennial supply of water, while Pishon corresponds to the name of no known river. It seems to be a purely artificial creation modeled on Gihon. Whether this be so

[17] See Skinner, *Genesis*, p. 202, and Brown-Driver-Briggs, *Hebrew–English Lexicon* (Oxford, 1959), *s.v.* "*Ḥᵃwîlāh*," p. 296.

[18] See C. Rabin, *Ancient West-Arabian* (London, 1951), pp. 26-28, and D. S. Margoliouth, *The Relations Between Arabs and Israelites Prior to the Rise of Islam.* Schweich Lectures, 1921 (London, 1924), pp. 8, 25-26.

[19] H. Wehr, *A Dictionary of Modern Written Arabic*, ed. by J. Milton Cowan, Ithaca, 1961.

or not, the similarity in pattern of the two names suggests that the author thought of them as forming a natural pair, like the Tigris and Euphrates mentioned in the following verse. If he did think of them in this way, the land of ha-*ḥᵃwîlāh* around which the Pishon flowed may have been regarded by the author as an African region comparable to the land of Cush around which the Gihon flowed. The two rivers would then be two great African rivers comparable to the two great Middle Eastern rivers.[20] In favor of an African locale is the fact that Havilah is made a son of Cush.[21]

The myth of the common source of the four great rivers may have arisen following the establishment of an Ethiopian dynasty on the throne of Egypt *ca.* 722 B.C., an event which brought with it an increased knowledge of the Ethiopian homeland. A feature of this homeland which caught the imagination of Isaiah was that it was divided by rivers:

> Ah, land of whirring wings
> which is beyond the rivers of Ethiopia;
> which sends ambassadors by the Nile,
> in vessels of papyrus upon the waters.
> Go, you swift messengers,
> to a nation tall and smooth,
> to a people feared near and far,
> a nation mighty and conquering,
> whose land the rivers divide. (18:1-2.)

Vs. 7 of the same oracle also refers to the tallness of the Ethiopians and to the fact that their land was one divided by rivers. It is natural to think in this context of the White Nile, the Blue Nile, and the Atbara.[22] In Gen. 2:10-14 the number of the great African rivers has been reduced to two, possibly to get a parallelism with the two great Middle Eastern rivers. A distinctive feature of these two rivers was that they each enclosed a tract of territory. Although neither the White Nile, the Blue Nile, nor the Atbara encloses such, the latter two (which take their rise in the same general area), taken together, do embrace a great oblong area.

[20] Speiser would identify Gihon and Pishon with the Diyala and Kerkha or, if Havilah be in Arabia, with the Kerkha and Wadi er-Rumma; see *Oriental and Biblical Studies. Collected Writings of E. A. Speiser* (Philadelphia, 1967), pp. 23-34. For earlier views, see J. A. Montgomery, *Arabia and the Bible* (Philadelphia, 1934), pp. 93-94.

[21] The use of the definite article with *ḥᵃwîlah* in Gen. 2:11 may be a subtle touch on the part of J2 designed to differentiate this Havilah from the Arabian Havilah.

[22] Ullendorff, *op. cit.*, p. 6, is of the same opinion.

The above evidence favors locating Havilah in Africa but the statement in Gen. 2:12 that Havilah was noted for its gold, *bedōlaḥ*, and *shōham* stone seems to point to an Arabian locale, for in Hebrew literature gold, spices, and precious stones are the three products for which South Arabia was famous.[23] Yet neither *bedōlaḥ*[24] nor *shōham* stone is mentioned elsewhere as an Arabian product, so that the case for an Arabian locale is not so strong as it appears at first sight.

If one turns to the African side of the Red Sea and seeks the location of Havilah there, a name which attracts attention is *Avalites* (mod. Zeila). According to the *Periplus* (pars. 1-7), the chief ports on the African side were (from north to south) Mussel Harbor (Myoshormos), Berenice, Ptolemais, Adulis, and Avalites, the latter being situated beyond the Red Sea, about eighty miles east of the straits of Bab el-Mandeb.[25] The author of the *Periplus* says that the journey from Arabia to Africa is shortest at this point. This does not mean that the African and Arabian coasts were nearest together at this point— this would be true only at the straits of Bab el-Mandeb—but that Avalites was the nearest African port to the Arabian ports of Ocelis and Muza. There were exported from Avalites, "sometimes by the Berbers themselves crossing in rafts to Ocelis and Muza on the opposite shore, spices, a little ivory, tortoise-shell, and a very little myrrh, but better than the rest." [26] Since the great gulf northwest of Avalites was called "the Gulf of Avalites," it may well be that a considerable stretch of the coast and hinterland in this area was known as "the land of Avalites" ("the land of Havilah" of Gen. 2:11).[27]

The *Periplus* (par. 5) conveys the further information that between Adulis and Avalites there was a very deep bay, identified by Schoff with modern Hauakil (Howakil) Bay (south of Massawa), "at the

[23] See I Kings 10:2, 10 (=II Chron. 9:1, 9), and Ezek. 27:22.

[24] An aromatic gum exuded by a small tree found in northwestern India, Arabia, and East Africa. According to W. H. Schoff, *op. cit., Periplus,* pp. 163-64, the best kind came from India.

[25] For the location of these ports, see the *Oxford Bible Atlas,* p. 67; and *Western Arabia and the Red Sea* (British Admiralty. Naval Intelligence Division, London, 1946), pp. 68-126. Although the foundation of at least the first three of these ports is attributed to the Ptolemies, the "founding" may have taken the form of enlarging old harbors which, under other names, had been in use from time immemorial. There is every reason to believe that the Red Sea was the scene of thriving commercial activity from very early times.

[26] *The Periplus,* par. 7. *Par.* (=paragraph) is used to refer to the text of *The Periplus; p* (=page) refers to Schoff's annotations on the text.

[27] *The Periplus,* p. 66. Josephus identified the Evilaeans (=the Havilites, see St. J. B. Thackeray, *Josephus,* IV, The Loeb Classical Library, p. 65, n.°) with the Gaetulians. But this is manifestly incorrect since the Gaetulians were the nomadic peoples south of Mauretania and Numidia (*CAH* x, 346-47).

bottom of which the opsian stone is found, and this is the only place where it is produced." In view of the statement in Gen. 2:12 that one of the products of Havilah was *shōham* stone, this passage in the *Periplus* takes on more than ordinary significance, all the more so since apart from the alabaster exported from Muza, this is the only stone referred to in the *Periplus* as an article of export from any African or Arabian port. It is probable that the *shōham* stone of Genesis is to be identified with this "opsian stone." Schoff quotes Henry Salt, *A Voyage into Abyssinia,* pp. 190-94, to the effect that he picked up at this bay specimens of black stone with very high polish which was later analyzed in England and found to be obsidian.[28]

The result of the above investigation is to show that the term *Hᵃwilah* was used in Hebrew to denote two distinct regions: (a) in Gen. 2:11 and 10:7 it denotes the region around the port of Avalites in northeast Africa; (b) in Gen. 25:18 it denotes the great Arabian desert known as the Empty Quarter.

3. Sabtah. See under no. 5.

4. Raamah.

Ezekiel, writing in the sixth century B.C., mentions only two South Arabian states, Sheba and Raamah, as engaged in trade with Tyre (27:22). It is evident from this that in the sixth century B.C. Raamah was not only a well-known place but was sufficiently important that it could be mentioned in the same breath with Sheba. In view of the large number of South Arabian inscriptions preserved, and in view of the large number of towns and districts mentioned in them,[29] it is inconceivable that a place as important as Raamah is not referred to somewhere. The only name in the inscriptions which at all resembles Raamah (Heb. *Ra‘mah*) is RGMT, a city located in the district of Najrān. In an inscription left by a fifth-century B.C. ruler (*mukarrib*) of Saba' (Sheba), RGMT is called "the city of La‘dhar'il, the king of Muha'mir." [30] This *mukarrib* claims to have burned and destroyed it,

[28] According to Pliny (*Nat. Hist.* xxxvi, 196-97, and xxxvii, 177), the "obsian stone" of Ethiopia was used for jewelry and statues.

[29] For a list of many of these, see G. Ryckmans, *Les noms propres sud-sémitiques,* I (Louvain, 1934), chap. IV.

[30] RÉS 3943=Gl. 418/419. See H. von Wissmann and M. Höfner, *Beiträge zur historischen Geographie des vorislamischen Südarabien* (Wiesbaden, 1953), pp. 9-11.

together with other towns in the Najrān area, but it revived, for it is mentioned again in a Minaean inscription (RÉS 3022) dating from *ca.* 340 B.C. In later years the city came to be called Najrān, after the name of the district in which it was located, and figures prominently in South Arabian history.[31]

The identification of *Ra'mah* with *RGMT* [32] is not without difficulty, for it requires us to believe either that South Arabian *g* could become ' in Hebrew (the strong *'ayin,* as the Greek transcription *Regma* indicates), and of this there are no other examples, or that the name was incorrectly transmitted. In any case, there seems to be no escape from the conclusion that the two places are identical.

According to the Cushite genealogy, Sheba and Dedan were both sons of Ra'mah. It is highly unlikely that J2 would have invented such a tradition; he must have derived it from an Arabian source. The tradition is inherently probable, for Ra'mah-Najrān is situated on the northern border of the Yemen, and thus between Dedan to the north and Sheba to the southeast. It could well be that some of the Najranites migrated north along the trade route leading to the Mediterranean area and established themselves at Dedan, while others moved southeast and eventually developed the kingdom of Saba (Sheba). It has long been recognized that the Sabeans had a different origin than the other South Arabian peoples since their dialect employed the prefix *h-* to denote the causative, whereas the other South Arabian dialects employed the prefix *s-*. The postulated migrations must have taken place at a relatively early period.[33]

Although there is no difficulty in accepting the tradition that the Sabeans and Dedanites had a common origin in the district of Najrān, it is more difficult to accept J2's assertion that they were originally of Cushite stock. The close physical resemblance between the modern Southern Arabs and the Abyssinians across the Red Sea has often been remarked. The same may have been true in ancient times, even before the Southern Arabs established colonies in Abyssinia, and it may have been reports of their similarity which led J2 to place Ra'mah where he did in his Table of Nations.

[31] See A. Moberg, "Nadjrān" (*EI*[1]).

[32] See Skinner, *op. cit.,* p. 203 (where the Minaean form of the name is incorrectly given), and Driver, *op. cit., Genesis,* 2nd ed., p. 119.

[33] Skinner (*op. cit.,* pp. 203, 350) and Driver (*op. cit.,* pp. 119, 240) interpret the coupling of Sheba with Dedan to mean that the Sabeans were at that time resident in the north, or that there was a northern offshoot of the Sabeans settled near Dedan. This seems a quite unnecessary inference.

5. Sabteca (Heb. *Sabtᵉkā'*).

Sabta and Sabteca are almost certainly to be identified with Shabaka (*ca.* 712-701 B.C.) and Shabataka (701-690 B.C.), the first two members of the twenty-fifth (Ethiopian) dynasty of Egypt, as M. C. Astour has shown.[34] These identifications would no doubt have been suggested earlier if biblical scholars were not so obsessed with the early date of J, or at least if they had been willing to recognize the existence of a late as well as an early J. J2, writing over a century after the fall (in 663 B.C.) of the Ethiopian dynasty, seems to have experienced difficulty in constructing a Cushite genealogy and found it necessary to utilize the names of the first two members of the Ethiopian dynasty.

II.

THE SONS OF JOKTAN

Joktan became the father of Almodad, Sheleph, Hazarmaveth, Jerah, Hadoram, Uzal, Diklah, Obal, Abimael, Sheba, Ophir, Havilah, and Jobab; all these were sons of Joktan. The territory in which they lived extended from Mesha in the direction of Sephar to the hill country of the east. (Gen. 10:26-30; I Chron. 1:20-23.)

1. Joktan

The first object of interest in this genealogy is the eponym himself. The name Joktan (Heb. *Yoqṭān*), unlike the name of the eponym Keturah in Genealogy III, has no obvious meaning and is, therefore, unlikely to have been invented by J2. We may be reasonably certain, then, that in Gen. 10:26-30 we have a tradition which was current among the Southern Arabs in the sixth century B.C. according to which they were descended from a common ancestor named Yoqṭān. Later on, in the Islamic period, Arab genealogists give the name of the eponym of the Southern Arabs as Qaḥṭān.[35] It would seem that either an original *Yoqṭān* became modified in the course of time to *Qaḥṭān*, possibly out of a desire to get an assonance with '*Adnān,* the eponym of the Northern Arabs according to the Muslim genealogists,[36] or an

---

[34] "Sabtah and Sabteca," *JBL* LXXXIV (1965), 422-25. Attention had already been drawn to the similarity of Sabteca to Sabataka by Glaser (*op. cit.,* II, 331), and by H. von Wissmann and M. Höfner (*op. cit.,* p. 109). I had come independently to the same identification.

[35] See *EI²*, p. 536*a*.

[36] When the Arabs became acquainted with the Hebrew *Torah,* they harmonized their own genealogical tradition with the scriptural tradition by making 'Adnān a son of Ishmael.

original *Qaḥṭān* was modified by the Hebrews into *Yoqṭān*. The latter of these alternatives seems the more probable since it is easier to explain a development from *Qaḥṭān* to *Yoqṭān*, with loss of the *ḥ* after the *q* sound, than to explain how an original *Yoqṭān* would become *Qaḥṭān*.

The settlements of the sons of Joktan are said to have extended "from Mesha all the way to Sephar *(bō'ᵃkāh sᵉphārāh)*, the mountain to the east *(har ha-qedem)*." The RSV rendering of this verse by "from Mesha in the direction of Sephar to the hill country of the east" is scarcely correct since the *h* appended to *sᵉphar* indicates that the latter was the eastern terminus. The words *har ha-qedem* must, therefore, be taken as in apposition to *sᵉphārāh*. Skinner[37] seems to favor an identification of Sephar with Zafār, the capital city of the Himyarites, although his treatment of the subject is far from clear. In any case, an identification with Zafār is questionable since it is far from certain that the city was in existence in the sixth century B.C.[38] Furthermore, since the genealogy embraces Hadramaut, Zafār, situated about 125 miles north of Aden, does not lie far enough east to meet the requirements of the narrative. If it was the *city* of Zafār which the author had in mind, it is strange that he should refer to it as the *mountain* to the east. It seems more likely that the author was referring to the mountainous region of Zufār (Dhufar, Dhofar), the frankincense-producing region, which lies northeast of Hadramaut.[39] The representation of South Arabian *ẓ* by *s* in Hebrew presents a difficulty for which it is difficult to find a satisfactory explanation.[40]

If we are to think of the territory occupied by the Joktanid tribes as extending from a well-known point in the west to a well-known region in the east, such as Zufār, it is natural to think of Mesha (Heb. *Mēshā'*) either as a region or a port along the sourthern part of the Red Sea. The only place with a name which at all resembles Mesha is Muza (modern Mukha, Mocha).[41] In the first century A.D. it was one of the busiest of the South Arabian ports, as we know from the *Periplus*,[42] and the same may have been true in a much earlier period. If so, a reference to Muza would be meaningful to a Hebrew

[37] *Op. cit.*, p. 222.

[38] See H. von Wissmann and M. Höfner, *op. cit.*, p. 33.

[39] For a description of Zufār, see Bertram Thomas, *Arabia Felix* (New York, 1932), chaps. I-IX. The Qara mountain range rises to a height of 3000 feet.

[40] For the representation of SAr. RGMT by R'MH in Heb., see p. 180.

[41] See the *Oxford Bible Atlas*, p. 67, and H. von Wissmann and M. Höfner, *op. cit.*, map facing p. 64.

[42] See *The Periplus*, pp. 25, 28, 30, 33, 34, 106, and 109; also H. von Wissmann and M. Höfner, *op. cit.*, pp. 61, 69, 74, 88-90.

ear. The inaccurate reproduction of the name in Hebrew is in line with other incorrect transcriptions of South Arabian names in these genealogies.

2. The Sons of Joktan

Only a few of the thirteen sons of Joktan can be identified. *Almodad* and *Sheleph* are unknown. Hazarmaveth could be either a topographical term denoting the great *wādī* of that name, or a political term denoting the kingdom of Hadramaut. Our knowledge of the ancient history of Hadramaut is still rather rudimentary,[43] but the kingdom was flourishing toward the end of the fifth century B.C. In view of its control of Zufār, the principal frankincense-producing region in Arabia, it is inherently probable that it was flourishing for a considerable time before that. Thus there is no difficulty in seeing in the mention of Hazarmaveth in Gen. 10:26 a sixth-century B.C. reference to a kingdom of Hadramaut.

Jerah (Heb. *Yerah*), Hadoram (Heb. *Hᵃdôrām*), and Uzal (Heb. *'Ûzāl*), the fourth, fifth, and sixth sons of Joktan, have sometimes been identified with the Hurarina, Iarki, and Azalla mentioned in an Assyrian inscription which describes a campaign of Ashurbanipal's army in Arabia,[44] but the Joktanids were Southern Arabs, and it is highly improbable that an Assyrian army ever penetrated as far south as the Yemen. An old Arab tradition identifies Uzal with the city of Ṣan'ā' (today the capital of the Yemen), but the trustworthiness of the tradition is uncertain.[45] Some have thought to find a reference to a South Arabian Uzal in Ezek. 27:19 where the text of the first part of the verse is probably to be emended to read "and wine from Uzal." But this Uzal was manifestly in Syria, not in Arabia, for the passage in which the reference occurs begins with a mention of Syrian towns in vs. 18 and works southward to a mention of places in South Arabia in vss. 22 and 23. A mention of a South Arabian place in vs. 19 would be out of harmony with the structure of the passage.[46]

Diklah (Heb. *Diqlah*), Obal (Heb. *'Ôbāl*), Abimael (Heb.

---

[43] For the history of Hadramaut, see *ibid.*, pp. 77-144.

[44] See *ANET*, p. 299, and Skinner, *op. cit.*, p. 221 n.

[45] Glaser (*op. cit.*, II, 427) is inclined to regard the tradition as the creation of Jews living in Arabia. See "Ṣan'ā'" (*EI¹*).

[46] An Assyrian ritual text published in *ANET*, p. 343, refers to "wine from the land of Azallu." This was probably the Syrian Uzal which, according to Ezek. 27:19, was noted for its wine. According to E. Ebeling in *Altorientalische Texte zum Alten Testament*, 2nd ed., ed. by H. Gressmann (Berlin and Leipzig, 1926), p. 306, Azallu was a region north of Harran.

ᵃbîmāʾēl), and Jobab (Heb. *Yôbāb)*, the seventh, eighth, ninth, and thirteenth sons of Joktan, have not yet been identified. *Sheba* (no. 10) is, of course, the South Arabian kingdom of Saba', centered at the cities of Mārib and Ṣirwāḥ.[47]

Ophir (Heb. *'Ôphir)*, the eleventh son of Joktan, was renowned in Hebrew tradition as a rich gold-producing center. It was primarily with the aim of obtaining gold that Solomon and Hiram dispatched vessels to Ophir (see I Kings 9:26-28 [II Chron. 8:17-18], and 10:11). Since gold would not form a bulky cargo, the vessels brought back other things as well. "Once every three years the fleet of Tarshish ships used to come, bringing gold, silver, ivory, *gôphîm*, and *tukkîyîm*"[48] (I Kings 10:22; II Chron. 9:21). According to I Kings 10:11, the ships also brought back "a very great amount of *almug* wood and precious stones."

The reference to *almug* wood (Heb. *ᵃṣê 'almuggîm)*[49] is of particular interest because in the Arabic form of the legend of Solomon and the Queen of Sheba it is related that when Solomon paid a visit to the city of Ṣanʿā' in the Yemen, Queen Bilqīs who resided at Maʾrib, the Sabean capital, three days' journey away, sent him gifts of "musk, ambergris, al-ʿūd (aloes-wood) and al-ʾalanjūj."[50] The last word[51] has a curious resemblance to Heb. *'almug* and may well provide a clue to an understanding of it.

'almug itself seems to be a Canaanite word, for it occurs (once) in Ugaritic. It denoted some species of tree found in the Lebanon mountains.[52] The *'almug*-wood brought back from Ophir was scarcely the

---

[47] See G. Van Beek, "Sabeans" *(IDB)*.

[48] For these much debated terms, see W. S. McCullough, "Ape" and "Peacock" *(IDB)*, F. S. Bodenheimer, "Fauna, A2k" *(IDB)*, and W. F. Albright, *Archaeology and the Religion of Israel* (1946), pp. 133-34.

[49] The parallel passage in II Chron. 9:10-11 calls it *algum*-wood (*ᵃṣê 'algummîm)*.

[50] See A. Socin, *Arabic Grammar*, 2nd Engl. ed. (London, 1895), p. 58. For an excellent discussion of the legend, see E. Ullendorff, *op. cit.*, pp. 131-45.

[51] The word occurs in Arabic in a great variety of forms, testifying to its non-Arabic origin. Thus: *alanjaj, alanjāj, yalanjūj, yalanjaj, yalanjūjī*. Steingass, *Persian-English Dictionary* (London, n. d.), gives the further forms *ālanjūj* and *anjūj*.

[52] The evidence for the existence of a Lebanese *'algum*-wood has led J. C. Greenfield and M. Mayrhofer ("The 'algummîm/'almuggîm-Problem reexamined," in *Hebräische Wortforschung. SVT* XVI, 83-89) to attempt to divorce the references to *'almug*-wood from the Ophir tradition. Thus they reject the explicit assertion in I Kings 10:11 that *'almug*-wood and precious stones were obtained from Ophir, adopting the shorter LXX reading which omits the second *mēʾōpîr*. In dealing with II Chron. 9:10 they suggest that the source of the *'algum*-wood and precious stones was not indicated "because they were assumed to come from the storehouses and workshops of Hiram." But surely the context of II Chron. 9:10 is such that there can

same as the *'almug*-wood to be found in Lebanon. It was manifestly an exotic wood of some kind, prized for its fragrance or its appearance or both. The name which it bore, while scarcely the same as that of the Lebanese article, must have been one that could easily become confused with it. Possibly in *'alanjūj*, the name of a rare wood presented to Solomon by the Queen of Sheba, we have the word we are looking for. It may have been because the Chronicler realized that the wood brought back from Ophir could not be the same as the wood procured from Lebanon that he altered the word in his version of the Ophir episode to *'algum*.

According to Lane (*Arabic-English Lexicon*, London, 1863-93), the word *'alanjūj* is of Persian origin. Freytag (*Lexicon arabico-latinum*, Halis-Saxonum, 1830-37) says it is "a fragrant Indian wood, which is commonly called agallochum." Jastrow gives two meanings: (i) "a species of cedar tree, probably coral wood"; (ii) "the aloe-wood (agallochum)." There is no indication that *agallochum* was native to South Arabia. It was a wood of Indian origin which must have been picked up by the Hebrew and Phoenician sailors at one of their ports of call. The *gôphim* and *tukkîyim* were not necessarily products of Ophir either. They may have been obtained somewhere en route. At any rate, it would seem unwise to lay too much stress on the mention of these objects in seeking to determine the location of Ophir.

The whereabouts of Ophir was evidently well known in the time of Jehoshaphat (*ca.* 873-849 B.C.), a century after Solomon's time, for this monarch planned to send an expedition there for gold (see I Kings 22:49 [EV 22:48]). From the following century comes the inscribed sherd from Tell Qasileh which mentions "gold of Ophir." [53] In the seventh and sixth centuries there are references to "gold from Ophir" in Jer. 10:9 (reading *Ophir* for *Uphaz*), Job 22:24, and 28:16. Thus there is evidence that Ophir continued to be known as a source of gold down to the sixth century B.C., the time of J2. Whether this means that a knowledge of the exact location of Ophir also persisted is not certain. If J2 had known of any tradition associating Ophir with Africa, he would surely have placed it among the sons of Cush.

We must reckon, however, with the possibility that J2 was mistaken

---

be no reasonable doubt that the *'algum*-wood and precious stones, as well as the gold, were thought of as having been obtained either in Ophir itself or picked up at some port *en route* to Ophir. The article by Greenfield and Mayrhofer is one of the finest discussions of the *'almug*/*'algum* problem which has yet appeared, but it is doubtful if their attempt to divorce the references to this exotic wood from the Ophir tradition can be accepted.

[53] See *JNES* X (1951), 264-67, and *IEJ* I (1950-51), 209-10.

in including Ophir among the sons of Joktan. One fact which militates against an Arabian locale for it is that there is no mention of Ophir in any South Arabian inscription. This is hard to understand in view of its fame as a gold-producing center. Another fact to be taken into consideration is that the number of Southern (Joktanid) tribes is thirteen rather than twelve as in the Northern (Ishmaelite) group. This awakens suspicion that an intruder is present in the Southern group, and the suspicion naturally falls on Ophir. J2 could not ignore Ophir, but being ignorant of its exact location he may have decided to include it among the sons of Joktan, because he knew at least that in order to get to it one went in the direction of South Arabia.

Van Beek[54] would identify Ophir with Somaliland, with a possible extension to the neighboring coast of South Arabia, on the ground that the products of Ophir are the same as those of Punt which, as Egyptian reliefs show, was in the vicinity of Somaliland. But, as pointed out above, it is unwise to place too much stress on the kinds of trade goods brought back from these expeditions, since the articles mentioned may have been picked up not at Ophir itself but at ports along the way.

Solomon's dispatch of an expedition to Ophir implies that in some way word had reached him that tremendous quantities of gold were to be had in this land. Possessing neither vessels large enough for such an expedition nor the sailors to man them, he turned to his royal friend, Hiram of Tyre, and persuaded him to join him in the proposed venture. One wonders from what source Solomon had learned of Ophir, since there is no indication that Ophir gold had been reaching Palestine before his time. If Ophir were in Africa, it may well be that the informant was his Egyptian wife, the daughter of one of the last Pharaohs of the twenty-first dynasty (see I Kings 3:1; 9:15, 24).

In view of the tendency of place-names to persist, and the failure of scholars to find any name on either the Arabian or the African coasts resembling *'Ôphîr*, it is probable that the location of Ophir should be sought inland. The region which has naturally suggested itself because of its rich gold deposits is the one now known as Southern Rhodesia. The oval structures of Zimbabwe, which bear a resemblance to some of the temples of Saba', were thought to furnish concrete evidence of early connections between South Arabia and this area. However, the earliest traces of occupation so far found at Zim-

---

[54] "Ophir" (*IDB*). See also the excellent discussion by G. Ryckmans in F. G. Vigouroux, *Dictionnaire de la Bible. Supplément*, Vol. 6 (Paris, 1960), cols. 745-51.

babwe date, according to radiocarbon tests, to about A.D. 700.[55] The rich gold fields of Southern Rhodesia meet the requirements of the Ophir tradition better than any other known gold deposits in Africa, but unless archaeological support for the identification is forthcoming, the location of Ophir must be sought elsewhere.

Since there is no mention of any Hebrew expedition to Ophir after Solomon's time, the Ophir gold which continued to reach Palestine down to at least the sixth century B.C.[56] must have been obtained through the Arabs. This presupposes early Arabian contacts with the East African coast, assuming that Ophir was in Africa rather than in Arabia. According to the *Periplus* (par. 16) this coast as far south as Rhapta (= Zanzibar or Kilwa or Dar es-Salaam) had been under Arab control since ancient times. It was subject under some ancient right to "the sovereignty of the state that is become first in Arabia." The fact that the East African coast down to Rhapta was called "Ausanitic" indicates that Arab control dated from a time when the South Arabian kingdom of Ausān flourished, i.e. before 400 B.C. Doubtless the Arabs had trading relations with East Africa before bringing it under their political control. Solomon's sailors may have obtained the services of an Arab pilot, but if information regarding Ophir had reached him by way of an Egyptian source, it is more likely that the pilot was an Egyptian familiar with the Red Sea. This man may have guided them along the East African coast to a point such as Rhapta where they were able to get in touch with Africans who were exploiting some rich gold deposit.

What happened after the sixth century B.C. to bring about the apparent cessation of traffic in Ophir gold is unknown. The gold field may have become exhausted, or political upheavals in Ophir may have put an end to the mining operations. At any rate, Ophir became cut off from the rest of the world, and knowledge of its whereabouts was lost.

The examination of the names of the sons of Joktan undertaken above has disclosed that eight, and possibly nine,[57] cannot be identified. The high proportion of names which find no correspondence in the South Arabian inscriptions may possibly be due to the fact that the genealogy presents the tribal situation prevailing in South

[55] See Roger Summers, "The dating of the Zimbabwe ruins" (*Antiquity*, XXIX [1955], 107-11) ; *The Periplus*, pp. 96-99; A. Grohmann, *Arabien* (München, 1963), p. 178; and H. von Wissmann and M. Höfner, *op. cit.*, pp. 74-75.

[56] See above, p. 185.

[57] The number depends on the authenticity of the tradition which identifies *Uzal* with Ṣanʻāʾ.

Arabia in the preinscriptional period. It may equally be due to the fact that many of the "sons" mentioned were insignificant tribes with which sailors became acquainted during their journeys along the coast, tribes which have left no epigraphical remains.

III.

THE SONS OF KETURAH

Abraham took another wife whose name was Keturah. She bore him Zimran, Jokshan, Medan, Midian, Ishbak, and Shuah. Jokshan was the father of Sheba and Dedan. The sons of Dedan were Asshurim, Letushim, and Le-ummim. The sons of Midian were Ephah, Epher, Hanoch, Abida, and Eldaah. All these were the children of Keturah. (Gen. 25:1-4; I Chron. 1:32-33.)

1. Keturah

The figure of Keturah is generally recognized to be a later importation into the Abraham tradition. The J1 version knows of only one wife, Sarah, and one concubine, Hagar. Keturah appears for the first and only time in Gen. 25:1-6, a passage which I regard as the work of J2.[58] There are several reasons, besides the secondary character of the passage, for regarding Keturah as a creation of J2 rather than as a figure drawn from Arab tradition. In the first place, it is unlikely that a group of Arab tribes would trace their descent from a woman. The fact that Hagar is presented as the mother, or rather grandmother, of the Ishmaelite tribes might seem to constitute evidence to the contrary, but Ishmael, not Hagar, was regarded as the real ancestor. Secondly, the name Keturah (Heb. *qᵉṭûrah*), meaning "frankincense," might have been appropriate for the eponym of a group of South Arabian tribes but was not so for a group living far from the frankincense-producing area, even though its members may have been involved as carriers in the frankincense trade (cf. Isa. 60:6). A foreigner like J2, however, might regard such a name as appropriate in view of the close association of Arabia with frankincense in the popular mind.

One is inclined to wonder why J2 felt it necessary to create the figure of Keturah. Was it because the Joktanid and Ishmaelite circles were "closed," leading him to create a new circle or category for other tribes with whose names he was familiar? It is of interest in this

---

[58] See pp. 172 and 175. J2's use of the plural form "concubines" in vs. 6 shows that he regarded Keturah as having the same social status as Hagar.

connection to recall that the Qaḥṭān-'Adnān scheme of the Muslim genealogists did not include all the Arabian tribes known to tradition either, peoples such as 'Ād, Thamūd, Iram, Jurhum, Ṭasm, and Jadīs, who were regarded as the original inhabitants of the Peninsula.[59] It may be that the groups listed as "sons of Keturah" were similarly regarded as more ancient than the rest, but this must remain a matter of conjecture.[60]

2. The Sons of Keturah

1. Zimrān, the first-named son, has not been identified.[61]
2. Jokshan is said to have been the father of Sheba and Dedan. This creates a problem since in the Cushite genealogy Sheba and Dedan are declared to be the sons of Raamah. A futher complication arises from the appearance of Sheba in Gen. 10:28 among the sons of Joktan. The seeming discrepancy between 25:3 and 10:28 can be explained by the fact that in the latter genealogy the South Arabian tribes are viewed from a larger perspective. Since there was a tradition that all the South Arabian tribes were descendants of Joktan, Sheba was so listed. But there was another tradition, more limited in scope and therefore probably more historical in character, which attributed a common origin to the Sabeans and Dedanites in the city of Raamah (in the district of Najrān),[62] and J2 preserved this tradition also. A more serious problem is presented by the statement in 25:3 that Sheba and Dedan were sons of Jokshan. Since it is impossible to equate Jokshan (Heb. *Yoqshān*) with Joktan (Heb. *Yoqṭān*), a solution of the problem must be sought in some other direction. I would suggest that the inhabitants of Raamah (from whom both the Sabeans and Dedanites sprang) regarded themselves as descended from an eponymous ancestor named Jokshan. If so, the existence of three seemingly different and contradictory traditions regarding the origin of Sheba and Dedan is explained.

3. The Sons of Jokshan

A feature of the genealogy in Gen. 25:1-4 which attracts attention is the extra detail given in the case of Midian and Dedan, five sons

[59] See *EI²*, I, 544.
[60] Note that they are represented as sons of Abraham whereas the Ishmaelites are grandsons.
[61] For some speculations regarding his identity, see Skinner, *op. cit.*, p. 350.
[62] See above, p. 180.

of the former being listed and three of the latter. This may be an indication that J2 was particularly interested in these two, or it may mean that they alone of the sons of Keturah represent states, entities composed of several elements, and that the other names are those of mere Bedouin tribes.

(a) Sheba. See n. 47.

(b) Dedan. For the history of Dedan, see F. V. Winnett and W. L. Reed, *Ancient Records from North Arabia* (Toronto, 1970), pp. 31, 99-101.

4. The Sons of Dedan

The names borne by the sons of Dedan in Gen. 25:3, unlike the other names in the Keturian genealogy, are in the plural form. This led W. F. Albright[63] to suggest that they denote classes or professions. He would give to (a) Asshurim (Heb. *'aššûrîm,* which he would re-vocalize as *'ašērîm*) the meaning of "peasants" or "warriors," to (b) Letushim (Heb. *leṭûšîm,* which he would revocalize as *lôṭešîm*) the meaning of "craftsmen," and to (c) Leummim (Heb. *le'ummîm*) the meaning of "tribesmen, clansmen." In Gen. 10:4, 13, 14, J2 employs plural forms to denote peoples (e.g. Dodanim, Ludim, and others); hence it is possible that the plural forms in 25:3 should be interpreted in the same way. It may be that the population of Dedan, a thriving commercial center on the frankincense route, was composed of three main groups. Although "Asshurim" can scarcely denote "Assyrians," as Albright has pointed out, it can denote "Syrians," since *'aššûr* is used at least once elsewhere for "Syria." [64] The presence at Dedan of

---

[63] "Dedan," in *Geschichte und Altes Testament,* "Beiträge zur historischen Theologie," XVI (*Albrecht Alt Festschrift* [Tübingen, 1953]), 9-11.

[64] In my opinion *'SR* is so used in Balaam's oracle on Kain in Num. 24:24: "But ships shall come from Kittim and shall afflict Asshur and Eber; and he also shall come to destruction." In view of the fact that the oracle on Amalek in vs. 20 is only one couplet in length, it seems odd that the oracle on Kain should be composed of two couplets (vss. 21-22 and 23-24), each with its own introduction. This leads me to suspect that the second couplet is a later expansion, designed to have some invasion from the Greek world (Kittim), such as the invasion of Alexander the Great, foretold by Balaam. If this theory be correct *'SR* must denote Syria rather than Assyria. The author of Daniel reinterpreted the oracle (see 11:30) to make it apply to the checkmating and humiliation of Antiochus Epiphanes by G. Popilius, the Roman envoy to Egypt, in 168 B.C. (see J. A. Montgomery, *Daniel,* p. 455).

The form *'SR* occurs in three Minaean inscriptions; *RÉS* 2771 (4th century B.C.), in association with *MṢR* (Egypt) and *GZT* (Gaza); *RÉS* 3022, in association with Egypt and *'BR NHRN* (Mesopotamia); and *RÉS* 2930 (fragmentary context). Mlaker, *WZKM* XXXVIII (1931), 102-3, suggested that the name had

an inscription (JS 64 lih.) referring to the god Ba'lsamīn (the Syrian Ba'alshāmēm, Be'elshāmîn) suggests that there was a colony of Syrian merchants established at Dedan in the sixth century B.C., just as there was a colony of South Arabian Minaean merchants resident there later, from the later part of the fifth to the second century B.C. The fact that the Syrians are mentioned first among the sons of Dedan may indicate that they played a leading role in the life of the city.

If "Ashhurim" is an ethnic term, it is likely that the other two terms are also. "Letushim" may well be the name of the principal Arab element in the population of Dedan. I am inclined to doubt that it denotes a guild of craftsmen in spite of the fact that Syriac *lāṭūšā* means "one who sharpens his sword." In Ezek. 27:20 the only article of manufacture for which Dedan is noted is saddle blankets. "Leummim" would denote other mixed elements in the population of the town.[65]

3. Medan (Heb. *Medān*) has not been identified.[66]

4. Midian (Heb. *Midyān*) was the name applied in ancient times to that part of northwestern Arabia which lies east of the Gulf of 'Aqabah. The principal oasis there today is Bad'. Ancient tradition knew of five Midianite towns or oases, for Num. 31:8 refers to "the five kings of Midian." These "kings" were doubtless each the lord of an oasis.

5. The Sons of Midian

(a) Ephah (Heb. *'êphāh*), the first named son of Midian, has been plausibly identified with Ghwāfah,[67] a site on the Hismah plateau, about one hundred miles southeast of Bad'. There are extensive ruins there, including a Nabataean temple erected about A.D. 165.[68] It may be the Arabian *Ḥaiappa* whose inhabitants paid tribute to Tiglath-pileser III (744-27 B.C.).[69] Sargon II (721-705 B.C.) claims to have crushed the tribe of *Ḥaiapa,* along with the Thamud, Marsi-

---

something to do with Shur on the northeastern frontier of Egypt. G. Ryckmans (*op. cit.*, I, 324) takes it as denoting "Assyria," but Albright (*op. cit.*, p. 10, n. 1) is certainly correct in interpreting it as "Syria."

[65] The omission of the names of the sons of Dedan in I Chron. 1:33 may be due to the fact that the political and social situation at Dedan had changed by the Chronicler's day.

[66] See Musil, *The Northern Ḥeǧāz* [=NH] (New York, 1926), p. 290.

[67] Musil, *NH*, gives the name as *Rwafa*, H. St. J. B. Philby, *The Land of Midian* (=*Midian* [London, 1957]) as *Rawafa*.

[68] For a description of the ruins, see Musil, *NH*, pp. 185-89, 255, and 291; Philby, *op. cit.*, pp. 130-56, and Grohmann, *op. cit.*, pp. 42, 49, and 71.

[69] See Skinner, *op. cit.*, p. 351, and *ANET*, pp. 283-84.

manu, and Ibadidi,[70] but it cannot have been completely crushed for Ephah was apparently in existence in J2's time. Isa. 66:6 refers to "the camels of Midian and Ephah" as though Midian and Ephah were separate entities. This was to some extent true, for Ghwāfah lies some distance southeast of the Midianite territory proper, but the genealogy in Gen. 25:1-4 shows that it was reckoned as Midianite. In fact, its position at the head of the sons of Midian in the genealogy may indicate that some tradition of priority was attached to it.

(b) Abida was identified by Musil [71] with the tribe of Ibadidi mentioned in the inscription of Sargon referred to above. It seems more probable, however, that in the modern name *Bad'* we have a worn-down form of Abida (Heb. *'ᵃbîdā'*). As stated above, Bad' is today the principal settlement in the old Midianite territory. The road which runs along the Red Sea, when it comes to the lower part of the Gulf of 'Aqabah, turns straight north, passing through the midst of Midian, and touches Bad' on the way. To the Arab geographers, Bad' is the second station on the pilgrim road from Ailah (near 'Aqabah). At Bad' Muslim pilgrims were shown the well from which Moses watered the flock of his father-in-law Shu'aib, the ancient prophet of Midian, who is identified in Islamic tradition with Jethro. In the vicinity of Bad' is a group of Nabataean tombs called *Maghā'ir Shu'aib,* "the caves of Shu'aib," evidence of the flourishing condition of the oasis in the Nabataean period (2nd century B.C.–2nd century A.D.) .[72] Since it is inherently probable that the Midianites were involved as carriers in the frankincense trade passing up from South Arabia, Bad'-Abida was no doubt flourishing at an earlier period as well. How far back the association of this spot with Moses goes is uncertain. Josephus (*Antiq.* ii. 257), writing in the first century A.D., calls the town to which Moses fled *Madian.* Ptolemy, Eusebius, and the Arab geographers also knew of a town *Madyan* on the east side of the Gulf of 'Aqabah. Probably it is to be identified with Bad'.

Since the two "sons" of Midian who can be identified turn out to be towns or oases, the other three names in the genealogy, (c) Epher (Heb. *'ēpher*), (d) Hanoch (Heb. *Hᵃnôkh*), and (e) Eldaah (Heb. *'eldā'āh*), were doubtless towns or oases also. The Midianite Hanoch may be the place mentioned in Gen. 4:17 as the first town ever built.

[70] See *ANET*, p. 286.

[71] *NH*, p. 292.

[72] See Fr. Buhl, "Madyan Shu'aib" (*EI¹*); Musil, *NH*, pp. 111-16, 278-96; G. M. Landes, "Midian" (*IDB*); Philby, *op. cit.*, A. F. L. Beeston, "The 'Men of the Tanglewood' in the Qur'an" *JSS*, XIII (1968), 253-56; Grohmann, *op. cit.*, pp. 36, 40, 41.

About fifty miles east-northeast of Bad' is a large field of ruins marking an ancient settlement. The modern name is *al-Quraiyah*, "the little village"; the ancient name is unknown.[73] It may well mark the location of one of the three Midianite towns which have not yet been identified.

5 and 6. Ishbak (Heb. *Yishbāq*) and Shuah (Heb. *Shuah*), the fifth and sixth sons of Keturah, are identified by some scholars with the *Yasbug* and *Subu* mentioned in Assyrian inscriptions.[74] The identifications are not above suspicion in view of the fact that these names are associated with northern Syria rather than with Arabia. Shuah was, of course, the tribe to which Job's friend Bildad belonged (cf. Job 2:11, etc.).

IV.

THE SONS OF ISHMAEL

These are the names of the sons of Ishmael, named in the order of their birth: Nebaioth, the first-born of Ishmael; and Kedar, Adbeel, Mibsam, Mishma, Dumah, Massa, Hadad, Tema, Jetur, Naphish, and Kedemah. These are the sons of Ishmael and these are their names, by their villages and by their encampments, twelve princes according to their tribes. (Gen. 25:13-16; I Chron. 1:29-30.)

Although a case can be made for thinking that Ishmael was once mentioned by name in both the J1 and E narratives, there is nothing to indicate that either of these narratives gave a list of his descendants. In fact, the form of these narratives is against any such assumption since they allow no place for the introduction of such a list. J2, on the other hand, introduced genealogies frequently, a fact which heightens the probability that he gave a list of Ishmael's descendants. There appear to be only two places where he could have introduced it: one is the Table of Nations in chap. 10; the other is chap. 25. But chap. 10, where some Arabian peoples are mentioned, was ruled out as a possibility since the story of Hagar and Ishmael is not related until chap. 16. So it must have appeared in chap. 25.

It is questionable, however, that the Ishmaelite genealogy now occupies the position in chap. 25 given to it by J2. The use of the plural form "concubines" in vs. 6 implies that a list of the sons of Ishmael ben Hagar once stood at the beginning of the chapter. P

[73] See B. Moritz's description of it in *Mélanges de la Faculté Orientale de Beyrouth*, III (1908), 403-15 and Plate 4; Philby, *op. cit.*, pp. 169, 171-87, and "The Lost Ruins of Quraiyah," *GJ* CXVII (1951), 448-58. Philby estimated the ruins to cover twelve and a half acres.

[74] See Skinner, *op. cit.*, p. 350, and Albright, *op. cit.*, p. 9, notes 4, 5.

shifted the list to its present position in vss. 12-16 apparently because he wished to rearrange the order of events so that the death and burial of Abraham would be related first, followed by a brief reference to his son Isaac, and ending with the list of his descendants by his other son Ishmael.

Whether P modified the Ishmaelite genealogy in any way when he shifted it to its present position must remain a matter of conjecture. If not, the genealogy gives us the tribal situation in North Arabia in J2's day, the sixth century B.C. Otherwise, it gives us that situation as it existed in P's time, the fifth century B.C.

Of the twelve sons mentioned, six (Nebaioth, Kedar, Adbeel, Dumah, Massa, and Tema) appear in Assyrian inscriptions of the eighth and seventh centuries B.C. Nebaioth is said to have been Ishmael's firstborn. Since there would be no point in J2 (or P) inventing such a statement, it may be taken for granted that we have here an ancient Arabian tradition. The Assyrian annals indicate that Kedar, second in the genealogy, was the leading tribe in North Arabia in the eighth and seventh centuries B.C. The primacy accorded to Nebaioth must reflect a more ancient political situation.[75] The Kedar appear to have had their grazing grounds in the Wādī as-Sirḥān. The homeland of the Nebaioth is more difficult to determine. A search for traces of them in the Ḥā'il area which Professor Reed and I carried out in 1967 resulted in the discovery of about two hundred ancient inscriptions, but in none of them is there any mention of the Nebaioth. During our earlier expedition in 1962, we found on Jabal Ghunaym near Tema two inscriptions which mention the *NBYT* (**Nabayāt*),[76] but where the tribe dwelt remains uncertain.

Six of the other sons of Ishmael, that is, Adbeel, Dumah, Massa, Tema, Jetur, and Naphish have been identified and require no further comment.[77] The remaining four sons: Mibsam (Heb. *Mibśām*), Mishma (Heb. *Mishmā'*), Hadad (Heb. *Ḥᵃdad*), and Kedemah (Heb. *Qēdᵉmah*) do not appear elsewhere, although Jebel Misma' (about 160 miles east of Tema) may mark the homeland of the Mishma tribe.[78]

[75] Similarly the primacy accorded to the tribe of Reuben in Hebrew tradition reflects a prehistoric situation.

[76] For these, see F. V. Winnett and W. L. Reed, *Ancient Records from North Arabia* (Toronto, 1970), pp. 38-39, 113-20.

[77] For Adbeel, see Albright, *op. cit.*, p. 9, n. 7; for Jetur, see E. W. Saunders, "Ituraea" (*IDB*); Naphish is found associated with the Hagrites of Transjordan at the time of Saul (see I Chron. 5); for Dumah, Massa, and Tema, see the work referred to in n. 76.

[78] See Driver, *Genesis*, 2nd ed., p. 242. It is curious that the names *Mibśām* and *Mishmā'* appear in I Chron. 4:25-26 as Simeonites.

An examination of the four genealogies in the book of Genesis which have to do with Arabian peoples shows that they preserve ancient traditions of undoubtedly Arabian origin. This is particularly true of Genealogy II which gives a list of 13 (originally 12) South Arabian peoples, and Genealogy IV which gives a list of 12 North Arabian peoples. The division of the Arabs into two main stocks is in basic agreement with Arab tradition as it appears in the works of the later Muslim genealogists and shows that this tradition is of very ancient origin. Genealogy I, on the other hand, seems to be the work of J2 himself. Attention has been drawn to the difficulty which he seems to have experienced in trying to construct a Cushite list. The seemingly fictitious character of Keturah suggests that Genealogy III is also J2's handiwork, although there is an interesting parallel with later Muslim genealogical tradition which knows of ancient peoples who stood outside the 'Adnān-Qaḥṭān scheme.

The somewhat scattered position of the genealogies is due to the limitations imposed on the author by the nature of his narrative. He could scarcely refrain from any mention of the Arabs when giving the descendants of Shem in chap. 10. Hence he placed there those Arab peoples who were not regarded as sons of Abraham. The others he could only mention after he came to deal with Abraham. Thus the scattered position of the genealogies is not an argument against unity of authorship. Nor are the different traditions regarding the origin of Sheba and Dedan to be regarded as such since the same author may have preserved variant traditions. In any case, it has been shown that these variants are capable of being reconciled.

The date assigned to the author is dependent, of course, on one's view of the literary structure of the book of Genesis as a whole, and it has not been possible here to enter into a discussion of such a large topic. There is nothing in the epigraphical Arabian sources which is opposed to the sixth-century B.C. date here proposed for the genealogies. The latter know of Sheba and Hadramaut (probably as kingdoms) but make no mention of Qatabān or Ma'īn. This is in agreement with the epigraphical evidence which indicates that these kingdoms did not come into existence until the fifth century B.C.

The tribal picture presented by the genealogies is not necessarily complete, but it gives us such information on the subject as J2 was able to collect, and doubtless few important tribes are missing. If some peoples such as the Thamud, Ibadidi, and Marsimanu, who figure in Assyrian inscriptions of the eighth century, are missing, it is necessary to remember that Sargon II claims to have crushed them and deported the survivors to Samaria.[79]

Perhaps the most significant finding of the present study is that, whereas the names of the North Arabian tribes are reproduced with meticulous accuracy (wherever they can be checked), the reproduction of the names of South Arabian tribes and places often leaves much to be desired. Thus we find *Ḥᵃwîlah* instead of *Ḥāli*, *Raʿmāh* instead of *Ragmah*, *Yoqṭān* instead of *Qaḥṭān*, *Sᵉphār* instead of *Ṣufār* (Ar. *Zufār*), *Mēshāʾ* instead of *Muza*. The only conclusion to be drawn from this is that J2 derived his information about things South Arabian from a source, or sources, that was not always reliable. Pushing back the genealogies to a date earlier than that adopted here will not solve the philological problems involved.

---

[79] See *ANET,* p. 286.

Midianite Donkey Caravans
WILLIAM F. ALBRIGHT

In early 1968, I found once again that I had been snared in the habitual patterns of biblical criticism. For many years I had considered Num. 31 as a priestly document of late date and had not troubled to analyze its content. In this chapter we have an account of a war between Israel and Midian shortly before the death of Moses. We have also a detailed record of the booty taken after the defeat of Midian, which included some 5,000 donkeys for every tribe of Israel, plus the stipulated number of animals which went to the service of the Tabernacle—61,000 in all. Not a single camel is mentioned anywhere in this chapter, nor for that matter in any of the narratives of Exodus, Numbers, or Deuteronomy, except once in a list of all possible domestic animals smitten with an epizootic plague just before the Exodus. Since in the story of Gideon (Judg. 6–8) camels appear, in different contexts, no fewer than four times, we are faced with an odd dilemma. Is it possible that between the time of Moses and Gideon the camel came into use as a caravan animal in West Arabia, whereas donkeys were still used exclusively in the Mosaic period? While the hieratic character of the narrative does suggest stylization, this is just as plausible in early times as later, since there is no known date limit on formal listing or repetitive inventories anywhere in the ancient world. Moreover, it would have been virtually impossible for any later writer or editor to have credited the nomadic Midianites with donkeys and no camels, whereas in our oldest pertinent Near-Eastern sources, after the end of the second millennium, camels were universally associated with the desert.[1]

I communicated my observations to my old friend Otto Eissfeldt,

[1] See my references in *Yahweh and the Gods of Canaan* (London [cited as YGCL] and New York [cited as YGCNY], 1968), pp. 70-73, 179, 270-71, and *passim*. See now also E. Anati, *Rock-Art in Central Arabia*, I-II (Louvain, 1968); he has proved that the "oval-headed" and "realistic-dynamic" phases of rock-art in southwestern central Arabia date from the late third and much of the second millennium B.C.

and we then planned a joint article, which was changed to two separate articles as material began to accumulate. Professor Eissfeldt's article appeared in *JBL* LXXXVII (1967), 383-93, under the title "Protektorat der Midianiter über ihre Nachbarn im letzten Viertel des 2. Jahrtausends v. Chr.," with text by him and with several long quotations from my letters. Eissfeldt and I have both come to the conclusion that these chapters preserve extremely archaic features. The harshness of the rules of war which then prevailed was no longer acceptable by the seventh century B.C., though it was undoubtedly still practiced, as it has unhappily been all too often since those days. It is difficult to exaggerate the bitterness of warfare between nomad raiders on a *ghazū* and the settled peoples whom they raided. The hostility which existed between the raiders and the raided is often illustrated in the Assyrian inscriptions and may still be observed today in various parts of the world. As late as 1925, I remember how bitterly the settled Arabs of eastern Syria recalled the bloody raids of the 'Anezeh during the rebellion against the French. The kindest word for them heard from the settled Muslim Arabs of the region east of Ḥumṣ was *el-wuḥûš*, "the wild beasts." In ancient times there was rarely opportunity for resort to any form of pacifism. Either people resisted such aggressors or they, together with their families, were destroyed.

In fact, the only way to put a stop to interminable bloody aggression was to weaken the foe to such an extent that he could not continue. This was done by various forms of decimation—a third of the enemy being punished with death and the rest enslaved,[2] or by still more drastic methods. Early Israelite customary law was, however, generally much less harsh than that of the surrounding peoples, just as the traditional law of Moses was much milder than that of the ancient Near Eastern law codes.

We have in the latter chapters of Numbers some extremely archaic traditions which probably received their final editing, at least for practical purposes, with the JEP redaction in the early seventh century B.C.[3] In 1944 I published my study, "The Oracles of Balaam," in

---

These people were mostly hunters, hunting wild animals of all kinds, including camels and large cattle. Tame camels and camel riders do not appear with certainty until well along in the first millennium B.C., in the same phase as Proto-Arabic graffiti. See further n. 11 below.

[2] See A. Alt, *ZÄS* LXXV (1939), 16-20. There is an interesting passage in a Middle Assyrian royal inscription which throws light on the situation, and which I hope to treat elsewhere.

[3] For my position on the nature of the "sources" *JEP* in the Pentateuch and beyond, see YGCL (n. 1 above), pp. 25-36 and YGCNY, pp. 28-41. Concerning recognition of the mutual dependence of the "sources," which are recensions of

which I pointed out that the poetic text is much older than the prose and was almost certainly put into writing in the tenth century B.C.[4] Since then a number of discoveries have confirmed its early date and have shown that the prose narrative also contains very archaic material. In addition to the points which I have brought up on various occasions since this article was published, Eissfeldt (*loc. cit.*) has shown that the collection of Moab and Midian is also historically sound, and in preparing an encyclopedia article on Balaam recently, I was able to include a number of points made by other recent scholars confirming details of its antiquity.[5] As demonstrated in detail by Eissfeldt, the Midianites at that time exercised a kind of protectorate over Moab and Edom, which were vassal states under their domination. In Num. 27 we have a narrative which seems to be etiological in origin but which also goes back to very early tradition. The five daughters of Zelophehad were then identified with five subdistricts of Hepher. The various genealogical traditions about Manasseh in the Old Testament are explained by the names of districts and subdistricts in the ostraca of Samaria from the eighth century B.C., where some of these five daughters were the names of districts with feminine names.[6] One of these names (Tirzah) is included among Canaanite towns whose kings were conquered by Joshua, according to Josh. 12 (Hepher also appears in the same list). Then we have several chapters which contain cultic provisions of definitely archaic type with regard to observance of various feasts. Chapter 31 is followed by more old material which obviously came from different sources but was included, regardless of the heterogeneity of its content. In short, Eissfeldt is quite right in recognizing the archaism of much of the prose

---

the same original as well as separate collections, I owe most to the two late Old Testament scholars Martin Noth and Sigmund Mowinckel, but my view of the ultimate sources depends much more heavily on recognition of oral tradition, as seen in verse quotations and reminiscences.

[4] *JBL* LXIII (1944), 207-33. See further, on the identification of Balaam's homeland, *BASOR* CXVIII (1950), 15-16, n. 13, and YGCL 13, n. 38. On the adjacent pages (YGCNY, pp. 15-16) will be found further updating of my 1944 paper.

[5] Especially in the paper of Manfred Lehmann, *ZAW* LXXXI (1969), 78-79, on the seven bullocks offered three times (with seven rams) by Balaam and the seven oxen (and seven rams?) mentioned on the broken fifteenth- (or fourteenth-) century tablet from Gezer (on which see my treatment, which still stands, as far as it goes) in *BASOR* XCII (1943), 28 ff. In both cases they would solemnize a treaty (or other formal compact).

[6] See my detailed treatment in *JPOS* V (1925), esp. pp. 38 ff.; it was corrected substantially in *JPOS* XL (1931), 241-51, with further corrections by F. M. Cross, Jr., and G. E. Wright; see the latter's paper in *Eretz-Israel* VIII (E. L. Sukenik Memorial Volume, 1967), esp. pp. 60*-64*.

content of the Balaam narrative as well as of the account of the war between Midian and Israel before the death of Moses.

Since the publication of Eissfeldt's article new archaeological material of great importance has come to light, thanks to the energy of Yohanan Aharoni and Beno Rothenberg, at the site of Mene'îyeh in the 'Arabah south of the Dead Sea, made famous by the exploration of Nelson Glueck. They discovered, in early 1969, a small Egyptian temple, containing Egyptian inscriptions and other objects, as well as pottery of the same type as they have been finding in the 'Arabah in recent explorations. The inscriptions show that the temple was built by Sethos I (*ca.* 1315-1304 B.C.), then destroyed, and rebuilt later in the time of Ramses III (*ca.* 1198-1167 B.C.). Inscriptions of Merneptah and Sethos II of the 19th Dynasty are also reported to have been found. Incidentally, this yields the same general picture of Egyptian occupation in the Jordan-'Arabah Valley that we find at Beth-shan and Tell Deir'alla (probably Succoth) in the middle Jordan valley, excavated by H. J. Franken. This picture of close inter-relationship between Midianites, Moabites, and Edomites in the latter part of Moses' lifetime, presumably during the third quarter of the 13th century B.C., presents us with a new political pattern, which Eissfeldt was the first to grasp.

It now becomes clear that the Pharaohs of the 19th and early 20th Dynasties were very much interested in the exploitation of the mineral resources of Northwest Arabia as well as its trade routes. A very important route for Egypt during the period between 1225 and about 1175 B.C. ran from the northern Jordan Valley south to the Gulf of 'Aqaba. We must remember that at that time the level of the Dead Sea was not nearly so high as it is today, thanks to the constant accumulation of silt as well as to the deposit of mineral salts on its floor.[7] There was little break in the continuity of travel except when raiders from the mountains attacked the caravans. This explains why we have such flourishing settlements at that time in the upper and middle Jordan Valley as well as south of the Dead Sea. The Nauri inscription of Sethos I [8] tells us that state slaves were employed in the

---

[7] See esp. *AASOR* VI (1926), 53 ff.; Ralph Baney, *Search for Sodom and Gomorrah* (Kansas City, 1962). There were some unfortunate aspects to Baney's undertaking, but I was at the time in close touch with him, and there can be no doubt as to the value of his elaborate sonar maps and the submarine finds which he made (and which are described in the book by competent specialists). Cf. also my remarks in *The Scrolls and Christianity* (London, 1969), pp. 12-13.

[8] See *JEA* XIII, 193 ff., and XXXVIII, 24 ff., together with Sir Alan Gardiner, *Egypt of the Pharaohs* (Oxford, 1961), pp. 251-52, and my discussion, YGCNY, p. 271 (=YGCL, p. 234)—correct the mistake "late thirteenth century" in both editions to "late fourteenth century."

mining operations of Pharaoh; we also have lists of different categories of workers, including donkey drivers (*šwyw*). The term *šwy*, "donkey driver," as well as *šwwty* (Coptic *ešōt*), "trader," are almost certainly derived from *šw*, "wild ass, onager," eight of which appear among the funerary offerings to one *Bby*, who was the provisioner of the ruler of the district of el-Kab, together with thirty-two bubalis antelopes.[9] The word has the determinative "donkey" and cannot easily be separated from the homonym meaning "desert." Wild asses or onagers, were highly prized, as we know from ancient and modern records, for breeding purposes; they were often crossed with tame donkeys for larger and stronger progeny (just as was then beginning to be done with mares and donkeys, producing sterile hybrids which possessed much more strength than donkeys and more docility than onagers or horses).[10]

In spite of overwhelming evidence that domesticated camels were still unknown in the literate areas of the ancient Near East until the end of the Bronze Age or the beginning of the Early Iron, many scholars still insist that this idea is somehow wrong and that camels were used for caravan purposes much earlier.[11] The evidence from occasional finds of camel bones (often intrusive) or figurines representing camels (more often merely alleged to be camels against the results of critical inspection) is quite useless in differentiating between tame and wild camels. On the other hand, there are no contemporary references to the use of camels in carrying goods or persons until well after the beginning of the Iron Age (twelfth century B.C.), whereas

[9] See both editions of YGC, cited above.

[10] Dr. Stephen J. Lieberman has called my attention to some Ur III texts which describe the importation of onagers (ANSE LIBIR=dusú) into Babylonia from the West (*Amurrû*), and I have also learned recently about a European traveler in the early nineteenth century who referred to the breeding of the onager (which was highly prized) with the small tame donkey (*burro*) in the Môsul area. In addition to the literature cited in YGCNY, p. 61, n. 22, and p. 269, n. 1 for the large black (dark brown) donkeys so highly preferred by the Old Assyrian merchants, see now Mogens Trolle Larsen, *Old Assyrian Caravan Procedures* (Istanbul, Nederlands Historisch-Archaeologisk Instituut, XXII, 1967), *passim*. That both the Old-Assyrian donkeys and the more modern Damascus breed were originally the product of crossbreeding is now being recognized more and more.

[11] It would be unfair to single out individual scholars who have followed their teachers or the *communis opinio*, since the evidence against them is fast becoming decisive to any informed student. I should, however, like to thank Mr. Schnayer Z. Leiman for sending me an article in the *Yavneh Review* for 1967 (pp. 16-26) on the subject, "The Camel in the Patriarchal Narratives." In it he gives a long series of statements and arguments against my well-known theses. Not a single one is valid, and most of them drop out at once because I have never disputed the existence of wild or only partially tamed camels for thousands of years before the end of the Bronze Age. I have always insisted on the late date of "effective domestication of the camel" (i.e., for caravan and military use).

there are literally thousands of such references to donkeys and donkey caravans. In the Iron Age the situation is literally reversed, with steadily increasing numbers of references to the use of both Arabian and Bactrian camels. These are facts, and the contrary allegations are pitiful in their lack of solid evidence *of any kind.*

Of course, no one now denies that wild camels were common in Arabia during this early period.[12] It is also more than probable that herds of semi-domesticated camels were allowed to roam free in the territory of a given nomadic group, which used the milk and hair of living camels and the flesh and hides of dead camels. They could easily be collected by driving them into the now famous "kites," the remains of which are found scattered over the North-Arabian desert.[13] That there was already a well-developed caravan trade between Midian and South Arabia seems to be virtually certain. In our two campaigns at Timnaʻ and Hajar Bin Ḥumeid (1950-51), Richard L. Bowen discovered clear evidence for successive stages of irrigation before and after the foundation of the town of Hajar Bin Ḥumeid, directly opposite the Mablaqah Pass leading from Wâdi Beiḥân to the next big parallel valley to the north, Wâdi Ḥarîb. In later centuries this was a very important point on the caravan route leading from Qatabân through Saba', Maʻîn, and Nejrân northward past Mecca and Yathrib (Medina). On the basis of these data, which we established with the aid of pottery and carbon 14, we were able to date the foundation of the fortified town itself no later than about 1000 B.C., and by careful figuring of the rate of deposit of silt we could fix the beginning of irrigation *ca.* 1600-1400 B.C. in round numbers.[14] In the light of what we learned through intensive surface exploration, this would represent the period when caravan trade between South Arabia and the north began. In early times occupation was chiefly restricted to the Wâdi Ḥaḍramôt and the lateral *wâdis* emptying into it, where there was plenty of water available just under the surface. In the regions to the west (Saba', Qatabân, and Maʻîn) it was necessary to subjugate the *suyûl* (plural of *seil,* "flash flood") which brought down the heavy rains from the mountains of Yemen. The harnessing of the *suyûl,* with the aid of elaborate irrigation works based on the deflector dam principle, took a great deal of capital investment which did not become

[12] See esp. above, n. 1.

[13] For convenient orientation, see Yigael Yadin, *IEJ* V (1955), 1-16.

[14] For the chronology, see my survey in the Eissfeldt jubilee volume, *Von Ugarit nach Qumran* (Berlin, 1959), pp. 1 ff., with Richard LeBaron Bowen's detailed analysis, *Archaeological Discoveries in South Arabia,* ed. W. F. Albright (Baltimore, 1958), pp. 43 ff., and esp. 64-68. The date then proposed for the foundation of Hajar Bin Ḥumeid (Baltimore, 1969), esp. pp. 355 ff.

available until the development of caravan trade.[15] In Qatabân and Awsân, together with adjacent territory, myrrh flourished. Further east in eastern Ḥaḍramôt, Šaḥr, and especially in Zofâr frankincense was at home. This is still true today, and in antiquity (as we know from Greco-Roman authors) it was even truer.[16] In other words, the myrrh and other aromatics of Arabia Felix were carried north, as a rule, by different routes. The myrrh trade followed the western route, while the frankincense trade generally took an eastern route, since the sources of frankincense lay relatively closer to the sea.

Frankincense, which probably reached Babylonia by sea as well as by land, is attested from the Cossaean period (*ca.* 14th century B.C.) on down.[17] It does not appear in the canonical Babylonian vocabularies, which in their extant form date substantially from the First Dynasty of Babylon (19th-16th centuries B.C.). On the other hand, myrrh is listed in the canonical vocabularies[18] and is also mentioned in the Amarna Tablets (*ca.* 1380-1360 B.C.): Twice it appears among gifts from Tushratta, king of Mitanni, to Pharaoh, and once Milkilu, prince of Gezer in Palestine, asks Pharaoh to send him myrrh (glossed *murra*) as a medicament (*ana ripūti*); it was evidently very expensive.

The time at which the linear alphabetic script was borrowed from the northern Semites by the South Arabians can now be quite closely fixed by comparison of the oldest known lapidary forms of the latter (from about the ninth century B.C.), as well as of the oldest graffito forms from western Ḥaḍramôt, with datable sequences in Sinai and Palestine. This comparison fixes the time of borrowing securely in the 14th-13th centuries B.C., more probably in the 14th than in the 13th.[19] The Midianites certainly played a decisive part in the movement of script since, like the later Nabataeans, they were at the re-

[15] Bowen, in the publication cited in n. 14, pp. 82-85. I agree with his position, but would stress the importance of caravan trade even more strongly.

[16] See A. Grohmann, *Südarabien als Wirtschaftsgebiet* (Vienna, 1922), pp. 114-55; R. LeB. Bowen, in *Archaeological Discoveries in South Arabia* (Baltimore, 1958), pp. 60-63, as well as G. W. Van Beek in the same volume, pp. 139-42.

[17] For the Accadian word *labanātu, lubunītu* (South Arabic *lbnt*, Heb. *lebōnā*, Ar. *lubān*), see W. von Soden, *AHW*, pp. 552a and 560b (1965). The most important occurrence is in the dream book published by A. Leo Oppenheim, *The Interpretation of Dreams in the Ancient Near East* (Philadelphia, 1956), p. 328, reverse, col. i: 9 (with transcription as corrected by von Soden: "If frankincense rains upon a man, that man will f[all] in the desert, and upon him . . . (?)." Oppenheim cautiously dates the composition of this text in the Cossaean period, on the basis of an adjacent list of place-names. This is perhaps safer in some ways, but a date in the 18th century B.C. must also be considered seriously. Under no circumstances can the list be dated after the 14th century B.C.

[18] For references, see W. von Soden, *AHW* DCLXXVI (1967). Note *šaman murri* =Ugar. *šmn mr* (see above).

[19] On the graffiti from Ḥaḍramôt, see provisionally A. Jamme, *BASOR* CLXXII

ceiving end of the nascent caravan trade in spices, and most hitherto discovered Bronze Age specimens of linear alphabetic writing come from Midianite territory in southern Sinai.

It is quite true that Philby's exploration of Midian proper, between 1950 and 1953, did not yield a trace of graffiti antedating the middle centuries of the last millennium B.C.[20] Yet it is obvious that writing, once available in alphabetic form, would be quickly put to use by Arabian caravaneers, just as it was by the Greek traders of the Iron Age after they had seen how the Phoenicians used it. So again we are justified in dating the beginnings of the donkey caravan trade between South Arabia and Egypt=Syria no later than the 15th century B.C. In fact, it may well have been the success of Queen Hatshepsut (between 1490 and 1470) and her successors in sending naval expeditions to Punt (Somaliland) in search of frankincense and other exotic articles, which stimulated the peoples of western Arabia to organize overland trade in myrrh and frankincense. The *šmn mr* which appears in the 14th-century ritual texts from Ugarit is, of course, "oil perfumed by myrrh," but it proves the antiquity of the use of this substance in religious cult (cf. Exod. 30:23).

The trading caravans presumably started in Ḥaḍramôt, swung around the Empty Quarter (*er-Rubʿ el-Ḥâlī*) through Qatabân, Saba', the region later called Maʿîn, and Nejrân, past Mecca and Yathrib (Medina), thence to Dedan (el-ʿUlā) and on through Midian proper. Owing to the great distances covered, and the frequent lack of water, fodder, and grain for the donkeys, the time consumed was probably much more than the three months (or even less) required by the camel caravans of early Roman times. As a reasonable hypothesis we may assume that the southernmost phase of the caravan route was arranged by the Ḥaḍramis and the Sabaeans,[21] with the

---

(1963), 41-54, with my comments on p. 54. See most recently Frank M. Cross, Jr., in *Eretz-Israel* VIII (E. L. Sukenik Volume, 1967), 19*.

[20] See his report in *The Land of Midian* (London, 1957), and his completely negative results (pp. 5-6). Incidentally, I had encouraged him to explore northwestern Arabia for this purpose, though I was pessimistic about chances for success, since graffiti had no practical commercial value and assume a rather high degree of literacy on the part of nomads.

[21] If A. G. Loundine (Lundin) is right in his reconstruction of the now famous list of Sabaean eponyms (see most recently *JAOS* LXXXIX (1969), 533-41 (with all necessary bibliography), as well as in his dating, the people of Sheba kept exact chronological records back to the eleventh century B.C. However, I consider the dating as much more problematic than the reconstruction, which seems to be substantially correct. In agreement with Hermann von Wissmann (letter of Jan. 25, 1969), I do not think that the extant list goes back before the early eighth century B.C. On the other hand, there is epigraphic proof going back to about the ninth century B.C. for caravan trade between Ḥaḍramôt and Bethel; see G. W. Van Beek and A. Jamme, *BASOR* CLI (1958), 9-16, and *BASOR* CLXIII (1961), 15-18. The

central part under Dedanite[22] (or other) control and the northern in Midianite hands. Needless to say, the donkeys would have to be replaced by fresh beasts from time to time. In short, the entire operation was more complex and expensive than after the introduction of camels, and the high value placed on myrrh in the Amarna letters may thus be easily explained.

The foregoing observations have again illustrated the fact that there is no general rule applicable to the "historicity" of any given datum in our extant text of the *Hebrew* Bible. The narratives about Abram omit any reference to the camel, and those about Isaac and Jacob, demonstrably archaic in customary law, modernize in substituting "camels" for "donkeys" in describing long journeys across the desert between Palestine and Upper Mesopotamia. Aside from one such touch at the beginning of the Joseph story (Gen. 37:25), and a single mention of camels in Exod. 9:3, no camels appear in subsequent narratives before the late twelfth century. On the other hand, donkeys and donkey caravans are very often mentioned. We have seen that the sudden appearance of vast numbers of donkeys among the Midianites of Moses' time is perfectly in keeping with the actual situation then, just as are the donkey caravans of Joseph's brethren in Gen. 42–47, or the Israelite donkey caravans of the time of Deborah (Judg. 5:6-11).[23]

---

identity of the baked clay stamps from Bethel and Mešhed is almost complete, and the straw temper in the Bethel stamp was certainly South-Arabian in origin. Subsequent examination of the markings on the back of the stamp convinced two eminent archaeologists (neither an expert in South-Arabian matters) that the Bethel stamp is identical with the Mešhed one (unfortunately there can be no confrontation, since the latter disappeared at some time in the past, leaving only the squeeze in Vienna). However, the incredible difficulties raised by supposing that the Mešhed stamp somehow made its way from Europe to Bethel, where it was excavated in 1957 by James L. Kelso, who was probing in ancient debris outside the Bronze Age wall of the town, raises so many more unanswerable questions than the apparent coincidence in straw marks on the back of the stamps that I do not have the slightest doubt about the authenticity of both stamps.

[22] See provisionally my paper on "Dedan" in *Geschichte und Altes Testament, Albrecht Alt Festschrift* (Tübingen, 1955), pp. 1-12, where I identify it with Old Babylonian *Tidnum* and *Tidanum* (to be read *Didnum* and *Didanum*). To these writings may now be added Ur III *Dadnim* (gen.), as well as *Dadanu* as name of el-'Ulā in the inscription of Nabonidus describing his expedition in West Arabia (sixth century B.C.). Since I plan to write a substantial new paper on Dedan, I shall limit myself here to pointing out that the uncertainty as to whether the people or place came first, to which I refer at the end of my paper on Dedan, was probably unnecessary. We have the people of Midian in the time of Moses and later, and the town of Madyan in the Classical and Arab geographers—with a span of 2500 years between them. Accordingly, there is no real problem in identifying the name of the people *Did(a)n* in the 21st century B.C. with the place-name *Dedān* in the sixth-second centuries B.C.

[23] See YGCL (above, n. 1), pp. 43-44, and YGCNY, pp. 48 ff.

Nationalism-Universalism and Internationalism in Ancient Israel

HARRY M. ORLINSKY

Our topic is particularly pertinent for a volume that honors Herbert Gordon May, for it has long been of major interest to him; see, for example, his discussion of "Theological Universalism in the Old Testament," *JBR* XVI (1948), 100-107. It is hoped that a close reading of his article and the present essay that is warmly dedicated to him will indicate that not infrequently it is a matter of definition that marks our difference in attitude toward a biblical passage; on such passages as Isa. 19:18 ff. and Mal. 1:11 we see eye to eye.

It has long been a commonplace, both in Jewish and in Christian circles, among scholars no less than among laymen, that the authors of the Hebrew Bible in general and the prophets in particular were internationalistic in their outlook. It is widely asserted that their concept of God and of the non-Israelite, non-covenanted peoples of the world embraced, quite beyond the population and boundaries of ancient Israel, all mankind. Yet it is a fact that no one has attempted to test systematically this universally assumed and accepted view. No one has gone directly to every pertinent biblical passage and examined it per se within its context, and then brought together all the individual conclusions reached in order to determine whether an integrated whole, a clear pattern, has emerged.

In the course of a paper read by invitation at the one hundred and third annual meeting of the Society of Biblical Literature (New York, December 29, 1967), I dealt with this matter under the general title, "Some Problems of Eisegesis and Exegesis in the Bible." I noted there at the outset that very few areas of scholarly research in the Humanities have been so exposed to outside, nonscholarly pressures as the biblical, both the Hebrew Bible and the New Testament. The Hebrew Bible has long constituted living reality to both the Jewish and Christian communities of the world, in a manner that ancient Mesopotamian or Egyptian or Canaanite or Greek or Roman religious texts have not been. No one devotes a lifetime of careful study to these writings conscious of anyone looking over his shoulder to see how he interprets them; that is, whether his interpretation of these texts will reflect favorably or otherwise on their original authors or on the society that produced them. There is no significant institution or group in existence today that has a vested religious interest in these texts and their interpretation.

Small wonder, then, that biblical research has long been a battle-field for the forces of eisegesis as against exegesis and, what is even more to the point, that hostile eisegesis has not always been recognized by scholarship for what it really is. It has, instead, been accepted as friendly exegesis. It is therefore incumbent upon biblical scholars, more than upon most others, always to be on the alert to recognize and practice the methodology that marks the study of, say, the ancient texts of Mesopotamia, Canaan, Egypt, Greece, and Rome.

It is significant that some half dozen passages constitute the parade examples for the internationalistic view attributed virtually unanimously to the Old Testament authors, and in every one of these passages it is clear, on close scrutiny, that incorrect eisegesis has been permitted to dominate correct exegesis.[1]

One of these passages, as everyone knows, is Mal. 2:10. This says[2]: "Have we not all one father? Has not one God created us?"[3] Yet it is a fact that non-Israelites are in no way involved in this passage. The prophet is addressing himself directly and exclusively to the sacerdotal elements (the priests and levites) in restored Judah, and

---

[1] See the "Introductory Statement" in H. M. Orlinsky, *The So-Called "Servant of the Lord" and "Suffering Servant" in Second Isaiah, Supplements to VT* XIV (Leiden, 1967), pp. 3-4, where some pertinent passages from H. J. Cadbury's paper on "Motives of Biblical Scholarship" (*JBL* LVI [1937], 1-16) are quoted, and where further reference is made to essays by E. R. Goodenough and M. S. Enslin.

[2] The translations employed in this essay, where they are not my own, derive from *The Torah* (New York, 2nd ed., 1967), *The Five Megilloth and Jonah* (New York, 1969), or the RSV. In no case have I parted company with these translations when an important interpretation was involved.

[3] *hᵃ-lo av ehad lᵉ-khull-anu//hᵃ-lo el ehad bᵉra ánu.* The system of transliteration has been simplified as much as possible without, it is hoped, loss of clarity. Thus *v* and *kh* (as distinct from *b* and *k*) represent spirant *beth* and *kaf*, whereas *g* and *d* do service for both spirant and mute *gimel* and *dáleth*. The length of the vowels has been disregarded, and only the penult accent has been indicated.

he is rebuking them vigorously for acting improperly and arrogantly vis-à-vis the nonsacerdotal, the lay elements in the Judean community, as though they were not equally the covenanted partners of God:

> "And now, O priests, this command is for you. If you will not listen, if you will not lay it to heart, to give glory to My name," says the Lord of Hosts, "then I will send the curse upon you. . . . So shall you know that I have sent this command to you, that My covenant with Levi may hold. . . . True instruction was in his mouth, and no wrong was found on his lips. . . . But you have turned aside from the way; you have caused many to stumble by your instruction; you have corrupted the covenant of Levi. . . ." Mal. 2:1-8.

It is this denunciation of the priestly class which leads directly into our vs. 10. Indeed, the second half of our verse goes on to say: "Why then are we faithless to one another, profaning the covenant of our fathers?" It is only by suppressing this latter part of the verse, with its clear reference to "the covenant of our fathers" (*berith 'avothénu*)—which could embrace fellow Israelites only—that the first part, now wrenched wholly out of context, can be made to refer to all the peoples of the earth. This is a clear case of eisegesis.

In the process, one must also not forget that the only time a non-Israelite people is mentioned by Malachi is when Edom is referred to at the very beginning of the book. What the text says is this:

> The oracle of the word of the Lord of Israel through Malachi. "I have loved you," said the Lord. But you [namely, Israel] have said, "How have You loved us?" The Lord replies, "Esau is Jacob's brother; yet I have favored Jacob, and I have rejected Esau. I have made his hill-country a waste, and given his heritage to jackals of the desert." If Edom says, "We are shattered, but we will rebuild the ruins," the Lord of Hosts says, "They may build, but I will tear down, till they are called the wicked country, the people with whom the Lord is angry forever." Mal. 1:1-4.

That is what the text of the book of Malachi says about what its post-biblical readers assert to be an expression of internationalism.

It is rare for a verse to be made the basis for a creed. Yet Lev. 19:18 has been used in this manner with reference to internationalism and the "Golden Rule." This passage, traditionally rendered "You shall love your neighbor as yourself" (for a more precise and less misleading translation, see below) has long been used as the basis for the concept of world brotherhood.

Disregarding the implications of the negative and positive forms of expressing it, this concept reads "And what you hate, do not do to any one" in Tobit 4:15; "Just as you do not wish evils to befall you, but to participate in all that is good, so you should deal with those subject to you and with offenders . . . for God deals with all men with gentleness" in the Letter of Aristeas[4]; and "What is hateful to you, do not do to your fellow man. This is the whole Law (*Torah*); the rest is commentary" is credited to Hillel (first century B.C.) in the Babylonian Talmud, Shabbat 31a (in reply to the request of a heathen convert to Judaism for a brief exposition of his newly adopted religion). In similar manner, Jesus formulated the Golden Rule by "So whatever you wish that men would do to you, do so to them; for this is the Law and the Prophets" (Matt. 7:12; cf. Luke 6:31). And the answer he gave to the question, "Teacher, which is the great commandment in the Law?" is recorded in Matt. 22:37-40:

"You shall love the Lord your God with all your heart, and with all your soul, and with all your mind (Deut. 6:5). This is the great and first commandment. And a second is like it, You shall love your neighbor as yourself (Lev. 19:18). On these two commandments depend all the Law and the Prophets."

Already Sirach (Ecclesiasticus; about 200 B.C.), at 17:14, had alluded to the Leviticus passage: "And He gave commandment to each of them concerning his neighbor." So did Paul several centuries later: Now I Paul say to you. . . . For the whole Law is fulfilled in one word, "You shall love your neighbor as yourself" (Gal. 5:2, 14); with which compare Rom. 13:8-10: ". . . for he who loves his neighbor has fulfilled the Law . . . ," and subsequently James 2:8 ff.: "If you really fulfill the royal law, according to the Scripture, 'You shall love your neighbor as yourself,' you do well. . . ." Akiba, apparently a contemporary of James, likewise expressed the prevailing Jewish belief that Lev. 19:18 was the supreme principle in the Bible (see Sifra, *ad. loc.*).[5]

[4] Section 207, in M. Hadas (ed.), *Jewish Apocryphal Literature* (Philadelphia, 1951), where additional reference is made, *inter alios*, to Isocrates (436-338 B.C.), Nicocles 3.61 ("Do not do unto others that which angers you when others do it unto you"), and to the rabbinic and early Christian formulations mentioned by H. G. Meecham (*The Oldest Version of the Bible: "Aristeas" on Its Traditional Origin* [London, 1932], p. 292), and by H. L. Strack-P. Billerbeck (*Kommentar zum Neuen Testament aus Talmud und Midrasch*, I, "Das Evangelium nach Matthäus," 459-60).

[5] For additional data and discussions, the reader should consult the chapter on "The Greatest Commandment" in I. Abrahams, *Studies in Pharisaism and the Gospels* (reissue, New York, 1967), pp. 18-29 (with its reference to Philo, etc.); G. F. Moore, *Judaism in the First Centuries of the Christian Era: The Age of the*

There can be little doubt that early in the postbiblical period, first among the Jews and later among the Christians also,˙ Lev. 19:18 became the biblical cornerstone of internationalism, of the concept of world brotherhood and the essential equality of all mankind. But is this outlook, noble and worthwhile as it may be, really what the text of Leviticus says? Alas, it requires no great learning or ingenuity, only objectivity—the determination to let the Hebrew text speak for itself —to read the text and its immediate, pertinent context and to note that its author had no one but fellow Israelites in mind.

In vss. 11, 15, and 17 he speaks of *ᵃmithékha*, traditionally rendered "neighbor," the same as *reᵃkha*, but probably a more intimate (family?) term[6]; in vs. 16 he employs the term *bᵉne ᶜammékha* "your countrymen" traditionally "your people"; in vs. 17 he uses the expression *'aḥikha* "your brother, kinsman"; and in vs. 18, immediately preceding our own phrase, he asserts: *lo'-thiqqom wᵉlo'-wᵉlo'=thiṭṭor 'eth-bᵉne ᶜammékha*, "You shall not take vengeance or bear a grudge against your countrymen" (RSV: against the sons of your own people). Reading the chapter as a whole, it is crystal clear that the author was addressing himself to fellow Israelites alone:

> The Lord spoke to Moses, saying: Speak to the whole Israelite community (*dabber 'el-kol-ᶜadath bᵉne-yisra'el*) and say to them: You shall be holy, for I, the Lord your God, am holy. . . . You shall not steal; you shall not deal deceitfully or falsely with one another (*'ish baᶜamitho*). You shall not swear falsely by My name, profaning the name of your God: I am the Lord. You shall not defraud your fellow (*reᵃkha*). . . . You shall not render an unfair decision: do not favor the poor or show deference to the rich; judge your kinsman (*ᵃmithékha*). Do not deal basely [meaning of Hebrew uncertain] with your countrymen (*bᵉ'am-mékha*). Do not profit [meaning of Hebrew uncertain] by the blood of your fellow (*reᵃékha*) : I am the Lord. You shall not hate your kinsman (*'aḥikha*) in your heart. Reprove your kinsman (*ᵃmith-ekha*), but incur no guilt because of him. You shall not take vengeance or bear a grudge against your countrymen (*bᵉne ᶜammékha*). Love your fellow as yourself (*wᵉ'ahavta lᵉreᵃkha kamókha*) : I am the Lord. You shall observe My laws. . . . Lev. 19:2-19.

Tannaim, II (Cambridge, 1927) , 79-88; G. B. King, "The 'Negative' Golden Rule," *JR* VIII (1928) , 268-79; and see the comments by Malbim (Meir Leibush ben Yehiel Michael, nineteenth-century commentator on the Bible, author of *Ha-Torah wᵉ-ha-Miṣwah*) at Lev. 19:18, and by S. Zeitlin in "Love Your Enemies," pp. xxiii-xxvi of his "Prolegomenon" to the 1969 reissue of G. Friedländer, *The Jewish Sources of the Sermon on the Mount* (1911) .

[6] While the dictionaries and commentaries generally adduce Akkadian *emūtu* as a cognate, the extra-biblical history of Hebrew *ᶜamith* is hardly certain, and is in need of close analysis.

As indicated above, it is not easy to find in the English language a single word as the precise and clear equivalent for *ré'a*. The traditional rendering "neighbor" lends itself too readily to misinterpretation, and far too many readers of the Bible fail to recognize that " 'Neighbor' in the Old Testament generally denotes a fellow member of the people of the covenant; it is therefore similar to 'brother'. . ." (H. F. Beck, "Neighbor," IDB III, 534-35). The term "fellow Israelite" expresses the idea accurately.

Furthermore, it may be noted that in the covenanted Israelite societal structure in the holy land of Israel, where all the inhabitants, non-Israelite as well as Israelite, were subject to the laws of the covenant, the non-Israelite who lived in the land had numerous privileges and responsibilities (see the convenient discussion of "So-journer" by T. M. Mauch in IDB IV, 397-99). Since our section of Lev. 19 involved Israelites only, it was necessary, later in the chapter, to make special reference to the non-Israelites who resided (a better term than "sojourned," which denotes a brief or temporary stay, a "visit") in the land; accordingly, vss. 33-34 read:

> When a stranger resides with you in your land (*wekhi-yagur 'ittekha ger*), you shall not wrong him. The stranger who resides with you shall be to you as one of your citizens (*ke'ezrah mikkem yihyeh lakhem ha-ger ha-gar 'ittekhem*); you shall love him as yourself, for you were strangers in the land of Egypt: I the Lord am your God.

It is only because he resides among Israelites in the land of Israel that the non-Israelite receives this status; the same non-Israelite, were he a resident of Moab, or Ammon, or Assyria, or Egypt, or Edom, or Babylonia, etc., would have no such status, for the non-Israelite outside the land of Israel was outside the scope of the covenant between Israel and God.

A third classical case in point is the passage in Amos 9, where the statement is made (vs. 7):

> "You are to Me the same as the Ethiopians, O children of Israel," declares the Lord. "I brought up Israel from the land of Egypt, and the Philistines from Caphtor, and the Arameans from Kir."

Amos is commonly understood to manifest here internationalism on the highest level: Ethiopians, Israelites, Philistines, Arameans—all are regarded equally by the God of Israel.

But does Amos really assert, or even imply, either here or anywhere else in his book, that the God of Israel is at the same time and equally

211

the God of the Ethiopians and of the Philistines and of the Arameans? This is hardly what Amos says or implies in 2:4:

> Thus said the Lord:
> For three transgressions of Judah,
> For four, I will not revoke it,
> Because they have rejected the Teaching of the Lord
>   (*'eth-torath YHWH*)
> And have not kept His laws (*ḥuqqaw*).

None of the six non-Israelite nations mentioned previously (1:3–2:3—Arameans, Philistines, Phoenicians, Edomites, Ammonites, and Moabites) was accused of rejecting God's *torah* or of transgressing his *ḥuqqim*. How could they be, when they had no such obligation to Him in the first place?

Even more positive and pointed is Amos' statement in 3:1-2:

Hear this word that the Lord has spoken concerning (or: against) you, O children of Israel, concerning (or: against) the whole family that I brought up from the land of Egypt:

> You only have I recognized (or: acknowledged)
> Of all the families of the earth;
> Therefore I will punish you
> For all your iniquities.

The fact that God brought up the Philistines from Caphtor and the Arameans from Kir in no wise indicated that these peoples and God had entered into a contract, as Israel and God had done previously. Indeed, God's contract with Israel was a mutually exclusive one, and forbade Israel to recognize and worship any other god—on penalty of various kinds and degrees of punishment—and barred God from recognizing and prospering any other people.[7]

As a matter of fact, the very phrase "I brought you up (*he'eléthi 'ethkhem*) —or: "brought you out," "freed you" (*hoṣé'thi 'ethkhem*) —from the land of Egypt," frequently occurs in the Bible in place of the term *berith* ("covenant") to indicate God's exclusive covenant with Israel. Thus Amos employs this phrase three times (2:10; 3:1; 9:7) for the covenant relationship, whereas in its single occurrence (1:9) the term *berith* is employed in a less exclusive sense, concerning the "covenant of brotherhood" (*berith 'aḥim*) between Phoenicia

---

[7] Note, e.g., how often the *niph'al* form of *shaba* "to swear, vow," is found in the Bible with God as the subject and his covenant with Israel as the context; see S. Mandelkern, *Concordance*, 5th ed. by (F. Margolin-) M. Goshen-Gottstein (1962), p. 1144. God could not act counter to his voluntary vow, unless Israel transgressed.

(Tyre) and an unnamed people which the former violated. Similarly, the expressions "I/He (God) led you (cf. 2:10, *wa-'olekh 'ethkhem*) through the wilderness (for forty years) ," and "I/He (God) destroyed the Amorites/Canaanites (cf. 2:9, *we-'anokhi hishmádti 'eth-ha-'emori*) before you," and "I/He (God) dispossessed the Amorites/Canaanites (*wa-yóresh 'eth-ha'emori*) before you," are all expressions of the covenant relationship between God and Israel, never between God and any other people.[8]

What, then, is the relationship between God and the non-covenanted, non-Israelite peoples of the world, in view of the undeniable fact (e.g., Amos 1:3–2:3) that God, and none other, punishes them for transgressions? Further, what is the nature of these transgressions, seeing that God's *torah* and *huqqim,* that is, his covenant, are not involved?

To the biblical writers, from first to last, God is not only Israel's God alone, exactly as Israel is God's people alone, but he is at the same time, and naturally so, also the God of the universe, the only God in existence in the whole wide world, the only God who ever existed and who will ever exist. As God of the universe, he is the sole Creator and Master of all heavenly bodies (sun, moon, stars) , of all natural phenomena (lightning, thunder, rain, drought, earthquakes) , and of sky, earth, waters, and all living beings therein, human and animal. All natural phenomena, all heavenly bodies, all living creatures, all people, nations and individuals alike, are subject to his direct supervision and will. He is their Master in the fullest sense of the term.

And so, the God of Israel is at the same time the sole God and Master of the universe without being the God of any nation but Israel: the *natural* God of biblical Israel is a *universal* God, but not an *international* God. With no people other than Israel did God ever

---

[8] James Muilenburg has made use of these expressions in his discussion of "The Form and Structure of the Covenantal Formulations," *VT* IX (1959) , 347-65, though they hardly demonstrate an amphictyony; on the nonexistence of this institution in ancient Israel, see J. G. Vink, "The Date and Origin of the Priestly Code in the Old Testament" in *The Priestly Code and Seven Other Studies, Oudtestamentische Studiën,* XV (1969) , 128 ff.: ". . . the idea of *amphictyony.* Recent studies tend to do away with the concept altogether. . . . An all-out attack on the amphictyonic hypothesis was launched by H. M. Orlinsky ('The Tribal System of Israel and Related Groups in the Period of the Judges,' *Oriens Antiquus,* I [1962], 11-20) . . . . We agree with Orlinsky's view, not with Noth's widespread theory . . ."; and see further reference there to R. Smend, S. Herrmann, G. Fohrer, J. Maier, and others. H. G. May, in *The Bible in Modern Scholarship,* J. P. Hyatt, ed. (Nashville, 1965) , p. 73, had expressed the opinion that ". . . deserving further discussion . . . is the amphictyonic organization of early Israel, almost axiomatic in contemporary biblical scholarship even though variously interpreted, and concerning which Orlinsky has raised serious questions."

enter into a legally binding relationship. To the biblical writers God was never the God of Moab, or of Egypt, or Canaan or Assyria or Aram or Ethiopia or Philistia, *et. al.* He was the God of Israel alone; and just as Israel was to have no other god, just so was God to have a legal obligation to all his creation, embracing not only all non-Israelite peoples of the world, but also the living creatures of sky, earth, and waters, all the heavenly bodies, and the like.

What is this universal legal obligation of God's? According to the Bible (Gen. 8–10), after God destroyed the world (a world that had become too lawless to merit preservation) he assured the survivors (Noah and his family and all the animals with them, and their descendants forever) that never again would he bring destruction upon life on earth. But mankind, in turn, had to respect human life; wanton murder and the shedding of blood would not be tolerated. God further fixed the careers of all heavenly bodies, of the seasons, of the use of animals as food for man, and other matters that we have come to subsume generally under the term "natural law." As a result, while no nation other than Israel owes allegiance to God and his Teaching (*Torah*), and while God has committed and restricted himself exclusively to the interests of his chosen people, Israel, he has the power, as the God of the universe, to regulate and to interfere in the affairs of all peoples everywhere. He will not tolerate murder, excessive brutality, wanton conduct; such action is contrary to God's ordered universe, to what has aptly been called by the rabbis the "Noahide Laws."

J. H. Greenstone wrote a clear and compact article on this subject in the *Jewish Encyclopedia* in 1904.[9] These are "Laws," he wrote,

which were supposed by the Rabbis to have been binding upon mankind at large even before the revelation at Sinai, and which are still binding upon non-Jews. The term Noachian indicates the universality of these ordinances, since the whole human race was supposed to be descended from the three sons of Noah, who alone survived the Flood. Although only those laws which are found in the earlier chapters of the Pentateuch, before the record of the revelation at Sinai, should, it would seem, be binding upon all mankind, yet the Rabbis discarded some and, by hermeneutic rules or in accordance with some tradition . . . introduced others which are not found there. . . . They declared that the following six commandments were enjoined upon Adam: (1) not to worship idols; (2) not to blaspheme the name of God; (3) to establish the courts of justice; (4) not to kill; (5) not to commit adultery; and (6) not to rob. . . . A seventh commandment was added after the Flood—not to

[9] "Laws, Noachin," II, 648-50; recently reissued.

eat flesh that had been cut from a living animal (Gen. ix. 4). Thus the Talmud frequently speaks of "the seven laws of the sons of Noah," which were regarded as obligatory upon all mankind, in contradistinction to those that were binding upon Israelites only. . . . In another baraita . . . the seven Noachian prohibitions are enumerated as applying to the following: (1) idolatry; (2) adultery; (3) murder; (4) robbery; (5) eating of a limb cut from a living animal; (6) the emasculation of animals; (7) the pairing of animals of different species. . . .[10]

Postbiblical rabbinic discussions apart, the fact remains that the Bible does tell us quite a bit about these universal laws. In Gen. 9:1 ff. we read:

God blessed Noah and his sons, and said to them, "Be fertile and increase, and fill the earth. The fear and dread of you shall be upon all the beasts of the earth and upon all the birds of the sky . . . and upon all the fish of the sea. . . . Every creature that lives shall be yours to eat; as with the green grasses, I give you all these. You must not, however, eat flesh with its life-blood in it. But for your own life-blood I will require a reckoning: I will require it of every beast; of man, too, will I require a reckoning for human life, of every man for that of his fellow man!

> Whoever sheds the blood of man,
> By man shall his blood be shed;
> For in His image
> Did God make man."

And God continues (vss. 9 ff.):

"I now establish My covenant (*'eth-berithi*) with you and your offspring to come, and with every living thing that is with you—birds, cattle, and every wild beast as well. . . . Never again shall there be a flood to destroy the earth. . . ."

[10] An interesting recent discussion of "Do Noachites Have to Believe in Revelation? A Passage in Dispute Between Maimonides, Spinoza, Mendelssohn, and H. Cohen; a Contribution to a Jewish View of Natural Law," by S. S. Schwarzschild, may be found in *JQR* LII (1961-62), 297-308; LIII (1962-63), 30-65. Incidentally, to Maimonides, the seven Noahide commandments are: the prohibitions of (1) idolatry, (2) the improper use of the name of God, (3) murder, (4) sexual immorality, and (5) theft, (6) the injunction to establish laws and courts, and (7) the prohibition to eat meat from a living animal. But whereas it had generally been held that (p. 301) "Everyone who accepts the seven Noachite laws and is careful to fulfill them is one of the righteous men of the nations of the world and has a share in the world to come," Maimonides introduced the condition that the "Noachite" must also believe that these seven laws were revealed by God to Moses in the Torah, and that he thus merely reaffirmed an earlier injunction to Noah and his children.

Or when Isaiah denounces King Sennacherib of Assyria and assures him ignominious defeat, it is because of his blasphemous treatment of God (II Kings 19:22 ff.; Isa. 37:22 H.) :

> Whom have you blasphemed and reviled
> (*'eth-mi heráfta we-giddáfta*) ,
> Against whom raised your voice
> And insolently raised your eyes?
> Against the Holy One of Israel!
> . . .
>
> Because you have raged against Me,
> And your tumult has reached My ears,
> I will put My hook in your nose
> And My bit in your mouth,
> And I will take you back by the road
> By which you came.

Turning back to Amos, chaps. 1 and 2, it is, again, God's universal, "Noahide" laws which have been violated by Israel's Gentile non-covenanted neighbors. Again, it is in his capacity as the God of the universe (not as the national God of Israel, since Israel was not the object of these violations) that he will punish the transgressors. In 1:3-5 it is the inhuman treatment that Damascus meted out to Gilead ("because they threshed Gilead with threshing sledges of iron") that will result in the former's punishment. In vss. 6-8, Gaza will suffer the consequences for "carrying into exile a whole people." According to vss. 9-10, God will destroy Tyre "because they delivered up a whole people to Edom and did not remember the covenant of brotherhood"; while vss. 11-12 assert that God will devastate Edom "because he pursued his brother with the sword and cast off all pity." God will destroy Ammon and exile her leaders, say vss. 13-14, "because they ripped up women with child in Gilead"; and, finally, in 2:1-3, God will cut off the leaders of Moab "because they burned to lime the bones of the king of Edom."

All these crimes are clearly violations of the "Noahide" laws, the universal laws of nature, involving as they do mass murder, exile, and excessive and unnatural brutality—man's inhumanity to man. It is because God promulgated these laws that they exist (at least the biblical writers believed this to be so) , and it is God alone who will punish the violaters. Indeed, who else is there to execute judgment—the "no-gods" of Syria, Philistia, Phoenicia, Edom, Ammon, and Moab? Then, after having hammered home to his Israelite audience the fact that Israel's God is the only and all-powerful Deity in the world, Amos turned directly to his fellow countrymen and warned them, as God's only covenanted people, that far and beyond their non-covenanted neighbors, they would be called to account "for having rejected the Teaching of the Lord and for not having kept his laws" (*'al-mo'osam 'eth-torath YHWH we^huqqaw lo' shamáru*) —for it is Israel alone upon whom the *torah* of God was binding. And this is exactly the import of 9:7. As the sole Deity of the universe, Israel's God is responsible for the migrations and careers of all peoples of the world, be it those of the Ethiopians, or of the Philistines, or of the Arameans, or others, as well as of those of his own chosen people. This did not, however, make Israel's God (nor is it ever so asserted in the Bible) also the God of the Ethiopians, or of the Philistines, or of the Arameans!

To prove that the expressions *'elohe ph^elishtim, 'elohe 'aram, 'elohe mo'av,* or *'ammon* or *'edom* or *'ashshur* or *bavel* or *misráyim,* etc., never refer to the God of Israel, it is scarcely necessary to refer to such a passage as Judg. 10:6: "The Israelites again did what was evil in the sight of the Lord. They served the Baalim and the Ashtaroth, and the gods of Aram, and the gods of Sidon, and the gods of Moab, and the gods of the Ammonites, and the gods of the Philistines; but they forsook the Lord and did not serve Him" (. . . *wa-ya'avdu 'eth-ha-be'alim we-'eth-ha-'ashtaroth we-'eth-'elohe 'aram we-'eth-'elohe sidon we-'eth 'elohe mo'av we-'eth 'elohe vene-'ammon we-'eth 'elohe ph^e-lishtim . . .*).

It is worth noting here that it may well be that the term *'elohe* in connection with, say, Moab and Ammon, ought to be translated "god" rather than "gods." The evidence that the Moabites and Ammonites regularly served more than one deity (more than, respectively, Chemosh and Milcom) is hardly any greater than that the Israelites regularly served more than one (YHWH). Thus the Moabite Stone and the Book of Kings, so far as monotheism is concerned, are not greatly different. What the term *'elohe* conveys here, and frequently elsewhere in the Bible, is not "gods" to indicate gross polytheism, but simply "a no-god," "an alleged god." So that the expression *'elohim 'aherim* may very often be rendered simply "another god" with even more justification than "other gods." The idea is simply that the biblical writers complained that God was not being obeyed, not that more than one other god was being worshiped. Whether the common expression accusing Israel of worshiping "other gods" (or perhaps "another god"; see Mandelkern's *Concordance,* s. *'aherim*) really constituted an accusation of idolatry or was, rather, a cliché expression for "You are not obeying God, whose spokesman I am and whose orders I bring you; obey Him by heeding my (i.e., His) words" (the speaker being anyone who claimed to be a spokesman of God: Moses, Samuel, Nathan, Ahijah, Elijah, or any of the prophets, etc.), is a very basic problem that I hope to deal with elsewhere. Be it also noted that just because a Gentile people worshiped only one god was no indication to the biblical writers that he was a real god and comparable to their own God, or that such a people, like the Israelites, was also monotheistic. Such a people was a heathen people that worshiped "a no-god."

In line with this understanding of the biblical concept of God (that is, that God was national and universal but not international), other passages such as Isa. 2:2-4, Mic. 4:1-4, and Isa. 56:7 fall readily and naturally into place. As the only real God in the world, and with Israel as his exclusive partner in covenant, the biblical writers believed that sooner or later the peoples of the world would come to recognize these two covenanted partners as representing the only true religious force. Thus Isaiah and Micah (perhaps deriving from a common source) declare:

> In days to come,
> The Mount of the Lord's House shall be established
> As the highest mountain,
> Rise above the peaks;
> And all the nations shall stream to it,
> And many peoples shall go and say:
> "Come, let us go up
> To the Mount of the Lord,
> To the House of Jacob's God,
> That He may instruct us in His ways
> And that we may walk in His paths."
> For instruction *(torah)* shall come forth from Zion,
> The word of the Lord from Jerusalem.
> He will judge among the nations,
> Arbitrate for many peoples;
> And they shall beat their swords into plowshares,
> Their spears into pruning hooks:
> Nation shall not lift up sword against nation,
> And never again train for war.

Whether this declaration is to be understood literally or figuratively, and even though the precise historical circumstances for it will probably not be determined, these two prophets expressed unequivocally the nationalism of God and the superiority—rather, the uniqueness—of his teaching *(torah)* which he gave to his people, Israel. Further, it is to Zion, and to no other capital city or religious center, that the peoples of the earth will stream, and it is from Jerusalem, and from no other spot on earth, that God's message *(davar)* will emanate. Yet strange as it may seem, this passage has been comprehended by nearly everyone as the very essence of internationalism, as though there were a single aspect of the beliefs and practices of any people in the world except Israel—the language, or the prayers, or the sacrifices, or the shrines, let alone the gods—that was worthy of the slightest consideration for incorporation into God's *torah*.

As for Isa. 56:7, "for My House shall be called a House of prayer for all peoples" *(ki vethi beth-tᵉphillah yiqqare lᵉ-khol-ha- 'ammim)*, the whole passage, far from articulating internationalism, simply asserts that those non-Israelites (vss. 3-6 make mention of "foreigner[s]" *ben [bᵉne]-ha-nekhar* and "eunuch[s]" *saris[im]* who adopt and demonstrate their obedience to God's commandments and institutions would be permitted to become members of his covenanted community in the land of Israel:

Thus said the Lord:
Observe what is right and do what is just,
For soon My vindication shall come,
My deliverance soon to be revealed.
Fortunate is the man who does this,
The person who holds fast to it:
Who keeps the sabbath and does not profane it,
And stays his hand from doing any evil.
Let not the foreigner say,
Who has attached himself to the Lord,
"The Lord will exclude me from His people,"
And let not the eunuch say,
"I am but a dry stick."
For thus said the Lord:
To the eunuchs who keep My sabbaths,
Who choose what I delight in
And hold fast to My covenant:
I will give to them
In My House and within My walls
A monument and a name
Better than sons and daughters.
I will give them an everlasting name
Which shall never perish.

219

And the foreigners who attach themselves to the Lord,
To minister to Him and to love the name of the Lord,
To be His servants—
All who keep the sabbath and do not profane it,
And who hold fast to My covenant—
I will bring them to My sacred Mount
And let them rejoice in My House of prayer.
Their burnt offerings and sacrifices
Shall be accepted on My altar;
For My House shall be called
A house of prayer for all peoples.
Thus declares the Lord God,
Who gathers the dispersed of Israel:
I will gather still more to those already gathered.

Note that only those Gentiles—even eunuchs!—who have already been observing the laws of the sabbath and fulfilling the covenant in every respect are eligible for membership in God's select community, membership that takes effect when they have emigrated from Babylonia to Judah and entered the service of God in his Temple in Jerusalem.

Even a cursory examination of our section is sufficient to point to an adherent of the priestly hierarchy in power in restored Judah as the author. This is evident, for example, from the *combination* of the following items: (1) The emphasis on the observance of the sabbath (vss. 2, 4, 6) is typically priestly. The term *shabbath,* not part of Second Isaiah's concern or vocabulary, is found otherwise only in 66:23, in a similarly late and specifically priestly context:

"And from them (namely, the Gentile nations mentioned in vs. 19: Tarshish, Put (Pul, H.), Lud, Tubal, Javan, and the distant coasts) likewise I will take some to be levitical priests (lit., priests Levites, la-koh*a*nim la-l*e*wiyyim) ," said the Lord.

"For as the new heaven and the new earth
Which I will make
Shall endure before Me,"
Declares the Lord,
"So shall your seed and your name endure.
And new moon after new moon,
And sabbath after sabbath (*u-midde shabbath b*e*shabbatho*) ,
All flesh shall come to worship Me."

Note in this connection that the phrase *shabbeth b*e*-shabbatho* occurs only here (in vs. 23) and in Num. 28:10 (a *P* passage) ; also that all thirty-one occurrences of the plural form *shabbathoth* in the Bible are found in *P* or otherwise late contexts: Exod. 31:13; Leviticus (eleven times); Ezekiel (twelve times); Neh. 10:34; I Chron. 23:31; II Chronicles (four times); and our Isaian (56:4) passage.

(2) It is not acceptability of Gentiles or proselytism in general that the author has in mind here (as one might argue, say, for Isa. 2:2-4 [Mic. 4:1-4]), but the legalization even of castrated Gentiles for sacred work in the Temple of Jerusalem. This is contrary, for example, to the older law (Deut. 23:2 [1]): "No one whose testes are crushed or whose member is cut off shall be admitted into the congregation of the Lord." Indeed, even an animal with such defects is excluded as a sacrifice to the Lord, especially when offered by a *ben-nekhar,* "a foreigner" (Lev. 22:24-25): "You shall not offer to the Lord anything [with its testes] bruised or crushed or torn or cut; you shall have no practices [i.e., mutilations or sacrifices] in your land. Nor shall you accept any such [animals] from a foreigner for offering as food for your God; since they are mutilated, they have a defect, they shall not be accepted in your favor."

(3) It is not easy to deny a direct connection between a passage such as Num. 18:1 ff. and our passage in Isa. 56. The Numbers passage reads:

> The Lord said to Aaron: You with your sons and your ancestral house shall bear any guilt connected with the sanctuary. . . . You shall associate with yourself your kinsmen the tribe of Levi, your ancestral tribe, to be attached to you and to minister to you (*we-yillawu ᶜalékha wi-share-thúkha*), while you and your sons [serve] before the Tent of the Pact. They shall discharge their duties to you and to the Tent as a whole, but they must not have any contact with the furnishings of the shrine or with the altar, lest both they and you die. . . . No outsider (*zar,* i.e., an Israelite not of priestly-levitical stock) shall intrude upon you as you discharge the duties connected with the shrine and the altar. . . . I hereby take your fellow Levites from among the Israelites; they are assigned to you in dedication to the Lord . . . , while you and your sons shall be careful to perform your priestly duties in everything pertaining to the altar and to what is behind the curtain. . . . Any outsider (*zar*) who encroaches shall be put to death.

In Isa. 56:6 note the expression *u-vᵉne ha-nekhar ha-nilwim ᶜal-YHWH lᵉsharᵉtho* ("And the foreigners who attach themselves to the Lord to minister to him") in connection with vs. 2 in the Numbers passage reproduced above; and 56:7, *ᶜolothehem wᵉ-zivhehem lᵉrason ᶜal-mizbᵉhi* ("Their [viz., the foreigners'] burnt offerings and sacrifices shall be accepted on my altar") is to be noted for the contrast with vss. 3, 5, 7 in the Numbers passage.

A closer study may well uncover other associations that are pertinent. Thus, is *lo^c yikkareth* in Isa. 56:5 (". . . I will give them [the eunuchs] an everlasting name which shall never perish [lit., be cut off]"), a deliberate play on *karuth*, "one whose member (or testicles) is cut off" (Deut. 23:2 *k^{e}ruth shaphkha; karuth* for animals in Lev. 22:24)? The eunuch's manliness may be cut off, but not his name! Or when Isa. 56:6 talks of " (the foreigners who attach themselves to the Lord to minister to him . . .) to become his servants," should this expression, *lihyoth lo(w) la-^{c}avadim*, recall at once Lev. 25:55, *ki-li v^{e}ne-yisra'el ^{c}avadim ^{c}avaday hem*, "For it is to Me that the Israelites are servants: they are My servants . . ."? It is significant that only Israel and Israelites are God's servants (*'eved, '^{a}vadim*) in the Bible, with the sole exception of the eunuchs in this passage, and Nebuchadrezzar[11]; all other *'^{a}vadim* are servants to mortals.

There is, of course, much more to the problem of "levitical priests" than our immediate preoccupation with nationalism-universalism; for example, the date of the sections quoted above and the period and circumstances in which Aaron and the tribe of Levi (not the craft of the levite, as in Judg. 17–18[12]) were introduced in the Bible. But enough argument has been presented here to indicate that, far from being a model expression of internationalism, Isa. 56 presents the clerical-nationalist interests of the priestly group in power in post-exilic times, interests that are somewhat less than internationalistic.[13]

As a matter of fact, it is not certain that Isa. 56 is even universal, let alone internationalistic. The priestly element that came to dominate in little Judah in the post-exilic period manifested all the chief characteristics that are usually associated with clerical interests: narrow political, social, and cultural views, an attitude of superiority toward the nonclerical elements of the population, the kind of arrogance that comes from a belief that the priestly authority derives directly and exclusively from God himself, a ready reinterpretation and rewriting of history and law codes to provide antiquity and justification for what is really but contemporaneous priestly innovation and revision; and so on. The purpose of Isa. 56, then, is primarily

---

[11] See chap. I, "The Biblical Term 'Servant' in Relation to God," pp. 7-11 in H. M. Orlinsky, *The So-Called "Servant of the Lord," op. cit.,* with the "Additional Note" on "King Nebuchadr/nezzar of Babylon, My Servant" in Jer. 25:9; 27:6; 43:10.

[12] See Section D, "The Seer-Priest in Ancient Israel," in my chapter (XXIV) on "The Seer-Priest," *The Patriarchs and the Judges,* B. Mazar, ed., II, 144 H., in the series *The World History of the Jewish People,* due to appear in English in 1969-70/5730 In the Hebrew version of 1967/5727, see pp. 290-96, 366-70, 387.

[13] See the monograph by Vink (*op. cit.*) on the priestly treatment of history and historical materials.

to justify and legalize the incorporation and use of what had been palpably impermissible and illegal previously, specifically no less, but no more, than the use of eunuchs and other aliens in the Temple service of God. There was no universalistic—not to speak of inter-nationalistic—ideology present in the priestly outlook, nor did it develop such ideology in its subsequent career in power. Indeed, what characterized its outlook was the vigorously nationalistic attitude toward non-Judeans, precisely the attitude against which the authors of Ruth and Jonah wrote so forthrightly and eloquently.

The nineteenth chapter of Isaiah has long been troublesome to scholars. The whole first part of the chapter, vss. 1-17, speaks of the crushing and humiliating defeat that Egypt will suffer at the hands of God, and this theme is repeated in vss. 22-23 of the second part of the chapter. But in the midst of these dire pronouncements, at the beginning of the second part, there appear statements in which, according to many scholars, "Old Testament religion reaches its zenith and . . . we find the crown of biblical theology." [14] Verses 18-25 read:

> In that day, there shall be several (lit. five) cities in the land of Egypt speaking the language of Canaan and swearing allegiance to the Lord of Hosts. . . . In that day, there shall be an altar to the Lord in the midst of the land of Egypt. . . . And the Lord will make Himself known to the Egyptians; and the Egyptians shall acknowledge the Lord in that day and worship with sacrifice and burnt offerings, and they shall make vows to the Lord. . . . In that day, there shall be a highway from Egypt to Assyria, and the Assyrians shall come into Egypt and the Egyptians into Assyria. . . . In that day, Israel shall be the third with Egypt and Assyria, a blessing in the midst of the earth, whom the Lord of Hosts has blessed, saying, "Blessed be My people Egypt, and Assyria the work of My hands, and Israel My heritage" (*barukh 'ammi miṣráyim u-ma'aseh yaday 'ashshur we-naḥalathi yisra'el*).

I regard this passage (along with the essential message of the books of Ruth and Jonah, on which see below) as evidence for the beginning of the development of internationalism as a flourishing factor in biblical Israel's outlook, and I should date this second part of Isa. 19 (vss. 18-25) to the Seleucid-Ptolemaic period in Judean history. It was then that an altar was actually erected to Israel's God on Egyptian soil; namely, the temple of Onias at Heliopolis. This historical setting is especially probable, if not indeed obligatory, if the preserved reading in vs. 18, *'ir ha-héres*—which is baffling as it stands (so that the entire phrase *'ir ha-héres ye'amer le-'eḥath* was left un-

[14] H. G. May in *The Bible in Modern Scholarship*, p. 100.

translated above, and is meaningless in the translations which reproduce it literally) —represents original *'ir ha-ḥéres* (with *ḥeth* in place of *he*), "City of the Sun"=Heliopolis. This reading is accepted by many scholars on independent grounds: A number of Hebrew manuscripts read *ha-ḥéres,* as do the Targum (on which see, for example, Rashi and David Qimhi), Summachus, the Vulgate, and the Arabic translation of the Septuagint. On the overall background, see S. Zeitlin, *The Rise and Fall of the Judaean State,* I (Philadelphia, 1962/5722), 76-80, and n. 76 on p. 463.

This is the period and region—the commercial routes and the Mediterranean shores of Asia and Egypt, the heart of the Jewish diaspora at the time—which marked the beginning of genuine and consistent international thinking in ancient Israel. It is not the forced Exile in Babylonia, consequent on the destruction of Judah and Zion, that brought about this outlook. Nor yet is it the antinationalistic reaction of a considerable portion of the nonpriestly segment of the Judean population, as expressed by the authors of the books of Jonah and Ruth that brought about this outlook. It was the presence of hundreds of thousands of Judeans in Egyptian and Syrian Mesopotamian territory (*miṣráyim* and *'ashshur* in the Hebrew text) earlier conquered by Alexander. In these lands, Jews lived a relatively free life, free to remain where they were and free to return to Judea whenever they wished and for as long as they desired. This would be the time and place for a new attitude, beyond the nationalistic-territorial-universalistic attitude of the prophets and of the pre-exilic period generally, according to which God could be worshiped anywhere, not just on Zion in Jerusalem in the holy land of Israel. An Egyptian (let alone a Judean) could remain in Egypt and be a full-fledged Jewish worshiper of Israel's God; and even an altar could be erected in Egypt for sacrifice to God.

Contrast this new, late post-exilic attitude with the late pre-exilic attitude, as exemplified by Deut. 4:28 and Jer. 16:13. The former reads (Moses addressing his fellow Israelites):

(If . . . you act wickedly and make for yourselves a sculptured image in any likeness . . . the Lord will scatter you among the peoples. . . .) There you will serve man-made gods of wood and stone, that cannot see or hear or eat or smell.

And Jer. 16:13 (Jeremiah addressing his fellow Judeans):

(You yourselves have acted more wickedly than your fathers. . . .) So I will cast you out of this land to a land you have not known, you or your fathers, and there you will (have to) serve other (or: alien) gods (*wa-ʿavadtem-sham ʾeth-ʾelohim ʾaherim*) day and night, for I will show you no favor.

In pre-exilic times, one of the most severe punishments that God's chosen people could suffer for transgressing the covenant with God was not alone the devastation of their homeland and the destruction of the Temple but, perhaps even more, exile from the holy land to an unclean land (cf. Amos 7:17), where they could not worship the Lord properly, that is, with sacrifice.[15]

It is wrong to lump together Isa. 2:1-4 and Mic. 4:1-4, on the one hand, with Isa. 19:18-25 on the other. The former insist that it is to Zion that all nations will come streaming, whereas the latter has it that an altar will be erected to God's worship in Egypt. It is the latter that is internationalistic, not the former.

Withal, my main purpose in quoting the latter part of Isa. 19 was not primarily to indicate the circumstances and period in which internationalism became a significant part of Israel's thinking. That would belong properly, it seems to me, to the domain of the competent scholar of the Second Jewish Commonwealth and the Hellenistic era. My intention was but to illustrate a basic aspect of methodology.

There are, literally, hundreds, not just tens and scores, of passages in the Hebrew Bible, from Genesis through II Chronicles, that assert positively or at least reflect the relationship of God and Israel as being purely nationalistic. Amos put it this way (3:1-2):

> Concerning the whole family that I brought up from Egypt:
> Hear this word, O children of Israel,
> That the Lord has spoken concerning you,
> You alone have I acknowledged (or: recognized; *raq ʾethkhem yadaʿti*)
> Of all the nations of the earth (*mi-kol mishpᵉhoth ha-ʾadamah*);
> That is why I call you to account (*ʾefqod ʿalekhem*).

---

[15] The theory that the synagogue—as a house of prayer, not of assembly or sacrifice—originated in Babylonia during the Exile is quite without foundation; all the pertinent biblical, intertestamental, and early rabbinic literature, together with the results of archaeology, rule this out. See S. Zeitlin, "The Origin of the Synagogue," *Proceedings of the American Academy for Jewish Research*, III (1932), 69-81; E. Rivkin, "Ben Sira and the Nonexistence of the Synagogue: A Study in Historical Method," pp. 320-54 of *In the Time of Harvest: Essays in Honor of Abba Hillel Silver* (1963), with full bibliography; and I. Renov's (unpublished) doctoral dissertation (Hebrew Union College-Jewish Institute of Religion [New York, 1952]), *Some Problems of Synagogal Archaeology*, chap. II. "Development of the Ark," p. 58, and nn. 58-59 on p. 235.

Deut. 32:8-9 expresses it as follows:

> When the Most High gave nations their homes
> And set the divisions of men,
> He fixed the boundaries of peoples
> In relation to Israel's numbers.
> For the Lord's portion is His people (*ki ḥéleq YHWH 'ammo*),
> Jacob His own allotment (*ya'ᵃqov ḥével naḥᵃlatho*).

And Second Isaiah declares to his fellow Judean exiles (49:22-26):

> Thus said the Lord God:
> I will raise My hand to nations (*hinneh 'essa' 'el-goyim yadi*)
> And lift up My ensign to peoples.
> And they will bring your sons in their bosoms
> And carry your daughters on their shoulders.
> Kings shall be your attendants,
> And their queens shall serve you as nurses;
> They shall bow to you, face to the ground,
> And lick the dust of your feet. . . .
> I will make your oppressors eat their own flesh,
> And they shall be drunk with their own blood as with wine.
> Then all flesh shall acknowledge (*wᵉ-yadeʿu*)
> That I the Lord, the Champion of Jacob,
> Am your Savior and Redeemer!

Similarly, as Herbert May has noted in the work previously cited, "the post-exilic writer in Micah depicts the Gentiles licking the dust like serpents . . . ," Mic. 7:16-17:

> The nations shall see and be ashamed of all their might;
> They shall lay their hands on their mouths,
> Their ears shall be deaf.
> They shall lick the dust like a serpent,
> Like the crawling things of the earth;
> They shall come trembling out of their strongholds,
> They shall turn in dread to the Lord our God,
> And they shall fear because of You.

Or take as another example Isa. 14:1-2 (generally recognized as post-exilic) and Zech. 2:14-16. The former asserts that the alien may become attached to triumphant and restored Israel, whereas the Gentile peoples who had held them captive would become their slaves. The latter declares that only the Gentiles who join Israel in her restored homeland can become part of God's people and that only in Zion will God dwell. The text of Isa. 14 reads:

226

The Lord will have compassion on Jacob
And will again choose Israel,
And He will set them on their own soil;
And aliens shall join them (*wᵉ-nilwah ha-ger 'alehem*)
And cleave to the House of Jacob.
And the peoples (*'ammim;* the Gentiles) shall take them
And bring them to their homeland (*mᵉqomam,* lit. place);
And the House of Israel shall possess them
On the soil of the Lord
As slaves and handmaids:
They shall become captors of their captors
And shall rule over their taskmasters.

And the passage in Zech. 2 reads:

Shout for joy, Fair Zion! For lo, I come and will dwell in your midst,"
declares the Lord. "Many nations will attach themselves (*wᵉ-nilwu
goyim rabbim*) to the Lord in that day and become My people, and I
will dwell among you." Then you will know that the Lord of Hosts
Himself sent me to you. And the Lord will take Judah to Himself as
His portion in the holy land, and He will choose Jerusalem once more.

Such passages—it bears repeating—may be readily multiplied by
many, many scores throughout the Bible. And if such other, allegedly
internationalistic expressions as *navi' la-goyim nᵉthatikha* "I appointed (or: "designated") you a prophet to (or: "for") the nations"
in Jer. 1:5; *wᵉ-'ettenkha livrith 'am lᵉ-'or goyim* "I will make you a
covenant of people, a light of nations" in Isa. 42:6; and *u-nᵉthatikha
lᵉ-'or goyim* "I will make you a light of nations" in Isa. 49:6, are not
being dealt with here, it is only because I have discussed them in
some detail in my study, *The So-Called "Servant of the Lord" and
"Suffering Servant" in Second Isaiah.* The conclusions reached there
may be cited here, in part (pp. 116-17):

However such expressions as [the three passages cited above from Jeremiah and Second Isaiah] are translated, all the contextual data in these
[two] Books make it amply clear that nothing international was implied
in them. These prophets, God's spokesmen all, were not sent on any
mission to any nation other than their own . . . to God's covenanted
partner, Israel. When they were not simply the means by which God
punished His erring people, the pagan peoples were merely helpless
witnesses—just like the heavens and the earth and the mountains—to
God's exclusive love and protection of His people. This is the essential
meaning of such passages as Jer. 26:6 and 4:2 . . . i.e., the heathen nation shall say: May we be as prosperous and protected as Israel—if all

goes well with Israel; but: Cursed shall you be like Israel—if Israel is in degradation at the hands of God for her sins.

In a word: Israel will be "a light of nations" in the sense that Israel will dazzle the nations with her God-given triumph and restoration; the whole world will behold this single beacon that is God's sole covenanted people. Israel will serve the world at large as the example of God's loyalty and omnipotence.

Something ought to be said about the books of Ruth and Jonah in relation to our theme. I fully agree with the considerable majority of scholars who date both these books in the post-exilic Persian period. I understand these books to constitute a vigorous rejoinder to the views of the priestly establishment in power at the time, views clearly set forth in the books of Ezra and Nehemiah. Thus it is hardly a coincidence that in inveighing against the mixed marriages current in restored Judah and their consequences, Ezra calls for the rejection of the "foreign women" (*nashim nokhriyoth*) and their progeny (cf. Ezra 9:12; 10:2, 10, 11, 14, 17, 18, 44). This stand Nehemiah shared completely (Neh. 10:31; 13:1-3, 23-30). Ezra 10:10-11 puts it forthrightly (after RSV):

And Ezra the priest stood up and said to them, "You have trespassed and married foreign women, and so increased the guilt of Israel. Now then make confession to the Lord the God of your fathers, and do his will; separate yourselves from the people of the land and from the foreign women."

And Nehemiah declares (13:23 ff.):

In those days also I saw the Judeans who had married Ashdodite, Ammonite, and Moabite women. . . . And I contended with them and cursed them and beat some of them and pulled out their hair; and I made them take oath in the name of God, saying: "You shall not give your daughters to their sons, or take their daughters for your sons or for yourselves. Did not King Solomon of Israel sin on account of such women . . . ? Foreign women made even him sin. Shall we then listen to you and do all this great evil and act treacherously against our God by marrying foreign women?"

The point of the book of Ruth is that a "foreign woman" (cf. *we-'anokhi nokhriyah* in 2:10)—and a Moabite at that!—is not only perfectly acceptable to God and to Israel, but she can be worthy enough to become the ancestress of King David, Israel's greatest hero and God's chosen ruler and founder of Judah's great dynasty. But this is true only if she adopts wholeheartedly the beliefs and practices of Israel. Within the short space of eighty-five verses, where the word

"Ruth" occurs a total of twelve times, the term *mo'ᵃviyah* is employed along with the name no less than six times (*ruth ha-mo'ᵃviyah:* 1:22; 2:2, 21 (quite strikingly, in replying directly to her mother-in-law, Naomi) ; 4:5, 10; and cf. 1:4, *nashim mo'ᵃviyoth . . . wᵉ-shem ha-shenith ruth*). Also, in 2:6, one of Boaz' servants, in reply to his master's question, "Whose girl is that?" says, "She is a Moabite girl" (*na'ᵃrah mo'ᵃviyah hi*—not "She is Naomi's daughter-in-law" or the like) who came back with Naomi from the country of Moab. In 2:10, in thanking Boaz for his acts of kindness, Ruth says, "Why are you so kind as to single me out, when I am a foreigner (*wᵉ-'anokhi nokhriyah*)?" Boaz' reply is most revealing, in that it sets forth clearly the acceptability of a genuine convert—even a Moabite—to Israel's God and religion (vss. 11-12):

> "I have been told of all that you did for your mother-in-law after the death of your husband, how you left your father and mother and the land of your birth and came to a people you had not known before. May the Lord reward your deeds. May you have a full recompense from the Lord, the God of Israel, under whose wings you have sought refuge!"

No less significant in this connection is the blessing bestowed upon Ruth by the entire Bethlehemite community, after they bore witness to Boaz' acquisition of "Ruth the Moabite" in his role of levir (4:9-11):

> And Boaz said to the elders and to the rest of the people, "You are my witnesses today that I am acquiring from Naomi all that belonged to Elimelech. . . . I am also acquiring Ruth the Moabite, the wife of Mahlon . . . , that the name of the deceased may not disappear from among his kinsmen. . . ." All the people at the gate and the elders answered, "We are witnesses. May the Lord make the woman who is coming into your house like Leah and Rachel, both of whom built up the House of Israel! Prosper in Ephratah and perpetuate your name in Bethlehem!"

It is a considerable accolade to be blessed by God "like Leah and Rachel," and further to be described as a "daughter-in-law who . . . is better . . . than seven sons" (4:15) !

It is hardly for the purpose of discussing the institution of levirate marriage, or to tell a beautiful story about devotion or romance, or to provide David with a genealogy, or the like, that the book of Ruth was brought into being. Whatever the origin of the materials which our author employed, they were chosen and utilized for a purpose. That purpose could hardly have been anything other than a direct attack on one of the main planks of the program advanced by the Ezra-Nehemiah school of thought.

Likewise, the book of Jonah—also a product of the post-exilic period, a date accepted on various grounds by most scholars[16]—was hardly composed to tell the story of a shipwreck and a whale, or of a man who refused to accept God's call to be his spokesman, or of a great people and city becoming converts to Israel's God and a part of his covenanted people, or the like. Without going into detail, and admitting that here the data are less specific and clear, one can assert with some confidence that the primary purpose of the author of Jonah was to demonstrate that the entire world, man and beast, is God's creation and concern. Moreover, any non-Israelite people which repents of its wickedness—the kind of wickedness that deserves God's punishment (see above on Amos 1–2 and the Noahide Laws)—may be forgiven by God if it repents:

> The word of the Lord came to Jonah son of Amittai, "Go at once to Nineveh, that great city, and proclaim judgment upon it; for their wickedness has come before me." (1:1-2.)

> The word of the Lord came to Jonah a second time, "Go at once to Nineveh . . . and issue to it the proclamation that I tell you." Jonah went at once . . . and proclaimed: Forty more days, and Nineveh shall be overthrown! (3:1-4.)

> The people of Nineveh believed God. They proclaimed a fast, and great and small alike put on sackcloth. When the news reached the king of Nineveh, he rose from his throne, took off his robe, put on sackcloth, sat in ashes, and had the word cried through Nineveh: "By decree of the king and his nobles: Man and beast . . . shall cry mightily to God. Let everyone turn from his evil ways and from the injustice he has committed. Who knows but that God may turn and relent . . . so that we do not perish." God saw what they did, how they were turning back from their evil ways. And God renounced the punishment He had planned to bring upon them, and did not carry it out. (3:5-10.)

> The Lord said [to Jonah], "You cared about the plant, which you did not work for and which you did not grow, which appeared overnight and perished overnight. And should I not care about Nineveh, that great city, in which there are more than a hundred and twenty thousand persons who do not yet know their right hand from their left, and many beasts as well!" (4:10-11.)

[16] See the discussions and references in O. Eissfeldt, *The Old Testament: An Introduction,* trans. from the 3rd German ed. by P. R. Ackroyd (New York, 1965), pp. 403-6 and 477-83, with "Additional Literature and Notes" on pp. 760-61 and 765-66.

A close reading of Ruth and Jonah shows that the view of their authors is in keeping with the outlook of their pre-exilic predecessors. Once again a position is put forth which holds that God is Israel's God alone, and that he is the only God in the universe; in short, a national-universal God. In the latter capacity, he metes out punishment to all Gentile peoples who transgress the laws of the universe, but is ready to remit punishment if they repent. (Interestingly, the terms used in Jonah for the transgressions by the Ninevites, *ra‘ah* [1:2; 3:8] and *ḥamas* [3:8], are the same as those employed in Gen. 6:5, 11, 13 for the generation that was responsible for God's decision to bring the Flood upon the earth.) In every essential respect, the concept of God in his relation to Israel and to non-Israelite peoples is the same in Ruth and Jonah as in Amos and all the other pre-exilic prophets. If Ruth and Jonah mention some specific events not found in pre-exilic literature, for example, the total acceptability of Ruth the Moabite, or the cancellation of punishment for repentant Nineveh, it is simply because historical conditions brought on the presence of the one in one period and its absence in another; but there is no contradiction in basic concept.

Concepts do not originate and function in a vacuum. They are part of the social process, subject to social forces. The historian cannot be content with such generalizing statements as those of Eissfeldt[17]: "We may only say that the breadth of outlook towards another nation which appears here [in the book of Ruth] as in the book of Jonah is more readily intelligible in a later than in an earlier period"; and, "We can only say with certainly that the broad universalism and tolerant humanity which give the book [of Jonah] its attractive tone, belong to the compiler and his time. . . . In the pre-exilic period such far-reaching universalism and such unconditional tolerance are difficult to imagine." What is one to say, then, of the book of Esther, which is no less post-exilic than Ruth and Jonah, yet is hardly characterized by "broad universalism and tolerant humanity"? Indeed, Eissfeldt, and everyone who operates with abstract concepts in a vacuum, without regard to time and place, is so much the theologian and moralist, rather than historian, that he would insist that

> in the assessment of the book [of Esther], we must distinguish between its aesthetic and its ethical and religious value. As a narrative it deserves full recognition. . . . But Christianity, extending as it does over all peoples and races, has neither occasion nor justification for holding on to it. For Christianity Luther's remark should be determinative . . . :

[17] *Ibid.*, pp. 483, 405.

"I am so hostile to this Book [II Maccabees] and Esther that I could wish that they did not exist at all, for they Judaize too greatly and have much pagan impropriety." [18]

A scholar who moralizes demoralizes history.

The pattern of nationalism in the Bible, clear and pervasive, can be gauged from another angle. One may draw up a list of every Hebrew word or expression in the Bible that is used in describing the relationship between God and Israel on the one hand, and between God and non-Israelite peoples on the other. In the case, say, of the book of Isaiah (all sixty-six chapters) I have in mind *'elohe yisra'el* "the God of Israel" (not of any other people), *Bore' yisra'el* "Creator of Israel," *yoṣer* (*yisra'el/ya'aqov*) "He who fashioned (Israel/Jacob)," *mélekh* "King," *ṣur* "Rock," *qedosh* "Holy One," *mehoqeq* "Lawgiver" (for Israel), *ro'eh* "(Israel's) Shepherd," *ba'al* "be the Husband of, espouse," *'av* "Father," *ne'eman* "Faithful One," *'avir* "Champion," *nish'an* the One on whom Israel alone can rely, etc. It is Israel alone whom God "chose" (*bahar*), "gathers" (*'asaf*), "glorifies Himself in" (*yithpa'er*), "ransoms" (*padah*), "redeems" (*ga'al*), "assembles" (*qabbeṣ*), "shields" (*magen*), "shows compassion to" (*merahem*), and a number of others. One will search in vain for such terms to be employed with reference to non-Israelite peoples, except in such passages as those in Isa. 19, discussed above.

Instructive in this conection is the work compiled by Jesus son of Sirach. The Judean author of Ecclesiasticus, as is evident from a careful reading of his text, represents the priestly establishment in power in Judea in the third/second century B.C. His attitude toward the Gentiles is a direct continuation of the nationalism-universalism of his predecessors. It is not the internationalism manifest in the viewpoint of the author of Isa. 19:18-25. Sirach writes (16:24–17:32; after RSV):

> Listen to me, my son, and acquire knowledge,
> And pay close attention to my words
>
> . . .
>
> The works of the Lord have existed from the beginning
> by His creation (or: judgment),
> And when He made them, He determined their divisions.
> He arranged His works in an eternal order,
> And their dominion (or: elements) for all generations.

[18] *Ibid.*, pp. 511-12.

. . .

> After this, the Lord looked upon the earth
> With all kinds of living beings He covered its surface,
> And to it they return.
> The Lord created man out of earth,
> And turned him back to it again.
> He gave them few days, a limited time . . .
> . . . And granted them dominion over beasts and birds.

. . .

> He filled them with knowledge and understanding
> And showed them good and evil.

. . .

> He bestowed knowledge upon them,
> And allotted to them the law of life.
> He established with them an eternal covenant,
> And showed them His judgments.
> Their eyes saw His glorious majesty.
> And He said to them, "Beware of everything unrighteous,"
> And He gave commandment to each of them concerning
>   his neighbor.
> Their ways are always before Him.

. . .

> He appointed a ruler for every nation,
> But Israel is the Lord's own portion.

Sirach conceives of God as the only God in the world, the God of the world, the God of the universe and everything and everyone in it. At the same time, he is the God of Israel alone, and of no other people. As 17:17 puts it:

> He appointed a ruler for every nation,
> But Israel is the Lord's own portion.

After the first, and much briefer, form of this essay was read in public, a question was asked from the floor: "What do you do with Mal. 1:11 in the light of your paper?" The verse reads:

"For from where the sun rises to where it sets, My name is great among the nations, and in every place incense and pure oblation are presented to My name. For My name is great among the nations," said the Lord of Hosts.

The fact is that such representative scholars as S. R. Driver and Eissfeldt,[19] among many others, see nothing in this verse (at least, they

[19] S. R. Driver, *Introduction to the Old Testament*, 9th ed. (London, 1913), pp. 355-58; Eissfeldt, *op. cit.*, pp. 441-43.

make no specific mention of it) to upset or modify their view that Malachi, like Ezra and Nehemiah, emphasizes observance of the cult and national exclusiveness. How else is this passage to be taken in the context of both the chapter and the entire book if not as rhetoric? The same question can be posed for vs. 14*b:* "For I am a great King," said the Lord of Hosts, "and My name is feared among the nations."

But something more basic is involved here; namely, the very essence of scholarly research: the matter of methodology. It should be axiomatic that one must first deal with what is unequivocal and straightforward so as to comprehend as clear and consistent a pattern as possible. If such clear data are available in some abundance, so much the better. Then, and only then, does the scholar proceed with the difficult and less clear, the elusive passages, dealing with each passage in its own right. If this analysis brings forth a picture that is not consistent with that produced by the seemingly unequivocal and straightforward, the scholar must then proceed to determine whether the two patterns of thought existed side by side, at the same time and in the same region, but among different strata in the societal structure. Is the element of chronology involved, one outlook being later than the other? Or is it a matter of geography, different regions or countries? And so on the investigator must look at various possible factors. Under no circumstances is it permissible to dismiss a clear-cut pattern in favor of an interpretation arising from elusive and unclear passages. Yet it is amazing how often in our field of research it is rather the principle of *ignotum per ignotius* that is followed. Exegesis is pushed out by eisegesis. More than one scholar blandly accepts Isa. 19:18-25 as genuinely Isaianic. It is described in such terms as: "This prophecy (is) Isaiah's last and noblest 'testament to posterity,' " "The prophecy is a remarkable one . . . for the grand catholicity of the picture . . . ," and as "remarkable prophecy (which) has no equal in biblical literature. . . ." Ignored in the process are all the other passages to the contrary, overwhelming in quantity and in clarity, not only in the Bible generally but in the book of Isaiah itself, including the group of chapters (13–23) in First Isaiah that deal with the foreign nations: Babylon, Assyria, Philistia, Moab, Syria, Ethiopia, Egypt, against Egypt and Ethiopia, against Babylon, Edom, Arabia, and Phoenicia. This, it should be noted, includes the entire first part of chap. 19 itself. So what is uncertain to put it mildly, namely, the presence of the concept of internationalism in the Bible as a whole and in Isaiah in particular, is explained by what is even more uncertain, namely, the historical context of Isa. 19:18-25. This is hardly an acceptable methodology.[20] In this connection, it is worth repeating what Henry J. Cadbury once wrote on "Motives of Biblical Scholarship":

> Another bias of our procedure is the over-ready attempt to modernize Bible times. This tendency . . . arises partly from taking our own mentality as a norm and partly from a desire to interpret the past for its present values. . . . A third defect . . . arises not from a modernizing but from a conservative tendency. When new conceptions force us from old positions we substitute for the old positions imitations or subterfuges which are not better supported than their predecessors but which we hope are less vulnerable. . . . We are afraid to follow the logic of our discoveries and insist that we are retaining the old values under a new name.[21]

Very few of us biblical scholars, *qua* scholars, are free of the influence of our upbrnging and general environment. The Hebrew Bible means nowadays, as it has in the past, different things to different people. Some would seek and find in it proof texts for post-biblical rabbinic interpretation. Others would like to see in it the kind of declarations that point to and demonstrate the truth of Christianity, each scholar understanding the term in his own way.[22] Still others would prefer to discover in the Bible, especially among the prophets, the most progressive and liberal ideas and ideals in all human experience. For one reason or another, nearly all who belong to these different groups would like very much to find internationalism, not nationalism, in the Bible. Certainly this is the temper of much of the world since World War II. And so if the biblical outlook is nationalistic-universal rather than internationalistic, biblical Israel is regarded as having been far behind our own times and our progressive outlook.

Apart from the fact that it is not the concern of scholarship to deal in judgment value and to mete out awards for backward- or forward-looking views, we tend to overlook all too readily that our own outlook

[20] In the process, Amos, Isaiah, Jeremiah, Second Isaiah, and the rest, not to speak of their audiences, are made to look foolish, contradicting themselves from one statement to another. Thus Second Isaiah is made to say one thing in 49:1, 6 and the very opposite in climaxing the chapter in vs. 26. But then, I suppose, the ancients, unlike ourselves, must have been primitive folk, gullible and illogical. Or were they?

[21] Henry J. Cadbury, "Motives of Biblical Scholarship," *JBL* LVI (1937), 1-16.

[22] See, e.g., H. J. Cadbury, "Gospel Study and Our Image of Early Christianity," *JBL* LXXXIII (1964), 139-45; C. T. Craig, *passim* in "Realized Eschatology," *JBL* LVI (1957), 17-26, and "The Identification of Jesus with the Suffering Servant," *JR* XXIV (1944), 240-45.

in this area is still virtually identical with that of the Bible. We like to believe that we think and act internationalistically rather than nationalistically. Did we not, for example, create the League of Nations after World War I, and the United Nations after World War II? Yet who can deny that it was precisely the nationalistic interests of each member nation that brought the League of Nations into being and that determined the vote and actions of each of them? Was it not for self-protection and self-advancement that each nation joined the League and maneuvered within it, or did not join it, or voted to keep another nation out of it altogether? And finally the League of Nations died because of the clash of mutually exclusive nationalistic interests, yet the United Nations was achieved. How many would undertake today to seek to prove that pure unselfish internationalism motivates the joining, or not joining, or not being permitted to join, the United Nations? And if a nation, large or small, is too weak to have its way, it will create or join one bloc of nations or another. This is not internationalism at all. It is nationalism pure and simple, not more and not less than biblical Israel's nationalism. When Isaiah and Micah looked forward to the transformation of swords into plowshares and spears into pruning hooks, it was surely because of their nationalistic interests. Surely because of the constant overrunning of their beloved land and people they looked forward to the cessation of war. Never again would an Asiatic power invade them (whether them specifically or simply en route to Egypt), nor would Egypt ever again overrun them (whether them specifically or en route to the conquest of Phoenicia-Syria-Mesopotamia). Their outlook and motivation were no different from our own today. Most of the European nations after World War I wanted war abolished because each of them had just experienced the brunt of it. Most of the nations of the world after World War II want war abolished because nuclear weapons can annihilate every one of them in a matter of minutes, no matter where they may be located. The motivation against war and for peace has long been and still is nationalistic. And if anyone wishes to designate biblical Israel a Founding Member of the League of Nations or of the United Nations, that is all right with at least one writer.

The Significance of Cosmology in the Ancient Near East

WALTER HARRELSON

Two distinct cultures, brilliantly portrayed in *The Intellectual Adventure of Ancient Man*,[1] dominated the ancient Near East. The cosmologies of Egypt and Mesopotamia have a number of similarities, but the differences are much more striking than the similarities. Egyptian cosmology exercised little influence upon biblical cosmological reflection. I am choosing, therefore, not to deal with it in this paper, except now and again by way of contrast.

By 3000 B.C., Sumerian culture in lower Mesopotamia had already worked out, it seems, a view of the universe which was to endure with only minor modifications for over 2000 years. The threefold division of the universe with which we are familiar from the Bible is found in Sumerian culture. Heaven, consisting of various regions, is the abode of the gods. The earth, conceived of as a disc, and the underworld complete the divisions of the universe. The primeval waters are located both above the vault of heaven and below the earth. The upper and lower seas (the Mediterranean and the Persian Gulf) represent the limits of the earth. The vault of heaven rests upon the outermost bounds of the earth, thus enclosing man in an earth which is protected from destruction by the firm underside of heaven and by the under-earth mountains which support the disc-earth over the lower primeval waters. This cosmological picture is precisely that found in the Old Testament.

We are all familiar, I suspect, with the classical creation story from

[1] H. and H. A. Frankfort, John A. Wilson, Thorkild Jacobsen, and William A. Irwin, *The Intellectual Adventure of Ancient Man, An Essay on Speculative Thought in the Ancient Near East* (Chicago, 1946).

Mesopotamia, the *enuma elish*.[2] Older Sumerian versions have been preserved only fragmentarily, but the story certainly had its Sumerian prototype. The creation is portrayed as having occurred as a result of conflict among the gods. We are introduced first to the situation which gave rise to the very existence of the gods themselves. Only the two realities Tiamat (the salt water) and Apsu (the sweet water) are there from the beginning, uncreated. From their commingling, pairs of deities are born. Chief among them are (in this text) Anu (the sky god), Ea (the god of sweet water and of earth's fruitfulness), and Marduk (the chief god of Babylon, the equivalent of the Sumerian storm god Enlil). The creation story has little place for the goddesses of the pantheon; we hear nothing specifically of Inanna (later called Ishtar) the goddess of love and war, or of the mother goddess Nin-hursag (also known by many other names).

The lesser gods are so noisy and unruly that they disturb the divine principles Tiamat and Apsu. Apsu is the more violent in his rage against his descendants and determines to destroy them. The gods discover Apsu's plans, and Ea (ever the wise god) casts a spell over Apsu and slays him. Ea thus becomes in fact the god of the sweet waters and of agriculture. But Tiamat learns that her consort has been slain and prepares to destroy the gods. The gods choose their champions to do battle with Tiamat, but none is successful until Marduk is commissioned. Marduk secures the promise of full authority over the gods, arms himself with dread weapons, and slays Tiamat. From her body the vault of heaven is created and the bounds of the seas surrounding the earth, as well as the earth itself, are established. The lower half of Tiamat apparently provides the seas and also the firmament (Tablet IV, end). The gods are then given their places in the universe: Anu to govern the sky and remain as the chief, but somewhat inactive, god in heaven; Enlil to rule over storm and wind (although Marduk is really exercising the Enlil functions in Babylon), and Ea to govern fertility and the sweet waters in place of Apsu. The stars, constellations, and other divinities are assigned their tasks, the flood gates of heaven are secured, the calendar is constructed, and the movement of sun and moon regulated. Nothing is heard of the underworld in the material now available from Tablet V.

Man is then created from the blood of Kingu, the god who is adjudged by the assembly of the gods to have been the one chiefly responsible for Tiamat's "rebellion." The creation of man is the work

[2] James B. Pritchard, ed., *Ancient Near Eastern Texts, Relating to the Old Testament,* 2nd ed. (Princeton, 1955), pp. 60-72.

of Ea, and it is skillful and wonderful to behold. The purpose of man's creation is clear: He is created to serve the gods and relieve them of toil. The gods are arranged into two groups: 300 govern in heaven under Anu's lordship; 300 rule in earth, presumably under Marduk's authority. The gods then build a magnificent house for Marduk in Babylon, the temple Esagila, to which all the gods come for the festival of the New Year. The gods confer upon Marduk the full authority of the pantheon. Fifty divine names are attributed to him; he is thus exercising the functions of these gods and *is* in fact these gods operationally. Some scholars have seen in this attribution of powers to Marduk a tendency in the direction of monotheism. The tablet closes with instructions that Marduk's fifty names be taught to all and their meanings explained.

The creation story, in its various versions, portrays the establishment of order out of chaos. The cosmos came into existence as the consequence of conflict within the pantheon. The creation of man is the result of a brilliant idea of Marduk (in *enuma elish*): The gods should not have to labor so hard to maintain order in the cosmos; let creatures be formed who can take over the hard service of the gods. But the lifeblood of man must be provided by a divine being, if man is to live and be able to serve the gods appropriately. So man is fashioned from the inert Tiamat materials and from the blood of the rebel Kingu. The clever work of Ea in fashioning man is praised, but the story quickly turns to the establishment of a divine guard in heaven and on earth. Man is referred to again in connection with Marduk's rule on earth. Marduk is to be the shepherd of men, is to regulate their lives, eliciting from them praise of the gods and requiring them to maintain the food offerings for the gods. Man is to care for the temples, improve the land, and be diligent in waiting upon the needs of the gods. The life of man has a clear-cut purpose: He is the servant of the gods and is charged to be faithful in this service. He has been created by the gods, he has divine lifeblood in his veins, but he is clearly not a divine being. Gilgamesh is to learn (Babylonian Flood Story, Tablet X) that man is made to die; the quest for immortality must end in failure:

> Gilgamesh, whither rovest thou?
> The life thou pursuest thou shalt not find.
> When the gods created mankind,
> Death for mankind they set aside,
> Life in their own hands retaining.
> Thou, Gilgamesh, let full be thy belly,

Make thou merry by day and by night.
Of each day make thou a feast of rejoicing,
Day and night dance thou and play!
Let thy garments be sparkling fresh,
Thy head be washed; bathe thou in water.
Pay heed to the little one that holds on to thy hand,
Let thy spouse delight in thy bosom!
For this is the task of (mankind) ! [3]

The creation story contains one line which is of profound significance for an understanding of Babylonian cosmology. Earth is to provide a "likeness of what (Marduk) has wrought in heaven." [4] The vast collection of mythological materials from the Sumerian, early Babylonian, Assyrian, and late Babylonian cultures makes abundantly clear that heavenly existence is the prototype, or the archetype, for life on earth. The temple Esagila in Babylon is a model of that built by the gods in heaven. It is a point of connection between heaven and earth. The old Sumerian city state culture seems to have provided the analogy for the picture of the heavenly assembly. The gods talk over the decisions which must be made and come to a consensus, just as did the full citizens of a Sumerian city state in southern Babylonia. The establishment of order in heaven was succeeded by the establishment of an analogous order on earth. But order in heaven and on earth must be maintained. The early "democratic" heavenly government is succeeded by the conferral of full authority upon one of the high gods (in the creation story this is Marduk). And order on earth is maintained by the conferral of full authority upon one of the governors of the old Sumerian city state. Kingship is established in heaven first, and then it is "lowered from heaven." [5]

The very classification and arrangement of the material elements of Mesopotamian culture have their explanation in the lives and deeds of the gods. The Sumerian myth entitled "Enki and Ninhursag" [6] has a number of motifs. Chief among them, it seems, is the explanation of how certain plants came to be what they are. For each of the eight plants created from the semen of Enki by Ninhursag, eight deities are later created to govern these plants. The conflict between pastoral and agricultural modes of existence is portrayed in the story of the conflict between Dumuzi and Enkimdu, a story of two suitors for the hand of

---

[3] *Ibid.,* p. 90 (Tablet X, col. III) .

[4] *Ibid.,* p. 69 (col. VI, l. 113) .

[5] See the Sumerian king list, *ibid.,* pp. 265-66; Thorkild Jacobsen, *The Sumerian King List,* "Assyriological Studies," No. 11 (Chicago, 1939) , pp. 71 ff.

[6] Pritchard, *Ancient Near Eastern Texts,* pp. 37-41.

the goddess Inanna (later Ishtar), who are finally reconciled, it being acknowledged that the life of both is indispensable to human existence.[7] The tools used by man are gifts of the gods, and their prototypes are probably understood to be in heaven. Building materials were first employed by the gods, and the technique of building is no discovery of man but a divine creation. Warfare is first waged in heaven; mankind engages in war, not alone in obedience to the gods, but also following the pattern of divine warfare.

Earthly existence, in short, is participation in heavenly existence. The life of man is not simply understood to follow the natural rhythms and changes of the seasons and to have its legitimation in the fact that this rhythm has been decreed by the gods. Too little attention has been focused upon the fact that, for Mesopotamian culture, every day, every activity of man, every thought he has, every tragedy he suffers, represents his participation in the life and work and fate of the gods. It is true that the great festival of the New Year constituted the occasion for the renewal of the cosmos, for the reestablishment of the heavenly order in which earthly order participated. This great cultic act was the very center of Mesopotamian life. But the remainder of the year was lived in the conviction that there *was* order on earth, precisely because there was an established heavenly order. Every event in human life had its meaning; the meaning might be hidden, but it was known to the gods.

This point is particularly clear in the Mesopotamian understanding of law. The law collections, of which there are several,[8] were given by the gods to the kings under whose reigns they were promulgated. Law was established in heaven, and the regulations of life on earth, even the most detailed commercial regulations, had not merely the sanction of the gods but were the creation of the gods. Hammurabi, it is true, speaks of having established justice in the land, having decreed the laws found in the collection. But the scene portrayed on the law stela shows Shamash giving ring and rod to Hammurabi, the symbols of judgment and lawmaking.[9] Hammurabi's laws are committed to him by Shamash, as the Epilogue makes clear.[10] They are his

---

[7] *Ibid.*, pp. 41-42.

[8] Notably the code of Ur-Nammu, ca. 2050 B.C.; the code of Lipit-Ishtar of Isin, ca. 1850 B.C.; the code of the city of Eshnunna, possibly as old as that of Lipit-Ishtar; the code of Hammurabi, ca. 1700 B.C. Translations of the laws are found in Pritchard, *Ancient Near Eastern Texts,* pp. 159-98. See also G. R. Driver and John C. Miles, *The Babylonian Laws,* Vols. I, II (Oxford, 1952, 1955).

[9] See James B. Pritchard, *The Ancient Near East in Pictures, Relating to the Old Testament* (Princeton, 1954), p. 77 (fig. 246).

[10] Pritchard, *Ancient Near Eastern Texts,* p. 178 (col. XXIV, ll. 84-89, col. XXV, ll. 95-99).

copy of the heavenly tablets. The prototype of all law is the heavenly law, of which earthly law is a copy, an earthly equivalent.

The ethical significance of Mesopotamian cosmology has not been dealt with very fully in the literature I know. If it is correct that the life of man is patterned in every respect upon the life of the gods, then man is certainly summoned to take cognizance of this fact as he lives. The cosmology thus provides man with orientation for his overall life. He is a descendant of the first man created by the gods. He is charged to serve the gods, to be faithful in making his offerings and sacrifices, responsible in drawing up contracts (for the god of writing supervises contracts), diligent in repairing dikes (for Ea is the god of the sweet waters and dikes), quick to return the runaway slave (for the divine law given by Shamash says to do so), and courageous in battle (for Marduk himself is prosecuting the battle and will not tolerate slackness). The only difficulty with this religious view of ethics is that the gods are known to be rather capricious in their actions. Order is established in heaven, to be sure, but that order is precarious even in heaven. In early Sumerian thought, the cosmos was full of beings who sought to undo the life of gods and man. The underworld (*arallu*) was the abode of Ereshkigal, older sister of Inanna the goddess of love and war. Ereshkigal had around her monsters who could and did work destruction upon those who fell under their power. In the story of Inanna's descent to the underworld, a recently discovered text relates that various monsters followed her out of the underworld, seeking to take captive the divine rulers of the various cities. Only Dumuzi (Tammuz) seems not to have pleaded for mercy and been freed by the demons. Thus he is apparently carried off to the underworld, causing the fertility of the land to come to an end. The story must then have related how Inanna (Ishtar) rescued him from the underworld. The newly discovered text [11] is not preserved to the end of the story, but this text does offer the best sequel to the Inanna story. It appears that Inanna's first descent to the underworld was to provide her with the knowledge of the region that she would require when later she returned to rescue Dumuzi and restore fertility to the land.

[11] See Pritchard, *Ancient Near Eastern Texts,* p. 52, n. 6; Samuel N. Kramer, ed., *Mythologies of the Ancient World* (New York, 1961), pp. 109-15; *The Sumerians, Their History, Culture, and Character* (Chicago, 1963), pp. 153-60; "Cuneiform Studies and the History of Literature: The Sumerian Sacred Marriage Texts," *Proceedings of the American Philosophical Society,* 107 (1963), pp. 485-516. The new text (*PAPS,* 107, pp. 492-93) does provide a conclusion to the story, at least a preliminary conclusion, but it does not give us any reason for Inanna's initial trip to the underworld. The story closes with Dumuzi's sister mourning her brother's fate—in true tragic style.

The underworld is the place of death, the "land of no return." All human beings are destined to go there; the only exceptions being the flood hero(es), the Sumerian Ziusudra, the Babylonian Utnapishtim, who were given "life like the gods" because they had been spared in the deluge which destroyed mankind.[12] Thus the life of man is lived out under the protection of the cosmic order with its prototype in heaven, but this order is subject to the capricious conduct of the gods in heaven. It is a life subject also to the baleful influences of the netherworld, influences which can be warded off only with the help of the gods. It is of paramount significance for man, therefore, that he know how to enlist the aid of the gods. Specialists in the interpretation of dreams, in the reading of hidden messages from natural events (the flight of birds, the pattern made by water poured on the ground, the shape of the livers of sacrificed animals, etc.), in the offering of incantations and prayers, were indispensable for Mesopotamian culture. The firm conviction of Mesopotamian society (at least in the middle and later periods) was that the gods could help, if only they could be prevailed upon to do so.

The Mesopotamian cosmological speculations include a number of myths which portray primordial men who have sought to go beyond the limits appointed to mankind. Gilgamesh's quest for immortality is a case in point. The Adapa legend tells of Adapa's having cursed the south wind for having sunk his boat while he was fishing.[13] The curse was, of course, effective, and the south wind ceased to blow. Anu is aghast and calls for the culprit to be brought to him. Ea, however, wishes to befriend Adapa. He advises him how to flatter the gods as he makes his way to Anu's throne, and thus enlist their help before Anu. But Ea also tells him that he must not eat the food or drink the drink set before him; they will be poisonous. Actually, the gods intercede so powerfully for Adapa that Anu offers him the food and drink of immortality. But Adapa refuses them and thus forever loses his opportunity to become immortal.

The myth of Zu,[14] imperfectly preserved, seems to tell of how the bird-god Zu from the lower world gained possession of the tablets of destiny and thus was about to overthrow the entire cosmic order. One of the high gods is finally enabled to overthrow Zu, it seems (perhaps

---

[12] Pritchard, *Ancient Near Eastern Texts,* pp. 90, 95 (the Epic of Gilgamesh, Tablet X, col. III, ll. 3-5; Tablet XI, ll. 193-94); *ibid.,* p. 44 (the Sumerian deluge, ll. 257-58); W. G. Lambert and A. R. Millard, *Atra-Hasis, The Babylonian Story of the Flood* (Oxford, 1969), p. 133 (the flood story from Ras Shamra, reverse, l. 4).

[13] Pritchard, *Ancient Near Eastern Texts,* pp. 101-3.

[14] *Ibid.,* pp. 111-13.

it was Marduk), and order is restored. This is a good instance of the precariousness even of the heavenly order which served as the guarantee of order on earth.

The Etana legend [15] also shows us that divine kingship could be imperiled. Etana has no son and heir. Kingship thus is threatened with extinction unless Etana can secure the plant of life and, through its power, produce an heir. An eagle is induced to bear him to heaven, where, it appears, he was finally victorious in his quest. In this case, the daring act of Etana is successful, but not without great travail.

Prophets in Mesopotamian society employed the power of the divine Word revealed to them to guide the kings and leaders of society in their participation in the divine purpose. Prophets accompanied the kings in battle; they gave oracles indicating when the time was propitious for the building of temples and public buildings; they were the counselors of the kings in diplomatic and commercial undertakings. It is particularly important for biblical studies to note that some of these Mesopotamian prophets exercised tremendous freedom in the interpretation of the will of the gods for man. Prophets did not have to be consulted; they would bring their oracles on occasion even when they had not been summoned to inquire of the gods. And what they had to say could be bluntly critical of the kings. In the days of Sennacherib, an unnamed high official (almost certainly in the name of the god) challenges the action of the monarch, who has designated his younger son Asshurbanipal as his successor, in the following words:

> What had never been done even in heaven, the king, my lord, hath brought to pass on earth, and hath made us witnesses of it. Thou hast robed one of thy sons in the royal robes and hast named him as ruler of Assyria, and hast named thy elder son to succeed to the throne of Babylon. What the king my lord hath done for his son is not for the good of Assyria. . . . The lord my king has conceived an evil plan, and thou hast therein been weak.[16]

Earlier, at the northwest Mesopotamian city of Mari in the eighteenth century B.C., prophets, speaking directly in the name of the god and without bidding, could condemn the king of Mari for his failure to consult the deity as he should:

> A muhhum-man came from the god Dagan and said to me: Hurry, send to the king the word that he should consecrate sacrifices to the spirit of Iahdun-lim (the dead predecessor of the current king Zimri-lim).

[15] *Ibid.*, pp. 114-18.
[16] Georges Contenau, *Everyday Life in Babylon and Assyria* (London, 1954), p. 216.

Another prophet had a dream in the temple of Dagan in Tirka. The god told him to bear the following message to Zimri-lim:

> Send your messenger to me and lay your entire situation before me.[17]

The form of these prophetic oracles is virtually identical with that found in the Old Testament. The content seems to consist primarily of summonses to the rulers of the state to be more diligent in consulting the gods, but there is quite clearly a rather sharp reproof leveled against these royal agents of the god. The story of the Egyptian Wen-Amon in Byblos is another example. The king of Byblos has treated Wen-Amon contemptuously as the latter sought to get cedar to repair the barge for the god Amon. Wen-Amon is about to depart without his cedar when a young man is suddenly overcome with ecstasy and cries out, "Bring up (the) god! Bring the messenger who is carrying him! Amon is the one who sent him out! He is the one who made him come!" [18] The king of Byblos then grudgingly complies with Wen-Amon's request. He had been rebuked by his god for having been so uncooperative with the Egyptian visitor.

Jacobsen[19] has called attention to the note of pessimism and critical reaction against the authority of the gods which appears in some late Mesopotamian texts. The "righteous sufferer" describes his fate in terms analogous to those of the book of Job. He has been righteous all his life, gladly serving the gods, doing justly to his neighbors, but all sorts of misfortunes have befallen him. There can be no question that the gods could help him if they chose to do so. But he receives no help. How can such a thing be? The answer given is that the ways of the gods are beyond the full comprehension of man; man cannot expect to penetrate the will and purpose of the gods. But the sufferer then affirms that he must continue to hope and trust in divine deliverance, and the poem closes with this hope fulfilled.

Another text [20] (among several) is even more bitterly pessimistic about life's meaning: the dialogue of the master with his slave. The master states directly opposite judgments on the goods of life, and the slave gladly agrees with him throughout. Love is a good thing;

[17] Martin Noth, "Geschichte und Gotteswort im Alten Testament," *Gesammelte Studien zum Alten Testament,* 3rd ed. (München, 1966) , p. 236. E.T.: "History and Word of God in the Old Testament," *The Laws in the Pentateuch and Other Studies.* Trans. by D. R. Ap-Thomas (Philadelphia, 1966) , p. 184.

[18] Pritchard, *Ancient Near Eastern Texts,* p. 26 (ll. 39-40) .

[19] *Intellectual Adventure of Ancient Man,* pp. 212-18.

[20] "A Pessimistic Dialogue Between Master and Servant," Pritchard, *Ancient Near Eastern Texts,* pp. 437-38.

no, love is a bad thing. Libations offered to the gods are praiseworthy; no, they count for nothing. Almsgiving is good; no, it is worthless. It is not even clear that it is better to live than to die. The analogies with the book of Ecclesiastes are evident.

Mesopotamian hymns, prayers, and laments have been found in abundance. Many of the hymns praise the gods in the most extravagant language, but before they conclude they state the petition of the worshiper—which seems to be the whole point of the hymn of praise to the gods. The gods must be "softened up," helped to see that it is a good thing to grant the requests of petitioners. Again we can see that decisions are made in heaven; the gods must be prevailed upon to alter conditions on earth by making their heavenly judgments and then putting them into effect on earth. Communication between heaven and earth is indeed open, but the life of man has meaning and the fate of man can be altered only on the basis of the establishment of contact between heaven and earth. Man must share in the divine life if he is to live at all; man must live and work on the basis of heavenly archetypes of life and work; the gods may be gracious to man, but they must be persuaded to be so. The whole end of man, then, is to live in his appointed place in the cosmos in such a way as to participate in archetypal reality—in the heavens.

Mesopotamian cosmology enables mankind to discern and to fulfill his place in the world. The meaning of life is provided by analogy with the world of the gods. That which is ultimately real, then, is heavenly existence, but this ultimately real existence can only be shared by man to the extent that he models his earthly life upon that in the heavens. Finally, he must die and descend to the underworld. Immortality is not open to him. Nor does the Mesopotamian citizen appear to have found real significance in the continuance of his family, his city, his nation after his death. He must make the most of the life he has, by sharing as fully as possible in the life of the gods. Religion, then, is the most significant reality in his life. It *is* his life.

The comparisons and contrasts between Mesopotamian and Israelite cosmology are quite evident. The general cosmological scheme of the Israelites is precisely that of the Mesopotamians: heaven, earth, underworld, with the primeval waters held in check by the vault of heaven and by the restraining underside of earth. The seas are held in check by Yahweh just as they are by Marduk (or Enlil) (Pss. 46; 104; etc.). Yahweh is portrayed as the storm god (Enlil, Marduk, Hadad, Baal, etc.), riding upon the clouds (II Sam. 22:11). Before him the mountains quake, the breath of his nostrils brings devastation, and chaos threatens its return. But these great theophany hymns, of which there are several in the Old Testament (Judg. 5; Deut. 33; Ps. 68; Hab. 3, etc.), have been radically reshaped by the Israelite community. They speak much more of Yahweh's coming to deliver his people than they do of the natural phenomena. They portray Yahweh coming, not from heaven, but from the southeast—the wilderness of Paran, the mountain of Sinai. They have been historicized, set into the context of Yahweh's earthly deeds of salvation.

Even more striking is the way in which the creation motif has been recast. Gen. 1:1–2:4a, the priestly creation narrative, has not a thing to say about the life of God in heaven. God created the heavens and the earth, but the priests concentrate their full attention upon the earth. The sun, moon, and stars are simply God's "lamps," hung on the underside of the vault of heaven. What transpires above this vault of heaven is not once alluded to. Furthermore, all vestiges of the conflict of Yahweh with other powers in the universe have been eliminated in the story as it now stands. Cosmos is established out of chaos, but even that chaos is apparently being presented simply as the situation within which God begins his work after having called into existence the future elements of heaven and earth by the Word. The significance of the creation story is not exhausted by the fact that man lives in an orderly and reliable universe, although that is certainly important. Of even greater significance is the command to man, not to serve God but to subjugate and rule over the earth. The story closes with God at rest in the heaven; but when God rests, so also does man.

Man's life in Old Testament terms involves no quest for immortality. It is evident, nonetheless, that the motif of immortality once played some significant part in Israelite cosmological speculation. Where was the tree or the plant of life? Not in heaven, but on earth in the garden of Eden. Even this reference to the tree of life seems to rest upon the blending of two traditions concerning the origin of man. It seems fairly clear from a number of Old Testament passages (Ezek. 28; Isa. 14:12-14; Ps. 46; Isa. 2:2-4, and Mic. 4:1-4) that a West Semitic version of the mountain city (the equivalent of the Ziggurat in Mesopotamia) was known and used by Israel. According to this story, a city was built by the gods upon the highest mountain. From the city flowed the waters of life; there was located the tree of life. But man rebelled against the gods and was expelled from the city, doomed to die, denied the fruit of the tree (or plant) of life. Elements of this old story still appear in the Babylonian flood story (Tablet XI). But as Gerhard von Rad has shown,[21] the old garden story in **Gen.** 2–3 has virtually replaced this West Semitic story. The garden was an oasis in a wilderness, not a city upon a high mountain. The rivers still flow from the garden, which shows the unevenness of the blending of the two traditions. The tree in the midst of the garden is now two trees, the tree of knowledge and that of life. The old oasis version of the story probably simply referred to a tree in the garden, the fruit of which was not to be eaten on penalty of death. It is actually very difficult to interpret the whole story on the assumption that it constitutes a unity.

What has happened, it seems, is that the early narrators of Israel adapted a myth about the first man living in a city upon a high mountain. They greatly altered it, making the city a garden on flat ground, laying emphasis upon the requirement of simple obedience to Yahweh, and showing sin to consist fundamentally in a lack of trusting obedience to a gracious deity. But there is a further and significant elimination. Yahweh comes to the garden daily, it appears, but this garden is quite clearly an earthly reality. Yahweh has no heavenly garden which is the prototype of the earthly one. Paradise is on earth, on this earth. Its location is simply "somewhere to the east," but it is clearly below the vault of heaven. This "garden of God" (Ezek. 28: 13; 31:9) is no heavenly reality. Even when the old West Semitic version returns in eschatological passages (Isa. 2:2-4; Mic. 4:1-4) it is still an earthly reality. Jerusalem is to become the city on the mountain, the center of the universe (Ezek. 38:12), raised up above all other hills. The nations will be borne back to this city, flowing to it as once the rivers flowed from the mountain city at the beginning. Thus we see the myth of creation to have been radically transformed, the mythological motifs severely reduced or eliminated, and the story given a setting as firmly rooted in "history" as was possible.

The conflict motifs from the old Near Eastern creation stories are found here and there in the literature (Isa. 27:1; Job 26:12-13; Ps. 89:10, etc.). But these are motifs in the theophany hymns and belong with those discussed above. The Second Isaiah, as has been pointed out often, goes even further in historicizing the conflict motif (51:9-10). The real monster slain by Yahweh was the Pharaoh and his forces. The cosmos-chaos scheme is laid squarely upon the plane of history, as indeed it is in the theophany hymns generally. The forces of chaos are those found among the nations. Chaos results when mankind fails to be obedient to the covenant requirements; the land

[21] *Genesis, A Commentary*. Trans. by John H. Marks (Philadelphia, 1961), pp. 71-99.

mourns when Israel sins, when there is no knowledge of God in the land (Hos. 4).

More fundamental for an understanding of the contrast between Mesopotamian and Israelite cosmology, however, is the fact that the Israelite people so persistently resisted the temptation to explain their lives on the basis of analogy with the life of Yahweh. What is the true meaning of the name of Yahweh? The Old Testament will not say. Contrast the fifty names given to Marduk, which are to be taught to the children. How do we understand the techniques of agriculture, of craftsmanship, of statesmanship, or warfare? What are the models for all these? Absolutely none are given. Even the temple in the city of Jerusalem is modeled, not after its heavenly archetype, but (according to late tradition) on the model of the tent (tabernacle) in the wilderness. The model for that tabernacle is given by God to Moses on the mountain, but there is not the slightest suggestion that the archetype is located in heaven (Exod. 25:9). In fact, the temple model was Phoenician or Syrian; almost identical temple types have appeared in northwest Phoenicia and elsewhere.

How are Israel's laws given? They are transmitted to Moses, written by the finger of God (Deut. 9:10). This does seem to be a noteworthy parallel to the giving of the law in Mesopotamia. But note the differences. Moses is not a king, not the guarantor of the law on earth. In fact, Moses is sufficiently disobedient to Yahweh that he is not permitted to enter the land of the Promise. And *all* the laws of Israel are affirmed to have been given to Israel in the days of Moses: primarily at Sinai, with a few additions in the wilderness. No king of Israel is reported to have promulgated a single law; this is really remarkable, given the fact that the kings simply would have been required to revise, reissue, and add to the laws of Israel. But the community insisted that the law of God came at the time when Yahweh made a covenant with Israel on Mt. Sinai. All the laws came with Israel into the land of the Promise. They are firmly rooted in the saving work of God connected with the Exodus, Sinai, and the wilderness wanderings.

Was kingship lowered from heaven? On the contrary, kingship was a latecomer into Israel. There was a time when there was no king save Yahweh alone. Various traditions relate the establishment of kingship, but the kingship which prevailed (David's) is described in almost secular terms.[22] The seat of government in Jerusalem was also

[22] See Martin Noth, "God, King, and Nation in the Old Testament," *The Laws in the Pentateuch and Other Studies*, pp. 145-78, esp. pp. 161-66.

a relatively late thing. Jerusalem was taken from the Jebusites by stealth (II Sam. 5). David made the city his capital, and this city continued to remain a kind of no-man's-land in Israel, despite all its later sanctity. The prophets regularly distinguished between the "men of Judah" and the "inhabitants of Jerusalem." Hostility against Jerusalem was no less real than affection for it, in the early days of the kingship. The promise to David (II Sam. 7) and the work of the prophet Isaiah probably led to the sanctification of Jerusalem. But the holy city, the center of the universe, was once no Israelite city at all. Ezekiel can speak of its mixed origins: "Your father was an Amorite and your mother was a Hittite" (16:3).

Even the people of Israel themselves were relative latecomers on the human scene. Once they were no people. When Abraham was called, he was singled out without a word being said about his merits, his noble lineage, his "religion." When Egypt gave up her slaves, the latter emerged as a "mixed multitude"; they whined and bickered in the wilderness. When Yahweh made a covenant with them they broke it; in fact, during the very period in which the covenant law was being given, according to tradition, the people were engaged in breaking it and making gods for themselves at the foot of the sacred mountain.

But surely the kings came to have the status of "divine representative." This is entirely probable, in my view. Nevertheless, the description of these kings is one which by no means calls for the people's adulation. Their relative merits are catalogued. The greatest of them is condemned as an adulterer and a murderer. As for the prophets, they stand before king and people not to remind them of the supervision of some cultic duty, not to tip the scales in favor of one man's cause as over against that of another man. They proclaim in season and out the sovereign Word of Yahweh, a Word which challenges the total life of Israel, which denounces king, priest, other prophets, the temple, the sacrifices, the city of Jerusalem, and every prized institution or possession or custom in Israel. Yahweh is constantly busy, it seems, in tearing down even the "religion" of his people.

Mesopotamian cosmology, as we have seen, really accounts for the world in which mankind lives. The temples, the kings, the arts and crafts, the crops and fields, the rivers and mountains have their fixed and recognizable place in the cosmos. They draw their significance from their being representatives of their respective heavenly archetypes. This mode of thinking seems to have left few traces in Israel. It is true that the prophets know the reality of the divine assembly, that they get their revelations through their having stood in Yahweh's council (*sodh,* Jer. 23:18, 22). But what they have to say belongs entirely to this world. The call of Yahweh is to concrete obedience in the here and now. The meaning of existence is discerned in the ongoing pilgrimage of Israel in her history. The real archetypes for the understanding of a given situation are found in earlier situations, earlier deeds of salvation. The promise of God is affirmed, reaffirmed, fulfilled, reaffirmed as promise. The deliverance from Egypt, the wanderings in the wilderness, the entrance into the land, life under the charismatic leaders during the period of the judges—these events and experiences provide the center for Israel's understanding of herself. Later on, the earlier patriarchal traditions and the creation stories are employed in the same way. But the archetype is never a heavenly one. It is given in the historical or historicized experience of the people, illuminating later historical experiences.

Old Testament eschatology also has its points of connection with Mesopotamian cosmology. But even the eschatological pictures have been historicized. The coming savior-king of Isa. 9; 11; Mic. 5:1-5; Zech. 9:9-10, etc. is portrayed by means of imagery drawn from the divine kingship tradition of Mesopotamia and of Egypt. But interwoven in this imagery are motifs from Israel's early history. The king who is to come is in a number of respects a charismatic leader of the old premonarchical type.[23] The picture of the fulfillment of life's meaning found in Ezek. 40–48 is equally historicized. The twelve tribes of Israel will be reconstituted on the land. Who knows where those tribes actually are? No one but Yahweh. Yet they are to be restored. Even the language of apocalypse cannot get away from the historical dimension of Israel's faith: The Son of Man in Daniel must be identified with the "saints of the Most High," with the remnant of Israel. And the Suffering Servant of II Isaiah is depicted not in the language of the dying-rising god, no matter whether this myth was actually influential (as some believe) in the formation of this figure. His work is to provide a light to the nations, the real nations of this world. He causes astonishment to the kings of the nations when they see his exaltation, but he does so not as a heavenly being but an earthly one who has been exalted by Yahweh alone.

The cosmology of the Old Testament, in short, is a radically demythologized version of Mesopotamian cosmology. Cosmology has been subordinated to the historical consciousness of Israel. But it has

[23] See Walter Harrelson, "Nonroyal Motifs in the Royal Eschatology," Bernhard W. Anderson and Walter J. Harrelson, eds., *Israel's Prophetic Heritage, Essays in Honor of James Muilenberg* (New York, 1962), pp. 147-65.

not been eliminated. Israelite man lived in an ordered universe. Yahweh, the only God (or the only God who significantly acted in the world), maintained this order both through his own presence and activity and through the agency of his creatures. Divine and demonic forces operative in the world were entirely subject to the will of Yahweh, and man was strictly charged to lend no credence to the powers of divinity around him; they were "no gods," they were "emptiness," "worthlessness." The strictures against idolatry have been explained by Yehezkel Kaufmann[24] as reflecting a popular monotheism from the very beginnings of Israelite history, and also reflecting the fact that Israel never really understood polytheism and image-making. This is highly doubtful. The greatness of the Israelite spokesmen consists in part in their readiness to acknowledge that the rites and images and aspirations of "religious" man are of high significance. They were able to adopt, transform, and give concrete historical rootage to the mythological and cosmological speculations of their neighbors and of their own people. Cosmology remains, but it is a reduced, a "minimalized" cosmology. The world was being guided by Yahweh to a fixed purpose: the acknowledgment of Yahweh's lordship to the ends of the earth. It was impossible to portray this goal of the historical process without resort to mythological and cosmological imagery. But in comparison with Mesopotamian cosmology, that of Israel would have been considered utterly secular. Perhaps this is one of the reasons why the Jews were so often considered to be unreligious, atheistic, by their neighbors.

This minimal approach to cosmology is instructive for contemporary theology. Too much knowledge of the world can be devastating, for the "knowledge" has a way of turning out to be extremely problematic or illusory. Nothing weighed down Mesopotamian man more than the experience of disorder and chaos in his ordered universe. Our situation is no different today, I suspect. Leaving aside the implications of the Second Law of Thermodynamics (which, happily, I do not understand very clearly) and the threat of thermonuclear annihilation, I suspect that we may sometimes be almost overwhelmed with the thought that our civilization, our "world," may turn out to be on a level which could only be viewed as primitive in the eyes (if they have eyes) of the beings on other planets. It might be good for us if we could learn to live with as little cosmology as the Bible contains.

---

[24] *The Religion of Israel, from Its Beginning to the Babylonian Exile.* Trans. by Moshe Greenberg (Chicago, 1960), pp. 7-20, 122-49.

The Geography of Monotheism
DENIS BALY

Shema' Israel, Adonai Eloheinu Adonai ehadh. Credo in Unum Deum, Patrem Omnipotentem, Creatorem coeli et terrae. Lā ilah illā Allah, wa Muḥammad rasūl Allah.

These are the three classic statements of monotheistic belief, and they all come from the Middle East; there is nothing parallel in any other part of the world. Why this should be so is the theme of this paper.

There are those who would argue that there is little or no connection between this phenomenon and the geographical environment, however broadly this may be conceived. Indeed, any form of determinism is rejected in principle by possibly the majority of American geographers today, as well as by many of their European colleagues. "Admirons de loin," insists Pierre Gourou, "la simplicité d'une formule comme 'le désert est monothéiste'; restons méfiants devant ceux qui voudraient expliquer le foisonnement de la pensée religieuse hindouiste par la chaleur tropicale et la luxuriance de la végétation. L'influence du milieu géographique ... s'exerce plus modestement sur la naissance et la diffusion des religions universelles." [1] Other European scholars, however, would not go so far, and the most recent geographical study of the Middle Eastern area to be published in Britain argues for a close relationship between certain religious beliefs and the environment: The Central Plateau of Turkey

offers for human habitation the most forbidding environment of any part of the plateau. It was in this region that there evolved the characteristic pattern of Anatolian village life and its associated religious philosophy of submission to the awful and capricious power of nature, which have survived in essentials from Neolithic times to the present. ... There grew up in pre-Christian times a belief in a supreme goddess

[1] Pierre Gourou, *L'Asie* (Paris, 1953), p. 83.

253

of wild nature, remote and unpredictable, who granted her bounties haphazardly, in some places but not in others, in one season but perhaps not in the next. So closely linked was this cult with the endemic conditions of climate and topography that some of its features, and in particular those connected with the sacred associations of certain awesome localities, have survived all external changes of religion until the present time.[2]

That any form of religious belief is *required* by the environment is, of course, certainly false. Nevertheless, one must recognize that what men believe is unquestionably conditioned by the environment in which they find themselves. Among the most primary problems to which any group of people must seek an effective solution are the problems of how to maintain physical life, and how to preserve an orderly society, and to maintain these, moreover, within the limitations imposed (this word is used advisedly) by the geographical environment in which they live. At first they find themselves confronted by a collection of natural phenomena, amidst which they must seek to discern an orderly pattern of relationships if they are to survive. It is these physical facts, and no others, with which they have to deal, and to this extent at least their beliefs are the product of their environment. The conclusions they draw, while not dictated, are equally not altogether free, and the more precarious the conditions of life, the less man is able to impose his will upon nature. It is not surprising, therefore, that men tend to accept what they understand to be the facts of nature, and to derive their concepts of life and order from these facts. Almost all religion is essentially nature religion.

Absolute monotheism is alone in rejecting, in uncompromising terms, the apotheosis of any aspect of the natural world. Even ethical Confucianism, with its concepts of "heaven" and "earth," accepts to some extent the subordination of mankind to the pattern imposed by the realm of nature. Only in the Middle East, where "submission to the awful and capricious power of nature" was in earlier days by no manner of means confined to the Anatolian plateau, was this yoke broken, and the lordship of nature emphatically and publicly disowned. We are bound to ask, in consequence, whether anything in the nature of the Middle East itself either permitted or encouraged this extraordinary breakthrough in religious thought.

Many people have sought this liberating factor in the wilderness, and have claimed that monotheism is a response to the desert environment, to the utter and incredible vastness of it, the wide horizons,

[2] William C. Brice, *South-West Asia* (London, 1966), pp. 145 and 148.

the enormous inverted bowl of the sky, unobscured by clouds or mist, and the terrifying sameness of the landscape, for mile after dusty mile, uninterrupted by forest or marsh, village or city. "Le désert est monothéiste" has been an oft-repeated assertion first made by Renan, and even in the 1930's the celebrated British geographer P. M. Roxby urged this concept upon his pupils. But this is a romantic and sedentary view of the desert, which desert dwellers themselves do not share. What forces itself upon *their* consciousness is the infinite *diversity* of the desert, and polytheism is found in deserts no less than in cultivated lands. Muhammad condemned the Bedu of his day for their refusal, and even their inability, to recognize the One God. "The dwellers in the desert are the hardest in disbelief and hypocrisy, and most disposed not to know the limits of what Allah has revealed to His messenger." [3]

It is, moreover, a complete misunderstanding of the problem posed by the desert environment to assume that because natural life is so markedly absent, man is thereby liberated from the necessity of believing that his continued existence is dependent upon the forces of nature. Quite the contrary, in fact. In the passage already quoted Brice argued that the philosophy of submission to nature was dominant in the most barren part of the Anatolian plateau. It is true that the blatant worship of nature is no less a feature of the better watered regions, and no part of the Anatolian plateau is true desert, cultivation being everywhere possible, though threatened in the central basin by drought and desolation. Nevertheless, the increasing severity of the environment, as one moves from steppe to desert, seems to impose still more effectively on man his bondage to the unpredictable phenomena of nature, and consequently to render increasingly difficult that redemption from nature which is a necessary concomitant of monotheism.

We must indeed go further and assert that fully developed monotheism has *never* arisen in a desert but always in an urban situation, and that simplicity of environment is an obstacle rather than a prerequisite to monotheistic belief. Belief in only one God does not, it would seem, come easily to the human mind, for it is attended by serious intellectual problems, notably the problem of evil, and one of the most marked characteristics of a monotheistic God is his tendency to retreat into the infinite distance, and there to be completely lost to sight. Many of those primitive peoples who believe in a high god think of him as no longer active, and for some he is, as it were, a court

[3] *The Qur'an.* Sura 9:97.

of last resort, to be turned to only in an extreme crisis. This is a tendency also of the more sophisticated religions, where surrogates for God are a persistent accompaniment of supposedly absolute monotheism: The Word of God, both in Judaism and Islam, personified Wisdom in Hellenistic Judaism, the Blessed Virgin and the Saints in Christianity, angels in all three religions, and so on. I remember a devout Spanish woman telling me that she had been taught in her youth to bring her personal petitions to the Blessed Virgin, for God the Father could be concerned only with the infinitely vast problems of the total universe. In eighteenth-century theism God was clearly dormant, and in modern American society he has withdrawn to the vanishing point. Hence ninety-five percent of the population of this country claim to believe in God but at the same time dismiss him almost entirely from their minds.

Indeed, one is driven to wonder whether monotheism is compatible with a pluralistic society, and whether pluralism is not something of a polite and noncommittal word for polytheism. When a society accepts, both in principle and in fact, the view that the various groups of which it is composed should hold widely divergent beliefs about what constitute "life" and "truth" and "meaning," has it not in reality broken with a necessary requirement of monotheism? Such a society would seem required to assert, as the transcendent reality, the final unifying factor "which all men can accept," something other than an almighty but invisible and nonportrayable God, and to put in his place some "more natural" concept as, for instance, the nation or common humanity. In this connection it is interesting at the present time to observe a recrudescence, among the youth of the United States, of a belief in the efficacy of magical practices, and in the not altogether unconnected methods of inducing ecstasy by means of drugs. Once more mankind shows signs of succumbing to a fear of nature and of seeking, therefore, to manipulate it. "The decisive consideration was and remains: who is deemed to exert the stronger influence on the individual in his everyday life, the theoretically supreme god, or the lower spirits and demons?" [4]

Monotheism has been defined as "the belief in an uncreated, Supreme Deity, wholly beneficent, omnipotent, omniscient, and omnipresent; it demands the complete exclusion of all other gods. The world in its most minute details is regarded as His work, having been created out of nothing in response to His wish." [5] This necessarily

[4] Max Weber, *The Sociology of Religion* (Germany, 1922), trans. by Ephraim Fischoff, with introduction by Talcott Parsons (Boston, 1963), p. 20.
[5] Paul Radin, *Monotheism Among Primitive Peoples* (London, 1954), pp. 15-16.

involves, as we have seen, total exclusion of the possibility that "any thing that is in heaven above, or that is in the earth beneath, or that is in the water under the earth" [6] can effectively represent the ultimate and final Reality, that Absolute in terms of which, or rather of whom, everything that exists acquires meaning and significance. "The depth saith, It is not in me: and the sea saith, It is not with me." [7] Admittedly, supernatural beings other than this one God are not necessarily excluded, and in Islam belief in angels is specifically required. But all beings, whether natural or supernatural, are strictly subordinate and derivative.

This definition, however, is highly sophisticated, and at one time it was taken for granted that all monotheism had this character, for it was understood that monotheism must have evolved out of primitive animism, through the intermediate stages of polytheism and henotheism. It is true that before the turn of the century Andrew Lang had already demonstrated that primitive peoples frequently believe in a distant, kindly, and moral Supreme Being, but his ideas did not win acceptance at the time, partly because he also wrote comic verse and fairy tales for children, which earnest continental scholars took to be evidence of a regrettably shallow and flippant mind, such as they discerned only too often in the British islands, but even more because the concept of a primitive monotheism contradicted the evolutionary character of all historical development, which until about forty years ago was held to be almost beyond dispute. In 1925 W. L. Wardle said, "It may still be regarded as the prevailing view that Israel's religion passed gradually from an elementary stage of animism, totemism, fetishism, through the stage of tribal deity, to the stage represented by the religion of the prophets, and that this stage was reached only under their influence." [8]

Now we know that Lang was right, and that belief in a "high god" is widespread among primitive peoples. Indeed, monotheistic and monistic tendencies appear at various stages in religious development and are by no manner of means the climax of a long evolutionary process of refinement and sophistication.

We must probably recognize four different types of monotheism: *primitive monotheism, proto-monotheism, pseudo-monotheism,* and *absolute* or *transcendent monotheism.* Primitive monotheism need no longer concern us here, for there would seem to be no geographical

[6] Exod. 20:4.
[7] Job 28:14.
[8] *ZAW*, Neue Folge II (1925), 195. Quoted by H. H. Rowley in *From Moses to Qumran* (New York, 1963), p. 36.

feature involved in its appearance. Contrary to the expectation of certain anthropologists, it is not characteristic of the simplest and most isolated societies, but is almost always found where there is a "hierarchy of three or more sovereign groups in the society," [9] and, moreover, in those societies "which have the most stable sources of food, namely a settled agriculture which produces grains." [10] It may merely be noticed that even at this early stage monotheism is not primarily associated with desert, or semi-desert, environments.

By proto-monotheism I mean those marked monotheistic tendencies in a developed religion, which do not, however, lead to true monotheism, for example, the tendency in ninth-century B.C. Phoenicia to regard all gods as manifestations of Astarte or Baal Hadad. It is true that this is not universally admitted, but we should probably accept John Gray's argument that no distinction should be made between Baal Melqart, "the Lord of the City," and Baal Shamem, "the high god who controlled thunder, lightning, and rain, and the consequent order of nature." [11] Gray has also suggested that it was "in fact in the kingship of God . . . that the influence of Canaanite on Hebrew thought was strongest." Pointing out that "Jewish tradition associates the Enthronement Psalms with the New Year Festival," he suggests that these Psalms "and their Canaanite prototype were relevant to this supreme crisis in the agricultural year." [12] If, therefore, it was the desperate need of the Canaanite farmers for the renewal of the winter rains which caused them to elevate Baal Shamem to a position of royal authority, and if also the Israelites borrowed and developed this concept in relation to Yahweh as absolute lord of the seedtime and harvest, then we must recognize that one of the most important contributory concepts in the development of Hebrew monotheism derives, not from the desert, but from the Levantine agricultural communities.

Similar unitary philosophies developed in the period of Hellenistic Greek thought, in the monism of the Upanishads, which, admittedly, can hardly be described as "monotheistic," and subsequently in the more truly monotheistic, or at least henotheistic, Hindu *bhaktism,* in which one of the traditional gods, Krishna, Vishnu, Siva, or Rama, is regarded by his devotees as the supreme reality.

It is this almost evangelical fervor to which Ramanuja gave an intellectual basis, commenting upon the text of the Gita as a Christian might

[9] Guy E. Swanson, *The Birth of the Gods* (Ann Arbor, 1964), p. 81.
[10] *Ibid.,* p. 77.
[11] John Gray, *I & II Kings* (Philadelphia, 1963), p. 352.
[12] John Gray, *Archaeology and the Old Testament* (New York, 1962), pp. 107-8.

upon the Gospels, and defining the nature of Deity, His relation to the Universe, and the relationship existing between Him and finite selves. Deity is the Creator, and stands in a causal relationship to the world which He emits, sustains and reabsorbs.[13]

Proto-monotheism seems also to have characterized the desert world of Arabia immediately before Islam, and men were tending at that time to regard all the gods of the Arabian desert and the oases as manifestations of the same god. Nevertheless, true monotheism appeared only in Mecca, and Allah achieved preeminence in Arabia only by right of conquest.

Pseudo-monotheism differs from proto-monotheism in that it is more conscious, for there is a deliberate attempt to promulgate, and even impose, religious beliefs of a new and unitary type. Such was Atonism, the religion of the heretic Pharaoh Ikhnaton in the fifteenth century B.C., Zoroastrianism in the period of the Achaemenid empire, and that strange amalgam which the Mogul Emperor Akbar attempted to promote in the sixteenth century A.D. in India. Behind this last, as behind the thinking of Ramanuja, there was certainly the true monotheism of Islam, but it is important because it illustrates the tendency for such pseudo-monotheism to appear in imperialist situations. Somewhat parallel to this was the Assyrian demand in the eighth and seventh centuries B.C. that all the conquered peoples should worship the Lord Asshur, the Roman insistence upon devotion to the Emperor as god, whatever other gods were worshiped, and in India the spread of Buddhism, and the "conquests of the Dhamma," under the great Asoka. We find it also in the letter from the Mongol ruler which William of Roubrouk brought to the king of France: "Such is the order of the eternal God: In heaven there is only one eternal God, and there is to be only one master on earth, Genghis Khan, son of God." [14]

We must class both Atonism and Zoroastrianism as pseudo-monotheisms, because neither in fact issued in a true and effective monotheism, and because both were strongly dualistic, though the dualism was of a different type. In Zoroastrianism it was a true dualism, for there were two opposed powers, independent of each other, though Ahura Mazda would ultimately triumph. Yet even Ahura Mazda himself was apparently forced to choose.

> Between these two the wise one chose aught, and the foolish one not so. And when these twain spirits came together in the beginning, they

---

[13] A. C. Bouquet, *Comparative Religion* 3rd ed. (Harmondsworth, 1950), p. 145.
[14] Mircea Eliade, *Patterns in Comparative Religion* (Cleveland and New York, 1963), p. 62.

established Life and Not-Life, and that the last, the Worst Experience shall be the followers of the lie, but the Best Thought to him that follows right. Of these twain Spirits he that followed the lie chose the worst things; the holiest Spirit chose the Right, he that clothes him with the massy heavens as a garment.[15]

Some scholars, it is true, have argued that the original thrust of Zoroastrianism was strongly monotheist rather than dualist.

Contre les forces du malin, le prophète appelle sans trêve, et en toute confiance, l'aide d'Ahura Mazda. Confiance qui nous permet d'évaluer a sa juste valeur l'adjectif "dualiste" . . . le Seigneur Sage et l'Esprit du Mal ne sont nullement sur pied d'égalité: *Angra Mainyu* (l'Esprit Mauvais) est seulement l'antithèse de *Spenta* Mainyu (l'Esprit Saint) lequel, a l'origine, est l'un des Sept Immortels Bienfaisants (*Amesha Spenta*) donc subordonné au Seigneur Sage.[16]

Be this as it may, the dualist concept seems so soon to have predominated, and to have been so remarkably enduring, that one is bound to speak of Zoroastrianism, i.e. the form taken by the religion founded upon Zarathustra's teaching, as dualist rather than monotheist. This dualism persisted in Iranian thought, and it seems to have been not unrelated to the equally persistent conflict between the desert and the sown, for in Persia, alone in the Middle East, the two societies were more or less equally balanced, and neither could dominate the other. What is certainly beyond question is that Zarathustra himself belonged to the world of the agricultural oases, and not the desert, and if indeed we are to speak of the prophet himself as monotheist, then we must recognize, here again, that this concept arose, not in the desert, but outside it. The Bounteous Immortals were very early identified with the physical world, "the Good Mind with cattle, Truth with fire, the Kingdom with metals, Right-mindedness with the earth, Wholeness with water, and Immortality with plants." [17] Zaehner calls this identification "arbitrary," but surely we must see here a very close association of the physical necessities of an oasis culture with the supposedly eternal values.

To what extent the Achaemenid rulers were themselves Zoroastrian believers is still, of course, a matter of dispute, but Zoroastrianism would appear to have been the official religion of the early Persian empire, and there is no doubt at all that we must recognize once again

---

[15] *Yasna*, XXX, 3-5, quoted by E. O. James in *Comparative Religion* (New York, 1961), p. 188.

[16] Jean Varenne, *Zarathustra et la Tradition Mazdeenne* (Paris, 1966), pp. 52-53.

[17] R. C. Zaehner, *The Dawn and Twilight of Zoroastrianism* (New York, 1961), p. 46.

the imperial situation, not only of the period in which the religion first came to prominence, but also of that later period in which it was revived as a matter of policy by the Sassanid rulers. The dualism was of great importance, for Zoroastrianism was the first Middle Eastern religion which saw conflict as a necessary part of order and society and therefore, as long as it remained within reasonable bounds, not something to be ruthlessly suppressed. There was, in consequence, a flexibility in the Persian system which we do not find in either Assyria or Egypt.

Atonism was no less an imperialist religion, though the efforts to promote it greatly weakened the Egyptian empire. The Eighteenth Dynasty in Egypt (ca. 1580–1321 B.C.) had seen the creation of this empire, and the expansion of control over Palestine and Syria, as well as southward into Nubia, in an effort to prevent any repetition of the shattering disaster of the Hyksos period, when, for the first time in Egyptian history, foreigners had ruled in the land of the Nile. Amon-Re, the Sun-God of Thebes, became in consequence an imperial god, exercising sway from the Euphrates to the Fourth Cataract of the Nile. He was the "sole lord, taking captive all lands every day, as one beholding them that walk therein." [18] Moreover, "he was the 'Hidden One' by name, the invisible god . . . who might be everywhere, and thus easily became the god of far-flung empire and the universal deity when the fortunes of the Empire carried him abroad." [19] Nevertheless, ancient Egyptian religion remained thoroughly polytheistic, and it was the authority of the Pharaoh, as being in his person all the gods, that was imposed upon the subject peoples.

Amenhotep IV, who came to the throne about 1375 B.C. and took the name of Ikhnaton, made no attempt to change this, for the absolute authority of the Pharaoh as god was basic to the entire Egyptian system. It is true that he swept away all the gods and their priests from the land of Egypt, closing their temples and erasing their names from inscriptions, and set in their place the Aton alone. Yet only he and his family worshiped the Aton; his subjects were still to worship him, the Pharaoh, as god. There were thus two gods, though not in opposition to each other. In fact, Ikhnaton was trying to establish the Egyptian system, with the Pharaoh as the absolute central authority, throughout the empire, on what he understood to be a sound foundation. Max Weber has argued that "the devaluation of the traditional religion by the monotheistic campaign of Amenhotep IV (Ikhnaton) immediately

[18] James, *op. cit.,* p. 192.
[19] John A. Wilson, *The Culture of Ancient Egypt* (Chicago, 1951), p. 170.

stimulated naturalism," [20] but surely the reverse was the case, and the naturalism was the driving force rather than the derivative. The essence of this new religion, which has its roots before Ikhnaton's time, was that the basic reality with which men have to deal is that of the visible, empirical facts, and not the hidden truth believed to lie behind these facts. The Aton was the visible disc of the sun, and this was now proclaimed to be the reality which gave life to Egypt, rather than the mysterious and hidden Amon-Re. Painters and sculptors were told to represent the Pharaoh and his family as they actually saw them, though he might be ugly and deformed, while his wife was breathtakingly beautiful; they were not to portray an idealized Pharaoh. In this religion there was, strictly speaking, no supernatural Supreme Being at all.

Nevertheless, two things must be recognized: First, Atonism was sufficiently monotheistic for Ikhnaton's famous hymn to the Sun to be used, with relatively few changes, as the basis for one of the greatest of the Hebrew psalms, Ps. 104. Second, there was evidently already a strong tendency toward proto-monotheism in Egypt, and Ikhnaton was by no means the original mind he has sometimes been called. The Cairo hymn to Amon in the fifteenth century B.C. had itself been the basis for his hymn, and the trend had been toward unification of all the gods under the supremacy of Amon-Re. This monotheistic tendency in Egypt has a long history and is certainly in large measure a direct response to the Egyptian environment. The first impact of the religion of ancient Egypt upon the unwary student must surely be one of complexity and diversity, of a "huge, rambling, unmanageable property with innumerable rooms," [21] but further knowledge will reveal strong tendencies both to polarity and to unification. There was a steady awareness of the "Two Lands" (the Delta and Upper Egypt), of the desert and the sown, of life and death, each always set over against the other, and yet at the same time a conviction that all meaningful existence was essentially one and eternal, held together by one everlasting Sun, one everflowing Nile, one undying Pharaoh. But it was the unity of an agricultural world where a single system of crops prevailed from one end of the long ribbon of black earth to the other, watered by one life-giving flood, a system initiated and maintained by the Pharaoh himself. The desert as such contributed nothing, for the desert was "the land of death," a world where neither existence nor meaning was

[20] Weber, *op. cit.*, p. 8.
[21] A. de Buck, *Bi. Or.*, 1944, in a review of G. van der Leeuw, *De godsdienst van het oude Aegypte* (1944), quoted by Th. C. Vriezen in *The Religion of Ancient Israel* (Arnhem, 1963); trans. by Hubert Hoskins (London, 1967), p. 45.

possible. The most that can be claimed is that the inalterable aridity of the climate assisted this sense of unity, for here is no variableness, and whether there will be rain or no is never a material question.

Similarly, there lies behind Zoroastrianism a movement toward the recognition of Varuna as the ethical god par excellence. This brings us back to proto-monotheism, which we have now recognized in at least Egypt of the Eighteenth Dynasty, India of the post-Vedic period (as well as much later), the Iranian plateau before the time of Zarathustra, Phoenicia in the ninth century B.C., the Aegean in the Hellenistic period, and the Arabian plateau before Muhammad. What all these have in common is relatively rapid expansion across a wide territory, bringing people in touch with many different environmental situations, and new, sharply differing concepts of society, and of right and wrong, and therefore with new "gods." These peoples are not making this encounter for the first time. Indeed, there is always a long history of movement, and confrontation with different environments, and they have already been required, not once nor twice, to bind together into a coherent unity varied interpretations of reality. Each of these peoples is aware of a whole pantheon of gods.

None of these peoples is autochthonous. No group started in the place where it is found in the time of which we are speaking. Even the Egyptians, that seemingly most static of nations, must at one time have moved into the hostile Nilotic jungle and marshes, out of the disappearing grasslands of the plateau, bringing memories of a totally different experience into a new and exotic situation. Nor was this the end. Settlement began at different points in the long ribbon of the Nile; similar, but not identical, societies developed, and a number of distinct gods made their appearance. These societies remained separate, though in increasing contact with each other, for a long period, and it was not until about 3000 B.C. that the process of unification was completed and the Delta and Upper Egypt bound together into one country. The stimulus to this final unification seems to have been, at least in part, confrontation by means of trade with the older Sumerian civilization of southern Mesopotamia.

It was therefore an already highly complex culture and religion which, thirteen hundred years later, was shaken to its foundations by the Hyksos conquests, and then embarked upon a grand imperial adventure to prevent a renewal of this humiliation. Southward they expanded to the tropical lands of the Fourth Cataract, westward to the green plateau country of Cyrenaica, and north-eastward through rain-fed farmlands to the Euphrates, so topsy-turvy a world in Egyptian eyes that the river, they said, "flowed backward." In this region they met the Hittites from the Anatolian plateau, and the Mitanni from the foothills of the high Armenian mountain ranges. From the temple of Deir Bahari, we know, they ventured also as far as the forests of East Africa.

In this same period occurred the migrations of the "Sea Peoples," coming from the steppes of southern Russia, and perhaps ultimately from central Asia, through the Aegean peninsula into the Mediterranean lands as far apart as Sicily and the Levant coast, where we meet them later as the Philistines and the Phoenicians. In neither Greece nor the Levant did these peoples find uninhabited territory, for in Greece were the Myceneans, in contact with Crete and the Levant, and the Phoenician coast had been occupied for thousands of years by a whole variety of peoples and had had a long history of communication with the outside world.

Similar movements of Indo-European peoples had brought the Iranians, the Aryans or "Noble" people, onto the great Persian plateau, into the mountains round Lake Van and Lake Urmia, and down the Khyber Pass into the fertile Indus Valley, where the Harappā civilization had long been in contact with Lower Mesopotamia. The cultures these migrating invaders encountered were everywhere diverse, and every region was heir to an exceedingly long and complicated history, stretching back for millennia.

The vicissitudes of the history, and the varied patterns of the environment, are reflected in the manifold pantheons of these societies. Hinduism is the product of a marriage between the Indo-European Aryan culture and the irrigation culture of the Indus Valley. But the religion and culture of the invaders themselves were already complex, and they had three distinct groups of gods, considered by some to be heavenly gods, gods of the atmosphere and gods of the earth, and by others to be related to the three classes of Aryan society, priests, warriors, and commoners. This process of expansion and incorporation of new territory, new types of society, new ideas, especially new concepts of good and evil, of what it is that sustains and what that destroys, the social order, involves also the incorporation of the gods, for the effective "god" of any group is that which it understands to be its ultimate good.

He is always the "life-giver," the ultimate and vital reality which endows all that is with significance. Theophoric names given to children bear witness to this, for he it is in terms of whom anything can be named. Where he does not prevail there is no life, for though beyond the boundaries of his power life may be technically and inexplicably possible, it is a meaningless existence not worth living, and does not, in fact, comprise "life" in any terms which people within the boundaries could understand. This conviction that those beyond the pale are without order, or meaningful existence, is both pervasive and persistent. Even as late as the end of the nineteenth century the peasants of northern Russia were convinced that beyond their western frontier lay only a vast, inchoate, dismal realm called "Germania," without roads, railways, or even villages, whose inhabitants were deaf and dumb and totally unable to communicate with one another. Not even the evidence of their own eyes and ears, when they were confronted by actual foreigners, with their books and newspapers, served to convince them to the contrary, for to admit that the world outside was a meaningful world would impose upon them far too great a disorientation, and a rearrangement of their ideas about everything.[22] Yet expanding horizons always mean that other peoples, with their different ways of life, their different values, and their different gods, must somehow after all be taken seriously.

The mythological struggles between the gods reflect these tensions, and the process of multiplication of gods and their incorporation into a polytheistic culture continues until saturation is reached and further incorporation becomes too great a strain. This strain has long been apparent, and with it the necessity for the equation of the gods, and we find universally in these societies a tendency for the gods to become merged, and for the qualities of all to be ascribed to that one who at the moment is being addressed.

It is when such a society or culture becomes involved in a further, and frequently cataclysmic, expansion that this tendency to equation takes on a strongly monotheistic aspect, in the effort to subordinate mutually exclusive and even violently opposed cultural patterns to an overruling authority, and thus bring law and order to a dangerously chaotic and even rebellious situation. The establishment of the Egyptian Empire, the foundation of the Phoenician colonies in the ninth century b.c., the Greek conquests under Alexander, the spread of the joint Aryan-Hindu culture into the Gangetic plain and to the even more different world of the Deccan south of the Satpura Hills— all of them had this explosive character. The rapidity of the expansion, the inclusion within one world of cultures so strongly opposed that equation is well-nigh impossible, the realization that men can no longer call "barbarian" or "disorderly" that which they had once so

[22] Frederick Hamilton, *The Vanished Pomps of Yesterday* (London, 1919; 27th ed., 1937), pp. 117-19.

named—all these are factors urging men toward the adoption of a monotheistic system. Pseudo-monotheism, as distinct from proto-monotheism, occurs when a strong ruler attempts to impose this pacification from above, seeking to bind together into one his disparate dominions, by the imposition of a common and universal system.

These, however, are no more than *tendencies*. In every case, with the establishment of reasonable agreement, there was reversion to polytheism, in Egypt, India, Phoenicia, the Hellenistic world, and in Iran. Vriezen, indeed, insists that it is wrong to speak of monotheism at all in this connection. Admittedly, in Mesopotamia, Egypt, and in Phoenicia,

> the headship of a single god can evolve into a firmer unity in the divine world, so that it approximates to a particular form of monotheism or rather, monarchism. The chief deity is then the bearer of every divine name and likewise of every divine attribute. . . . On the score of unity within the pantheon there were widely divergent contributions and . . . the polytheism of the ancient East hovered between two poles: the one extreme was an unintegrated collection of many gods, the other involved the recognition of an all-embracing godhead. For the latter the word "monotheism" is hardly appropriate. Monotheism, as a form of religious belief, is not a matter of acknowledging a particular phenomenon in nature as having prior place above all others, but of a wholly peculiar and underived spiritual being or essence of godhead, qualitatively of a different character from anything in nature.[23]

This is certainly true, and his warning is apposite. Nevertheless, it is neither unreasonable nor inaccurate to speak of "monotheistic tendencies," or "proto-monotheism," in this context, if one recognizes clearly that there never at any time evolved, or developed, a true monotheism out of these tendencies. Indeed, one must insist that no form of proto-monotheism can produce a breakthrough into true monotheism, if there is not already provided the means for man to escape from his otherwise inevitable bondage to the phenomenological world as the bestower of significance. Only the Jewish people made this breakthrough, and it was not until they were in exile in Babylon that a thoroughgoing or transcendent monotheism was clearly expressed and fully accepted. In those days they were the very opposite of a great imperial or commercial power. They were but a fragment of what once they had been; they had no territory; they were strangers in a strange land.

Their history had been fully as long and as complex as that of any of the peoples we have so far considered. The land of Canaan had first

[23] Vriezen, *op. cit.*, pp. 35-36.

known the triple distinction of pastoralism, agriculture, and even embryo commerce, six millennia before the days of Abraham. Wave after wave of new peoples had passed across the Levant bridge, and the sound of movement to and fro had never been stilled. Their own movements had been related to that complicated series of migrations already mentioned. Some of them had gone down into Egypt, perhaps in the wake of the Hyksos, though this is disputed, and perhaps at other times as well, and they had left the Nile Valley shortly before the onslaught of the Sea-Peoples, the Philistines and the Israelites invading different parts of Palestine within about a century of each other. We must no longer think of a straightforward journey through Sinai to the Promised Land, and one must deprecate at present any attempt to reconstruct the route of the Exodus. Instead, it was a restless movement of people, regarded by those who were not of their number as stateless and subversive, into the wilderness where the Egyptian authorities could not reach them, and where the Egyptian gods held no sway. However the Exodus experience is to be interpreted, it is abundantly clear that the sphere of their wanderings was desert and not cultivated land, "all that great and terrible wilderness," [24] of which the desolation and hardship remained long in their memories, and that in some manner they came to know him who was in the future their God, Yahweh, as a result of their experience at the Mount. Whether this mountain is to be sought somewhere in the Sinai peninsula or, as seems more probable, east of the Arabah, is immaterial. They themselves traced the origins of their monotheism to this desert experience, and, despite the objections of such great authorities as Noth and von Rad, we must not attempt to separate the Sinai tradition from those of the Exodus and entry into Canaan. Their essential unity is evidenced in too many strands of the biblical tradition to permit us to reject it.

But were they, or even their leaders, in any valid sense of the word "monotheist" as a result of their experiences in the desert? This is the critical question. Certainly some notable scholars would claim this for them, and it is a thesis urged still by no less a master than W. F. Albright.[25] Yet it is surely inadmissible. All the time that the Israelites were in Palestine polytheistic tendencies were strong, and we have a great deal of evidence that the people continued to accept, and even to prefer, gods other than Yahweh right up to the fall of Jerusalem in 586 B.C. Both Jeremiah and Ezekiel had reason to protest

[24] Deut. 1:19.
[25] W. F. Albright, *History, Archaeology, and Christian Humanism* (New York, 1964), pp. 154-56.

against the adoration within the Temple itself of "the Queen of Heaven," against drink offerings poured out to other gods, and against "all the idols of the house of Israel" portrayed upon the Temple wall.[26] For something like six and a half centuries the Yahwists wrestled against the persistent polytheism of the ordinary Israelite, but at no point in this long history can one discern any clear pronouncement that the other gods are not to be worshiped because they do not exist. This scathing and decisive sword remained in its sheath, unused and apparently unsuspected, until the Exile. The prophetic community, it is true, unquestionably Yahwist in allegiance, was moving irresistibly toward absolute monotheism, but nowhere in their writings, until the Persian conquest of Babylon, and nowhere in the psalms, save only in two passages which are almost certainly late,[27] is it openly declared that the worship of the heathen is futility.

This polytheism, moreover, was not merely the religion of an ignorant and superstitious peasantry. Its repeated appearance in the sanctuaries dedicated to Yahweh, and the support given to it from time to time by the royal court, even in the more austere territory of Judah, force us to admit that the religious leaders themselves often saw nothing incompatible in the joint worship of Yahweh and other deities. Yahweh was for them but one among the gods of the world, though superior, and even this superiority was questioned in time of distress. For the more thoroughgoing Yahwists of the period of the monarchy, Yahweh still seems to have been one among the other gods, but he was emphatically never *primus inter pares;* he was from the very beginning peculiar, and it was natural to him to stand alone, aloof, apart. He was unable to mingle with the other gods, because he had nothing in common with them, and therefore those who named themselves by Yahweh could not properly worship these other gods. For those outside, however, the possibility remained open, and they incurred no blame for it.[28]

Nevertheless, the Sinai experience undoubtedly laid the groundwork for Hebrew monotheism in at least five important areas, all of which are related to the desert environment. The first is the rejection of the natural world as providing the framework of reality and meaning, that structure in terms of which everything that exists is named. As we have seen, all other societies seem to have taken it for granted that the phenomena of nature are the clue to meaning and order, because in the last resort life itself appears to be related to these phe-

---

[26] Jer. 7:18; Ezek. 8:10.
[27] Pss. 115:3-7; 135:15-17.
[28] Judg. 11:24; II Kings 5:15-19.

nomena. But the Hebrews had been catapulted from one environmental situation into its complete opposite, from the field into the wilderness, and for those who drew their life from agriculture the desert stood for death. This fundamental dichotomy in nature seems to have been one of the factors causing the Hebrews to embark upon a line of thought that was ultimately to subordinate the natural world entirely, and therefore to eliminate all the gods.

We are bound to conclude, not that the rejection of the nature gods is in any sense a consequence of the desert environment, but that it is consequent upon the fundamental *difference* between conditions in the desert and those in the intensely cultivated land of Egypt, so that continued life in the desert appeared to be a flat contradiction of everything that had been taken for granted in the Nile valley. The fact that the Israelites lived, and did not die, in the desert was therefore "unnatural," and it could not be explained, or "named," in terms of nature, but only because it had happened, that is to say, in terms of history.

Secondly, a new community came into being, held together by a new concept of that basic reality which binds men into a secure and unified society. The foundation of order is henceforth not royal authority, which is contrary to desert experience, but *agreement,* or covenant. This is, of course, not really new at all, and Gray is quite right to say that "the Hebrews were not unique in the ancient East, for they but reflected the characteristic tribal socialism of the desert." [29] The close relationship between covenant and law can also be found in Mesopotamia, though there perhaps it lacks the quality of an absolute principle.

Nevertheless, one must go further than Gray. It is of the first importance that the Israelites began in the desert to think of themselves and of their God as peculiar, in that they stood alone, separate, and apart, without any people to whom they could be compared—a peculiar people with a peculiar God. "He has not dealt thus with any other nation; they do not know his ordinances." [30] It is far from clear how this concept should have developed, if in fact the Israelites merely "reflected the characteristic tribal socialism of the desert." Perhaps we may reasonably find the roots of it in the crisis of identity into which the Exodus inevitably plunged the people. To be forced to take refuge in the desert was to be thrust into nonbeing, not merely in terms of the secure agricultural world, but in terms also of desert so-

[29] Gray, *op. cit., Archaeology,* p. 41.
[30] Ps. 147:20.

ciety itself. In the vast and limitless wilderness, where man is ever on the move, he cannot find his identity in a place, and it is not by towns and villages that men are named, as they are in the world of more settled communities. Instead, they identify themselves by their family, their clan, and their tribe. That which is meaningful and valid is that for which there are clear origins and relationships, and it is not by chance that this concept is utilized within Islam in establishing the authority of the *hadith*. Neither a man nor a thing has validity in itself, only by descent.

Not to be part of a recognizable tribe or clan is, therefore, to be without identity, to be without right to existence. If, as still seems most probable, the Israelites acquired their God from the Kenites, we must recognize that they acquired an understanding of their own significance among a group to whom the desert society accorded toleration but not recognition, a company of itinerant smiths. They did not, of course, take over Yahweh ready-made, so to speak, from the Kenites. In all cultural transfers a people give hospitality only to those concepts which they can relate to their own experience, and even then the concepts are molded to conform to this experience. In this reformulation of the Kenite ideas Moses surely played an important role, and we must grant to him the quality of a prophet like Muhammad, a man to whom is granted the power to see things in fundamentally new terms, and to establish an ordered and living community in the name of a reality hitherto unknown. Just as in the *umma* Muhammad bound together the *muhājirūn* and the *anṣār* in a new concept of relationship, so in the desert the Israelites were taught to recognize that nonbelonging conferred identity upon them more surely than belonging, and that the root of all significance and existence lay in otherness. Henceforth apostasy in Israel consisted in seeking to belong, in wishing to be like the other nations.[31] The absence of any partner for Yahweh, indeed of any trace of a partner, is a quite extraordinary feature of the biblical records, and if we did not have the evidence of Elephantine we would be quite unaware that the Israelites had ever ventured to endow him with a wife and family. This austere aloofness is not conceivably a devolopment out of the agricultural life of Palestine; it must have begun in the desert.

Closely allied to this is the third factor, which we may call the non-location of God. When fundamental reality is thought of as being closely related to the natural phonomena, whatever they are, there is inevitably a strong tendency toward identification of the god and the

---

[31] I Sam. 8:5, 19-20.

phenomenon. The two are in large measure inseparable, and this has taken place just as much in desert environments as in better watered regions. The gods, therefore, become located in the heavenly bodies, the atmospheric phenomena, in animals, or in particular places on the earth's surface, on mountains, in caves, in sacred springs, and so on. Yahweh, in the Exodus experience, is clearly in close relation to the Mountain of Sinai, which "quaked greatly," and "the smoke of it went up like the smoke of a kiln," [32] and to the pillar of fire by night and the pillar of cloud by day, all of which, despite the various objections that have been raised, can hardly be dissociated from volcanic activity somewhere in northwestern Arabia. Yahweh was, therefore, for the Kenites a nature god with his proper location, and to some extent this concept was taken over by the Israelites, though with two very important developments based upon their own experience: For them, though Yahweh "belonged" to Sinai/Horeb, he was in no sense tied to the site, and could move wherever he willed, and he was, moreover, not altogether to be identified with the Mount itself, for, at least in principle, the idea of a nature god had been rejected.

To what extent they were altogether, while they were in the desert, delivered from the domination of a nature god is very far from certain. Unquestionably, nothing in the desert itself encouraged such a conclusion, for the Bedouin shared with their counterparts elsewhere a lively fear of the unseen powers of the natural world. It would seem probable that pilgrimages to Sinai continued long after the entry into Canaan, but there was surely from the very beginning an uneasiness about identifying ultimate reality with nature, or with a place, and probably among the true Yahwists there was more than mere uneasiness. Later on, in the ninth century B.C., when Elijah went back to Sinai/Horeb to find Yahweh, he was said to be "in" none of the natural phenomena with which he had at first been associated.[33] The resistance to the divine location, which had been inherent and latent in the Exodus experience, now came into the open. It was not a necessary result of the desert sojourn, but we must perhaps recognize that nomadism may have rendered the breakaway somewhat easier.

The fourth factor is the concept of power as ultimate reality. This is quite basic to true monotheism, and from the beginning Yahweh was a god of power, manifested in violence and storm. Only a god of overwhelming power can become a sole and comprehensive god, and in the background of all proto-monotheism and pseudo-monotheism there is such a god. Originally he is always a nature god, but he must

[32] Exod. 19:18.
[33] I Kings 19:9-12.

be released from bondage to nature if he is to become absolute and supreme. But this understanding of a god of storm and power, which the Israelites evidently brought with them into Canaan, cannot in the least be regarded as a desert peculiarity. The awesome fury of the tempest is a universal Middle Eastern phenomenon.

Finally, it must be noticed that, whatever else the Israelites may, or may not, have brought with them out of the wilderness, they undoubtedly served a "jealous god" when they settled in Canaan, and inaugurated an era of religious intolerance and brutal exclusiveness. "The nature-cult of Canaan was universalistic, . . . it was a-moral and quite neutral, and, however much Hebrew prophets might condemn its licentious rites of imitative magic, they could not allege homicidal fanaticism." [34] Of the long tragic heritage of this intolerance it is not necessary to speak, save to insist that it is still a problem with which we have to wrestle, for exclusiveness and intolerance are necessary to monotheism, which can never permit a *deuteros theos*. Once triumphant, however, the only God can be merciful to his now powerless adversaries, and this seems to be something which his loyal followers find very difficult to grasp. The absolute intolerance, so unhappily necessary in the early stages, is indeed a product of the desert, of its harsh encouragement of the military virtues, of the absence of any central government which, by giving to the tribes themselves the function of self-protection, makes them only too easily judges in their own cause, and of the absence of any alternative way of life. Survival in the desert is always a blunt and brutal either-or matter.

It was to be characteristic of the Israelites, once they had entered the Promised Land, that though they never established a permanent empire or vast network of trade, yet they were exposed to one culture shock after another; they were to be constantly thrust into a situation in which they were forced somehow to incorporate into their experience the very opposite of what they had previously held to be true. In the Exodus they had been cast from the cultivated land and the hegemony of the Nile into the boundless desert, but with their settlement in Canaan they moved from the desert expanse into cities with gates and bars and into a world where landmarks were not an obstacle to the free movement of flocks but a necessity to secure society, and their removal was paramount sin. As long as Jerusalem stood, the desert lay close in upon one side of her and the farmland upon the other.

It was the tragedy of these small Levantine states that the peace

---

[34] Gray, *op. cit., Archaeology,* p. 119.

their people so much desired proved to be their enemy, for the land could not long support an expanding population, unrestrained by the savagery of war. To prevent famine another source of wealth had to be found, and, given their situation at the crossroads of the world, this was usually sought in trade. Unfortunately this led, almost inevitably, to territorial expansion in an effort to control and pacify the trade routes, and consequently to endless conflicts between the states, each intent upon establishing the same control.

It was in the ninth century B.C., in the days of Omri and Ahab, that the northern kingdom had to come to terms with the powerful commercial empires of Phoenicia and Syria, whose way of life seemed to the farmers and shepherds of Israel to be the enemy of all that they held sacred. It was, as we have seen, a time of proto-monotheism in Phoenicia, and probably in Syria as well, and Elijah fought to prevent the absorption of Israel into the empire of Baal Hadad. He did not, it is true, establish a full monotheism in Israel, nor, apparently, did he seek to, but he did capture for Yahweh the sacred promontory of Carmel by the sea, where fall the first autumnal rains, and demonstrate effectively the lordship of Yahweh over nature, a very important preliminary to monotheism.

The Israelites made three attempts to become a great commercial power, but each time they had no more than a temporary success. Yet, the great trade routes flowed through and around their territory, and they were ever aware of a world far exceeding their immediate horizons. Even a villager like Amos, from the edges of Jeshimon, could speak confidently of Egypt, Ethiopia, Hamath, Bit-Adini, Phoenicia, and Crete. He knew, moreover, that the Phoenicians had come from across the Great Sea, and the Syrians from Kir. There was hardly any time when the people were not exposed to foreign ideas infiltrating their country at the heels of the merchants or in the wake of military invasions.

The grim consequences of these endless conflicts between the kingdoms and the constant insecurity of the Levant weighed heavily upon the people, and the need for some unifying factor became increasingly felt, so that nation might no longer lift up sword against nation, or need to learn war any more.[35] To Amos belongs the distinction of seeing the breadth of the problem and to perceiving moreover that a universal order must be based upon covenant or agreement just as much as the order of a single nation. It is essentially for the absence

[35] Isa. 2:4; Mic. 4:3. Whoever may in fact have been the originator of this passage, it is surely a sound tradition that placed it in the eighth century B.C.

of covenant, or for its deliberate rupture, that he rebukes the nations in the celebrated first chapter. It is true that he sees Israel as the only nation whom Yahweh has directly "known." [36] but all nations have experienced Yahweh, and they should all, therefore, have grasped the basic principles of orderly and meaningful existence. Fundamental to his thinking is the proclamation that Israel was not alone in having had an exodus, but that this was the common experience of mankind.[37] Consequently, things throughout the world can be seen in true perspective only in terms of Yahweh, and right relationships be established only upon this basis. Yahweh is thus the Lord of the world, and Amos can properly be described as the first effective monotheist.

Of course, this was not thought out logically, and it was apparently taught for far too short a period for its revolutionary import to be understood. Much additional thinking and teaching still remained to be done by subsequent prophets, but the essential revelation had been made. It is not too much to say that all the rest is commentary.

The first efforts at creating a universal order were in fact made upon quite other principles, and in the name of Asshur men sought to establish a worldwide society in terms of absolute authority, and to maintain law and order by the exercise of military might and by the forcible scattering of rebellious populations. Very soon after the expulsion of Amos from Samaria[38] the people to whom he had preached fell victims to the dread Assyrian juggernaut. Whole sections of the population were transferred, to be replaced by other people, and the tiny state of Judah, which alone retained some measure of independent status, could take no independent action. As completely as any communist satellite, she had to accept the way of life imposed by her imperial master, and for nearly a century an Assyrian altar took precedence in the Temple of Jerusalem over that of the Hebrew God.

In the early years of the sixth century Jerusalem was destroyed by the Babylonians and the leading citizens carried into exile by the Euphrates. Here they had to begin all over again, utterly unable in the date groves of Babylon to repeat the patterns of society they had known in Canaan, or to continue those religious practices which until then they had understood to be divinely required. This is the meaning of that heartfelt cry, "How can we sing the song of Yahweh in a strange land?" [39] Once more they found themselves in a situation

[36] Amos 3:2.
[37] Amos 9:7.
[38] Amos 7:12-13.
[39] Ps. 137:4.

which spelled death to everything they had previously understood to be life.

It was in their effort yet again to comprehend in one inclusive system seemingly irreconcilable opposites that they made the great intellectual leap which dethroned the gods entirely and cast them forever into nonexistence. But this was not finally achieved, it would appear, until Babylon had fallen, an event which caused the whole Levant to shudder, and a much vaster empire had been established, from India to the Sahara, by a power which until that time had not even existed. Under Persian authority worldwide hegemony was claimed for Ahura-Mazda, the Good Spirit of Zoroastrianism, and the Second Isaiah's monotheism was apparently a counterclaim on behalf of Yahweh and the Yahwist understanding of the world. It was an absolute, and not a pseudo-, monotheism because exilic Judaism could have no conceivable imperial pretensions. It was perhaps the greatest triumph of the Persian imperial system that it tolerated the gods and permitted the existence of absolute values other than its own. There is the world of difference between the Egyptian and Assyrian inscriptions: on the one hand the display of the ruler savagely triumphing over his miserable enemies, and on the other hand those superb reliefs which adorn the staircase at Persepolis. These very people in the empire come in peace and tranquility to bring their diverse contributions to the maintenance of the universal order. It was, however, the greatest triumph of the exiled people of Judah, without territory or power, that they were able to be intolerant of all rival absolutes and to assert that there were no gods at all—only God.

There are only two other transcendent monotheisms, Christianity and Islam, and both derive from the Jewish achievement. Christianity is so completely the heir to Jewish experience that we need not examine it here. Nevertheless, we must give some attention to Islam, which is a new expression of monotheism and not a straightforward inheritance. It is true that Muhammad's thinking was strongly affected by what he had observed among the Christians and Jews of Arabia, and it must be presumed that he derived the principle of monotheism from them, especially the Jews. It was his contention that Abraham was the first Muslim, but in his thinking the undoubtedly debased Christianity of the Arabian tribes was not monotheism at all, for in the honors they paid to Jesus and his mother they had committed the cardinal sin of *shirk*, of "joining gods to God." The Judaism that he knew was certainly also debased, but it did assert the monotheistic concept and in all its worship spoke only to the One.

Muhammad apparently knew very little of the great prophetic tradition, and the word "prophet" does not mean in Islam what it means in the Old Testament. Moreover, he proclaimed monotheism, not within the Jewish community but wholly outside it, though he clearly expected Jewish support, a support which he did not in fact receive. We must therefore admit Islam to be a distinct restatement in the seventh century A.D. of that absolute monotheism which had first been enunciated in the eighth century B.C. and had triumphed in the sixth, that is to say, nearly twelve centuries before.

There lies behind Islam an Arabian proto-monotheism, as well as the true monotheism of Jewry, and there lies behind it also a long history, extending for thousands of years, of encounter with the outside world, by this time as far afield as East Africa, the Indies, China, and imperial Rome. It is a capital mistake to think of ancient Arabia as remote, and as pursuing its traditional nomadism unaltered by the surging tumults of the world at large. Nothing could be further from the truth. That the patterns of nomadic life remain constant is due to the stern conditions imposed by the desert environment, but the absence of change can be easily exaggerated. In fact Arabia has readily accepted what, within the limits of her way of life, she could profitably use, and in the ancient world her contacts with the surrounding nations were exceedingly widespread, both in time and space. Indeed, as with so much else, it would seem that we must place the beginnings of trans-Arabian trade much earlier than we had supposed, almost certainly long before the entry of the Israelites into Canaan. Islamic monotheism did not arise, therefore, in isolation or in simplicity, but in the conflict of world powers and the ebb and flow of international trade, in the struggle between Constantinople and Ctesiphon in Arabia and the head-on collision of contending systems and ideas.

It is true, however, that the three traditional ways of life in the Middle East—agriculture, pastoralism, and trade—did not easily mesh, though all were present and interacting upon one another. The diversity proper to monotheism was certainly characteristic of the peninsula, but the impulsion to bring them together into one system was not yet felt. Jewish monotheism was confined to the oases, and in the wastes of Arabia at large the dominant religious concepts were unashamedly polytheist and naturalistic. Nor could it easily be otherwise, for the phenomena of the natural world are here imperious. It cannot be said too often that the desert gives no encouragement at all to those who seek to escape from nature and defy her absolute authority. Nor does the desert ever suggest that life is simple. Life in the desert is exceedingly difficult, and as men move to and fro across *erg* and *hamada* they have to search diligently for life, and they are constantly threatened by the dire, mysterious *djinn* howling in the dark of night, haunting those strange, deserted ruins where once men lived but can no longer, enfolded in the midst of the sandstorm.

The immediate reason why monotheism should have been proclaimed when and where it was, in a world so hostile to it, seems to have been the establishment of the trading and banking city of Mecca, in the ancient halting place of the caravans, with age-old traditions of sanctity. It cannot be denied that, until that long distant day when the *haramein* shall be excavated, we cannot speak with certainty about the history of pre-Islamic Mecca. We must therefore accept, in the absence of any convincing evidence to the contrary, the Muslim tradition that no city existed there at all before the sixth century. Sacred the district certainly was, but it was a complex sanctity, reflected in the double and conflicting calendars, solar and lunar, and in the double pilgrimage to the Ka'aba and to Mount 'Arafat. The Ka'aba itself was constructed upon three sacred stones: the Black Stone in the southeast corner, the *maqām Ibrahīm* in the wall, and a third stone in the southwest, or Yemenite, corner. The pressures toward unification of the diverse systems had therefore already begun to be felt long years before.

After the construction of an actual city with permanent residents where previously men had lived together only temporarily, these pressures must have increased. It was, moreover, a city with a way of life and mores different from those of the existing settlements. It was entirely commercial, living by concepts previously associated only with the transient caravans, and consequently its establishment encouraged that breakdown in traditional morality which is reflected in the early suras of the Qur'an. The Qureish, guardians of the sacred areas and chief organizers of the trans-Arabian trade in which they invested heavily, sought to make this trade itself the dominant and unifying factor. The divinities whom the Meccans honored—Hubal, Manāt, Allāt, and al-'Uzzā—were associated with Muzdalifa, Qudaid, at-Ta'if, and Nakhla, all of them places on the vitally important trade routes, whose security the Qureish were anxious to preserve.[40] But this system proved insufficient, for the trade was threatened by events entirely external to Arabian experience and quite outside control or explanation in purely Meccan terms, that is to say the events of the unending conflict between Byzantium and the Sassanids, and in particular their

[40] Maurice Gaudefroy-Demombynes, *Mahomet* (Paris, 1969), pp. 48-55.

efforts to get at each other by capturing and controlling the Yemen. Behind the League of the Virtuous, in which as a young man Muhammad participated, lies a growing conviction of some of the younger inhabitants of Mecca that the crisis with which they were faced could not be dealt with merely by excluding the outsiders and maintaining, inviolate and unquestioned, the Meccan system and concepts. Some alternative and more comprehensive principle had to be discovered. To give the foreign gods a home in the Ka'aba, though some attempt to do this may well have been made, would in their view be no more than a palliative.

The most immediate crisis, however, was that the growth of Mecca introduced into the uneasy coexistence of desert and sown the third contradictory system, that of trade, a true rival for the mastery. In the wide expanse of Arabia the cultivated land was subordinate to the pasture, but the traders would accept no secondary position, and the commercial values strove for preeminence with those of the herdsmen. Now at Mecca, where Muhammad was born, they had a permanent base from which to conduct the struggle, and the sturdy individualism of the merchant began to replace the protective tribal socialism of the nomad. Medina, to which he fled with his faithful companions, was agricultural, and all around these cities was the desert in which as a child he had been reared. The three systems therefore met and contended in the person of Muhammad, and in his life and labor they were reconciled. The great achievement of Islam was the establishment of the *umma,* the new type of community. By this it broke down the ancient barriers between conflicting societies and brought about a new creation. Once again, it was in complexity and diversity that men submitted to *al-Wāhad,* the One, and this complexity and diversity are the very substance of the Middle East.

Historical Knowledge and Revelation*

G. ERNEST WRIGHT

I

The second edition of the Great Bible, published in 1540, contained a remarkable Preface by Thomas Cranmer, the archbishop of Canterbury and primate of all England. It is a sober and enlightening discussion of the reasons for Bible study and of the attitude in which the Scriptures should be studied. In the first half of the Preface he addresses himself to those who refuse to read the Bible in the vernacular and who discourage others from doing so on the ground that it is a dangerous religious innovation. He refers to the many earlier translations to show that the most ancient custom was precisely the reading of the Scripture "in the vulgar tongue. . . . And when this language waxed old and out of common usage, because folk should not lack the fruit of reading, it was again translated in the newer language." To indicate early Christian practice he quotes from a sermon of Chrysostom where people were urged to read the Scripture that they might be better prepared to understand and to remember what was preached. To those who replied that they could not understand what they read, Chrysostom had answered:

> Suppose you understand not the deep and profound mysteries of Scriptures, yet can it not be but that much fruit and holiness must come and grow unto thee by reading, for it cannot be that thou shouldest be ignorant in all things alike. For the Holy Ghost hath so ordered and attempered the Scriptures that in them as well publicans, fishers, and

---

* Sections I and II of this article are from the writer's paper "The Christian Interpreter as Biblical Critic," *Interpretation*, I (1947), 131-38, and are reprinted by permission of *Interpretation*. Other portions of this same article are also used but reworked for a different basic point than that of the original.

shepherds may find their edification, as great doctors their erudition: for those books were not made to vainglory, like as were the writings of the Gentile philosophers and rhetoricians, to the intent the makers should be had in admiration for their high styles and obscure manner of writing, whereof nothing can be understood without a master or an expositor. But the apostles and prophets wrote their books so that their special intent and purpose might be understood and perceived of every reader, which was nothing but the edification and amendment of the life of them that readeth or heareth it.

Cranmer concludes with a statement of what has ever been a basic proposition of Protestantism:

All manner of persons, of what estate or condition soever they be, may in this book learn all things what they ought to believe, what they ought to do, and what they should not do, as well concerning Almighty God as also concerning themselves, and all other[s]. Briefly, to the reading of the Scripture none can be enemy, but that either be so sick that they love not to hear of any medicine, or else that be so ignorant that they know not Scripture, to be the most helpful medicine.

In the second half of the Preface the archbishop addresses those who by their inordinate reading, indiscreet speaking, and contentious disputing, "slander and hinder the Word of God most of all other, whereof they should seem to be greatest furtherers."

There is nothing so good in this world but it may be abused, and turned from fruitful and wholesome to hurtful and noisome. . . . Wherefore I would advise you all, that cometh to the reading or hearing of this book, which is the Word of God, the most precious jewel and most holy relic that remaineth upon earth, that ye bring with you the fear of God, and that ye do it with all due reverence, and use your knowledge thereof not to vainglory and frivolous disputation but to the honour of God, increase of virtue, and edification both of yourselves and other[s].

Further to support this admonition, he again appeals to one of the Church Fathers, Gregory of Nazianzus, who wrote:

This contention and debate about Scriptures, and doubts thereof (specially when such as pretend to be the favourers and students thereof cannot agree within themselves), doth most hurt to ourselves. . . . We talk of Scripture, but in the meantime we subdue not our flesh . . . ; we go not about to pull down our proud and high minds . . . , and briefly, to reform our life and manners. But all our holiness consisteth in talking. . . . The learning of a Christian man ought to begin of the fear of God, to end in matters of high speculation; and not, contrarily to begin with speculation and to end in fear. . . Therefore, the fear of God must be the first beginning, and as it were an ABC, or an introduction to all them that shall enter to the very true and most fruitful knowledge of Holy Scriptures.[1]

This Preface is an excellent statement of the Protestant view regarding the use of the Bible by the Christian believer. Before the Reformation the church was accustomed to use the Scripture primarily as a source of proof texts for the doctrines expounded by the theologians. It was regarded somewhat as the papal decrees, which gave authoritative pronouncements in legal manner. The spiritual life of the ordinary Christian was nourished, not by the reading of the Bible, but by the ministry of the sacraments. The Mass was the chief means of grace, whereas the Bible was the source of theological knowledge for the citizen of the ecclesiastical state. The perspective of the Reformers was radically different. They opened the Bible for the layman and encouraged him to read it as the one source of a saving faith. It is often said that they substituted the authority of the Bible for the authority of the church. But the kind of authority uppermost in their minds was not the static authority of a book or even of a series of doctrines, but the authority of the God who reveals himself in his Word for the salvation of the believing reader. God has spoken by his prophets and apostles of old all that is needful to expel our darkness and bring us to his light. Let every Christian, whether he is learned or unlearned, give careful attention, therefore, to the study of the Scriptures as the chief means of grace and be nourished thereby in the faith which alone can save him from the bondage of sin!

In the sixteenth century, when the church was greatly in need of new life, these views came with all the force of a fresh discovery. As a result, people began to study the Bible with an intensity perhaps never equaled, and it is hardly possible to read anything from Protestant countries during the period that followed which is not heavily indebted in both word and thought to the Scriptures.[2] Public worship was reformed, and for Protestants the proclamation of the Word displaced the sacraments as the central focus of public worship. The preaching ministry was expected to be learned, and biblical scholarship began to increase and abound. As a biblical teacher, translator, and expositor, Luther is undoubtedly to be placed among the greatest figures in German history; and the commentaries of Calvin must

[1] See Harold R. Willoughby, *The First Authorized English Bible and the Cranmer Preface* (Chicago, 1942), pp. 38 ff.

[2] Cf. Peel in *The Interpretation of the Bible*, ed. C. W. Dugmore (London, 1944), p. 62.

surely be ranked among the chief monuments of Christian scholarship.[3]

II

It is indeed both surprising and significant, however, that notwithstanding their high view of the authority of the Bible, the Reformers were so free in their use of it. Their exposition of Scripture was a deeply religious one, but their conception of inspiration was such as to enable them on the one hand to appeal to the Bible as the only and all-sufficient guide to Christian faith and practice, and on the other to express views as a result of their intensive study which today might class them as "higher critics." To many this may appear as a strange contradiction, yet the fact is quite clear.

For one thing, they refused to accept the apocryphal books as canonical, though the Roman Church held them to be so. In his controversy with Eck, Luther declared: "A council cannot make that to be scriptural which is not of its own nature scriptural."[4] Calvin wrote that his opponents alleged "an ancient catalogue, which is called the Canon of Scripture, and which they say proceeded from the decision of the Church. I ask them again, in what council that canon was composed. To this they can make no reply. Yet I would wish to be further informed, what kind of a canon they suppose it to be. For I see that the ancient writers were not fully agreed respecting it."[5]

For practical purposes Protestants followed Jerome and the Hebrew Bible in omitting the Apocrypha, but the Reformers were by no means entirely committed to a static or objective dogma concerning the canon of Scripture.

Luther was perhaps the most outspoken on the subject. The supreme aim which God has in the Scripture is to awaken and nourish a saving faith which "arises in the heart, not by the authority of any, but by the *sole Spirit of God,* although man may be moved thereto by word and example."[6] Consequently, the authority which a writing has in

---

[3] The more one studies these commentaries, the more astonished he becomes at their scholarship, lucid profundity, and freshness of insight. Although biblical studies have moved a long way since the sixteenth century, there is still little which can be held to be their equal.

[4] Julius Köstlin, *The Theology of Luther*, trans. by C. E. Hay (Philadelphia, 1898), I, 318. H. H. Howorth, "The Origin and Authority of the Biblical Canon According to the Continent Reformers," *JTS* IX (1907-8), 188-230.

[5] *Institutes of the Christian Religion,* trans. by John Allen, 7th American ed. (Presbyterian Board of Christian Education, 1936), IV, ix, 14.

[6] Köstlin, *op. cit.,* I, 321.

itself to produce this faith is the mark of its value to the Christian. Thus to Luther the epistles of Paul, the First Epistle of Peter, and the Gospel of John are more of the gospel than Matthew, Mark, and Luke, though the latter form a good introduction, particularly for children. As is well known, the first book against which he employed internal criticism was the Epistle of James:

> Many sweat to reconcile St. Paul and St. James, as does Melanchthon in his Apology, but in vain. "Faith justifies" and "faith does not justify" contradict each other flatly. If any one can harmonize them I will give him my doctor's hood and let him call me a fool.

> Let us banish this epistle . . . , for it is worthless. It has no syllable about Christ. . . . The ancients saw all this and did not consider the epistle canonical.[7]

Luther would admit neither James nor Jude to have been written by apostles. The book of Revelation, he believed, was written by John the Evangelist, not John the Apostle; it does not teach Christ, and he held it in small esteem as uninspired. He did not believe in the Pauline authorship of Hebrews, and in his order of New Testament books the first twenty-four are successively numbered, while Hebrews, James, Jude, and Revelation are put unnumbered at the end in a class by themselves.[8]

With regard to the Old Testament, Luther was no less free in his criticism. "What does it matter," he asked, "if Moses should not have himself written the Pentateuch?" He noted the unchronological arrangement of the book of Jeremiah and thought it not unlikely that later editors had made additions to this book and those of Isaiah and Hosea. He believed that Chronicles was inferior as history to Kings, that Job was a drama, that Ecclesiastes was Maccabean in date, that the Song of Songs was not by Solomon, and that Esther were better outside the canon since it judaizes so much. While perfectly free in his criticism of the Bible, he believed that all such matters were of secondary importance. Thus, "when a contradiction occurs in Holy Scripture, so let it go."[9]

It has sometime been said that Calvin "was the real founder of the extreme doctrine of the inerrancy of Scripture."[10] While in the *Insti-*

---

[7] Quoted from Luther's table talk in Preserved Smith, *The Life and Letters of Martin Luther* (Boston, 1911), p. 269.

[8] Howorth, *op. cit.*, p. 207.

[9] For Luther's attitude toward Scripture, see esp. Köstlin, *op. cit.*, II, 223-73; R. H. Murray, *Erasmus and Luther* (London, 1920), pp. 146-47; and F. W. Farrar, *History of Interpretation* (New York, 1886), pp. 323 ff., with references there cited.

[10] So Preserved Smith, *Biblical World*, XXXVIII (1911), 244.

tutes a rigid doctrine of inspiration may possibly be inferred from occasional passages, it is obvious from his commentaries that Calvin held no such doctrine. Thus in various instances he recognized glosses in the sacred text (e.g., on John 8:3-11; I John 2:14; 5:7) and occasionally suggested the advisability of emendation (e.g., on Ezek. 16:45). On Matt. 27:9 he said that "the passage itself plainly shows that the name of Jeremiah has been put down by mistake instead of Zechariah." How this happened "I do not know, nor do I give myself much trouble to inquire." He freely recognized them as of no importance. On Heb. 11:21 he noted the deviation of the Septuagint from the Masoretic Hebrew text and remarked: "The Apostle hesitated not to apply to his purpose what was commonly received. He was indeed writing to the Jews; but they who were dispersed into various countries, had changed their own language for the Greek. And we know that the Apostles were not so scrupulous in this respect." He recognized the contrast in style between Ezekiel and Isaiah, frequently apologizing for that of Ezekiel. (On Ezek. 1:20: "Here he repeats what he had said, though he is rather prolix.")

While far more careful in statement than Luther about the canonicity of certain books, he doubted the Pauline authorship of the Epistle to the Hebrews and the Petrine authorship of Second Peter. He rejected the view that Samuel had written the books which bear his name, and with regard to Joshua he suggested that "a summary of events was framed by the high priest Eleazer, and furnished the materials out of which the Book of Joshua was composed." On Ezekiel he repeatedly asserted the necessity of historical knowledge: "Unless we know how God stirred him up we . . . shall be unable to receive any just fruit from his instruction." "The prophet's discourse cannot be understood without a knowledge of history." One of the significant features of his work was the judicious way in which he treated the Old Testament messianic prophecies and their fulfillment in the New Testament, though for this he was roundly criticized. In his comment on Gen. 3:15 he observed that "seed" is a collective noun and cannot possibly have been intended as a prophecy of Christ. In his Epistle Dedicatory to Romans he wrote: "It is therefore an audacity, closely allied to a sacrilege, rashly to turn to Scripture in any way we please, and to indulge our fancies in sport; which has been done by many in former times." [11]

[11] Considering the day in which he lived, Calvin's care and tact in exegesis are remarkable. To my knowledge, a careful study of his biblical criticism, based on his commentaries, has never been made. I am indebted, however, to F. A. G. Tholuck, "Calvin as an Interpreter of the Holy Scriptures," trans. by Leonard

In their comparatively free use of criticism, Calvin and Luther were by no means isolated in their time. Other Reformers shared this freedom in some measure, an extreme example being that of Karlstadt, who emphatically denied the Mosaic authorship of the Pentateuch.[12] Yet during the centuries which followed, dogmatic theology replaced scriptural exposition as the center of interest, and the Bible was again used chiefly as a source of proof texts and of rigid theological dogma rather than as a means of grace and of saving faith. With logical simplicity it was argued that only a belief in plenary inspiration and verbal inerrancy could provide the necessary certainty in matters of faith and conduct.[13] Cranmer's sober warning against the contentious disputing and indiscreet speaking which "slander and hinder the Word of God" was unheeded, and the Protestant controversies were prolonged and bitter.

Thoughtful and scholarly men began increasingly to see the need for intensive work among the biblical manuscripts in order that a more accurate text might be established. The Huguenot scholar Cappellus, for example, in his *Critica sacra* (1650) noted the variant readings in the extant Hebrew texts and the differences between the Masoretic text and the ancient versions. He was compelled to conclude that the vowel points and accents were not a part of the original Hebrew text but were inserted not earlier than A.D. 500, and that we therefore possess a fallible Hebrew text. The work of Benjamin

Woods, Jr., and published in the *Biblical Repository*, II (1832), 541-68 (reprinted in the Calvin Translation Society's publication of *Joshua* [Edinburgh, 1854], pp. 345-75); Louise Pettibone Smith, "Calvin as Interpreter of Ezekiel," in *From the Pyramids to Paul*, ed. L. G. Leary (New York, 1935), pp. 267-81; L. J. Evans in H. P. Smith, *Inspiration and Inerrancy* (Cincinnati, 1893), p. 67; Farrar, *op. cit.*, pp. 342 ff. Incidentally, in view of the later rigid interpretation of Calvin's doctrines of predestination and the irreversible decrees of God, it is interesting to read his comments on the passages which say that God repents (e.g., on Joel 2:13).

[12] *De canonicis Scripturis* (1520). So *Encyclopaedia Britannica*, 14th ed., IV, 880.

[13] Note, however, that in the Westminster Confession of Faith the chapter on Holy Scripture is so carefully worded as "1. To avoid mixing up the question of the canonicity of particular books with the question of their authorship, where any doubt at all existed on the latter point; 2. To leave open all reasonable questions as to the mode and degree of inspiration which could consistently be left open by those who accepted the Scriptures as the *infallible rule* of faith and duty; 3. To refrain from claiming for the text such absolute purity, and for the Hebrew vowel points such antiquity as was claimed in the Swiss *Formula Concordiae*, while asserting that the originals of Scripture are, after the lapse of ages, still pure and perfect for all those purposes for which they are given" (Mitchell and Struthers, *Minutes of the Sessions of the Westminster Assembly of Divines*, pp. xlix f.). It is quite clear that the Westminster divines attempted to produce a confession on which all Protestants of the day could agree (e.g., see *ibid.*, pp. 28, 151, 251).

Kennicott and I. B. de Rossi during the following century in publish-ing the readings of some 1459 Hebrew manuscripts proved this con-tention conclusively.[14] Yet it was a difficult view for Protestants of the time to assimilate. They felt that such a conception struck a death-blow at the doctrine of the Scripture's infallibility. Consequently, it was repeatedly asserted in the face of contrary evidence that the biblical text had not suffered in transmission and even the Hebrew vowel points were inspired.[15] During the eighteenth and nineteenth centuries, however, it became necessary to retreat from this position, though many continued to believe that the original documents were entirely pure. Textual criticism came to be accepted as an important and necessary discipline.

One example may be cited. In 1881, Professors A. A. Hodge and B. B. Warfield of Princeton Theological Seminary, the intellectual center of American theological conservatism at that time, published an important article on inspiration which seems to have been in-fluential and useful to the prosecution in the trials of C. A. Briggs and H. P. Smith a decade later.[16] In this article it was asserted that

> in all the affirmations of Scripture of every kind, there is no more error
> in the words of the original autographs than in the thoughts they were
> chosen to express. . . . Apparent inconsistencies and collisions with other
> sources of information are to be expected in imperfect copies of ancient
> writings; from the fact that the original reading may have been lost, or
> that we may fail to realize the point of view of the author, or that we
> are destitute of the circumstantial knowledge which would fill up and
> harmonize the record.

Yet Professor Warfield was also the author of a scholarly introduction to textual criticism in which it was admitted that both intentional and unintentional corruption exists in the present text of the New Testament, even that "some writers are ungrammatical, some are obscure, some are illogical, some are inconsequent, some are fright-fully infelicitous." [17]

---

[14] Kennicott, *Vetus Testamentum Hebraicum cum variis lectionibus* (1776-80) and *The State of the Printed Hebrew Text of the Old Testament Considered* (1753-59); de Rossi, *Variae lectiones Veteris Testamenti* (1784-98).

[15] See, e.g., John Owen, "Of the Integrity and Purity of the Hebrew and Greek Text of the Scripture . . ." (1658) in his collected *Works,* ed. William H. Goold (London and Edinburgh, 1853), XVI, 345-421.

[16] "Inspiration," *The Presbyterian Review,* II (1881), 226-60.

[17] *An Introduction to the Textual Criticism of the New Testament* (London, 1886), p. 86. See also p. 94.

III

It is difficult to account for the free attitude of Luther and Calvin toward both lower and higher critical matters in the Bible, *unless* we see that they put their basic emphasis in the conception of revelation at a very different point than did many of their followers in the succeeding creedal eras of Protestantism. For the great Reformers, the essential content of revelation is not every word of Scripture, every book of Scripture in equal measure with every other book. It is not in minor errors of quotation or in the acceptance of previous tradition regarding Mosaic authorship or the authorship of Second Peter. Such things to them seemed unimportant. What was important was the biblical content which had a saving power. Luther especially in the freedom with which he defined his own canon within the canon was employing theological considerations which had an experiential power, so that one's encounter with the Bible was not primarily in intellectual queries or disputations about the six days of creation, for example, but in existential issues that were salvation or damnation. Revelation thus had as central content *saving truth*.[18]

By contrast in the following centuries the splitting of Protestantism into so many factions, each claiming the Bible for itself, each insisting on its own truth as the only proper definition of revelation, brought a totally new situation. What to the Reformers was peripheral, inched into the center of considerations. Increasingly it was believed possible to state in intellectual generalizations, not tied as saving truth to any particular human situation, never historically specific but as timeless universals, precisely what the content of revelation is. The Bible became the new law book of doctrine for various Protestant groups.

Rebelling against this stance, whether in pietism or in rationalism, are the major authors of biblical study movements in their attempts to set the Bible free to speak its own piece in its own manner. In America the beginning of the movement for correct and independent exegesis of the Bible, based upon the very latest knowledge of grammar and lexicography, came with the work of Moses Stuart and Edward Robinson, both conservative Calvinists of the first theological school in this country, Andover Theological Seminary.[19] As a result of their

[18] For the Reformers' "saving truth," see esp. the excellent article of A. A. Hays, "The Ultimate Basis for the Authority of Scripture According to Calvin," *From the Pyramids to Paul* (New York, 1935), pp. 79-94.

[19] See W. F. Albright's articles on these men in the *Dictionary of American Biography* (New York, 1935); Roswell D. Hitchcock, in Smith and Hitchcock, *The Life, Writings and Character of Edward Robinson, D.D., L.L.D.* (New York, 1863), pp. 18-100; and G. Ernest Wright, "The Phenomenon of American Archaeology in

work and that of those who stand in their tradition, there have come into existence certain basic rules of exegesis and interpretation based upon solid grammatical and environmental study. Moreover, there has grown up in the churches a body of scholarship which insists that these basic rules be kept even when incomplete information may lead to disagreement about conclusions. As a result the Protestant tendency to divide into sects on the basis of claims to sole knowledge of what the Bible says has ceased. There is a higher authority that cannot be bypassed today, even by Roman Catholic theologians since Vatican II; it is based on correct and informed knowledge.

IV

Yet for all that, the task of the biblical historian is hardly finished. We would do well to analyze further the implications of Calvin's statement quoted above: "The prophet's discourse cannot be understood without a knowledge of history." It seems to me significant that the young Lutheran scholar, Samuel Preus, in his book, *From Shadow to Promise: Old Testament Interpretation from Augustine to the Young Luther*,[20] has been able to show that in spite of Luther's

> rigorous Christocentricity, his many unkind words about Moses, and the Marcionite leanings, both suspected and real, among representatives of the Lutheran tradition, . . . what separates Luther most decisively from the medieval hermeneutical tradition and further, what best explains the genesis of his Reformation theology, depends upon his peculiar appropriation of the Old Testament—his theological recovery of its history, its word, and its faith for the Church.[21]

The Old Testament, far from being a special world of divine happenings dimly foreshadowing the New Testament, a world set in olden times but having no real conjunction with our lives and times, except possibly in the cult, was rediscovered in its own right by the Reformers. It was found to be contiguous with our history, as being our history, and a world where we meet people like ourselves whose lives and events we can understand.

---

the Near East," *Glueck Festschrift* (New York, 1970), Chap. 1. The Boston liberals (later "Unitarians") made a substantial beginning but did not follow through when their interests turned to other issues: see C. C. Wright, *Three Prophets of Religious Liberalism* (Boston, 1961), pp. 13-17.

[20] Cambridge, 1969. For the thesis that the "Reformation restored a sense of the dynamism and divine purpose in history," see the essay by the historian E. Harris Harbison on "Calvin's Sense of History," *Christianity and History* (Princeton, 1964), pp. 270-88.

[21] Preus, *op. cit.*, p. 6.

When we use the term "history" in theology these days, it is very easy for the critic to point out how slippery a term it is for us, how varied its meanings are in any given work on faith and history. Yet one meaning is clear and important. Historical knowledge, which in the Bible is understood as the conveyor of revelation, is different from any other kind of knowledge. Knowledge of what are called bare facts, or of the world of objects or things, whether the moon, or electrons, or a Volkswagen, or 1066 and all that, is a different kind from that which one obtains when he reads about people and what they have done or are said to have done or will do in the future. There is a special identification that takes place, because of the similarity of personal beings, between a knowledge we now have of the Sumerians, their history, their myths and literature, their cities, temples, and palaces, than we have with soil problems in Iraq, past or present, or with the oil or mineral resources of the country. The huge foundation still remaining for the temple at Shechem is just a pile of stones for some people, but for me it is different. This is not only because I was a member of the Shechem archaeological team which worked out the history of the site, but also because the building they supported played an important role in the history of the people of Israel with whom I profess and possess a special affinity.

When people with different backgrounds read the various Gospels, they encounter a vivid impression of a powerful person. Imagination and intuition play a large role in breathing life into the words about another life. Study and reflection may revise preliminary intuitions, but the personal identification remains. And when one asks, "What does it mean?" he is asking a question intrinsic to every fundamental question about life: "What does it mean?" "What is happening?" These are questions about purpose, not merely the purpose of Jesus, but the purpose of human existence. In the case of Jesus the dominant impression has to do with a special way of speaking about the manifestations of power in, through, and around him at that moment, in his remembered tradition and in the future. His most frequent term for this was "the kingdom of God." And the happenings about Jesus and his people become intelligible only as a new beginning of previous experiences of power. In the words of my colleague Richard R. Niebuhr,

In this way, Jesus appears and acts in the gospel accounts as a concrete figure who makes Abraham and Moses and David and Elijah more real, not only because he is related to them by national religion and descent, but also because he is related to them directly through the sovereign decrees of God. And so he brings into the present the archetypal figures of covenant, the personal reality of covenant faith, and the palpability of the steadfastness of God, making all these things experientially real and convincing. As Jesus stands among his disciples, indisputably present in his mission, the decrees, promises, and rule of God appear as equally concrete . . . , emerge from cultic memory and scriptural tradition with a fresh immediacy. . . . Jesus is a restatement of the intentions that the lives of Abraham and Moses and the others served . . . ; he becomes a new embodiment of the covenant meetings of God and men. He lets his own life be so completely shaped by the steadfastness of God, that the Scripture portraits of the fathers wrestling in faith with covenant promises of God become more credible and attain a new meaning for all who suspect what is happening to Jesus . . . , a new beginning of all the great beginnings of faith between men and God.

In short, the Jesus of our evangelists, even of John, is the beginning again of . . . prophetic faith . . . , the recapitulator of their (the disciples') inherited faith-history. . . . Jesus does not promise life eternal but promises the time of the Kingdom of God.[22]

This is historical knowledge, gained by reading and hearing, in which one person encounters another human situation and cannot help sharing in it. There is at least a momentary attempt at identity, and whether the encounter reshapes my life depends upon how or whether the purpose, the reshaping power, the new beginning become my own in some way more or less permanent. I have a similar involvement at the moment with Thomas Jefferson, because I am reading a book which attempts to present him as a living force in the midst of living goals, purposes, aspirations. The experience enlivens me, commits me again to the Jeffersonian purpose and goals for our nation. It differs from the experience of the Bible, it seems to me, not in kind of historical knowledge, but in the purpose and power and ultimacy of the claim it lays upon me. That is, the Bible introduces me to a truly *ultimate concern,* in Tillich's sense, which undercuts or undergirds the Jeffersonian faith.

Historical knowledge thus is a kind of personal knowledge with which I, as a person, am involved. Attracted, converted, repelled, as the case may be, I am engaged in a sharing of life in historical study— and that is a different kind of knowledge than I have from a study of the horse or from the economics of England's foreign relations. Since people are involved, lines are blurred. Yet revelation clearly

[22] Richard R. Niebuhr, "Archegos, An Essay on the Relation Between the Biblical Jesus Christ and the Present-Day Reader," *Christian History and Interpretation: Studies Presented to John Knox,* ed. by Farmer, Moule, and Niebuhr (New York, 1967), pp. 79-100, citation from pp. 85-87.

belongs to the realm of historical knowledge after the manner in which I have just defined it, not to the world of things, nor even to the specially cultivated interior experience of mysticism.

V

The only way this historical knowledge can be conveyed is by means of narrative. Thus the revelation of the Bible concerns God's unveiling of himself, his identification of man's nature, of what he has done concerning the human problem. Its manner of presentation cannot be considered primitive because it comes from a supposedly primitive time, or because it is anthropomorphic, or because it reads to us like a kind of mythopoetry. Revelation as historical knowledge, that is, a knowledge of people and events including how they interpreted those events and their own purposes and roles within them, can therefore only be conveyed by a historical literature. There may be many different forms of the literature, and a highly selective group of types, but they all possess the historical center. Wisdom literature is not the center of the scriptural canon; it is peripheral to it. Yet the above generalization can apply even to it if we know that its moral affirmations, commonly shared, were highly refined as literature, and were probably the means by which scribes and the children of bureaucrats and of court were taught manners in ancient civilization so that they could be sent to the Jerusalem salons, to Egypt, to Phoenicia or Babylon. The Gospel of John seems to be like a "sayings source" in which traditional incidents are retold for teaching purposes only. Yet we need to recall that in the life of the early church it was one type of Gospel among many in which the teachings are merely the prologue to the Passion story which is told as straight narrative.[23]

Today there is surely no way to avoid the generalization that biblical revelation as saving truth is also historical truth, historically mediated, with narrative as the manner in which its variously employed literary forms are knit together.[24]

VI

In our ordinary uses of the theological term "revelation," we normally refer to something of ultimate importance for human life.

[23] See Helmut Koester, "One Jesus and Four Primitive Gospels," *HTR*, LI/2 (April 1968), 203-47.
[24] See further my discussion in Chap. 2, "Revelation and Theology," *The Old Testament and Theology* (New York, 1969).

This we say is, or is to be found in, the Bible. There is a great variety in our conceptions and ways of expressing what this is. The reason would simply be, it seems to me, that as human beings within the Christian—or Jewish—framework through which we look at reality, what is centrally important to us may not be what is centrally important to others. Even such a cliché as the term "Word of God" hides rather than exposes these differences. The reasons they exist are surely many, having to do with the biblical variety itself, with our heritage or tradition from our fathers whom we respect, with the differences between our day and any other preceding day, and the individual differences built into the structure of our groups and ourselves.

It is very likely that the exposition of the Bible by a person widely trained in the literatures of the ancient Near East will differ in perspective rather markedly from the exposition by one who knows nothing of the biblical environment. A Lutheran may place far more weight on Romans 7–8 and the Pauline problem of law and gospel as the key to the whole Bible than a Calvinist would be expected to do. An evangelist, whether Wesley, Moody, or Graham, in the tradition of the Anglo-American revivalist movement, would employ still another type of exposition of Scripture designed to bring about a speedy and radical change in its hearers. Moreover, the emotional life of an era or an individual brings differences in our views of what is most important in Scripture. The fear of the farmer about weather and prices, the anxiety of the executive for economic security with no union to protect him, the sense of inadequacy of a clergyman or a professor, all lead to differences in what we appropriate as most important to us from the Bible. Harry Truman did not claim that Bible or revelation was confined to the Sermon on the Mount. Matthew's collection of Jesus' teaching, set in the framework of a Moses-on-Sinai parallel, constituted for Truman what was most important in the Bible to him, thus in effect what essential revelation in the Bible is. Indeed, what is revelation to each of us can be gathered more from our *usage* than from our formal theological statements, which are often quite misleading and untrustworthy as a guide to our true beliefs.

In other words, both our conceptions of revelation and our expositions of it are greatly affected by the individuality of our background, our personal needs, our particular history as selves. Regardless of how our peculiar religious tradition defines revelation, the normal individual self will refract that definition in given ways, depending on his authentic selfhood. Yet that is precisely in accord with what we would

292

expect from the historical type of truth gained in the encounter with personal beings and human events.

A popular Christian theological position today, whether found in Barth, Bultmann, the United Presbyterian Confession of 1967, or the "Death-of-God" theologians, is the essential equation of revelation with Jesus Christ, so that whatever is said about God is virtually exhausted in Christology. This can be connected with Luther's famous dictum concerning revelation in the Old Testament: "Whatever leads to Christ." In practical effect, then, from this point of view one may do away with any meaningful relation of canon and revelation, as well as any essential importance for the Old Testament except as background. Certain exclusivist statements of Pauline and Johannine literature are often used to defend such a viewpoint, e.g., "No one has ever seen God; the only Son who is in the bosom of the Father, he has revealed him" (John 1:18); "He is the image of the invisible God (Col. 1:15). Christ is thus allowed to exist in history without history, and not infrequently is a radically "demythologized" being. The early church seems not to have read these verses in this christomonistic manner. Her attempt to put into current philosophical terms her understanding of the Bible gave a trinitarian statement of the manner of God's revelation. To summarize biblical history in philosophical categories requires a more complex and sophisticated formula than a mere monism of any kind could provide.[25]

Since the term "revelation," defined in any of the common senses in which we today use it, is not a biblical term but a product of our own attempt to simplify and generalize what would be particular in the Bible, we are faced with still a third subjective problem. If the term "revelation" is a shortcut to say what to us is normatively binding in the Bible upon us, then it is *our* theological construction, made because we must. It does no good simply to repeat biblical words alone, which received particular meanings from the crucible of a people's experience at one time and place. The theologian's task is to study that language and examine its meaning in the context of the experience of our time.[26] To repeat older creedal formularies is not necessarily helpful to faith now. That more often than not breeds new heresy because words have a historical setting and have to be constantly reinterpreted for a changing environment. To be stuck with a marvelous sixteenth- or seventeenth-century creed on a mountaintop

[25] Cf. H. Richard Niebuhr, "The Doctrine of the Trinity and the Unity of the Church," *Theology Today*, III (1946), 371-84; Gordon D. Kaufman, *Systematic Theology: A Historicist Perspective* (New York, 1968), esp. pp. 243-52.

[26] See Kaufman, *ibid.*, pp. 13-40, and esp. n. 3 on pp. 17-18.

is not especially helpful if that mountain is now jungle and historically significant action has moved far away from it.

VII

This is simply to say that by usage, if not by theoretical statement, what is central to our conception of revelation will vary. This, in turn, is not because we disagree radically on the Bible's central content, but because in dealing with historical testimony and encounter, our own selves, traditions, and current historical involvement affect what we see and grasp as most important.

Before and after the First Assembly of the World Council of Churches in 1948, the Study Department had gathered together a Bible Committee to discuss how Bible and current ethical decision could be brought together. At the Wadham College meeting in Oxford during the summer of 1949, the group seemed to find it impossible to find a common way along which to proceed. Finally Professor Walther Eichrodt suggested that one session be spent on the exegesis of Jer. 7:1-15, with various people contributing prepared statements as a basis for discussion. Perhaps then we could detect where and why we differed. Here were represented leading Protestant bodies in the West, together with a representative of Greek Orthodoxy. To our surprise we found no basic differences in approaching the text to find out what it says, nor in seeking what was basic truth, still valid, being conveyed by the pericope. Our differences derived from personal traits, levels of learning, different central interests currently before each person, diverse traditions, variations as to how the "message" applied directly or indirectly to our day, and by what route we traveled to bridge the gap between biblical times and now.[27]

Everyone there, however, was committed to what is generally called "the historical-critical method." This was developed in the Western World primarily during the last century and a half as a tool to write history fairly, without distorting the original meaning of the texts. It is a method of studying texts using to the full the most advanced

---

[27] For a selection of papers from two sessions of the Biblical Committee of the WCC's Study Department at Zetten, Holland and Wadham College, Oxford in 1948 and 1949, see A. Richardson and W. Schweitzer, *Biblical Authority for Today* (Philadelphia, 1951). The document produced as a result of Eichrodt's intervention was written by me with the aid of T. F. Torrance and revised by the full committee; it is to be found on pp. 240-43. A distinguished group of theologians as well as biblical scholars was present. For a paper and an address printed as a result of our discussion of Jer. 7:1-15, see Eichrodt, *Theology Today*, VII/1 (April 1950), 15-25; and Wright, *The Rule of God*, Lecture 5, pp. 79-92.

grammar, lexicography, comparative literature and religion, and the reconstruction of ancient history including biblical history in its context. The details of this method are too familiar to need spelling out here.[28] Its basic attempt is to exclude subjectivity as much as is possible by method and research, so that the Bible is not said to be saying what in effect it does not say. Cherished positions have to be surrendered occasionally, as for example by Catholic scholars on the amount of Mariology which is actually biblical, and by Protestant scholars on the complete spiritualization of Matt. 16:18 and the tendency to exclude any consideration of the probable fact that its actual context really was in the area of church discipline. Thus the method is a basic tool which attempts to recover the original context of the experiences spoken of in the documents, and making possible historical knowledge which can bridge the gap in time between the documents and ourselves.

One of the great stories of Western culture, a story every bit as important for the Western mind as the development of our technology, is the development of the historical sciences and of man's knowledge of himself. Inevitably, one result of nineteenth- and twentieth-century scholarship is the application of historical disciplines to the Bible and the question of how the Bible can be studied first of all in its own environment before we ask about its uses for theology, for our theology. The remarkable Protestant consensus on central issues which made the World Council of Churches possible had as one most important ingredient this agreement on the historical method as the first primary and indispensable tool in Bible study. A refusal to accept the historical method of biblical study was a basic ingredient in the decision of a number of Protestant churches to stay out of the World Council of Churches. An example of this is the great Southern Baptist Convention which at the moment has a debate within it reminiscent of the Fundamentalist-Modernist controversy experienced by some other Protestant bodies two generations ago. Southern Baptist biblical scholars and those educated in modern biblical research are for the most part participating warmly in the modern biblical movement, but opposing them within their denominational ranks are

[28] For an exposition of the historical method as used in Biblical Study, see James Muilenburg, "The Interpretation of the Bible" *Biblical Authority for Today* (see n. 27), pp. 198-218. For more general considerations, see Harbison, *Christianity and History* (see n. 20); W. F. Albright, *History, Archaeology, and Christian Humanism* (New York, 1964); E. H. Carr, *What is History?* (New York, 1963); C. N. Cochrane, *Christianity and Classical Culture* (London, 1944); and Gordon D. Kaufman, *Relativism, Knowledge, and Faith* (Chicago, 1960).

those to whom a thoroughgoing application of historical criticism is anathema. And it is paradoxically these latter who fail to see the appropriateness of historical method to historical knowledge.

One of the most striking characteristics of the conservative wings of the church during this century has been the weakness of their biblical scholarship. I once had great admiration for Carl F. Henry and his associates when they started *Christianity Today* as an attempt to "drive a wedge" for the new breed of scholarly conservatives, and to dissociate themselves from those who had lost all semblance of true scholarly learning, from those who were more given to sloganeering than to scholarship. Yet to speak of one field only, it was obvious that, with occasional exceptions for which one was grateful, biblical, especially Old Testament, articles and reviews simply did not measure up to the standard set by the editors for theological discussion generally. There is no word sufficiently eloquent to describe this weakness other than to say that it is pitiable. The rare exceptions only proved the rule.

Biblical scholarship which cannot relate itself to the ongoing community of biblical learning and at best feels it better to write only for in-group organs, will wither and fall behind. This is a simple statement of past experience, and it confronts the conservative movements with the question of the real seriousness with which their professions concerning the Bible are to be taken.

Many conservatives have little realization of the distance between biblical studies at the turn of the century and the scholarship of today. Many still think the historical-critical method is a choice between Wellhausen's views and biblical truth. The work of such scholars as Gunkel, Alt, Noth, von Rad, Albright, Bright, Cross and Freedman, Mendenhall, and others means that no one can conceive of the possibility of reconstructing Israel's history today according to the proposals of Wellhausen. Yet precisely how to do it is a problem on which there is no general agreement. Albright's influence on American, Israeli, and Roman Catholic Old Testament scholars has been so overwhelming that few scholars in these groups would consider attempting the task without the full use of the archaeological recovery of the ancient world as the primary setting in which the work is to be done. A dominant German assumption that primary historical data can be derived from inner literary analysis is rejected by this view on the grounds that internal literary analysis offers no *historical* data in itself without externally derived information around which to fix hypotheses concerning historical meaning. This is especially the case with the early traditions. Biblical archaeology and actual vigorous field work on the part of German biblical scholars have been a scarce commodity; this is vividly reflected in German biblical study. Primarily for this reason, those influenced by Albright's vision of biblical scholarship move in a different world in many respects from the heirs of a purely Germanic heritage.

The primary meaning of perhaps the greatest book in biblical archaeology, Albright's *From the Stone Age to Christianity*,[29] is relevant precisely at this point. Long convinced of the necessity of setting forth the archaeologically recovered framework for Israel's history, Albright only in the late 1930's thought that sufficient data, critically controlled, were available. It was then that he wrote the history of the ancient world in such manner as to enable one to fit the story of Israel's radically new political-religious movement within it.

Archaeology with its own methodologies is simply the historian's tool to get information to supplement and give setting for literary remains of a lost world. In some cases it provides the sole information about eras for which we have insufficient or no literary deposit whatever. Albright himself uses the term "archaeology" in the widest possible sense for the work being done in the area of the ancient world known to the Bible.[30] Thus to those who follow Albright's views it is virtually coextensive in biblical study with materials and data handled by the historical-critical method because it includes biblical archaeology.

VIII

Now we must ask whether the Bible as revelation can continue to be so received if it is also the object of archaeological and historical study. In 1966 the Calvary and Tacoma Bible Presbyterian Churches brought court proceedings against the Board of Regents of the University of Washington for offering a course entitled "The Bible as Literature." The plaintiffs had an inner contradiction in their argument. On the one hand, they charged the University of Washington with presenting the course in question from a biased point of view. On the other hand, they contended that before one could be considered qualified to teach Bible he must believe that it was inspired by God in a plenary manner, that it is the supreme revelation of the only

[29] Baltimore, 1940.

[30] From this perspective, see my review of "Biblical Archaeology Today" in *New Directions in Biblical Archaeology*, ed. D. N. Freedman and J. C. Greenfield (New York, 1969), pp. 149-65.

true God, and that there is no other way of salvation than through this revelation. In their view a teacher who in advance does not proclaim, confess, and truly profess this view is incapacitated as a teacher and should not be allowed to teach Bible. As a defense witness I stated that owing to language flexibility I, personally, could subscribe in general to the requirement just stated. Why, then, was I a defense witness against them? Their views amounted to a prejudice against all biblical scholarship which committed them to denunciation of all who did not come to the same conclusions as they did.

There are more sophisticated scholars who have adopted a comparable viewpoint to that of the plaintiffs in the Seattle trial. T. C. Vriezen in his *An Outline of Old Testament Theology*,[31] for example, protests against a purely descriptive approach to the Bible because it is not theological, and according to him one cannot interpret an Old Testament text without reference to the New Testament. Brevard S. Childs has emphasized this second point and has stressed that Christian exegesis can only begin and remain within "a framework of faith" which is defined in Christ.[32] If one begins as a descriptive historian and shifts to a theological position, "the possibility of genuine theological exegesis has been destroyed from the outset," Childs claims. He thinks of the descriptive task of critical-historical interpretation as "neutral criticism" which in advance defines the proper stance toward the Bible as that of one who is neutral toward its ultimate claims as revelation.

On one important point there is a similarity between the positions of Vriezen and Childs and that of the plaintiffs in Seattle. All agree that unless you take your stance in advance within a framework of faith, your biblical interpretation cannot be theological, a term which in these instances at least is defined as christological. Here the view is that historical exegesis is descriptive and neutral and therefore antithetical to Christian exegesis.

Such a position is not only wrong, it does not understand current historical method and, if pursued consistently, would enshrine not Scripture but tradition as Lord of the church and perpetuate errors and heresies in the name of Scripture, as has happened again and again since the Reformation.

Is "neutral criticism" a valid description of the historical method? For some it has been and is still. But it is out of fashion and can be

---

[31] Wageningen, Holland, 1958 (also Chas. T. Banford Co., Newton Centre, Mass.) .

[32] "Interpretation in Faith," *Interpretation*, XVIII (1964) , 432-39.

claimed to produce bad history. One calls to mind a certain American historian who has made a name for himself writing about American revivalism and revivalists. He derived great fun from his work, and it is enjoyable to read his accounts. Yet when one looks for careful exegesis he finds the author outside his material, a spectator enjoying himself, but not really understanding the personalities, their rootage, the history of European-American theology, which produced them. Therefore the work remains external, superficial; it does not truly convey historical knowledge. In his *History of Israel*,[33] Martin Noth confines himself to a surface survey of events as he reconstructs them. Their meaning for the participants or for subsequent people is completely omitted, and their outcome is carried into early Judaism, while any real consideration of their rootage for Christianity is simply rejected or at least omitted as irrelevant.

This is the sort of thing which comes to mind when the term "neutral" is used, though, as a matter of fact, neither of the authors mentioned is in the least neutral. Their prejudices are perfectly clear both from their manner of treatment and chosen content. By contrast a full, rich, far better history is, e.g., Carl Sandburg's *Lincoln,* where the author insofar as possible relives and participates in every facet of Lincoln's life, identifies with and absorbs himself in Lincoln. From the present perspective, it is possible for Sandburg to enter various critical assessments of Lincoln's attitudes and actions, but Lincoln remains his absorbing hero. In what way Lincoln's life is revelation of any type of ultimate truth, one will learn from Sandburg better than from anyone else. That is historical knowledge; it has no room for the term "neutrality" within it or about it. Sandburg is dealing with knowledge drawn from the life of one of history's greatest men. Can anyone claim that he did not use the tools of the historian for this work? Can anyone claim that those tools were or induced neutral criticism which destroyed its object's greatness?

But, it may be objected, we are talking about the Bible. One does not put the Bible in the same category as a book about the life of Lincoln. That is true, although Lincoln's life could scarcely be understood without the Bible, its influence on him personally or upon America's "civil religion." [34] Yet in our scholarly study of the Bible, are our methods different from those of Sandburg except insofar as

[33] Martin Noth, *The History of Israel,* trans. from the 2nd German ed. by Stanley Godman (New York, 1958).

[34] For discussion of this type of problem (i.e., the supremacy of the Bible over what can be understood only because the Bible has first existed), see what surely is the classic of our era in this area, H. Richard Niebuhr's *The Meaning of Revelation* (New York, 1941).

the material being studied is different? A scholar who holds his material in respect must work seriously with problems of text transmission, with the meaning of words and their inner relationships. He must make clear how they are or are not coextensive with the modern words used to translate them. These words must be brought into the context of the conceptual world of the Bible. The types and histories and usage of literary forms employed must be discerned. The forms of literature in prophecy, psalms, and wisdom materials call for some attempt to find their background and agents of transmission. The type of literature, its authorship, its historical setting, its personality interaction within history, and above all a sensitivity for the biblical world which produced the literature—all these are necessary if we would really understand the Bible.

Is neutrality a necessary ingredient of any of these procedures, or is it not rather in the make-up of a personality *before* he begins his work? He can be "neutral" in one sense only. He cannot presume to know all the answers before he starts. With all due respect to our fathers, does their work mean that we do *not* have to work? Is what they did for their day at all sufficient for us today, except that it is instructive of what we too should be doing for our own time? Yet we also should be doing new and different things. The world of biblical study is in the midst of an archaeological revolution which has produced new information at such a rate that increasing specialization among scholars has come into being; even a team can scarcely keep up. Furthermore, we live in a rapidly shifting environment which asks new questions and seeks new formulations. To this situation we must adapt to survive. A knowledge revolution in a rapidly shifting environment—either we lead with new methods and new adjustments, or we fall behind and die while others pass us by.

It is obvious that we must work on several different levels at the same time. Objective procedures, used publicly in a wide ecumenical community, aid in isolating our subjective opinions and throw them open to public scrutiny and critique. On a different level we must be asking what the Bible means for faith and fidelity now, and how our fathers' views must be further enriched or qualified or quite simply changed. To be a critical scholar and to hear the Word of God afresh in our moment demands work in which the Bible's meaning is continually discovered anew by one who is thoroughly alive and seeks the signs of the times now.[35]

[35] Professor Jay A. Wilcoxen of the University of Chicago has termed this "the prophetic analogy"; i.e., as a person studies the Bible, while living with expectancy

IX

Finally, a severe limitation is placed upon the scholar's work with the Bible when a popular line of current theology uncritically defines the Christian's "framework of faith" as Jesus Christ. This kind of statement, naïvely repeated, represents a real limitation, as I have attempted to explain elsewhere.[36] Christomonism is not a necessary form of christocentricity, and it is not helpful in Old Testament exposition.

Christomonism means that the content of revelation is confined to Christ and that, when the exposition of Christology is completed, all has been said that needs to be said theologically, as though the doctrine of God were *only thus* fully stated and nothing additional could or should be said. What Elton Trueblood has called "a unitarianism of the Second Person," or what H. Richard Niebuhr labeled "Christian henotheism" (Christology as a substitute for theology), is unfortunately perhaps the most popular mode of theologizing in Christianity ("One cannot talk about God anymore, but we do have Christ to talk about"). This is small help, in my opinion, when the problem is faith in God of any kind.

If the Risen Christ is the fulfillment of, the center of, and the key to, the unity of the Bible, then our most critical problem is the discovery of what he means for the church's task of interpretation. How, for example, are we to read the Old Testament in the light of Christ? Is Luther's phrase, "what leads to Christ" (*was Christum treibet*), a principle of selection between the eternal and the temporal? To make a simple assumption that it is such a principle may lead us to attempt an analysis of "the mind of Christ," whatever we may mean by that phrase, and then to use the result as a yardstick for measuring truth. Yet even the teachings of Jesus have a "situation-conditioned" nature, and our problem is not solved by the oversimplified supposition that everything we find in the New Testament is in itself more authoritative than anything we find in the Old Testament. Moreover, since the authority of the Old Testament as Scripture is

---

in the present as the meaningful period for him, the Bible comes "alive" and the past revelation becomes contemporary. See Wilcoxen, "An Interpretative View of G. Ernest Wright," *Criterion*, II/3 (Summer 1963), 25-31. A place where I have made the point most clearly is in the article "From the Bible to the Modern World," in *Biblical Authority for Today*, pp. 219-39. Here, I have sought to go beyond the position taken there in spelling out more definitely the special nature of historical knowledge which involves me in personal encounter with people and events.

[36] See G. E. Wright, *The Old Testament and Theology*, esp. pp. 13-38.

never challenged in the New Testament, we should find it most diffi-cult to use the latter as the real canon or measuring rod by which the Old Testament might be broken up into its authoritative and un-authoritative parts.

The unity of the Bible in Christ has been demonstrated more com-monly in the history of the church by the use of christological allegory and typology. Since Christ is the Lord of both Testaments, his Word is to be found in the Old Covenant as well as in the New. Yet in the Old Testament the passages which are clearly and unequivocally messianic comprise but a small part of the whole. Are we entitled to read in the remainder of the literature a Christology which the words themselves do not imply and of which the authors were seemingly unaware? Taken on its own terms, the Old Testament as a whole does not present Christ to us; it rather prepares the way for Christ. In the past, christological interpretation of the Old Testament has been tempted to read into the faith of Israel more than was actually there and to erase the biblical conception of time with its constitutent elements: promise and fulfillment.

To confess Christ as Lord of both Testaments is an affirmation of faith without precise content until it is further defined. We are compelled to explain what we mean by Christ in this connection, and to ask whether he achieves his true meaning apart from the doctrine of the Trinity. In itself the conception of the Trinity reveals an aware-ness of the complexity of the Godhead which defies oversimplified analysis. We are thus warned against the use of generalizing formulas in the interpretation of the Scripture. The belief in Christ as Lord means little unless God himself is first of all Lord. At a time when most Christians in the World Church are agreed on the lordship of Christ as the faith that binds the churches together, we must not be-tray the church's doctrine of Christ by a christomonism which in practice may resolve the complexity of the Godhead by a new kind of monotheism based on Christ.

If, on the other hand, the true meaning of Christ can be grasped only within the context of the Trinity, then we have taken at least one step forward in our search for valid hermeneutical principles. When in a trinitarian context we say that Christ is the Lord of the Old Testament, we do not infer the necessity of christological allegory or typology in interpreting the Old Testament. Instead, we are assert-ing that Christ shows us the true meaning of what God was doing with the Chosen People, Israel, because we see the end to which all was leading. Thus the initial and intervening steps in their history do not lose their meaning for us but instead are given new significance, because the end provides the key to their intended direction. One cannot set up route markers along a road until he knows the route. *Christ is the destination and at the same time the guide* to the true understanding of the Old Testament.[37]

---

[37] For the final four paragraphs, see my article, "From the Bible to the Modern World," in *Biblical Authority for Today,* pp. 226-28.

Form and Content:
A Hermeneutical Application
R. LANSING HICKS

INTRODUCTION

The meaning of the Old Testament for the Christian faith poses a paradox which has vexed both theologians and biblical scholars from the earliest days of Christianity. In principle, the Christian church has not only insisted that the Old Testament belongs with the New, but also that both show forth Christ. In practice, however, the church has always experienced difficulties in expressing exegetically the unity of the Scriptures which it confesses. Rooted in theology as well as in exegesis, this problem can be viewed as a basic hermeneutical issue. As such, it constantly presses its claim for serious attention.

Writing a generation ago about the problem of the unity of revelation in the Bible, Karl Barth asserted that "the cognition or recognition of this unity as it was alive in the whole Early Church, still confronts modern Old Testament science *as its chief task*." [1] But the task remains undone. To our own generation Walther Zimmerli has given notice that unfortunately the Old Testament now appears as "an alien factor in recent Protestant theology." [2] For when the systematic theologian attempts to elucidate the central affirmations of the Christian faith, he finds the Old Testament "an embarrassment"; and even when the New Testament scholar wishes to speak theologically about the authentic Word of God, "the Old Testament has to be silent." He warns us that "the situation can arise in which a hermeneutic, which attempts seriously to grasp the real content of the New Testament proclamation, no longer sees a need for the word and proclama-

---

[1] *Church Dogmatics*, I/2, trans. by G. T. Thomson (Edinburgh, 1936) , 79 (italics supplied) .
[2] *The Law and the Prophets: A Study of the Meaning of the Old Testament*, (Oxford, 1965) , p. 2.

tion of the Old." [3] The need is not now widely felt. Gerhard von Rad recently put the matter to us quite categorically by asserting:

> The coming of Jesus Christ as a historical reality leaves the exegete no choice at all; he must interpret the Old Testament as pointing to Christ, whom he must understand in its light. . . . *The only question is, how far can Christ be a help to the exegete in understanding the Old Testament, and how far can the Old Testament be a help to him in understanding Christ?* [4]

Here the issue is unmistakable and undeniable.

It is to one major aspect of the old but urgent issue concerning the unity of the Bible that this study is directed. We are now living in what we sometimes too arrogantly call "a world come of age," scientifically and theologically; and this poses for us a hermeneutical problem much more complex than that faced by the Fathers, for instance, or the Reformers. Now an old problem has been made more difficult by the unprecedented results of modern critical studies and more acute by the pressing demands of today's theological debates. In this situation we must ask ourselves whether, with integrity as historians and critics, we also can claim that the Old Testament not only anticipates and promises, but indeed shows forth and "preaches," Christ.[5] Accordingly, our concern is to suggest acceptable ways in which we ourselves, in this age of biblical criticism and theological skepticism, may better perceive and express the unity which the Bible possesses through Christ. Here, I will limit myself principally to a consideration of form and, more specifically, the interaction of form with content.[6]

[3] *Ibid.* It is equally clear, Professor Zimmerli observes, that Old Testament scholarship itself must assume a large share of responsibility for this acute situation. Accordingly, it faces the task of explaining properly the essential message of the Old Testament itself and also of showing to what extent the church is right in insisting upon the unity of the Canon (see pp. 2-4). His essay forms a penetrating study of these central issues and points out directions in which Old Testament research, New Testament scholarship, and systematic theology should move in order to come to a clearer understanding of the fundamental unity of the Bible.

[4] *Old Testament Theology,* trans. by D. M. G. Stalker (Edinburgh, 1965), II, 374 (author's italics). Here we see how strongly a skilled and committed biblical critic can emphasize the conviction that the Old Testament has to do with Christ.

[5] See Acts 8:35 and 2:29 ff.

[6] I first discussed this topic in the Winslow Lectures for 1968 ("Forms of Christ in the Old Testament") at the Seabury-Western Theological Seminary. There I also dealt with other expressions of form, with the use of the Old Testament in the New, and with the significance of this in ecumenical relations. The lectures were printed by the Seminary and distributed privately. I am grateful to the Dean of Seabury-Western and the editors of this *Festschrift* for the opportunity of pursuing further certain major aspects of the subject.

METHOD OF APPROACH

Preliminary considerations

The study of literature—ancient or modern, sacred and secular—has profited immeasurably from the analysis of form. Examination of forms has proved to be especially appropriate in literary studies because form is indigenous to language. Whenever we wish to communicate by speaking or writing, we are confronted with two related problems: what to say, and how to say it. There is the idea, the intellectual substance, to be communicated through language. There is also the word, the structure or shape, in which the thought is to be presented. At basis, we have to do with content and form.

Form criticism involves an analysis of individual words and literary structures in order to discern the meaning which they were intended to carry. We observe, for example, whether imperatives or conditionals, whether perfects or participles, are being used. For to ask what a thing is—what is its form, in what shape does it present itself to us—is already to inquire about its meaning. The same applies to larger literary units. To recognize that we are dealing with a myth rather than a chronicle, or with a parable instead of a biography, is essential for a proper evaluation of the literature being studied. The analysis is undertaken in the first place because of our assumption that form and content are fundamentally related. It proves profitable, because we find that in truth they are.

To move closer to the area of biblical studies, we may use an illustration from the book of Micah. The sixth chapter begins a third section in the present sequence of this little book. Both the authorship of the chapter and its relation to the other units are disputed among Old Testament scholars.[7] Critical analysis of vss. 1-8 identifies at least five forms: exhortation (1*a*), *rib* (1*b*), interrogation (3), soliloquy (6-7), and prophetic announcement (8). Recognition of these forms leads to an awareness of the author's intention in this particular unit. That much is obvious. But more is achieved than this: access is thereby gained to other parts of the book. To note, for instance, that some of these forms reappear in the second half of the same chapter is not merely to acknowledge continuity at the "reading level," but is to allow a logical presumption of unity of authorship for both sections of chap. 6. And to recognize further that these forms are also employed

---

[7] Consult the modern larger Introductions and Commentaries or, in briefer form, my preface and notes in *The Oxford Annotated Bible*, ed. H. G. May and B. M. Metzger (New York, 1962), pp. 1123 ff.

in the first chapter is to gain specific data for dealing with the problem of how chap. 6 is related to chap. 1, whose authorship is undisputed. All other tools of investigation must, of course, be applied to the problem and their results judiciously evaluated. The point here is that in addition to archaeological data, historical considerations, theological motifs, and the like, the analysis of form may also provide valuable information.

In the enterprise of literary criticism, therefore, we are obligated to deal with the forms in which thought is communicated, forms of speaking as well as forms of writing.

As valuable as it is, however, an analysis of form is only part of the critical endeavor of understanding a unit. Content must also be taken into consideration. At this point two observations need to be made. First, for the convenience of study, content may be separated from form and examined initially by itself. The evaluation of content has independent, if limited, merit and may be pursued on its own.[8] Accordingly, form may be separated from content to allow the one or the other to assist us in getting nearer to the core of meaning. Viewed with reference to its content, a unit in Old Testament literature, for example, may prove to be legal (Lev. 7:1-10) or prophetic (Amos 4:1-3) or sapiential (Prov. 2:1-22). So after examining form in relation to structure, i.e. to words (and to actions also, as we shall see later), it must be viewed in terms of its substance, its content.

But the divorce between the two can only be temporary and is, in a certain respect, unwarranted. If it is not universally valid, it is none-the less true in literary studies that form is intrinsically related to content. Thus, second, it should be noted that although separable, form and content cannot be permanently isolated without great loss. Ultimately form has to have content; it has to *contain* something. And conversely content has to take some shape; it has to *conform* to some recognizable or intelligible pattern. Therefore, to deal with one to the exclusion of the other is to surrender a significant part of the whole. Or, stating the process positively, in those instances when we press to discern the fullness of meaning, to deal with the one aspect is to invoke the other.

In principle, then, there is a whole consisting of form and content, which is ultimately inseparable, and of which the one aspect not only interacts with the other but also shares with it the totality of meaning.

---

[8] Of the two aspects (form and content) content is the more obvious and was long the principal area of investigation. Form criticism, employed consciously and scientifically with either secular or sacred literature, is a modern enterprise.

Literary studies in general and, for our purposes, biblical studies in particular have profited immeasurably from careful attention to form and content. For the whole area of literary scholarship this particular avenue of approach has shown itself intrinsically valuable because it deals with concepts and the words chosen to express them.

But in hermeneutical studies we are also concerned with the interplay between word and concept. "Word," "speech," and "event" are central terms in the vocabulary of today's hermeneutical debates. Moreover, it is precisely the term "word" that carries such profound theological weight in the Old Testament: the "Word of God" given by the prophets, pronouncing judgment and salvation, appears almost self-efficacious; it seems to embody an independent power which actualizes the purpose for which it is spoken (Isa. 55:11; cf. 44:26; 45:19, 23). The New Testament also contains, continues, and completes this emphasis. There the "Word of God" becomes actualized in the Incarnation and accomplishes its purpose, bringing judgment and salvation. In fact, the most significant term in the New Testament theological vocabulary, *logos,* offers a superb illustration both of the interaction between content and form, and of the unity of the Testaments. It conveys the idea of form, structure, and pattern as well as content and substance.

An approach which focuses on form and content has been found invaluable for literary and theological studies. I submit that it can also be useful in getting at the perennial problem of the unity of the Bible, which underlies many of the current hermeneutical discussions. Once again, however, my purpose is not to establish the fact that a unity exists which binds the two Testaments equally, or to prove that this unity exists most fully in Christ. The Christian church has held these claims from its earliest days. Rather, I wish to suggest that by delineating christological form and identifying soteriological content, ways may be found of affirming the unity of the Bible through Christ which are compatible to us in this hermeneutical age.

Analysis of Form

As already noted, in literary analysis form is examined in two major classes: forms of writing and forms of speaking. Both are *word* forms. So long as we investigate passages for their literary type we must necessarily deal with words. Here the method is obvious, clear, and rewarding. However, when the form-critical approach is adopted for hermeneutical purposes and an attempt is made to identify the theological meaning of a biblical passage, another important category must be dealt with: the form of *actions*. And if the necessity for this is not so obvious nor the method so clear, the results are nonetheless rewarding. Von Rad is right in warning that exact definition and classification of Israel's theological utterances still eludes us.[9] We need to recognize, nevertheless, that recent hermeneutical studies have been vitally concerned not only with the concept of "word" but also of "event." At times we view the two as united and speak of a "word-event" because we wish to show that word can have the character of event (as an *Ereignis* or *Geschehen*), and conversely that events themselves can be designated as "words" (of revelation).[10] But at other times, as is the case with content and form, individual treatment is needed. As speech may be separated from action so, for the purposes of our study, word may be distinguished from event. In the analysis of form this distinction is not only valid but valuable.

Forms of Words

Proceeding from the above arguments, the method here proposed requires a look at form in its relations to word and act, and an examination of it in relation to content. This prompts us to ask what the form contains, and to inquire what consequences follow from the observation that form and content are ultimately related. For we have already noted that form has to have content, that is, it has to contain something just as the reverse is true: content has to have some shape or assume some recognizable form. One does not merely know, for instance, that there is forgiveness for sins or that God's love reconciles. One sees that forgiveness comes at some point or through some institution, and that reconciliation is effected by some act or through some organ or agent. Form cannot be emptied of its content, nor can content be presented and transmitted without form. To see the one is to apprehend the other. Accordingly for our present purposes, to recognize, for example, true expressions of divine forgiveness in Israel's life is to perceive therein authentic forms of Christ.

[9] G. von Rad, *op. cit.*, p. 326. Perhaps it should be stated at this point that I had been working, unprompted, on a form-content approach to the problem of a Christian understanding of the Old Testament well before I read von Rad's section "The Old Testament and the New" in the 2nd vol. of his *Theology*. The sophisticated and extended articulation of his thought in this area has impressed me greatly, but what I offer here is, to the best of my knowledge, my own thought.

[10] This applies not only to single events (e.g., the capture of the Ark or the death of Josiah), but also to sequences of events and even to whole processes in biblical history (e.g., the Exodus or the oppression by the Philistines).

To illustrate, in Isa. 40:2,

> Speak tenderly to Jerusalem,
>   and cry to her
> that her warfare is ended,
>   that her iniquity is pardoned,
> that she has received from the LORD's hand
>   double for all her sins,

Israel receives the same gracious word of pardon, full and complete, which the men of the New Testament received in the forgiving Word-become-flesh, who said, "Your sins are forgiven," and, "Today salvation has come to this house" (Mark 2:5; Luke 19:9; cf. Rom. 10:5-13). Again, from the Old Testament we hear repeatedly words offering or promising life: "I have set before you life and death, blessing and curse; therefore choose life, that you and your descendants may live" (Deut. 30:19 [cf. vss. 15-20]); or, "Seek me and live" (Amos 5:4 [three times in this one chapter; vss. 6 and 14]). In these words we recognize the form of One, whose presence bestows life abundant (John 10:10), who himself acknowledged this true life under the Old Covenant (Luke 20:37-38), and whose resurrection manifests life eternal (John 11:25-26; cf. Heb. 11:17-19). For Christians, the speaker of these words of life to Israel bears upon himself the form of Christ.

As further examples of Old Testament words which are stamped with the form of Christ there are: the word of suffering (Job 16:18–17:2; 23; Pss. 22:1-2, 6-8, 14-18; 69:4-21; Lam. 3:1-24; and cf. Zech. 12:10-11); the word of forgiveness (Isa. 51:5-6; Jer. 31:34; Hos. 14:4-7; Mic. 7:19-20; Zech. 13:1); the word of salvation (Isa. 43:1-4; 61:1-4[11]; Jer. 23:5-6; 31:2-3; Ezek. 34:11-16; Zech. 8:13; cf. Ps. 22:30-31); and again the word of life (Isa. 25:6-8 [cf. Matt. 27:51; Heb. 6:19; 10:20]; 26:19; 55:3).

The presence of such words speaking through the pages of both Testaments constitutes a vital part of the divine revelation which unites the Bible. The manifestations of this revelation were multiform. It came through word and act; it was made known in speech and event. As word it was spoken "at sundry times and in divers manners in times past." [12] It cloaked itself in myth, legend, and saga, in law, proverb, and wisdom, just as it did in parable and epistle, in *kerygma* and *didache*. But it is the same word as that spoken "by the Son, whom

---

[11] The precise designation of this figure remains uncertain. Besides being an anointed and commissioned prophet and having other parallels with the Suffering Servant, he is unmistakably an *evangelist*. See Muilenburg's comments in *IB* V, 708 ff.

[12] Heb. 1:1 KJV.

(God) hath appointed heir to all things, by whom also he made the worlds." [13] Because of its unshakable conviction on this point, the early Christian church could assert that Moses and the prophets "preached Christ."

Forms of Actions

Since we must start with a written text, we meet some difficulties in attempting to draw a clear line between word forms and action forms. In biblical studies, of course, we do not have direct access to the action as such but only its description; and the description depends upon words. But for purposes of study a distinction can be drawn between words principally describing speech and those describing acts. Here we deal with the latter.

In the suffering of the obedient Servant of the Lord (Isa. 53:3-4), who

> was despised and rejected by men;
>   a man of sorrows, and acquainted with grief;
> has borne our griefs
>   and carried our sorrows,

Christians have discerned the form of Christ's sufferings (Matt. 8:17; Acts 8:32-35; I Peter 2:24-25). Here are forms of self-oblation and intercession. With Abraham's pleading for the salvation of Sodom (Gen. 18:20-33), with Moses' offering of himself for the transgression of his people (Exod. 32:11-14, 31-32), and preeminently with the Servant's vicarious oblation, the innocent for the guilty and the one for the many (see also Isa. 42:2; 50:4-9; 52:13–53:12),[14] we perceive as Christians the form of Christ's voluntary self-oblation, *that single act* by which all are made righteous.

Of the forms by which Christ is most clearly recognized, sacrifice is prominent. The story of Abraham's obedient offering of Isaac (Gen. 22:1-18) sets forth the form of innocent sacrifice with a clarity that seems to describe reality itself. In the depiction of the son sensing the solemnity and uniqueness of the occasion and yet walking confidently with a measure of faith which matches that of his father, while carrying the wood on which he is to be sacrificed, we find one of the more striking christological forms in the Old Testament.[15]

[13] Heb. 1:2 KJV; cf. John 1:1-5.

[14] It is not surprising to find several different forms in so rich and complex a unit as the Suffering Servant songs.

[15] See my brief exposition of this chapter in *IDB* II, 728 ff., "Isaac," 2c and 3, and the works by Schoeps and Lerch cited in the bibliography there.

Besides the act of self-oblation, there is also the act of self-limitation that exposes the form of Christ's own activity. Whether in making a covenant with Noah and promising that "never again shall there be a flood to destroy the earth" (Gen. 9:8-17; cf. 8:20-22), or in establishing a covenant with Israel and agreeing to a code of laws (Exod. 34:10-28; cf. chaps. 19–24) insuring communion (e.g. Exod. 20:24) and governing worship as well as dealing with judgment and justice, God voluntarily restricts himself on man's behalf. Instead of exercising his freedom to be arbitrary or capricious, God submits himself to structures of man's own dimensions. We might say that "for us men and for our salvation," the almighty Lord graciously limits his power to man's weakness and accommodates himself to man's needs. The action is similar to the granting of the tabernacle (Exod. 25, esp. vss. 8-9 and 17-22; cf. Heb. 9:11-12) and temple (I Kings 5:3-5; 8:20-21, 29; Ps. 132:13 ff.; cf. John 2:19-22). In God's selecting of a specific place and guaranteeing that *there* he will be really present and *there* man can truly meet him (Exod. 25:22; Deut. 12:5-14; Ps. 132:14; Ezek. 37:26-27), we see in Israel's life the form of divine limitation which reappears fully and finally in the New Testament (Phil. 2:6-7; Col. 1:19-20).[16]

Finally, there are instances in which the same unit possesses an unusual degree of correspondence of act with word. In these the totality of meaning is heightened as each form contributes its own value to the shared whole. A well-known passage from Exodus both serves as an example of this coalescence of word and act and illustrates forcefully the consequences which an analysis of form may carry for hermeneutics.

> Then the LORD said, "I have seen the affliction of my people who are in Egypt, and have heard their cry because of their taskmasters; I know their sufferings, and I have come down to deliver them out of the hand of the Egyptians, and to bring them up out of that land to a good and broad land.
>   Exod. 3:7-8

In the "seen . . . heard . . . known . . . come down . . . deliver . . . bring up" sequence, Israel saw the clear articulation of God's saving action accompanied by his gracious word. As Christians, we recognize further in this sequence the form of that act by which God will save all men, as we hear the word of redemption being spoken.

It is not enough to say of these two "salvific" acts that they show the consistency of God or the continuity of his purpose, although we

---

[16] Here we are also brought into the realm of incarnation and to a concept of the Real Presence.

312

must certainly affirm that much at the outset. But there is more. Assuming here the coalescence of word with event and the basal unity
underlying form and content, it can be affirmed that these two acts
are organic parts of a single whole. Hereby we derive reciprocal
benefits. First and more obvious, our Christian perspective deepens
the meaning which we find in the deliverance at the Red Sea. But
also and just as truly, our knowledge of God's appearance at Sinai
enriches our understanding of the Incarnation. In this unit, we are
enabled to perceive forms of Christ in the Old Testament. For there
are not two Saviors bringing forgiveness and redemption, but one.

Analysis of Content

In literary criticism a distinction can be made between form and
content for purposes of study. Taking again as an illustration forms
found in Mic. 6:1-8, we note that the *rîb* form occurs also, for instance,
in Jer. 25:31; 50:34; "interrogation," in Job 38:2 ff.; and soliloquy
in Exod. 3:3; Ps. 77:7-10 (H. 8–11). A literary analysis of these
passages chosen at random will indicate that each form is essentially
the same as its counterpart in Mic. 6. It is also obvious, however, that
in each case of the parallels just cited the *content* is different. Viewed
with reference to form, this second set of passages offers nothing intrinsically new. Viewed with reference to content, each passage presents
substantially new material. The newness gained by analysis of content
adds its own value to our total understanding of a passage, and we
may legitimately use it because of the reciprocal relations which exist
between content and form. Accordingly, for hermeneutical purposes
examination of the content of a passage may be made without reference, for the time being, to its form. Attention to the *content* aspect
of the form-and-content totality ought to assist our stated interest in
the christological unity of the Bible.

The form-content method here proposed utilizes the reciprocity
which operates between the two terms. Once again von Rad is right
in maintaining that "it would be too naïve to say that the form belongs to the Old Testament, but the content to the New." [17] But he
does not reckon adequately with the opposite movement of this formulation, nor does he proceed to explore the fuller possibilities inherent
in this approach.[18] To gain its full value the method must be worked
both ways. There *are* cases, as we have just attempted to show, where

[17] G. von Rad, *op. cit.*, p. 334.
[18] In fact, von Rad appears to deny these by certain comments; cf. *ibid.*, p. 333.

the Old Testament makes visible the form of salvation and the New Testament makes known its proper content. But not always. We must recognize that the movement linking the two Covenants also goes in the other direction. For in certain instances the Old Testament provides the content and the New Testament shows us its perfect form.

When it is realized that the interaction between form and content is reciprocal, and that the unity of the canon allows scholars to work equally in both sections, then analysis can begin with either Testament. In previous sections we have stood within the Old Testament and looked toward the New. Now let us begin with the Gospels. As an example, let us examine one form of Christ's work in the New Testament: his relation to sin. First, it is of the nature of Christ to *expose* sin. "Men loved darkness rather than light, because their deeds were evil" (John 3:19). His very presence convicted men of sin (John 16:22-25). Here is the form. Wherever we find passages whose content concerns the divine exposure of man's evil, whether leading to judgment or salvation, we are led methodologically to associate them with Christ. Accordingly, whenever the Old Testament exposes sin in this manner, it shares in the work of Christ. Thus all the prophets (e.g. Mic. 3:8) but also the law, as Paul well understood (Rom. 7:7-12). Second, it is of the nature of Christ to *forgive* sins. The Son of man has power on earth to say, "Your sins are forgiven" (Mark 2:1-12).[19] Wherever the Old Testament knows the forgiveness of sins, it knows Christ. Thus, again, not only in the prophets (e.g. Isa. 55:6; Mic. 7:18-20), but also in the law (e.g. Exod. 34:6-7; Jer. 31:31-34). Third, it is of the nature of Christ to *suffer* for the sin of others. Jesus showed his disciples that he must suffer and give his life as a ransom for many (Mark 8:31; 9:30-31; 10:33, 44). Wherever the Old Testament shows the innocent suffering and offering his life for the guilty, it shows forth Christ. Thus Moses (Exod. 32:31-32), Jer. (20:7-18; 37–38), and the Suffering Servant (Isa. 53:4-6). Fourth, it is of the nature of Christ to *redeem* from sin. Wherever the Old Testament proclaims redemption, it can be said to preach Christ. Thus throughout "in the law of Moses and the prophets and the psalms" (Luke 24:44; cf. Lev. 16:29-30; Isa. 2:2-4; 40:1-3; Ps. 130:7-8).

Down through the centuries Christians have had little hesitation in affirming that there is only one redemption and one Redeemer. It is equally true, as already noted, that they have constantly experienced difficulties in expressing this belief in their exegesis. Perhaps at this

---

[19] In the New Testament, this aspect of Christ's nature appears both in the form of words and the form of acts.

point the form-content approach can help in dealing with the essential unity of the Bible. In its soteriological passages the Old Testament presents the content of reconciliation and redemption. Though these may have been wrong in structure (e.g., in the *ritual* for expiation or the *imagery* of apocalyptic), they were right in substance. God in the Old Testament does reconcile and redeem. In its portrayal of Christ, the New Testament defines the form of the divine redemption and reconciliation. The reality between the two Testaments is one. Moreover, at basis, form and content, when they refer to the same reality, are united. When the totality is perceived, then to see one aspect of the whole is to know the other. To perceive the form of divine reality is to know its authentic content. To find its content is to be able to distinguish its true form. Therefore for Christians, wherever the Old Testament sets forth the content of redemption—the forgiveness of sins, or life in perfect communion with God—it shows forth Christ.

We started with the New Testament and looked back to the Old. But an analysis of content can also, of course, begin with the Old Testament. What may be of new value here is not the direction but the method.

The beautiful little *"torah* liturgy" in the nineteenth Psalm points its content strikingly beyond itself:

> The law of the LORD is perfect, reviving the soul; . . . sure, making wise the simple; . . . right, rejoicing the heart; . . . pure, enlightening the eyes; . . . clean, enduring for ever; . . . true, and righteous altogether.
>
> Ps. 19:7-9.

What is here claimed for the law, Christians say also of Christ. For the psalmist, the refreshing and edifying law illumines him and indeed brings him to life again.[20] For the Christian, Christ refreshes (Matt. 11:28), enlightens (John 1:4-9; 8:12), and restores to life (John 11:25-26; cf. I Cor. 15:22). And he accomplishes this, not in opposition to the law or apart from it, but by taking it into himself. In taking over this psalm as their own, Christians acknowledge a qualitative affinity between the *torah* as here idealized and Christ.

Again, it is notable in this connection that "for the poet the law is the point at which an encounter takes place with the living God who reveals himself in the law."[21] Therefore, it may be noted further that what the psalmist knows of man's encounter with God through the law, Christians say of Christ. Not only this, but "the 'law' comprises

[20] For an explanation of the adjectives and participles which Ps. 19 uses to describe the law, see F. James, *Thirty Psalmists*, rev. ed. (New York, 1965), pp. 30-31.

[21] A. Weiser, *The Psalms*, trans. by H. Hartwell (Philadelphia, 1962), p. 202.

the testimony which God bears to himself. . . . In the law the will of God is manifested to educate and to save. . . ." [22] In short, the psalmist calls the law perfect, knows it as the place where he meets God himself, and experiences God's saving will through it. This hymn offers specific content; following our method, may we not see a form of Christ here?

Earlier an example showed a coalescence of the form of words with the form of acts, and we noted the heightened value that such an interaction holds for the exegete. Similarly here an example can be cited illustrating the coalescence of content with form. The life and preaching of Hosea[23] bring together dramatically both these major aspects of our investigation. Seen in terms of suffering and obedience, the prophet's personal life is nothing short of an incarnation of the divine redemptive love. Hosea's suffering is personal and vicarious; the innocent one suffers internally and externally, in public and in private, for the guilty (1:2-3; 2:2, 4, 8; 3:1-3). And the prophet's obedience is immediate and constant (1:3; 3:2; cf. Exod. 4:1-13; Jer. 1:6). Hosea's message is the verbalization of his ministry, and both ministry and message, by form and in content, in word and by act, preach the gospel of redeeming love.

Many Christians see Christ in Hosea, hearing in his speech the word of grace and seeing in his life the act of grace. But those who hold this know, as did the early Christians, that Christ did not actually live during the time of Hosea, was not a contemporary of Jeroboam II. What, then? If it is too much to claim that either contemporary or early Christians believe Christ to have lived at that time, it likewise is too little to posit that he was somehow ideally present but without any trace. Salvation indeed belongs to Christ. But it does not exist in the abstract; it can be recognized by its form. It *conforms* to the reality which men have seen in Christ. In some of the Old Testament forms of speaking and acting—as certainly in Hosea's—can be seen the shape of Christ's own work. Nor does even this go far enough. We maintain that here we see this work not in abstraction nor even in anticipation but in its reality. Where the work of Christ is recognized, there Christ must be recognized at work. This, it seems to us, expresses the conviction of unity in Christ which the young Christians experienced when reading the Old Testament in the light of the New. Nor should we stop here. For if the form-content approach applied to the ministry and message of Hosea helps us to recognize the

[22] *Ibid.*
[23] See esp. Hos. 3:1-3; also 2:19; 11:3-4, 8-9; 14:4-8.

authentic work of Christ in this particular area which lies outside the pages of the New Testament, then it may also point us to the work of Christ *wherever* it occurs in the world.[24]

Intention

In examining the relationship between form and content, and exploring its significance for hermeneutics, we dealt with the form of words and acts. But there is another way in which attention to form may prove profitable in our study, and this becomes evident when we analyze further the area of action. In itself an action is not a simple but a complex entity and can therefore be examined on several different levels. For instance, an action can be classified either by its intention or its result. This distinction is more precisely limited by speaking of formal intention and immediate result. Previously we juxtaposed forms of action and content and were principally concerned with result. Here the aspect of intention is the central focus.

Like content, intention has to be expressed in recognizable shapes. To be known at all, it must be perceived. This is preeminently true, of course, when we deal with some other person's intention. With him it may be internal and latent; for us it must become external and patent. That is, it becomes known to us with, and through, a structure. It has to conform to some discernible pattern of expression; and here again, as with form and content, it may assume the form either of words or of actions, or appear in a combination of both. Viewed this way and judged by their immediate result, many of the acts which constitute God's dealings with Israel appear incomplete or inadequate. Viewed on the level of intention, however, they are not only full and sufficient, they are identical with the purposes of God as manifested in Christ. Our method which involves an analysis of form may enable us to view Old Testament acts and words through this perspective. What we have said, therefore, about the interrelations of form and content may assist us here in identifying the structure and substance of intention and, for our purposes, relating it to Christ.

Israel's history is shaped throughout by the intention of salvation. From the time of the Fall God has manifested this intention by offering man redemption and the grace of reconciliation: in the Cain story (Gen. 4:15 ff.), with Noah (5:29; 8:21-22), and unmistakably in the call of Abraham (12:1-3) and the covenant established with

---

[24] The implications here are of considerable value today, esp. for ecumenical theology.

him (15:7-21; 17:1-8). It becomes preeminently clear in the full "event" of the Exodus, which includes both the experience at the Red Sea and the institution of the law at Sinai. Here Israel experienced the divine "salvific" intention in two forms: act and word. The divine promise was dependable; Israel's response was not. Time and again Israel failed to respond in faith. She was stiff-necked and backsliding, rebellious and estranged. But her sordid history is punctuated by fresh expressions of God's desire to save. It was constantly formed and re-formed by the divine saving intention. It is seen in acts of discipline and forgiveness (for example, the opposition by the Canaanites and the conditional occupation of the land, the Exile and the Return); it is heard in words of judgment and grace ("cease to do evil, learn to do good; . . . though your sins are like scarlet, they shall be as white as snow" [Isa. 1:16 ff.]; "because you are precious in my eyes, and honored, and I love you, I give men in return for you, peoples in exchange for your life" [43:4]).

God's intention to save is repeatedly declared in the Old Testament both by what he says and does, in the forms of word and act. But also in the New Testament the divine intention is manifested in word and act, and both in the form of Christ. The saving act and the saving word are one. Certainly at the level of intention they are one within the Old Testament, just as we know them to be united within the New. Equivalently, we can acknowledge that on this basis they are the same in both Testaments. This is founded on our recognition of the uniformity of forms and identity of intention.

In principle, then, there is no division here. The Old Testament is not separated from the New either in reference to the "salvific" intention or in the reality of the redemptive acts. On the contrary, it is precisely the continuity of this saving intention, as expressed both in word and act, that binds the books of the Bible together. Here, in both Testaments, is salvation. And where salvation is offered, there is Christ.

To bring us closer to some of the hermeneutical implications of this approach, this line of reasoning should be pursued one step further. Where two forms are observed to be the same, whether of words or acts, there is uniformity. And where there is uniformity, there exists also the implication of unity. Therefore, when there are several forms in the Old Testament exhibiting such uniformity, we seek the possible basis of their unity. Within the bounds of the Old Testament itself, we certainly discover unity to exist at the level of intention. For example, in Exod. 32:31-32, Moses intends the same thing as the Suffering Servant in Isaiah, chap. 53—the offering of self on behalf of others.[25]

In our analysis the distinction between human and divine intention should not be ignored. Instead of being arbitrary, temporary, and vacillating, the divine intention, preeminently God's will to save, is consistent and unchanging. At every period in the *Heilsgeschichte* it remained fundamentally one and the same. As such, this intention possesses an intrinsic unity. Nor does this unity exist in isolation. It reaches out to incorporate within itself all divine acts born of the same intention, regardless of when, where, or how they came to be expressed. It appears certain that the writers of the New Testament understood this solidarity and voiced it quite clearly. In looking back upon Christ's self-oblation, the early Christians recognized that it shared with certain Old Testament acts a unity both of form (the voluntary offering of the innocent for the guilty) and intention (saving forgiveness). Accordingly, they affirmed this unity by calling those prior acts, acts of Christ.

Here we may again anticipate some implications of this argument. Since they were convinced of the authenticity of the old material and its unity with what they themselves had experienced in Christ, the New Testament writers could take it up and use it in their own proclamations. In fact, by actually quoting texts from the Old as part of the New, they bore permanent witness to their conviction that the two are one, and both are Christ's. In the terms of our discussion, they were expressing this conviction *formally* as well as theologically, that is, in literary form which instructs the eye and the ear. And when claiming the Old Testament material for themselves, the New Testament authors felt free to use only a brief portion of the larger unit they had in mind, not intending to take the verse out of its original context but choosing to invoke its fuller dimensions by quoting only a well-known part of it.

By employing this technique early Christian writers were, in fact, continuing both the theological position and the hermeneutical method of later Old Testament writers themselves. The prophets, for instance, often used older traditions as a basis for their own proclamations. They could rework and reuse this earlier material to legiti-

[25] One of the advantages of this approach is that it allows us to deal more easily with *institutions* than do other classical methods, like promise-and-fulfillment or typology. For instance, the author of the Epistle to the Hebrews, in chap. 9, recognizes and accepts as valid *on the level of intention* the purificatory rites and sacrifices in Israel's cultus, and thereby does not hesitate to associate them with Christ, although here in a "how much more" comparison.

mize what they themselves were proclaiming, because they perceived in these ancient traditions the reality of God's work in their world. Or, to use our language, they were able to re-form these older traditions because they recognized in them authentic forms of the divine activity.[26] Moreover, when drawing upon the older material, later Hebrew writers felt no obligation to cite at length; merely a reference, for instance, to "the offspring of Abraham, my friend; you whom I took from the ends of the earth" (Isa. 41:8-9), was enough [27] to call to the mind of the reader the mighty acts of God in Israel's past as well as her response to them. Neither aspect needed to be spelled out in detail by the poet, for each of them had long been part of the sacred history of his people. Both the divine action and Israel's re-action are evoked by the simple poetic reference; both are grasped as organic parts of a single whole; both now form part of the new "event" which II Isaiah is announcing. For "the Prophet of the Return," these prior events are not disparate, unrelated occurrences in the past but are constitutive elements of God's continuing "salvific" act. They do not merely form a background *for* his message; they belong *to* it. What appears on one level as a chronological gap separating the Patriarchal Age and the Exodus from the Exile and the Return, is closed on the theological level by the unity—we would prefer to say the uniformity—of God's acts.

IMPLICATIONS

In the foregoing analyses we recognized that there are forms of words and forms of actions; that these can be separated from each other to a limited extent, as word is distinguishable from event and speech from action; and that ultimately they are also related. But just as these are related to each other, so each is related in its own right to content. Now, the shape of an action allows it to be compared with other actions to determine whether they are similar or dissimilar. When an action by its form can be identified affirmatively with another action, the recognition of identity at this level allows the possibility of identity at other levels. That is, if two actions are the same in form and each bears a perceptible relation to substance or content,

---

[26] Concerning the re-forming and actualizing of the Old Testament saving hope, see von Rad, *op. cit.*, pp. 239 ff. and 327 ff. He shows rightly that the prophets used these traditions critically, holding fast to some and quietly passing over others, but that upon examination we find that this method "keeps remarkably close to the pattern used by earlier proponents of Jahwism" (p. 239).

[27] The same is still true today for a biblically literate person.

then a presumption of unity of content or identity of substance has been created, regardless of the chronological sequence or physical circumstances which may separate the two actions. Approaching the subject this way, we can transcend the usual limitations of time and space in our exegetical attempts to express the fullness of Christ's relation to the world.

In the New Testament we see the fullness of Christ, both in content and form, for "in him dwelleth all the fulness of the Godhead bodily" (Col. 1:19 KJV). At certain places in the Old Testament we discern forms which have a definite christological shape. At other places we meet material, the content of which is patently soteriological. On the assumption that form and content are fundamentally related, methodologically the recognition either of christological forms or of soteriological content in the Old Testament should allow us to associate them positively with Christ, as New Testament writers did in their several ways.

From our analyses of form and content we may now make some observations which have specific consequences for present-day hermeneutics.

There is only one "salvific" work going on in the world, and it is performed by one Savior. In the incarnate life of Christ we see bodily in unmistakable form the fullness of the divine saving activity. But though it is most clearly manifested there, it is not to be perceived there only. *Wherever* this action exhibits itself under one of its forms, it is identifiable as the act of Christ. And *whenever* anyone reacts to this act, he reacts to Christ. Beyond the province of exegesis, this carries implications for ecumenical theology.

The Old Testament itself also witnesses to God's saving activity, and indeed to the totality of it. To this testimony, and through it, man is called to respond in faith. Whenever the faithful response is made,[28] salvation is present regardless of the terms used to designate it.

In examining the form of acts and events, we found that intention is a prime factor uniting the various parts of the two Covenants. The Old Testament knows many manifestations of the divine will to save, given in the forms of word and event. Each has authority, urgency, and futurity; each is generated in love and given out of compassion. But the same conditions describe the offer of salvation in the New Testament. The coming of Christ is here also in word and deed. Here too it has authority and urgency and continues the note of futurity.

[28] See, e.g., Gen. 15:6; Deut. 30:15; Hab. 2:5; Joel 2:32. Cf. Paul's appropriation of the Genesis affirmation in Rom. 4, and of Joel's statement in Rom. 10, esp. vss. 10-13.

Here too its motivation is found in the divine love and compassion. Following our approach we may affirm that the intention to save, which is constantly expressed in the Old Testament by word and act, is identical with that encountered in the Christ-event. The intention is the same, the act is the same, and the Agent is the same. This is the position of faith from which New Testament authors viewed the Old Testament[29] and on which they based much of their exegesis.

In its ultimate proportions the claim which the early Christian authors sustain goes beyond the statement that the Old Testament prepares the way for Christ or that in Christ the expectations of Israel reach fulfillment. The claim boldly advanced in the New Testament is that there is only one redemption and one Redeemer. Thus God either offered redemption to man under the Old Covenant, or he did not. And if he did, he offered it through Christ.

Officially the Christian church has tried to follow its early leaders in maintaining this unity of the Scriptures through Christ. For it knows, as Alan Richardson has formulated it, that "God's saving activity in history is the theme of both Testaments, and neither Testament alone contains the complete record of it. Each Testament, however, testifies to *the whole of God's saving activity,* not merely to a part of it." [30] But today many Christian laymen would deny completely the validity of this assertion, and many theologians and biblical scholars honestly find it an embarrassment. By employing the concepts associated with form, perhaps we can more readily understand the position of the New Testament authors, and express it in our own exegesis. I suggest, then, that when reading the Old Testament, the early Christians recognized in its words and acts forms of the divine intention to save and, knowing that there is one salvation, not two, confidently believed them to be forms of Christ.

From the start, I have insisted that both form and content be examined. To bring theory and praxis together, a brief final example is offered that deals with content and carries implications for herme-

---

[29] In his provocative and detailed study *Jesus Christ in the Old Testament* (London, 1965), A. T. Hanson shows how thoroughly New Testament authors viewed the Old Covenant through Christ. He holds that "the central affirmation [of the New Testament writers] is that the pre-existent Jesus was present in much of OT history, and that therefore it is not a question of tracing types in the OT for NT events, but rather of tracing *the activity of the same Jesus* in the old and in the new dispensation" (p. 172, italics supplied).

[30] "Is the Old Testament the Propaedeutic to Christian Faith?" in *The Old Testament and Christian Faith,* ed. B. W. Anderson (New York, 1963), p. 18 (italics supplied). Note, however, that Richardson's conclusion differs from mine. His follows more along the historical line of promise and fulfillment.

neutical discussions. In Rom. 10:9, Paul asserts that if the reader can say with his mouth "Jesus is Lord" and believe in his heart that God raised him from the dead, he will be saved. To this, Christians can readily assent. But the *Old* Testament also realizes, as we have already seen, that God "kills and makes alive" (cf. Deut. 32:39); that he offers to man death or life (30:15); and that whoever seeks him honestly will live (Amos 5:6; cf. vs. 4). As a consequence of our method—here, uniting Old Testament content with Christian form— we maintain that when the Jew of the Old Testament said in faith that God is Lord, and that the Creator is also the Preserver and Re- storer, the Author and Giver of life, then he was saved. And that Jew was saved no less lovingly or fully than those Jews who encoun- tered Jesus "in the days of his flesh," or we today who profess the Christian faith. In these Old Testament affirmations we meet soterio- logical content. The form of each passage just cited differs from the others as each differs from the form in which Paul makes his declara- tion. But the content is the same and so is the intention: the gift of life abundant. And that life, wherever or whenever offered, is life with Christ and in Christ. The men of the New Testament believed this and felt under compulsion to say it. The fact that they expressed this faith in a language which today seems too naïve[31] or stereotyped,[32] is principally a hermeneutical, not a theological, problem.

CONCLUSION

Faced with the difficulty that for many Christians today the Old Testament seems irrelevant and has become an embarrassment, we need constantly to seek new ways of stating the unity which the Bible possesses through Christ. Here I have suggested a method that explores the relations existing between form and content, and have attempted to articulate some of its implications for hermeneutics. In its essence the present approach leads to this summary statement:

At many places in the Old Scriptures, the early Christians encoun- tered words and events, in the forms of which they recognized Christ.

[31] Two well-known examples would be John 12:37-41 and I Cor. 10:4. See Han- son's examination of these (*op. cit.*, pp. 104-8 and 10-23).

[32] We have in mind particularly the statement "that it might be fulfilled . . ." and its variants. The evangelists could take an Old Testament passage in which they discerned the forms of Christ and apply this formula to it because they were convinced of the *totality* of the Christ-event. That is, they saw its wholeness and could view its beginning and its end as a single reality. This position is argued cogently and fully by B. S. Childs in his article "Prophecy and Fulfillment" in *Interpretation*, XII (1958), esp. 268-70.

The "word" they confronted in Israel's sacred writings contained both judgment and forgiveness, just as they knew the *Logos* in the form of Christ to have spoken to them words of judgment and forgiveness. The divine actions which they saw as constituting Israel's sacred history were acts of discipline and redemption. In these they recognized the same "salvific" intention they discerned also in the life and death of Jesus Christ. Since they had come to affirm the basic unity existing between Israel's God and their own Savior and were also convinced of the continuity of the divine saving action in history, they could bring together form and content, intention and act. Acknowledging the reality of redemption in Christ, they could accept *all* authentic forms of redemption as Christ's.

As the evangelists bore witness *to* these forms, they also bore witness *through* them. They felt not only that they *could* express themselves through Old Testament forms but that they *must*. And where the Christian interpreter met in the Old Testament certain content whose intention was salvation, he particularized it and delineated it by stamping over it the form of Christ. For him the two parts, content and form, were halves of an indivisible whole. New Testament authors, like the earliest Christian preachers, felt both the propriety and the necessity of viewing the one as a constitutive part of the other. Affirming the continuity of the "word" and the totality of the "event," they could approach this single reality from either direction. From the one side they could read the Old Scriptures more clearly in the light of Christ; from the other they could understand him in greater depth and describe the extent of his saving work in wider range by the light which the Old Testament cast.

Incense Altars
NELSON GLUECK

Some small distinctive pottery and soft limestone incense altars were found in the uppermost Level V of Tell el-Kheleifeh (Ezion-geber: Elath). This shallow, largely eroded level can be dated mainly to the fifth century B.C., going back to the late sixth and forward to the early fourth centuries B.C.

There were two forms of incense altars at Tell el-Kheleifeh, one of plain cuboid blocks and another of decorated cuboid blocks with four stumpy, more or less rectangular corner legs. All of them had shallow troughs or basins on top for the incense, which, when burned, left black traces. The small four-legged incense altars bore dotted, wavy-lined, or dentiled decorations, which had, respectively, been pecked, incised, or impressed into the surfaces. The use of these altars and others like them, both contemporary and later, for the burning of incense, is highlighted at Lachish by the occurrence there, on one of the sides of one of them, to be dated to the fifth-fourth centuries B.C., of an Aramaic inscription, featuring the word *lbnt'*, "incense." [1]

Scratched on each side of a small, creamy buff, four-legged pottery altar was a crude representation of a camel, with some strokes on one side that might possibly represent a cameleer[2] (Pls. 1:3, 2:1; Fig. 1). On the partially remaining side of a fragment of another small,

[1] A. Dupont-Sommer, in O. Tufnell, *Lachish III, The Iron Age, Text* (London, 1953), pp. 358-59; *Plates*, Pl. 49:3; 68; W. F. Albright, *BASOR* CXXXII (Dec. 1953), 46-47; *The Archaeology of Palestine* (Harmondsworth, 1949), pp. 143-45; A. Jamme, *Bi.Or.* X (1953), Pl. XIV and pp. 94-95, discusses South Arabian incense altars, inscribed with names of different kinds of incense, which should be dated between the 3rd and 2nd centuries B.C.; cf. R. L. Bowen and F. P. Albright, *Archaeological Discoveries in South Arabia* (Baltimore, 1958), p. 150, n. 8. Uninscribed incense burners of the cuboid type extend down to the first three centuries B.C. in South Arabia; cf. p. 150 and p. 153, Pl. 96; cf. W. F. Albright, *BASOR* XCVIII (April 1945), 28; CXXXII (1953), 46; G. Caton-Thompson, *The Tombs and Moon Temple of Hureidha* (Oxford, 1944), pp. 46-51, and Pls. XVI, XVII.

[2] For other contemporary incense altars in Israel and Jordan with crude drawings of fauna, flora, and/or geometric designs incised on the sides, cf. nn. 7-17 below.

purplish buff, well-levigated pottery incense altar, only the corner of the top and one of the four legs of which are preserved, is an incised drawing showing two cranes (?), facing each other, antithetically, on either side of a (lotus?) plant or (palm?) tree.[3] It is framed on each of the two long sides by a border of a vertical ladder with horizontal rungs, and on the topside by a horizontal ladder with vertical rungs, which is surmounted by a horizontal row of triangles. Another series of triangles is repeated between the two lines of the arched row on the bottom, the ends of which (to judge from the one intact side) spring from the vertical ladders extending along the outer sides down to the middle of the bottom of the legs (Pls. 1:1, 2:3; Fig. 3:1).

A comparatively intact, small, grayish buff, four-legged pottery incense altar from Level V was heavily decorated above the stumpy rectangular corner legs with three horizontal zigzag lines incised above one another; the two rows of squarish spaces between them were filled with numerous dots pecked into the surface. The triangular spaces below the bottom zigzag line are almost completely empty of these dots, which, however, also tattoo the area of the surfaces of the legs and form a curved line over the arch between the legs. There are no dots in the triangular spaces above the top zigzag line, although there is a straight horizontal line of dots above it just below the outer edge of the rim[4] (Pls. 1:4, 2:4; Fig. 3:2, 3).

There was recovered a fragment of another small incense altar, of lime plaster with sand temper, which originally had four stubby rectangular legs, with an arched or vaulted opening or entrance between them on each side. The shallow basin at the top was blackened by fire presumably from the burning of incense. Near the top outer surface of each side are two horizontal rows of small triangular indentations. They are framed between the tops of two vertical rows of the same kind of small triangular indentations that on each side reach down to the bottom of the legs. Originally, there was also a double row of these indentations on the top of the flat rim on each side. Only one of the four legs and part of the rim on two sides and part of the small basin at the top remain (Pl. 3:1).

Still another fragment of a small pottery incense altar was found, consisting only of part of a corner of the top shallow basin and part of the rim of the sides of the existing corner. On top of the rim is impressed a horizontal row of a zigzag, double dentiled decoration with

---

[3] Cf. K. Galling, "Archaeologischer Jahresbericht," *ZDPV* LII (1929), p. 248 and fig. 12:5.
[4] Cf. G. A. Reisner, C. S. Fisher, D. G. Lyon, *Harvard Excavations at Samaria II, Plates* (Cambridge, 1924), Pl. 80:a,b,c.

opposite bands of outward pointed triangular teeth, looking something like a closed zipper (Pls. 1:2, 2:2; Fig. 2:1).

A nearly complete, intact example of a small incense altar of pottery, related in shape, size, and decoration to those from Tell el-Kheleifeh, was purchased by me at Jerusalem at the Baidun Antiquity shop on the Via Dolorosa (Pl. 4). It was made of coarse ware with numerous grits and had been completely covered with a hard, wet-smoothed, thick, grayish white lime slip, on which an intricate design of triangles, diamond-shaped squares, circles, and horizontal and vertical lines had been incised. The four squarish, stubby legs at the corners are separated by a low vaulted opening on each side. The top of the flat thick rim is decorated on all four sides with an encircling row of small incised circles.[5] They are similar to those occurring in horizontal and vertical rows framing vertical diamond-shaped squares set on edge or double triangles, between two vertical lines, which their side edges sometimes intersect, reaching down to the bottoms of the legs. Between the two inner vertical rows of circles, themselves framed between vertical incised lines, and below the same kind of horizontal row of circles running along the entire length of the upper outside surface, are horizontal bands of complete or half triangles separated by horizontal incised lines on two adjacent sides with a somewhat varying pattern on the other sides. This type of incense altar is very closely related to one found at Timnaʻ in Arabia, the outside of which was "completely covered with hard lime plaster (on which the decoration is found; the plaster covers the rim also)." [6]

In addition to the small incense altar from Timnaʻ in Arabia, other examples closely related to those of Tell el-Kheleifeh have been found at Gerar, Tell Jemmeh, and Tell Farʻah,[7] Ashdod,[8] Lachish,[9] Gezer,[10]

[5] L. Ziegler, "Tonkästchen aus Uruk, Babylon, und Assur," *ZA*, Neue Folge 13:3 (47), (June 1943) 3 Heft, p. 225, fig. 3 from Uruk; W. M. F. Petrie, *Gerar* (London, 1928), Pl. XLI:14.

[6] R. L. Cleveland, *An Ancient South Arabian Necropolis: Objects from the Second Campaign, 1951, in the Timnaʻ Cemetery* (Baltimore, 1965), pp. 119, 120, and Pl. 90:TC 1955.

[7] Petrie, *op. cit.*, Pls. XLII:5, 6; XL, XLI, and pp. 18-19; J. L. Starkey and G. L. Harding, *Beth-Pelet* II (London, 1932), Pls. LXXXVIII:14; XCIII.

[8] M. Dothan and D. N. Freedman, "Ashdod" I, *ʻAtiqot* VII (1967), p. 27, fig. 9:8 on p. 59, and Pl. IX:14.

[9] Tufnell, *op. cit., Text*, pp. 226, 358, 383; and *Plates*, Pls. 49:3; 64:7; 68; 69; Dupont-Sommer, *Text*, pp. 358-59, dates them to the 5th-4th centuries B.C.; cf. W. F. Albright, *BASOR* CXXXII (Dec. 1953), 46-47.

[10] R. A. S. Macalister, *The Excavation of Gezer* II (London, 1912), pp. 442-47; p. 442, fig. 524 (bottom three); p. 443, fig. 525; p. 444, fig. 526; Tufnell, *op. cit., Text*, p. 383, points out that "though they were attributed at the time of discovery to the Hellenistic period, the amended chronology for that site would date them to about 550 B.C."

Samaria,[11] Tell es-Sa'idiyeh in the Jordan Valley,[12] Petra,[13] Hureidha,[14] Thaj,[15] Aden,[16] Uruk, Babylon, Assur.[17]

The opinion expressed years ago by Sir Flinders Petrie that in the Palestinian incense burners was reflected the growth of Assyrian influences, seems to us to be substantially correct, except that the date he assigns them in the eighth-seventh centuries B.C. is, we think, too early.[18] This influence was especially strong in the seventh-sixth centuries B.C. and continued into the fifth.[19] Woolley and Mallowan have pointed out that the vast majority of the incense burners and incense altars from Ur belong to the Neo-Babylonian period.[20] And William F. Albright has correctly concluded that Palestinian incense altars date from the sixth (or late seventh) century to the fourth century B.C., to which period he has assigned the Hureidha incense altars excavated by Miss Caton-Thompson.[21] It is noteworthy that Dupont-Sommer dates the same type of incense altar at Lachish to the fifth-

[11] Reisner, *op. cit., Plates*, Pl. 80:a-c; J. W. Crowfoot, *et al., Samaria-Sebaste* III, Plates (London, 1957), fig. 119:2; H. T. Bossert, *Altsyrien* (Tübingen, 1951), p. 303, fig. 1018a-c.

[12] J. B. Pritchard, *Arch.* XIX/4 (Oct. 1966), p. 290, describes there "a small limestone incense altar . . . with the name of its owner in archaic Hebrew script. The altar also has incised geometric designs painted red and black, as well as the figures of a man and horse." He reports that it was found in a large building, the most recent occupation of which was toward the end of the 4th century B.C.

[13] The Tell el-Kheleifeh type of small, four-legged incense altars of the 5th century B.C. continued in use down into Nabataean times; cf. N. Glueck, *Deities and Dolphins* (New York, 1965), p. 425, Pl. 193; p. 614, n.1005; P. J. Paar, "Objects from Thaj in the British Museum," *BASOR* CLXXVI (Dec. 1964), p. 21, figs. 1:11, 12; pp. 24, 28.

[14] Caton-Thompson, *op. cit.*, pp. 47-50; W. F. Albright, *BASOR* CXXXII (Dec. 1953), 46, dates the soft limestone incense altars from there to the 6th-4th centuries B.C.; cf. *BASOR* XCVIII (April 1945), 28-29; G. Van Beek, "Monuments of Axum in the Light of South Arabian Archaeology," *JAOS* LXXXVII/2 (April-June 1967), 114, 119; "A New Interpretation of the So-Called South Arabian House Model," *AJA* LXIII/3 (July 1959), 269-73, and Pl. 70, fig. 7; Bowen, *op. cit.*, pp. 150-51 and Pl. 96; Cleveland, *op. cit.*, pp. 119, 120, and Pl. 90:TC 1955; 536; 1862; 1915; 2273; p. 120 and Pl. 91:TC 2011.

[15] Paar, *op. cit.*, p. 21, figs. 1:11, 12, and pp. 24, 28; H. R. P. Dickson and V. P. Dickson, "Thaj and Other Sites," *Iraq* X:1 (1948), p. 2.

[16] G. L. Harding, *Archaeology in the Aden Protectorate* (London, 1964), Pls. XIX:51; XXXIII:56, 62.

[17] L. Woolley and M. E. L. Mallowan, *Ur Excavations IX: The Neo-Babylonian and Persian Periods* (London, 1962), Pl. 36 and p. 103; Ziegler, *op. cit.*, pp. 224-39; Galling, *op. cit.*, pp. 247-50; L. Legrain, *Terra-Cottas from Nippur* (Philadelphia, 1930)), Pls. LXV:359; LXVI:360-63; LXVII:364-67.

[18] Petrie, *op. cit.*, pp. 18-19; Starkey, *op. cit.*, Pls. LXXXVIII, XCIII.

[19] N. Glueck, "Some Edomite Pottery from Tell el-Kheleifeh," *BASOR* CLXXXVIII (Dec. 1967), 27-38.

[20] Cf. n. 17 above.

[21] W. F. Albright, *BASOR* XCLXXX (April 1945), 28-29; CXXXII (Dec. 1953), 46; *Archaeology of Palestine*, pp. 143-45; Caton-Thompson, *op. cit.*, pp. 47-50.

fourth centuries B.C., as has already been noted, and that Tufnell assigns the Gezer examples to about 550 B.C.[22] This type of altar, as has been indicated, definitely continues into the Nabataean period.[23] Our conclusion regarding the Tell el-Kheleifeh incense altars, to judge both from the Level V in which they were found and from comparative material, is that they are to be assigned to the fifth century B.C., with the possibility that they may first have made their appearance there near the end of the sixth century B.C.

Belonging to this same level and period at Tell el-Kheleifeh was a fragment of a small incense altar, made of semi-porous stone. Only one face is preserved, showing two stubby legs at the corners, with a low flattened arch between them, and a deep horizontal groove along the upper face of each side. The bottom of the shallow basin at the top shows some blackening, possibly from the burning of incense (Fig. 2:2). Examples of small, square incense altars occur in Mesopotamia and Cyprus, bearing incised pattern decorations, with the area at the bottom, which would normally have been cut out between the legs, remaining intact, but also undecorated.[24]

One small cuboid incense altar of whitish, silty chalk, with a rounded basin at the top, was found in Level V (Pl. 3:2). Some horizontal and vertical lines scratched on its outer surface are faintly visible. Another small incense altar of the same type, made of reddish buff, coarse, well-baked ware, was found nearby (Pl. 3:3; Fig. 2:3).

Another incense altar (Pl. 5, Fig. 4) of uncertain provenance, perhaps from the Hebron area, of the general type described above, was purchased by me at Kando's antiquity shop near the American School of Oriental Research in Jerusalem. Made of well-fired clay, it is light red in color, with a thin pink slip over its outer surfaces. Each side and the rims are decorated with various combinations of grooves and dots. The grooves were accentuated with dark purplish lines of paint, now worn away in part. The dots on the sides and top rims were filled in with light red or dark purplish paint. The differences in color may stem from the manner in which the paint has lasted. On the underneath surfaces, the inside of the four legs was originally painted in red, and there is a faintly visible, red-painted cross on the bottom. This small incense altar is well made, slightly asymmetrical, with well-smoothed surfaces. The bottom and insides of the incense basin show traces of burning, visible also to a lesser degree on the four sides. This incense altar can also be assigned to the fifth century B.C.

[22] Cf. n. 9 and 10.
[23] Cf. n. 13.
[24] Ziegler, *op. cit.*, pp. 229, 230, and fig. 33a-d; p. 237, fig. 64.

PLATE 1

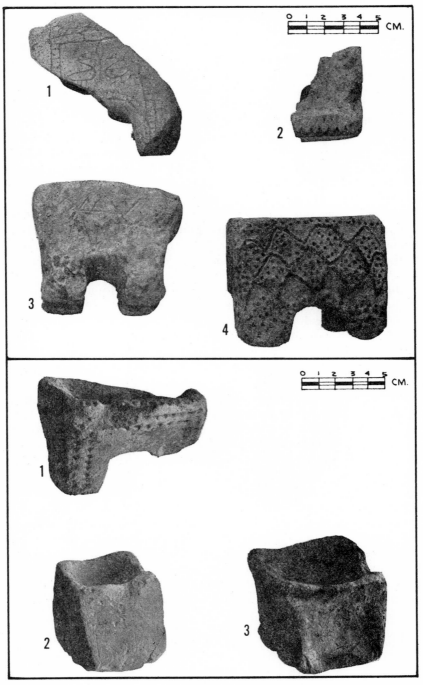

PLATE 3

PLATE 2

CMS

PLATE 4

CMS

5 CM

PLATE 5

5 CM

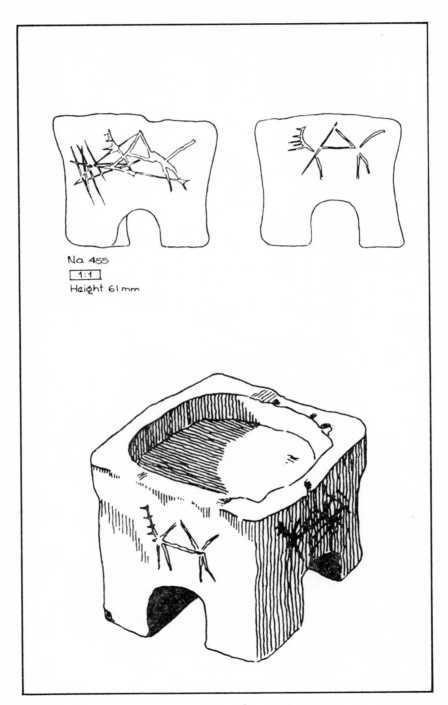

No. 455
1:1
Height 61mm

FIG. 1

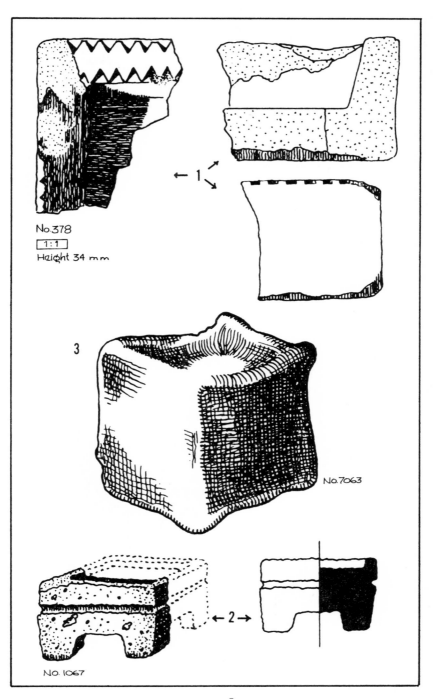

No. 378

1:1

Height 34 mm

1

3

No. 7063

No. 1067

2

FIG. 2

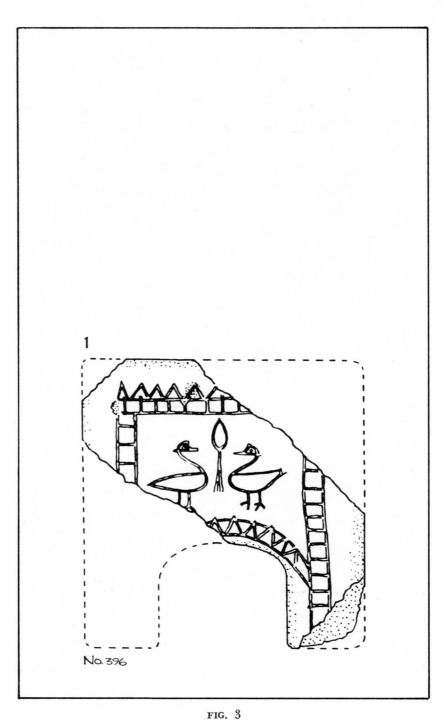

No. 396

FIG. 3

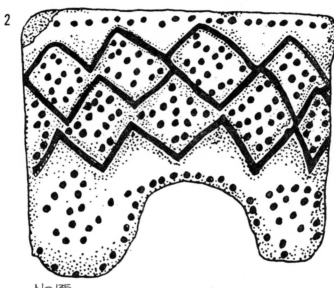

2

No. 135
1:1
Height 68mm

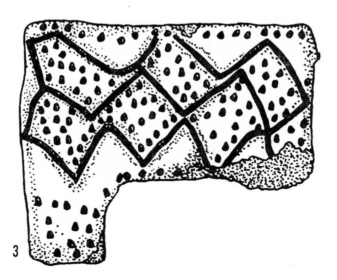

3

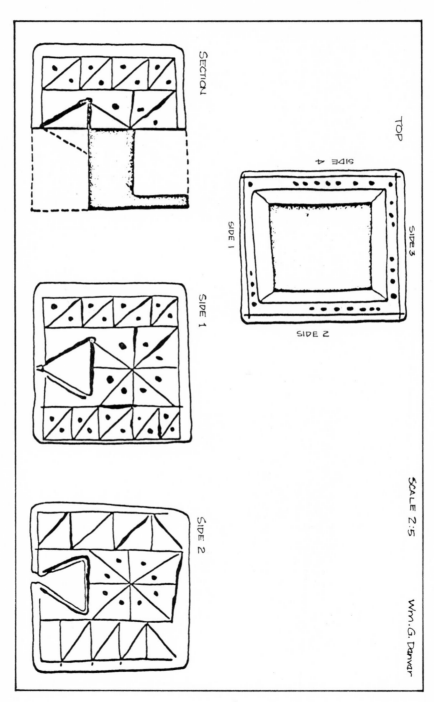

FIG. 4

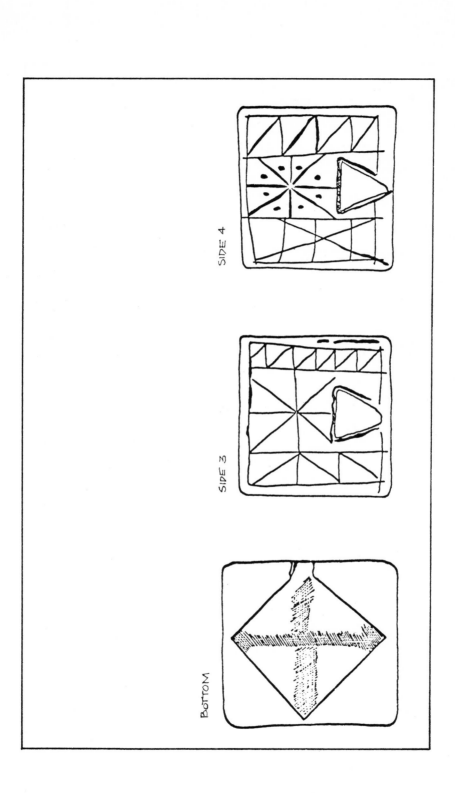

Index